EDITED BY HANK NUWER

The Hazing Reader

INDIANA
University Press
Bloomington & Indianapolis

Publication of this book was assisted by the Friends of Indiana University Press.

This book is a publication of

Indiana University Press
601 North Morton Street
Bloomington, IN 47404-3797 USA

http://iupress.indiana.edu

Telephone orders   800-842-6796
Fax orders   812-855-7931
Orders by e-mail   iuporder@indiana.edu

The paper used in this publication meets the minimum requirements of American National Standard for Information Sciences—Permanence of Paper for Printed Library Materials, ANSI Z39.48-1984.

Manufactured in the United States of America

Library of Congress Cataloging-in-Publication Data

The hazing reader / edited by Hank Nuwer.
    p. cm.
Includes bibliographical references and index.
ISBN 0-253-34370-4 (cloth : alk. paper) — ISBN 0-253-21654-0 (pbk. : alk. paper)
  1. Hazing—United States. 2. College students—United States—Conduct of life. 3. Initiations (into trades, societies, etc.) 4. Greek letter societies—United States. I. Nuwer, Hank.
  LA229.H32 2004
  378.1′98′55—dc21

                                                                            2003011797

1 2 3 4 5   09 08 07 06 05 04

The Hazing Reader

In memoriam:
Irving L. Janis, Josef Lysiak, Hank Nuwer Sr.,
Coach Steve Bania, and Irvin Howard.

In grateful appreciation:
Jenine Nuwer and Fraser Drew.
And for Louis Ingelhart,
in appreciation for all he has done to preserve
student press freedoms.

Operator: Nine-one-one. What is your emergency?
Caller: Yeah, we have someone down that's not breathing anymore.
Operator: Okay. Is this person with you at 811 Rio Chico?
Caller [*frantically*]: Yeah. Yeah. Exactly! Yeah.
Operator: Do you know why?
Caller: Uh, I think he's been drinking too much. We need help, right now.
Operator: Is there somebody there that can—
Caller: —Yeah, we got plenty of people here—
Operator: —that could stay on the line and talk to the paramedics?
Caller: Um, sure. Uh, let me get those guys that are out there trying to deal with him, 'cause he's all—
Operator: If you could get the phone to them, and I'll transfer you over, okay?

(*Voices in the background on the caller's end of the line begin shouting, terrified, as if the emergency has suddenly escalated to a new, more critical stage. Someone is giving frantic, desperate commands, which cannot be understood.*)

Caller: What's wrong?
Voices: Hey, hey, hey! He's—Fuck, he's going! He's going [to die] right now!
Operator: Okay, listen to me. The fire and the paramedics are on the way.
Caller: Okay.
Operator: If [there is] somebody that can calm down and listen to instructions on how to help that person, I want you to put them on the phone. Is that person you?
Caller: Okay. Okay. Tell me what to do here.
Operator: Okay. You stay on the line. I'm going to transfer you over, okay?
Voices in Background: One, two, three, four, five. (*They are maybe trying CPR or some other type of artificial resuscitation.*)

(*Dial tone and dialing beeps as the call is transferred to the rescue team.*)

Operator: Stay with me, okay? Stay with me. I'm going to tell them on the phone. I'm going to talk first, and then they'll tell you what to do. (*Sound of a phone ringing on the line.*) They're going to be there within just two minutes or so. You're doing okay.
Emergency team member answers: Communications. . . . Okay, what's going on there, guy?
Caller: Um, he's not breathing right now. He's been passed out right now.
Voices:
—Oh, my God. It's not working, Dude.
—Get him up! Get him up!
—Get him over to the bed!
—There's no way.
—Get him up! Come on!
Emergency: Okay. Sir? Listen to me, okay?
Voices:
—Does someone know first aid in here?
—I've been doing it! I've been doing it! It's not working, okay?
—What's wrong?

(*The voices grow louder in the background, as if people are moving about, closer to the phone, or the caller is carrying the phone closer to the voices. He has not answered the emergency worker. There is a sense of rising panic in the voices.*)

Emergency: Sir! You need to have everybody calm down in the background, right down.
Caller: Everybody? Shhhhh!
Voices (overlapping):
—Okay. What's up? What's up?
—No, no, no.
—I'm certified. Let me in. I'm certified. Let me in. Hold on. You go like this.
Caller: Okay. Hold on. Shhhh.
Emergency: You need to have everyone calm down. Listen. . . . In order for me to help you, you're going to have to have everybody calm down.
Caller: Everybody calm down. (*The voices get quieter. Only a few are talking, and they're not shouting.*) Okay?
Emergency: All right. What has he been doing to cause him to not breathe?
Caller: I think he's been, he's been drinking a lot.
Voices:
—Please!
—You motherfucker! I'm certified. You've got to—

(*Now come many other undistinguishable shouts and rhythmic noises, which might be counting again, as if they are trying fast CPR or something in a desperate manner; all this overlaps the phone conversation*).

—(*angry wail*) I'm certified.
Emergency: . . . You need to have those people in the background . . . get out of the room, so I can help you.
Caller: Okay. Hey! Everybody out! Everybody out! Out! Out! Out! (*They keep shouting, talking—everyone at once.*) Out! Out! (*They are not going.*) Get out! Out! Out!

(*The line goes dead. The rescue team arrives to find Adrian dead.*)

—911 emergency call excerpt
Victim: Adrian Heideman
Location: California State University, Chico, Pi Kappa Phi house
Time: 1:21 A.M., October 7, 2000
http://orion.csuchico.edu/Pages/Vol46issue4/online/911call.html

* * *

Ten days earlier, I had given a talk on hazing at Chico State. Mike Heideman, Adrian's father, later told me, "I think Adrian may have attended your talk at Chico State. My understanding is that everyone who rushed fraternities was required to attend. There is also a note in Adrian's day planner mentioning a talk. . . . "

—Hank Nuwer

Contents

Acknowledgments

I wish to acknowledge the assistance of the following who have helped this book come into being. First, I would like to thank Jenine Howard Nuwer, who transcribed and edited copy. I also owe a debt of gratitude to Kendra Boileau Stokes, Jane Lyle, Kate Babbitt, and Robert Sloan, my editors at Indiana University Press.

Also, these people contributed to the book you find in your hands:

Charles Eberly of the Center for the Study of the College Fraternity; James W. Brown; Michael V. Gordon; Robert G. Waite; John (Tony) William; Eileen Stevens; Rita Saucier; Jayne and Kevin Moore; Steve Rogers; Connie Clery and S. Daniel Carter of Security on Campus, Inc.; Brian Rahill of Stophazing.org; and the library staff members at the University of Illinois, Cornell University, Franklin College, Anderson University, Indiana University, Indiana University–Purdue University Indianapolis, Ball State University, Miami University of Ohio, Purdue University, and the Library of Congress. Finally, I received important words of support from Fraser Drew, Maryruth Glogoski, and Mary Karen Delmont of Buffalo State College.

I also had the benefit of participating in the August 1999 Alfred University national survey of initiation rites and athletics for NCAA sports teams under the research team of Nadine Hoover and Norm Pollard. Thanks also to Hank Dewey and other alumni fraternity brothers of mine at Buffalo State College who have supported my decision to write about fraternal reform measures. No one but myself is accountable if errors slipped into these pages.

Some of my work on hazing has been supported by a grant from the Gannett Foundation, designed to send journalism professors into the real world to write stories.

I gratefully acknowledge the pledge, as well as his parents, who allowed me an interview at their family home at a time of crisis, due to a hazing incident.

I sincerely thank the contributors who share their knowledge, opinions, and theories in the essays printed in this book. They, in turn, thank those who contributed interviews and ideas that were incorporated into their articles. Opinions expressed in these essays are those of the authors and may not necessarily reflect the opinions of the editor.

Hank Nuwer

Some sections of "Exterminating the Frat Rats" appeared in *NUVO Newsweekly* (1999) and *Beta Theta Pi Magazine* (Winter 2003): 8. Copyright © Hank Nuwer.

Some sections of "Military Hazing" by Hank Nuwer appeared in *The Ameri-*

can *Legion,* vol. 147, no. 1, (July 1999): 40–42; and in *Broken Pledges* by Hank Nuwer (Atlanta: Longstreet Press, 1990). Copyright © Hank Nuwer.

"Cult-like Hazing" appeared in slightly different form in *The Chronicle of Higher Education,* vol. 46, no. 14 (November 26, 1999), B7–8; and *Wrongs of Passage* by Hank Nuwer (Bloomington: Indiana University Press, 1999).

The editor and Indiana University Press gratefully acknowledge permission to reprint the following:

Selections from Lionel Tiger, *Men in Groups* (New York: Random House, 1969). Copyright © Lionel Tiger.

Ricky L. Jones, "The Historical Social Significance of Sacrificial Ritual: Understanding Violence in the Modern Black Fraternity Pledge Process," *Western Journal of Black Studies,* vol. 24, no. 2 (Summer 2000): 112–24. Reprinted by permission of *Western Journal of Black Studies.*

Donna Winslow, "Rites of Passage and Group Bonding in the Canadian Airborne," in *Armed Forces and Society,* vol. 25, no. 3 (Spring 1999), 429. Reprinted by permission of Transaction Publishers.

Scott R. Rosner and R. Brian Crow, "Institutional Liability for Hazing in Interscholastic Sports," *The Houston Law Review,* vol. 39, no. 2 (Summer 2002): 275–305. Reprinted by permission of *The Houston Law Review.*

Scott R. Rosner and R. Brian Crow, "Institutional and Organizational Liability for Hazing in Intercollegiate and Professional Team Sports," *St. John's Law Review,* vol. 76, no. 1 (Winter 2002): 87–114. Reprinted by permission of *St. John's Law Review.*

Michelle A. Finkel, "Traumatic Injuries Caused by Hazing Practices," *American Journal of Emergency Medicine,* vol. 20, no. 3 (May 2002): 228–33. Reprinted by permission of Elsevier Science.

Excerpt from Irving L. Janis, *Victims of Groupthink* (Boston: Houghton Mifflin, 1972). Reprinted by permission of Houghton Mifflin.

James C. Arnold, "Alcohol and the Chosen Few: Organizational Reproduction in an Addictive System" (Ph.D. diss., Indiana University, 1995). Reprinted by permission of James C. Arnold. The full text is available at http://www.addall.com/Browsa/Author/3077706-1.

Grateful acknowledgment is given for permission to use original photographs by Mike Heideman, Greg Danielson, and Alice L. Haben.

Chapters by D. Jason DeSousa, Michael V. W. Gordon, Walter M. Kimbrough, Jonathan R. Farr, Holiday Hart McKiernan, Gregory Danielson, Susan VanDeventer Iverson, and Elizabeth J. Allan, were commissioned especially for this book.

Hank Nuwer's editor's introductions to all chapters are published here for the first time.

Introduction:
Exterminating the Frat Rats

Hank Nuwer

When I belonged to a fraternity in college and was hazed and hazed others, I hated the term "frat rat." Now I try to exterminate frat rats. It's my job.

First, an explanation why that pejorative term "frat rat" applies here to hazers who commit criminal acts. I do not apply the term to those who do not haze or are part of the growing Greek anti-hazing movement. I've learned in my reading that a "rat" in older farming communities was a laborer hired to nibble patiently at an old barn's beams and supports with a small tool until the whole structure collapses—just as he escapes.

"Frat rat" describes all Greek members who abuse, degrade, and humiliate pledges, then graduate—like the frat rat you will meet in Chapter 4 who now has a position of trust at a U.S. college. Metaphorically, these few chew away at the foundations of Greek houses and threaten to bring the system crashing down on the heads of all. They leave, but their hazing practices stay. In May 2003, alumni of Psi Epsilon Chi at Plattsburgh State University of New York planned to celebrate the chapter's thirty-fifth anniversary. Instead, alums permanently shut the house, stunned and sickened by the death of Walter Dean Jennings, 18, who police said died following ten days of "water torture" in which he had to drink copious amounts of fluids. At a news conference, the city's mayor vowed that he would personally attend when the letters were torn off the fraternity house. Eleven members of Psi Epsilon Chi had been charged with criminally negligent homicide, a felony, and misdemeanor hazing.

My last book, *Wrongs of Passage*, opened with the 1993 death of Chad Saucier, a community college student from Mobile, Alabama. Auburn University's Phi Delta Theta allowed Chad to pledge even though he was academically ineligible by local and national rules. He died grotesquely, dressed in a goofy elf suit, after swilling liquor during a traditional Christmas party in which members "encouraged" new "men" (all of whom were under 21) to drink. Having swilled enough whiskey and Jägermeister® to flatten four strapping males, Chad's intestines twisted inside him as he convulsed on the fraternity-house floor. He may or may not have heard a hammering against his own chest as a brother slammed Chad's heart with his fists in a futile effort to bring him around.

Right up to the minute Chad died, the Auburn members and pledges were laughing. For them, hazing was a commonplace behavior without consequences. Others even argued that what Chad went through failed to meet their own personal definitions of hazing. In contrast, Chad's parents and Auburn administrators expressed horror that he died trying to please those fraternity brothers; they agreed that the bottle exchange between new and veteran members was a dangerous custom in need of abolishing.

Longtime Auburn student-life professional Deborah Shaw, an outspoken critic of hazing, could offer no assurance that the death would not be repeated. "I have dealt with five hazing cases in the last three months, all at Auburn University, all with some of our older, traditional chapters," said Shaw, director of Foy Student Union and Student Leadership, in an e-mail interview for *Wrongs of Passage.* "One in particular sounds so similar to what the Phi Delts were doing the night Chad died: a Christmas party with lots of alcohol, pledges getting drunk, pledges performing for the actives, etc. Why are things not different after Chad's death? I wish I had the answer."

Here may be the answer: Hazing is endemic in American schools from junior high through graduate and professional schools. It is also rampant in the military and is a hidden cancer for oil riggers, firemen, and others in the workforce. For example, an 18-year-old female ambulance driver died from a booze binge her new male colleagues asked her to endure as an initiation. Scholars and the general public alike long have searched for accurate information on hazing to explain a societal problem threatening the well-being of organizations as diverse as fraternities and sororities, the military forces of many nations, athletic teams, certain occupations, and some high school and collegiate clubs.

Initiation rites have been an important part of different cultures throughout history. Few of us go through life without taking part in some sort of rite of passage. My boss at the Indiana University School of Journalism—Indianapolis, James W. Brown, has for years tried to get me to investigate what is tantamount to hazing in Ph.D. programs by some advisors who put graduate students through hellacious mental ordeals. I have no problem with the validity and value of certain initiation rituals; the majority of people who take part in fraternal initiations are "normal" individuals, not sociopaths. What I am referring to are rituals that exhibit cult-like characteristics—monopolizing someone's time, robbing them of space, forcing them to accept an all-or-nothing group mentality. In short, I am opposed to rituals of a pathological nature—hazing, as we've collectively come to call these wrongs of passage.

Profane Celebrations

Hazing is an all-encompassing term that covers silly, potentially risky, or degrading tasks required for acceptance by a group of full-fledged members. Novelist Ralph Ellison once observed in a talk delivered at West Point that hazing is a profane celebration of the more formal and sacred values of an organization. Although hazing is mostly associated in the media with athletes and Greeks, the fingerpointing in the United States goes back to 1657, when Harvard fined upperclassmen for freshman hazing. Many early college presidents, preferring absolute order to the flourishing of individual identities, encouraged hazing. They saw it as a way to teach precedence, build school loyalty, and assimilate students from all economic classes. Other educators even then called it "a weed in the garden of academe," and nineteenth-century presidents at Amherst College, University of Michigan (Ann Arbor), Miami University of Ohio, and Indiana University condemned class hazings that resulted in hundreds of serious injuries and some deaths. With a few exceptions, until the mid-1920s, most campus hazing deaths (at Amherst College, Massachusetts Institute of Technology, University of Kentucky, Colgate University, Hamilton College, Franklin & Marshall College, Northwestern University, Purdue University, etc.) occurred in freshman-sophomore class scraps. But after 1928, hazing deaths in fraternities began to eclipse the total of class hazing deaths.

Attitudes haven't fully changed for the better since the nineteenth century. Too many college administrators have turned their heads while hazing goes on—performed by fraternity chapters whose members show unbridled school spirit and who contribute big bucks as alumni. These presidents and deans instituted the right policies, but students knew they could haze so long as they didn't rub things in an administrator's, advisor's, or coach's face.

Until the 1970s, hazing deaths occurred infrequently enough that college presidents who endured one could lament them as "isolated" accidents. But the presence of alcohol in the initiations of local and National Interfraternity Conference fraternities contributed to a documentable rise in initiation- and pledging-related deaths. Likewise, serious beating injuries and occasional deaths in African-American fraternities also began in the mid-1970s (although alcohol has been a factor in few deaths of black pledges). Sororities had two hazing deaths in the 1970s; most sorority women eschew physical hazing in favor of activities far less likely to cause deaths. However, alcohol-related deaths of sorority women in the 1990s and allegations, yet unproven, of sorority hazing deaths in 2002 have raised the vigilance of national sorority headquarters.

High School Hazing

The Alfred University/NCAA survey released in 1999 revealed that nearly half of all collegian athletes say they were first hazed in high school or even in middle school. Thus, hazing—a ritual that gives hazers a sense of power, entitlement, and occasionally sadistic pleasure—must also be addressed by educators who work with teens and preteens. Unfortunately, high school educators lag far behind collegiate Greek administrators and the heads of Greek headquarters when it comes to an awareness of hazing problems. In the last fifteen years, high school hazings have included acts of sodomy, sexual assaults and coerced sexual simulations, forced drinking, paddlings, coatings with foul or vile substances, and the eating of repulsive substances.

Why does hazing flourish in many high schools? It may have something to do with the fundamental drawbacks of the U.S. educational system, which is charged with serving the needs of a great many young people. Some teenagers are brilliant introverts who reject the hero worship of athletes and beautiful people rampant in high school. The students who attack these "outsiders" sometimes act on overt cues from teachers and administrators, and coaches at the college level can also turn a team against a nonconformist rookie whose willingness to turn in teammates for hazing labels him as a high-maintenance troublemaker. Often, the words and actions of these adults teach the students that nonconformists have two choices—assimilation or isolation. High school hazing of freshmen and rookies can be particularly vicious when directed toward nonconformists struggling to find an identity. In fact, hazing is part of a larger culture of violence and destruction.

Could it be that school shootings are just part of a destructive, self-fulfilling prophecy? That the Columbine High School trenchcoat mafia shooters acted from a misguided sense of revenge when they opened fire on athletes who had made their lives unpleasant? If so, all the more reason to end hazing and bullying to protect both the nonconformists and the school stars.

Those in authority may find it difficult to write a definition of hazing that adequately covers all demeaning or dangerous activities. I define hazing as any action required by full-status members of low-status, probationary members that in some way humbles newcomers who lack the power or wit to resist. The new members hunger for acceptance and go along with hazing because they want to experience a tradition they have been told is necessary for group camaraderie and solidarity. Other authors in this book will stress a far more formal definition of the term.

To be sure, many hazers argue that hazing is either beneficial or harmless. And hazing can be noncriminal. This occurs, for instance, when a professional sports team asks rookies to don silly costumes without requiring alcohol consumption or when a fraternity chapter drops a sober pledge off in the country. The problem with noncriminal hazing is that one or more members can be incited to foolhardiness or violence during the excitement of partaking in a group ritual. In addition, unintended consequences can occur because of the negligent nature of hazing.

As an example, consider that when a Swarthmore College chapter of Delta Upsilon dropped Peter Mertz off in the country, its members ought to have considered whether his being in unfamiliar territory might result in his being struck and killed by a passing automobile, as did occur. The incident officially was regarded as non-hazing, but one Delta Upsilon member later wrote a letter to anti-hazing activist Eileen Stevens in which he said this: "All of us—no matter how hard we told ourselves that it was an automobile/pedestrian accident rather than a hazing—have been unable to shake the realization that it would not have happened without the hazing."

Two other dangers can occur when members regard hazing as harmless tradition. One, the hazed and hazers become unlikely to intervene when an activity escalates and becomes hazardous. Likewise, passersby on or off campus are likely to shrug off any hazing they witness instead of reporting it.

Two, the newcomers themselves sometimes stage a rebellion and demand that a full-status group member perform potentially risky tasks. To distinguish hazing conducted by members from hazing conducted by probationary members, I call the latter "reverse hazing." It has led to deaths at the University of Texas, Eastern Illinois University, and several other institutions.

Professional Athletes

The general public is often confused by what it reads in newspapers about hazing or hears from those who have experienced it. Prohibitions and standards that apply to one group are missing from those applied to another group. Professional sports teams, for example, have been lax about punishing hazing infractions. Thus, pro football players who tape rookies to a goalpost or belt one made to run through a gauntlet not only are not held accountable but also often find these activities portrayed in a humorous or positive light by the media. Yet similar activities by high school or college athletes often result in sanctions against the veterans. There is no "one size fits all" yardstick that applies to all who haze.

Hazing offenses also can slip through the cracks when police and prosecutors decline to file criminal charges. Victims who survive, or the parents of victims who perish, sometimes take their accusations into civil court in an attempt to convince a judge or jury to regard the same reckless rituals as "hazing" and award a judgment.

How This Book Came to Be

I long have lamented the absence of a single book that could provide an interdisciplinary overview of hazing. Since no such book existed, I have compiled this collection of essays selected from a range of disciplines. The collection primarily lends itself to an understanding of hazing behaviors. Until the publication of this book, a good deal of what is available here was accessible only to expert researchers and was published in doctoral dissertations, low-circulation journals, and in single chapters from a number of books.

This one-volume collection synthesizes the best available information on hazing from writers whose diverse backgrounds are in the social sciences, law, medicine, student affairs, journalism, counseling, athletic administration, and cultural studies. While scholarly writings can sometimes show a very narrow focus—depending upon individual interests and specialties—the scope of this book is broad. Its contributors at all times help the reader demystify the practice of hazing.

The book begins with analytical essays by sociologist Stephen Sweet, anthropologist Lionel Tiger, "groupthink" psychology theorist Irving L. Janis, and by me, a journalism professor and author of three additional books on hazing. Sweet's essay takes a well-known sociological theory and links the dynamics of hazing in student groups to predictable processes of group interaction. In his view, hazing is not conducted by sadists but is tied into a desire for belonging that leads participants to justify such activities as necessary, even legitimate.

His conclusions lead to practical applications that may better enable student-affairs professionals to devise positive rituals that might be substituted for dangerous or demeaning hazing practices.

While Sweet's work is current, I found it also useful to include a pioneering piece by anthropologist Lionel Tiger that is drawn from his 1969 book *Men in Groups*. Tiger views hazing by collegiate males as a means for them to attain status and group acceptance. In his opinion, hazing is a sort of courtship dance in which outsider males preen for the insider males whose group they wish to join. These insiders are valued by the outsiders because the former are seen as possessing certain characteristics that high-status females might find attractive. Professor Janis's essay teaches us the dangers of loyalty to a group that can override common sense, rational thought, and moral qualms.

My own essay, "Cult-like Hazing," singles out the hazing organizations that pose the threat of physical and/or psychological harm to recruits. These are collegiate fraternal groups that employ cult-like rituals during the pledging process, minimizing the contact of newcomers with those who are not group members and controlling them to cultivate dependency. These are the dangerous and negligent Greeks I dismissed earlier as frat rats.

What follows then are four essays and an interview that look at hazing practices in a narrow but important segment of hazing collegiate groups. The writers in this section consider the behaviors of the worst hazing offenders, those most likely to cause hazing deaths or serious injuries. The first, by researcher James C. Arnold, provides a unique perspective on a single high-risk fraternity that he observes as a non-Greek outsider. Arnold concludes that fraternal groups whose pledging activities revolve around alcohol are "addictive organizations." Arnold's primary purpose in conducting research was to study alcohol in relationship to group norms in a fraternity, but the hazing he observed nonetheless pinpoints those extremist chapters that could conceivably lose a pledge from an alcohol overdose. I should also point out that Arnold disagrees with my in-print contentions that fraternal reform is possible, taking a far more unforgiving view of fraternities such as the particular chapter he studied. I find such debate, even strong disagreement with my views, healthy.

Three educators who are also fraternity members—D. Jason DeSousa, Michael V. W. Gordon, and Walter M. Kimbrough—next address the systematic beating or paddling of prospective members that have contributed to the deaths of African-American pledges. Their conclusions about the present-day conditions in African-American fraternities may intrigue or disturb readers. A companion essay, written by scholar Ricky L. Jones of the University of Louisville, demonstrates one way to approach these deaths to understand the behavior behind them. Jones is also a fraternity member.

A fourth essay, an excerpt contributed by a graduate student and student-affairs professional, Jonathan R. Farr, considers chronic offenders at a single university. While it may be questionable for a university to eliminate an entire Greek system for the sins of a handful of such perennial problem groups, Farr's essay may lead school officials and national fraternity headquarters to question the wisdom of keeping alive chapters that show little inclination to act as responsible campus citizens. Accompanying this piece is an analysis of sorority hazing today by Holiday McKiernan, counsel and past executive director of a large female fraternity and, like many national sorority leaders, an outright condemner of hazing and underage drinking on campuses.

Next comes my own essay on military hazing. I have addressed some of the more brutal patterns of hazing in the U.S. military. Participants in military hazing stress that they think there was a purpose to the hazing—the purpose of keeping them alive and establishing "to-the-death" camaraderie. Nonetheless, all U.S. military academies and branches of the service have sternly worded prohibitions against hazing at this time. In her valuable companion piece, Dr. Donna Winslow, a world-renowned expert on the regimental system and its relationship to the army ethos, has described the rituals of the Canadian Airborne and attempted to sort out the meaning of acts that those outside the regiment viewed as troubling or worse.

Without any reflection on the Airborne essay itself, which I considered a groundbreaking addition to the literature on military initiations, I must note that Dr. Winslow's definition of hazing as worded in the Airborne essay will no doubt stir debate, particularly among anti-hazing activists. With regard to fraternity hazing in the United States, a former Alfred University administrator charged with investigating pledge Chuck Stenzel's death in 1978 insisted and stressed in our interview that this could not be a hazing death because it occurred during an initiation rite called "Tapping Night" locally—not during a Hell Week or any other extended period of hazing. I have argued in my book *Broken Pledges* that an initiation rite can be an incident of hazing. Prof. Winslow's conclusion supports the definition of the Alfred administrator I interviewed. I suggest that this matter is one of the stickiest hurdles to get over as the military, fraternity leaders, and educators try to reach consensus on a single definition of hazing. I think debate on this issue of coining a definition is not only healthy for scholars but essential for those charged with overseeing groups of every sort.

Deeper into the book are three essays on hazing and the law and one on traumatic injuries that doctors need to look for to identify cases of hazing that end up in emergency rooms. The two law essays are the work of Scott R. Rosner, a lecturer in the Legal Studies Department at the Wharton School, University of Pennsylvania; and R. Brian Crow, a professor the Department of Sport Management at Slippery Rock University. The essay by Michelle A. Finkel, M.D., of Massachusetts General Hospital, examines traumatic injuries incurred by victims in hazing episodes. She recommends that doctors be more willing to suspect hazing in cases where severely intoxicated or badly bruised collegians show up in emergency rooms.

Next comes a section on athletic hazing. Herein is a first-person account by former soccer player Gregory Danielson. His experience of an alcohol-related initiation occurred while he was a first-year student at the University of North Carolina. Because I was unable to secure interviews with a coach and an athletic director involved in the Danielson incident, I have supplied a brief introduction that relies on news accounts and UNC records instead. The final two essays, also written specifically for this volume, are by Susan V. Iverson and Elizabeth J. Allan of the University of Maine. They write about changing a hazing culture and the differences in how males and females haze. Iverson and Allan both made important contributions to changing a hazing culture at previous institutions where they were employed. Like myself, they are far more hopeful that hazing can be contained.

I am indebted for suggestions on the editing of this book to Charles G. Eberly, president of the Center for the Study of the College Fraternity. "If we are to thoroughly understand the dynamics of hazing in order to change the culture in which it exists, we must do so from many and varied perspectives," said Eberly.

If the text in your hands succeeds in making hazing fully understandable to the scholar and general reader alike, I will have done my job as editor. I am accountable if any errors have crept into the text.

I hope that these essays inspire graduate students in similar disciplines to choose hazing-related research for their theses and dissertations, increasing knowledge of a topic that has been a scourge for centuries but studied intently only in the recent past.

To stop the problem of hazing in society, it will take large-scale, directed strategies by the public, legislators, educators, and Greek groups. Past fraternal solutions such as "Greek Week," "Help Week," bans on pledging, and dry houses were well intentioned (and may even have saved some lives), but they have failed to kill the roots of hazing. The problem—and student deaths—continue.

Hazing in U.S. Culture

Ending hazing in U.S. secondary schools and colleges would be an important step toward ending the wider acceptance of casual violence and alcohol abuse in our culture today. Before that occurs, educators, legislators, journalists, parents, students, and the public at large must examine the issue of hazing intellectually and unemotionally. A constant goal must be the desire to create civility in U.S. classrooms. Educators err when they call for a return to the values of founders and old-time students. Records of early schools show that our forefathers were inclined, as children and young adults, to partake in hazing acts few parents today would want their children to emulate. In fact, many fraternity chapters that haze rationalize their actions by calling them a part of tradition. They ignore the best of what these national fraternity founders strove to accomplish: a sense of community, a system of honor, the courage to live one's ideals, and a respect for the academic life of the mind and the benefits of exercise.

So why don't college presidents and trustees simply end hazing? The reality is that while academe contains some of the country's finest minds, its members have not, as an Alfred University professor I interviewed remarked, shown themselves to be a very heroic bunch. Likewise, the NCAA has been astonishingly lax through 2003 in its efforts to create hazing awareness and to establish a leadership position against hazing to guide coaches and athletic directors.

Too many people in academe (faculty uninvolved in student life, overworked administrators, and students looking for a ticket to a future job) act like members of a dysfunctional family. Fraternities that haze and abuse alcohol thrive in such a climate. They are unlikely to change the behaviors they think give them status on campus. It's only when a hazing death or disgusting incident occurs—something shocking that arouses the wrath of the press and shames administrators—that there is likely to be widespread campus acknowledgement that hazing is insidious and harmful.

In spite of dozens of hazing deaths, only Alfred and Auburn Universities and Chico State, to my knowledge, have shown remorse by inviting the mothers of deceased pledges to come to campus to speak of their grief or to get them involved in anti-alcohol or anti-hazing activities. Why don't the mass of students change their behavior even when more Chad Sauciers or Adrian Heidemans die? Our larger culture has become inured to violence. It elevates anyone who survives an ordeal such as hazing. It hates the "wimp" who says, "No, I'm outta here" or "tattles."

People Who Defend Hazing

I'm aware that many people despise the stand I took against hazing twenty-five years ago. These people tell me they want hazing to continue—despite its being illegal in forty-three states. I have received several e-mail messages defending hazing: "America is the land of the free [with] the freedom to join whatever group that you want," wrote a 23-year-old male, David [his real name]. "If I want to join a group that beats the crap out of me every day, I can. If I want to join a group that requires me to drink 6 gallons of wine in a day to join, I can. Pledging my fraternity was the best thing I did." "I think this is much ado about nothing," Suellen, a mother from Vista, California, wrote me. "No wonder there are so many wimps in society today. EVERYBODY WANTS TO BE A VICTIM! Unless there is extreme physical harm being done then hazing amongst teams, social clubs/groups, etc. is good and a bonding experience. Once you've 'been there, done that' you're proud of yourself and it is a brotherhood-bonding thing. I am the wife of a Marine officer (former college football player & frat guy) and mother of 3 sons—all athletes, in frats., college grads, etc. AND ALL HAVE BEEN THRU THIS STUFF MANY TIMES/ NO BIG DEAL!!!" "You are making a federal case out of nothing. I bet you a case of beer that more people are injured playing sports . . . than ever got hurt from [athletic] initiations," said fraternity alumnus Mike, who urged me to get a life. "Are you in a make-work program to find something to write about? Figure out how many people went down the road and got drunk but graduated and now have become successful, raised a family, pulled pranks and even survived an initiation."

Mike might have been speaking about George W. Bush, whose hazing activities as Delta Kappa Epsilon pledge and chapter president at Yale University have been well documented by *The New York Times*—although I find it a shame that the four young Delta Kappa Epsilon males from Yale who were killed in a 2003 car wreck on their way back from an all-night pledging ritual won't have the same opportunities that President Bush has enjoyed.

Even many members of the media defend hazing. Writers for *Sports Illustrated, Rocky Mountain News,* and other publications have praised the hazing which 80 percent of all surveyed NCAA college athletes say they have experienced." We're all for college and pro hazing," said *Sports Illustrated*'s Richard Hoffer in a September 13, 1999 opinion piece, saying it builds camaraderie and teaches humility. "All" presumably includes the two New Orleans Saints rookies hospitalized after a 1998 ritual beating and the family of Nicholas Haben, a Western Illinois lacrosse club rookie who died of drink during his initiation.

"I would laugh were I the Douglas County (CO) district attorney who gets handed the report on this so-called crime," wrote Bill Johnson, a *Rocky Mountain News* columnist, after some high school students were busted for taping first-year students with duct tape and making them kiss shoes. "I would remember my freshman and senior years of high school, when I got and gave what those kids received," wrote Johnson on September 3, 1999. "I would tell the police to bring me real crimes."

If Mr. Johnson wants "real" crimes, high school hazings in the 1980s, 1990s, and 2000s involve sodomy, sexual assault, and physical abuse. Such media critics who extol the pleasures of collegiate team hazing trivialize the death of Nicholas Haben and others like him. And while few people want to see kids who haze (with the exception of pledge deaths or serious injuries caused by negligence, beatings, or sadistic acts) packed in jails with sociopaths and hardened criminals, ignoring them is equally wrong. Charging hazers with a crime is an important step toward getting them into awareness seminars and community service–related programs where they can rethink their actions. What's also needed is nationwide reform that allows middle schools and high schools to hold back the diplomas of hazers and other students guilty of uncivil behavior —unless they can show evidence of remorse, such as the performance of meaningful community service—not the ridiculous poor excuse for community service performed by most of University of North Carolina soccer players in 1996, as is documented in Chapter 12.

Death of Hazing, Not More Hazing Deaths

All is not hopeless. Numerous educators, coaches, athletic directors, and students are pushing for idea-sharing and reform to end hazing and alcohol abuse. In part this is because several Greek executive directors, some school administrators, and a few coaches have personally attended the funerals of pledges. These individuals say they realize that Greek life may be fun, rewarding, and worthy in its mentoring—but it is not worth dying for. These leaders are sending undergraduates a no-nonsense message: Eat and be merry, but drink responsibly or tomorrow you—and your chapter or sports team—will die. Hundreds of chapters nationally have been shut down for hazing or alcohol violations. A few sports teams have had games forfeited and have even had seasons cancelled at the college and high school level. Many chapters that choose to go alcohol free get rewarded with foundation dollars to help them maintain their fraternity houses. Also tightening the screws are universities, with Chico State a prime example after experiencing the death of Adrian Heideman.

Dave Westol, chief executive of Indianapolis-based Theta Chi, has seen what happens when chapters endanger their pledges. Since 1997, four pledging-related (one of which involved a rushee) and/or alcohol-related deaths have occurred in New York, Indiana, and New Jersey chapter houses of Theta Chi. One wrenching case described by Sweet in this book involved 17-year-old Theta Chi pledge, Bini Oja, in a 1997 alcohol-related hazing at Clarkson University (Potsdam, New York). "The death at Clarkson was a terrible experience for everyone involved. Not a day goes by that I don't think about it," said Westol in an e-mail to me. "But, I also know that if we don't respond to it with education and emphasis, we are not acting in a responsible fashion."

Westol visits chapters and repeats the message that hazing is wrong and that alcohol can kill you if you abuse it. His former career as a Kalamazoo, Michigan, assistant prosecutor gives him a hard-edged approach to enforcement when a chapter deceives him or shatters rules. He says he gives a grace period to a chapter really trying to clean up its act, but his patience erodes "with groups whose members don't get it."

Of all the issues a Greek organization encounters, alcohol has caused the biggest problem for international or national headquarters and athletic teams. In spite of educational forums, the problem continues to escalate, according to studies conducted by the College Alcohol Studies Program at the Harvard University School of Public Health.

Dave Westol broods on finding ways to change the culture of drinking. He said that his job is made harder when older fraternity alumni and even parents view alcohol and hazing as romantic, college "fun things" to do. Alums and occasionally the fathers of members come to chapter houses to relive their student days by popping brews, giving undergraduates an unfortunate example. "One of the challenges we face these days is alumni and parents who say, 'Gee, I drank in my day. . . . ,'" said Westol said in an e-mail to me. "I answer, 'Yes, but not like they're drinking today.' . . . It's a different culture."

Unfortunately, not all undergraduate chapters voted to accept the ambitious National Interfraternity Conference/National Panhellenic Council Select 2000 (dry-house) plan, just as many black chapters continue to illicitly conduct hazing in so-called renegade pledging activities in spite of National Panhellenic Council (NPHC) anti-hazing measures passed in 1990. Some National Infraternity Conference (NIC) member fraternities voted to delay acceptance until 2003 or later. Former NIC head Jonathan Brant (he's taken a job with Beta Theta Pi Foundation in Ohio) stressed in an interview with me that the dry-house movement has been delayed but remains alive. "There is still a desire to address systematic change from entertainment-based chapters to purposeful [chapters] on campus," said Brant. But some observing the Greek scene are less than en-amored with plans to make houses alcohol free.

Activist Rita Saucier, whose son Chad died at Auburn University, fears that some chapters that signed on to be "dry" will break their vows. She wonders if reforms are designed more by fraternity lawyers to stop litigation than they are to stop pledging deaths. "I believe dry houses are yet another way that fraterni-ties protect themselves in lawsuits," said Saucier in a telephone interview with me. "It is just another means of not being held accountable for hazing."

Dave Westol insists that draining alcohol from the fraternal bloodstream is only a start. The real job of reform ahead means changing the student culture chapter by chapter—working in tandem with others hoping to make changes in society as a whole. Instead of serving as the nation's bartender and recruiting potential alcoholics, fraternities need to recruit members who find other, posi-tive ways to assert their maleness and individuality. "If we change the culture, we change the type of men who join," said Westol.

Hazing's End

Unfortunately, no reforms can bring new hope to the dead. Chad Saucier and his dreams will always be dead. He won't receive an Auburn degree. He won't marry and father his own children. He won't live the long, productive life of promise that his mother and father saw ahead of him. He won't experience any-thing positive the Greek system has to offer. To put it bluntly, that stinks.

While Chad remains in his grave, the frat-rat species continues to haze. That's unacceptable. One positive outcome, however, is that the national Phi Delta Theta organization has taken an unrelenting position toward fraternal al-cohol misuse since Chad's death.

During my own fraternity days at Buffalo State College, this is what I expe-rienced in addition to hazing: camaraderie, the introduction to my lifelong writ-ing mentor, leadership skills, a million laughs, and those after-midnight discus-sions about getting jilted, the meaning of life, and the deaths of buddies in Vietnam. In short, the Greek system introduced me to many good people.

I hope high-quality Greeks won't rest until frat rats are extinct. I hope Ameri-can public opinion can be mustered so that those who haze do so only under the peril of revealing themselves for the abusers, groupthinkers, and negligent beasts they really are.

Hazing must end. It *will* end.

A Chronology of Hazing Events

387 B.C.E.   Plato commented on the savagery of young boys he observed. Fraternity historian Frederick Kershner considered Plato's observations perhaps the earliest account of hazing-like behaviors.

371 C.E.   St. Augustine at Carthage described hazing-like taunting and bullying of newcomers by the *eversores* or "Overturners."

ca. 530   Justinian, the Byzantine emperor who codified Roman law, decreed that the hazing of first-year law students must be ended.

1340   The University of Paris forbade hazing under penalty of expulsion.

1441   Students at Avignon created the anti-hazing Fraternity of St. Sebastian. Hazing was rampant during the age of the rise of universities.

1481   The *Manuale Scholarium* described hazing customs at Heidelberg, including the wearing of ridiculous yellow-billed caps by new students.

1501   Martin Luther endured hazing at Erfurt as a student. Later, in 1539, at Wittenberg, he advocated hazing as a means of strengthening a boy to face and endure life's challenges.

1657   In the American colonies, two Harvard College students paid small fines for hazing John Cotton and John Whiting. Later, a member of the class of 1684 was expelled for hazing but was readmitted after repenting.

1838   A family history describes the death of John Butler Groves (born October 31, 1819) in a hazing at Franklin Seminary in Kentucky.

1846   The University of Heidelberg forbade the pelting of new students with garbage.

1873   Cornell first-year student Mortimer N. Leggett died in a fall into a gorge while wandering with Kappa Alpha Society members.

1874   The president of the University of Michigan sent a letter home to the parents of punished hazers to express his displeasure with the practice.

1900–1901   A U.S. House of Representatives committee investigated hazing at the United States Military Academy. Douglas MacArthur, then a plebe, testified. MacArthur failed to provide full disclosure of the savage hazing he endured.

1912	The death of first-year student Isaac Rand in a University of North Carolina frosh hazing led to the arrest of his hazers and a stern warning to the university president issued by the governor of the state.
1928	National Interfraternity Conference leaders issued a condemnation of hazing.
1940	A sub rosa fraternity at the University of Missouri required a drinking session that led to the death of Hubert L. Spake Jr.
1959	After Kappa Sigma pledge Richard Swanson choked to death on a slab of liver, a filmmaker used the event as the inspiration for the fictional movie *Fraternity Row.*
1969	In his book *Men in Groups,* anthropologist Lionel Tiger depicted hazing-like initiations as a form of men courting men.
1970	A female member of a national sorority died in an accident at Eastern Illinois University as pledges were dropping her off in the country far from campus. Her death marked the beginning of more than three decades of pledging-related and hazing deaths in fraternal organizations/athletic teams that were to occur every year through 2003.
1974–1975	Twelve young males died in miscellaneous hazing or pledging rituals.
1978	Virginia State College student Lynn Delk, 20, likely was the first sorority pledge to die in a "going-over" ceremony for a local African-American sorority. A fraternity male who tried to save her from drowning also perished. In an article for *Human Behavior* magazine, author Hank Nuwer interviewed Irving L. Janis, who commented on fraternal hazing rituals as a form of "groupthink" in which members put aside their moral qualms in the interest of what is perceived as tradition and unanimity. The same year, Eileen Stevens became a nationally recognized anti-hazing activist following her son's death in a hazing at Alfred University. National Lampoon's *Animal House* was released, portraying hazing as just one more comic misadventure in the Delta fraternity house.
1990	Although athletes had perished in fraternity initiations several times going back to 1928 at the University of Texas, the death of a rookie lacrosse-club player Nick Haben at Western Illinois University was likely the first conducted by an athletic team rather than by a fraternity. That year, the National Panhellenic Council, a national umbrella group of prestigious African-American fraternities and sororities, outlawed and condemned all acts of hazing.
1991	Television network CNN reported on a U.S. Marine Corps hazing ceremony called "blood-pinning," which aired in 1993, to raise an outcry against extreme hazing rituals in the mili-

tary. Those who were promoted during the ritual were shown screaming as their insignia pins were pushed into their chests.

1993   *Dazed and Confused* was released as a movie, depicting high school hazing as humorous.

1994   The death of Southeast Missouri State Kappa Alpha Psi pledge Michael Davis following a cruel pummeling in a hazing attracted widespread media coverage.

1998   Ann Landers printed a letter written by Rita Saucier about the death of her son Chad at Auburn University in a fraternity bottle exchange that led to increasing awareness of how alcohol and hazing too often are inextricably linked.

1999   Alfred University researchers published a national survey called *Initiation Rites and Athletics: A National Survey of NCAA Sports Teams* that estimated that one in every five athletes was subjected to grossly unacceptable and potentially illegal hazing.

2000   Adrian Heideman's death in a Chico State fraternity house leads to widespread scrutiny of hazing and drinking in the California system of colleges. In an initiative called Select 2000, the National Interfraternity Conference and National Panhellenic Conference step up previously introduced measures to control hazing and binge drinking.

2001   Arizona became the forty-third state to pass anti-hazing legislation.

2002   Foolish pledging events took the lives of male students at the University of Maryland and University of Nevada, Reno and the lives of two females at California State Los Angeles. All four deaths brought strong denials that the deaths fit the definition of hazing.

2003   Following a longstanding pledge tradition, members of Yale University's Delta Kappa Epsilon staged a night of reveling and bonding in New York. Four participants were killed and five were injured in an automobile accident on a poorly lighted Connecticut highway. The chapter was also that of President George W. Bush and former president George Bush. Fraternity members said the event did not meet their definition of hazing. No charges were filed.

Security on Campus, Inc., begins sending letters of inquiry to campus officials to ask why hazing incidents that appear to meet the definition of criminal hazing were handled by school judicial review instead of by police investigation.

Police charged eleven members of Psi Epsilon Chi fraternity at SUNY Plattsburgh with hazing and criminally negligent homicide on April 30 in the death of pledge Walter "Dean" Jennings. Police said Jennings died as a result of drinking massive amounts of water for ten days as part of an initiation.

The Hazing Reader

1   Understanding Fraternity Hazing

Stephen Sweet

Editor's note: *Stephen Sweet worked at New York State as a sociology professor in 1997, when a 17-year-old pledge for Theta Chi fraternity died during an initiation ritual involving the drinking of tremendous amounts of alcohol. Sweet, who was personally and professionally interested in the case, applies symbolic interactionist theory to hazing rituals in an attempt to make intellectual sense of a tradition that appears senseless to people outside the hazing fraternity.*

Sometimes students behave in ways that, on the surface, defy logic and reason. In many circumstances these behaviors can be attributed to immaturity and require little response from college counselors and administrators. In other circumstances, such as the events surrounding fraternity hazing, these behaviors are not so easily dismissed. In this chapter, I take a bit of methodological license and offer a rich account of how symbolic interactionist theory can be used to make sense of student life, using fraternity hazing as a means of illustration. The insights of symbolic interactionism reveal that fraternity hazing is not illogical, beyond reason, or the product of immaturity. I suggest that hazing is the result of group-interaction processes that are linked with students' need for belonging, their isolation from other social relations on campus, and subcultural definitions that legitimate hazing events as a necessary component of fraternity initiation rites.

This chapter is designed to operate on two levels. One level is specifically directed to fraternity and sorority advisors or administrators dealing with fraternity hazing problems. Although a complete set of prescriptions or policies to prevent fraternity hazing is beyond the scope of this chapter, I offer a theoretical explanation of the elements of the fraternity subculture that perpetuate hazing. My hope is that once this is understood, this information can be used to creatively work with students to minimize the problems that are endemic to some of these organizations. Although much of the following is critical of fraternities, please understand that my intent is not to muckrake or cast aspersions on these organizations. Fraternities and sororities do many positive things on and off college campuses. My concern is simply to offer information and a perspective that can help advisors ameliorate one problematic aspect of fraternity life.

On another level, this chapter is about symbolic interactionism, a perspective commonly used by sociologists who specialize in the study of face-to-face social encounters. Although some terms have migrated to mainstream discourse, relatively few individuals outside the fields of social psychology and sociology recognize the wide-ranging implications of this perspective. Therefore, as I explain the origins of fraternity hazing, I focus discussion on symbolic interactionist concepts, defining key terms and identifying the work of theorists central to the development of this perspective. Once they are conversant in the rudiments of symbolic interactionism, I hope that counselors and administrators find it a useful means of comprehending and addressing other aspects of student social behavior on campus.

Method

Studying fraternity hazing is methodologically problematic for a number of reasons. Greek organizations are secretive by nature. Members are reluctant to reveal information regarding initiation rites, according to Thomas Leemon's (1972) firsthand observations of a fraternity house. As a consequence, survey methods are not especially useful, and the responses those methods use are likely to be of questionable reliability. To seek formal interviews with participants involved in a fatal hazing is also ethically problematic, given the resulting trauma of these events and the ways in which responses could affect the subjects' well-being in lawsuits that commonly follow. Participant-observer methods are also not feasible, due to the ethical and time constraints that prevent researchers from situating themselves in a participant-observer role to gather information on the circumstances leading up to a hazing event. Content analysis of existing journalistic sources are also of limited use because these tend to reconstruct hazing events to fit familiar narratives. Although police reports can offer descriptions of hazing events, they offer little in the way of a cultural understanding of the context in which this behavior occurs. Another methodological concern is that these sources tend to focus solely on the immediate circumstances of the incident and therefore lack important information on events that precede the hazing incident by days or weeks.

Lacking the opportunity to study fraternity hazing with traditional methodology, I have been forced to adopt a piecemeal approach and have gathered data from a variety of sources to identify the contextual features that surround these events. The sources of my data (loosely defined) are informal unstructured interviews with approximately twenty current and former members of Greek organizations. Some of these individuals were students indirectly connected with Theta Chi, a fraternity that experienced a hazing death in February 1997, while others were members of other fraternities and sororities inside and outside the community of Potsdam, New York. This group constitutes a sample of males who willingly discussed their experiences in Greek organizations. Other information comes from my participation on the SUNY Potsdam Greek Life Task

Force, a committee consisting of faculty, administrators, fraternity and sorority members, and representatives from national fraternity and sorority organizations. The remainder of my information comes from scholarly research on fraternity culture, which I reframe within the lens of the symbolic interactionist perspective. The obvious limitations to this "methodology" are that I do not have a representative sample of fraternities or fraternity members. This being said, I am confident that sufficient data were collected to provide robust analysis.

Results

Frequency and Types of Hazing Events

On February 10, 1997, 17-year-old Clarkson University freshman Binaya ("Bini") Oja, along with twenty other students, began pledging Theta Chi fraternity in Potsdam, New York. As part of their initiation, the pledges gathered in a semicircle around a bucket and were instructed by fraternity members to take turns drinking hard liquor. If any pledges did not drink the liquor fast enough so that bubbles were seen rising in the bottles, they were instructed to guzzle a full glass of beer. The point of the game was simple: each pledge was expected to drink until he vomited. Bini drank a lethal amount of alcohol and was carried upstairs. The next morning he was discovered with his feet up on a couch and his face on the floor next to a garbage can. An autopsy determined that he died by inhaling his own vomit.

Students connected indirectly with the Theta Chi fraternity informed me that the fraternity brothers actually tried to stop Bini from drinking when they saw him "overdoing it." Newspaper accounts, on the other hand, suggest that he was pressured very strongly to drink heavily. One of Bini's fellow pledges reported in a police statement "[Bini] seemed to be drinking more than the others, and I think he wanted to impress others that he could drink a lot." Taking all of the information available, it seems clear that Bini deliberately and willingly engaged in actions that he thought would draw social approval from the people whose opinions he valued highly.

Bini's experiences conform to other hazing deaths documented in the most detailed descriptive study of fraternity hazing to date, *Broken Pledges* (1990). Hank Nuwer reveals hundreds of cases of pledges placed in, and willingly submitting to, psychologically and physically punishing conditions. A few case examples taken from his book reveal the creativity of fraternities and the compliance of pledges in this regard:

1974: Monmouth College, West Long Branch, New Jersey; Zeta Beta Tau
Members ordered five pledges to dig six-foot "graves" on a sandy beach on the Atlantic Ocean. The five then lay down in the graves while members threw handfuls of sand atop them. The grave of William E. Flowers Jr. collapsed, and he began inhaling sand. He died of asphyxiation. A grand jury called the death "accidental,"

clearing seven Zeta Beta Tau members who had been arrested on charges of manslaughter.

1980: Stetson University, Deland, Florida; Pi Kappa Phi
Several members of the Chi Chapter were expelled from the fraternity for shocking pledges with an electrical device. Seven years later the entire chapter was suspended for one year in a similar incident, possibly involving the same electrical device.

1986: Manhattan College, Bronx, New York; Beta Sigma
On one of the coldest nights of the winter, pledge Michael Flynn, 19, was abandoned naked on an isolated country road in Putnam County, New York. During the drive by automobile to the drop-off point, fraternity brothers poured beer on his feet, ignoring two pleas from Flynn that his feet were freezing. The windchill factor outside the car was 35 degrees below zero. Flynn's feet were seriously frostbitten. He was hospitalized for two weeks and suffered permanent health problems. A judge acquitted the four defendants, saying he could not determine that the brothers had knowingly subjected Flynn to frostbite.

In the context of discussions with current and former members of Greek organizations, I learned of toes being broken by hammers in games of "Fear," beatings with paddles, sleep deprivation, submersions in vats of filth, and drinking "games."

On the surface, these acts appear at worst sadistic and at best stupid. These terms, however, are flawed because they focus the sources of these problems within individuals rather than the interactional processes that happen between people. Sadism, for example, implies the existence of a psychological or moral abnormality in the character of the fraternity brothers or pledges. Although published accounts indicate that some hazed pledges had difficulty adjusting to college life, most appear to be normal, healthy young men, according to Nuwer's conclusion. Sadism also suggests that fraternity brothers harbor hostility toward the pledges. In fact, the opposite is true; fraternity brothers tend to care very deeply for their pledges and feel great regret when a pledge is actually seriously injured, as is the case with members of Theta Chi. The term "stupidity" implies that fraternity members and pledges are of below-average intelligence. Data do not seem to support the contention that hazing is a product of low intelligence or ignorance. As indication of this, the Greek Life Task Force at SUNY Potsdam found no difference between the grade point averages of Greeks (pledges and members) and their non-Greek counterparts. The SUNY Potsdam task force also identified that Greek members have a high level of awareness of what constitutes hazing and the legal consequences of infractions against hazing policy. With these insights in mind, apparently the source of hazing problems is not the result of personality or the intellectual shortcomings of pledges or fraternity members.

Despite difficulties in estimating how many nonfatal hazing incidents occur each year and go unreported, college administrators, counselors, and professors are all too aware of the problem of fraternity hazing. A literature review published in *Broken Pledges* found over 400 documented hazing incidents resulting in serious injury and death from 1900 to 1990; additional incidents are described in Nuwer's *Wrongs of Passage* (1999). A survey of 283 fraternity advisors revealed that over half of these advisors believed that hazing existed in some of their groups (Shaw and Morgan 1990). Another barrier to estimating the frequency of hazing is that students often do not recognize when they are being hazed or abused (Moffatt 1989). It is ironic that colleges and universities add to the problem of estimating hazing by deliberately avoiding inquiry into hazing incidents for fear of damaging institutional reputations or incurring financial liability to victims (Curry 1989; Nuwer 1990).

The problem of fraternity hazing does not seem to be abating. So little success has been achieved that the *Chronicle of Higher Education* declared in 1997 that most efforts to address fraternity hazing have failed.

The conclusion I have reached, supported by an extensive literature review on fraternity and sorority culture, is that hazings are quite frequent and are generally not characterized by sadism, stupidity, or even coercion. A full understanding of why pledges willingly participate in their own degradation involves delving into the sources of pledges' identities and their relationships with fraternity brothers. Symbolic interactionism offers a useful path to insights in these processes.

Symbolic Interactionist Theory

Probably more than any other individual, Herbert Blumer is responsible for introducing the symbolic interactionist perspective to mainstream sociology in a series of articles, which were later published in his book *Symbolic Interactionism: Perspective and Method* (1969). Although not the first symbolic interactionist, Blumer was the first sociologist to use the term symbolic interactionism as a way of linking a number of sociological studies into a theoretical camp. Symbolic interactionists are a heterogeneous group, and their perspective has been used to address a variety of social encounters. Although the research interests of these scholars vary, Blumer effectively identified a set of premises that link symbolic interactionists with one another. These premises include:

1. Human beings act toward things on the basis of the meanings these things have for them.
2. The meaning of things arises out of the social interaction people have with each other.
3. People engage in interpretation in dealing with the things they encounter.

Symbolic interactionists stress that selves are socially constructed and that people play an active role in shaping the direction of their own and each others' behaviors through the use of symbols. The symbolic interactionist perspective challenges many of the beliefs about the self, particularly the notion that people are made up of enduring personality traits. People commonly believe that they are a particular "type" of person, such as an introvert or extrovert. Symbolic interactionists assert that the self is highly malleable and is constantly being shaped and reshaped. To be more accurate, according to the symbolic interactionist perspective, the self is better characterized as a process than an object. Because relatively few outside of sociology are conversant in symbolic interactionism, I focus on a few concepts and metaphors central to symbolic interactionist theory, drawing from classic sociological research and theory, and apply these to fraternity initiation rites.

The Power of Material Selves and Social Selves

One of the most important features of symbolic interactionist theory is the appreciation that selves are constructed. William James (1890/1983) forcefully argued that the self is made up as much of social and material components as it is of inner drives and traits. The material self is constituted by tangible objects that represent who we are as individuals. These objects include things such as the type of car a person drives and a person's clothes, hairstyle, and bank account. These things demonstrate to us and others who we are as individuals and constitute our "identity kits," wrote Erving Goffman (1961).

Greek organizations manipulate the material selves of their members by constructing new identity kits for their recruits. During pledging, students are invariably given some of the following items: pledge pins, T-shirts, sweatshirts, rings, books, and paddles bearing the fraternity's insignia. Pledges and initiates also commonly decorate their rooms extensively with Greek paraphernalia. When pledges surround themselves with these items, it enhances the degree to which the fraternity becomes a part of their identity. A 1997 study of sororities by Arthur revealed that pledges often build their entire wardrobe around the colors and insignias of their organization. The study indicated that the clothing was an essential means by which the initiates and new members bolstered their identity to themselves and others in the sorority.

The social self, according to James, is the set of relations we have with other people, including our friends, relatives, and business associates. James points out that a great deal of any individual's identity is comprised of his or her social relationships. If a member's group experiences success, for example, the egos of the individual members inflate. Being a professor at Harvard, a computer engineer at NASA, or a brother in Phi Chi Epsilon may increase an individual's pride simply through association with a prestigious organization. Conversely, if an individual is socially affiliated with stigmatized groups, they often come to feel mortified and contaminated, observed Goffman. Fraternities deliberately and systematically limit the social relations of their pledges, forcing them to form tight groups with intimate contact. In this way, sociologists accurately describe them as "greedy organizations," noted Arthur. Greedy organizations are groups that set up strong boundaries between members and nonmembers and assert exclusivity. Fraternity initiation rites are designed to terminate or curtail many of the associations that pledges previously held outside of that organization. As the pledge becomes more isolated from other social groups, the identity of the individual becomes ever more closely tied with the Greek organization (Leemon 1972; Arthur 1997). As a consequence, "exit costs" increase because pledges literally lose a major part of themselves by withdrawing through depledging.

The Looking-Glass Process

Charles Horton Cooley's (1922/1970) concept of the looking-glass self is a metaphor to describe the process by which a person develops a self-concept. Cooley suggests that any person's self-concept is largely a product of what other people reflect to that person about himself or herself. At its most simple level, the theory suggests that if people consistently yawn or fail to make eye contact when a person talks, that person is likely to come to believe that she is uninteresting. Conversely, a person who is given trophies, awards, and praise will be more apt to believe that the self she possesses has talent and is worthy.

In fact, people often do not know what others think of them; the best they can do is interpret the gestures of others. A yawn, after all, may simply indicate that the other person is tired. In reality, individuals do not necessarily know what other people think of them, nor are they aware that they are constantly engaged in interpretation of other people's gestures. The looking glass, therefore, may be better conceptualized as a clouded mirror. We never know what is exactly going on in other people's heads; the best we can do is make informed judgments about ourselves based on the gestures that we perceive others to be making.

Cooley's theory suggests that individuals' selves can be built up or brought down if others send them signals that they are worthy or unworthy of respect. In an analysis of fraternity initiation rites, Leemon shows that fraternities manipulate pledges' definitions of self in a conscious manner during initiation. In the early phases of the initiation rites, during rushing and immediately following the acceptance of the pledge bid, fraternity members offer self-affirming gestures to the pledge. They are treated as special people and their egos inflate as a consequence. However, once pledges are effectively separated from their old connections outside of the fraternity, members then send pledges clear signals that they are of lesser status than fraternity members. Not only does positive contact decrease but also pledges are systematically degraded; for example, by being called upon to perform cleaning tasks around the house or to carry matches for members just in case they need a light. Why would pledges agree to do something that they ordinarily would resist? According to Cooley's theory, they do so in part because they strongly desire the affirmation of others.

Heavy alcohol consumption is promoted in many fraternities, and fraternity members are much more likely to binge drink in comparison to their non-Greek peers, according to annual studies by Henry Wechsler. Court records of hazing events document that pledges that resist fraternity members' commands to drink are met with teasing and ridicule (Curry 1989). At Alfred University's Klan Alpine house, the fraternity where pledge Chuck Stenzel died, considerable social pressure was put on pledges to consume alcohol in excessive quantities.

So important was heavy alcohol consumption to this fraternity's subculture that members would actually photograph each other vomiting. In these pictures, one can observe the sheer joy of the members watching other members get sick over the fraternity-house porch railing, according to Nuwer's *Broken Pledges*. The individual that conforms to this expectation will likely experience congratulations on being "a party animal." Bini Oja experienced very similar responses from the Theta Chi fraternity brothers. As he and the other pledges chugged liquor, they were accorded praise from the brothers. As members vomited, the brothers cheered. Not incidentally, the first pledge to vomit was also given a T-shirt.

Definitions of the Situations

In 1928, William I. Thomas introduced the importance of the definition of the situation and formulated a maxim now commonly referred to as the Thomas theorem: If people define situations as real, they are real in their consequences. The Thomas theorem implies that researchers need to examine the way in which hazing events are defined. Definitions of situations are produced, in part, through linguistics (Lakoff and Johnson 1980). Tobacco companies, for instance, define cigarette smoking as a "habit" and a "lifestyle," whereas critics of cigarette companies use the terms "addiction" and "death style." Shift the words and the definition of the situation shifts as well.

Fraternities do not tell their pledges that they are going to be "hazed," "beaten," or "abused," but pledges anticipate some degree of abuse during "hell week." Initiation rites are framed as a "tradition" involving "discipline" that is "character-building" and reveals "loyalty" and "commitment." The belief that hazing is part of a tradition is one of the most serious barriers in getting fraternity members to reform their initiation procedures. Colleges are also reluctant to use the word "hazing" to describe events that lead to the death or injury of fraternity initiates. For example, following the hazing death of Chuck Stenzel, the words "manslaughter" and "abuse" were notably absent from the public addresses of Alfred University officials. These officials were more inclined to use terms such as "accident" or "unfortunate incident." According to Nuwer's *Broken Pledges* and *Wrongs of Passage*, so long as hazing remains socially defined as "pranks" or "jokes" or in other benign terms, the practice will likely continue.

Cases of individual and gang rapes occurring in fraternity houses have been extensively documented. There is considerable evidence that a rape culture is endemic to some fraternity houses and that members and initiates in those houses are expected to either perform actual rapes or act out rape scenes (Sanday 1990). In these fraternities, gang rape is commonly termed "pulling train," referring to men lining up like train cars waiting to have sex with the same woman. Usually this woman has been deliberately drugged or made so drunk that she loses the ability to resist. Sanday argues that pulling train becomes possible, in part, as a consequence of the way fraternities often define women. Women are referred to as "sluts," "gashes," "heifers," "swatches," and "cracks." Terms such as these dehumanize the female in the mind of the male, enabling him to avoid thinking of her subjective experiences. Members also avoid feeling guilty by placing blame on the rape victim for the attack, wondering about the type of woman who would allow herself to be so drunk or stoned that she could not say what she wanted. Definitions of situations such as this carry tremendous weight in shaping behaviors of fraternity members and the social responses to their actions.[1]

Words are one way to define a situation. Another way to define a situation is to engage in packaging. Packaging involves the systematic linking of symbols and objects together in such a way that perceptions are shaped and managed, as Fred E. Katz noted in *Ordinary People and Extraordinary Evil* (1993). Cigarette companies package their products by linking cigarettes with images of freedom and sexuality, such as the smoker shown on horseback or lovers cavorting on a blanket. Nazi propaganda films packaged images of Jews with images of rats crawling out of sewers, supporting the cultural definition of Jews as dangerous elements in German society that needed eradication.

How do fraternities package hazing in the context of initiation rites? When fraternity members seek to define a situation as one of solemn importance, rooms are darkened, candles are lit, robes are worn, and fraternity symbols are displayed (Nuwer 1990). Any event that accompanies these cultural symbols, such as having initiates lie down in a coffin, will likely be defined as solemn simply by being coupled with those symbols. Situations can also be defined as festive by using bright lights and rock music. Once a situation is defined as a party, or, as in Bini Oja's case, "a game," initiates can enjoy the act of drinking to the point of vomiting.

Role Taking and Reference Groups

Charles Herbert Mead's book *Mind, Self and Society from the Standpoint of a Social Behaviorist* (1934) is largely concerned with developing a theory that accounts for the maintenance of effective social encounters. In simple terms, Mead wanted to identify the process by which two or more individuals could get together and interact. His explanation examined the concept of role-taking. Role-taking is the mental act of viewing oneself from the position of another person before engaging in a potential action. Tamotsu Shibutani (1961) enlarged upon Mead's concept of role-taking to highlight the importance of reference groups. Reference groups are subdivisions of society from the person's perspective. They could be groups that an individual belongs to or desires to belong to or any number of other social groupings such as race, class, or gender. In each case, the individual thinks about how his or her actions would be viewed from the perspective of that specific subgroup of society.

One thing stands clear in the analysis of fraternity hazing deaths and of pledging as a whole—the importance of the fraternity members as a reference group to pledges. When pledges are asked to do embarrassing or sometimes dangerous acts, apparently they are usually not thinking "What would my mother say?" or "What do those strangers think of me?" They are more concerned with how they might look to their fellow pledges and the fraternity members. The case of Bini Oja reveals the power of reference groups and role-taking. Bini's fellow pledge was probably accurate in his assessment that Bini's motives for drinking so much alcohol was that he wanted to impress others. Rather than just waiting for approval to emerge, Bini deliberately engaged in actions that he thought would draw social approval from his reference group.

Tattoos are a recent trend among fraternities and sororities, and members now sometimes obtain tattoos to display the organization's insignia on their body, as was the case with an entire pledge class for a fraternity at the University of Vermont. Some members of fraternities even brand fraternity letters on their forearms. The process of branding and tattooing is a symbolic display, not only of having the letters but also of being willing to endure intense pain for the organization. In all probability the individuals choose to do this because they believe that it will increase their status in the group.

Another aspect of Mead's theory bears emphasizing. Mead conceptualizes "the self" not as a thing but rather as a process. People think of their selves as objects, but that object is highly malleable and individuals are active in shaping the self that they call their own. For example, most people change their hairstyle only after considerable thought. Although as individuals we think of ourselves as being stable things, there is great potential to change if we want to redefine ourselves. The stability of the self is largely a product of maintaining stable sets of social relations and a stable definition of what one's self is. If the relations are reshaped or the self is redefined, the self will be reshaped as well. As an illustration, consider the profound change that occurs in people when they undergo a religious conversion such as becoming "born again" and start interacting with other people who define themselves in a like manner. A similar change occurs once individuals define themselves as "pledges" and "fraternity members."

Discussion

The symbolic interactionist perspective reveals that hazing is not simply the result of psychologically or morally flawed individuals; rather, it is the result of a confluence of symbols, manipulated identities, and definitions of situations that are organized in the context of fraternity initiation rites. Eliminating fraternity hazing is a challenging proposition because it is so strongly embedded in the subculture of some fraternity houses. The symbolic interactionist perspective offers alternate understandings of the actions of pledges and fraternity brothers and leads to very different approaches than those of some "common sense" solutions.

As a point of contrast, behaviorist theory suggests that most behavior is learned through a combination of rewards and punishments. Policy implications of this theory suggest that rewarding fraternity members for desirable behaviors and punishing them for undesirable behaviors would decrease the incidence of hazing. Unfortunately, this does not seem to work in practice, as Alfie

Kohn (1993), an advocate for teaching classroom values, has stressed. Instead of looking at rewards and punishments as solutions, symbolic interactionists suggest that the path for reform is through examining meaning systems that surround social encounters and the power these "realities" have in shaping individuals' decisions about their conduct.

Fraternity hazing results from definitions of situations that compel fraternity members to believe that abuse of recruits is a desirable part of entry into the fraternity. In fact, Greek organizations use the same type of strategy other groups use to cultivate strong commitment and loyalty, wrote Leemon in 1972. Of late, many newspapers have noted that doctors, for example, are commonly hazed (although this term is rarely used) during residency when they are expected to work incredibly long shifts that necessarily involve sleep deprivation. Changing a culture, of course, is not an easy matter.

Studies reveal that Greek subculture places a high value on secrecy and autonomy. This aspect of Greek society is especially problematic for college advisors and administrators because fraternities are not receptive to sharing their secrets with these outsiders. Fraternities are also not receptive to intrusion into what they perceive as internal affairs. Because college authorities do not constitute a salient reference group for Greek members, advice from advisors or administrators can go unheeded.

Given that college authorities are not a reference group, counselors may be well advised to mobilize resources to put campus groups in touch with insiders who will be accorded immediate respect. Representatives of national fraternity organizations are one such group. National representatives are insiders and therefore can offer reflections and advice that would otherwise not be well received. In lieu of a formal presentation by student-life professionals on how to conduct a good pledge program, offering financial support for such a presentation by alumni with Greek affiliations could be a strategically advantageous approach to disseminating needed information.

Another direct application of symbolic interactionist theory relates to reshaping definitions of situations. As discussed above, hazing occurs because fraternities define it as a necessary part of their initiation rites and package it carefully to pledges in order to produce compliance. Advisors can be instrumental agents in reshaping definitions of situations so that members of Greek organizations willingly accept the need for change. Rather than acting as policing agents, advisors can serve as "redefiners."

For example, a young woman came into one of my classes with a large paper clock tied around her neck. On the clock was written the phrase "Ask me what time it is." The student's head repeatedly dropped during the class and she obviously was struggling to keep her eyes open. At the end of class, I tactfully asked her to stay behind for a moment. With the other students gone, I told her that I knew she was being asked to stay awake by her sorority sisters. She did not deny this. I told her that I didn't expect her to break her vow of secrecy, but that I wanted her to recognize that she was being hazed. She responded that "it would be all over soon." I responded again, "I want you to recognize that you are being hazed." From her nonverbal response, I saw that this registered and a new reality was created. I then followed this statement by saying "I want you to recognize that right now it is a choice for you to submit to this abuse and that you can choose to go to sleep if you want to." After allowing her to process this, I asked her to reflect on how she plans to conduct herself as a sorority sister and if she will do the same type of thing when she is responsible for her own group of pledges. I suggested that if she wanted things to change, she would have to be responsible for producing this change. This encounter took about five minutes at the end of a class.

Advisors will vary considerably in their interaction styles, and the above example is not intended as a prescription of how to interact with students in the face of a suspected hazing event. I use it as a means to illustrate how advisors may take advantage of the symbolic interactionist theory by positioning themselves from the perspective of pledges, understanding their definition of a situation, and then interacting strategically to change that definition when appropriate. I did this by not challenging the student's solemn oath of secrecy or by demeaning her sorority or Greek society. At the same time, I attempted to redefine this student's perception that submission to hazing was unavoidable. I also redefined this particular pledging rite as abuse, and as a consequence possibly influenced this student's short-term response as well as her long-term conduct as a future sorority sister.

One other direct application of symbolic interactionism relates to the social nature of the self. The symbolic interactionist perspective reveals that pledges' willingness to submit to abuse is linked with their inability to think of themselves outside of their status as future fraternity members. Pledges literally lose their "old self" during the pledging process as they are given new identity kits and new social relations and definitions of self and shift to a new reference group. As pledges construct new identities to correspond with fraternity membership, they have greater difficulties envisioning alternate paths of action that contradict the desires of their reference group. Left unchecked, fraternities and sororities will likely exploit the advantages of socially isolating their pledges. Although this will not necessarily lead to hazing, it increases the likelihood that pledges will submit to being hazed.

Advisors and administrators can curtail this potential by limiting the power of fraternities and sororities to isolate pledges from other social groups. Student-affairs professionals can help prevent hazing by structuring policies to facilitate pledges' connections with other students outside of the Greek subculture. For example, following a recent hazing death, the Massachusetts Institute of Technology has begun restricting pledging to students who have already completed their freshman year. Possibly this policy will enable new students to build stronger relationships outside of fraternities, thereby making resistance to hazing a more tenable alternative.

Social problems such as fraternity hazing have no easy solutions. Symbolic interactionism offers some useful insights, though, in explaining this problematic social behavior. Maintaining sensitivity to the ways in which fraternities understand hazing and the ways fraternities shape pledges' abilities to define their selves may be the best way to construct programs and policies designed to prevent hazing.

NOTES

1.   See also Martin and Hummer 1989; Nurius, Dimeff, and Graham 1996; Rhoads 1995; and Strombler 1994.

2   Males Courting Males

Lionel Tiger

Editor's note: *Lionel Tiger has contributed his theories on hazing in essays for publications such as* The New Yorker *as well as in an interview for the* New York Times. *His 1969 work on hazing,* Men in Groups, *was perhaps the first attempt by a scholar to recognize that males endure hazing with the expectation of gaining approval from high-status males.*

Let us first set out a hard fact: observation and experience and extensive data allow us to say that [heterosexual] men prefer to be surrounded by beautiful and available women rather than by aloof and unattractive ones—the sense of manliness is enhanced in one situation, depressed by the other. This is obvious. What is also obvious is that profound and complex interactions occur between the enviable man and his choice harem and between the luckless other male and his less-exciting friends. In general, [heterosexual] men prefer attractive [heterosexual] women and women prefer men who are attractive and powerful. To use the term nonpejoratively, we are all sexual status-seekers, and this is an explicable and appreciable biologically based process.

An analogy exists here with the relations between males. Males will prefer to be with high-status males defined by their community as attractive rather than with the contrary. They gain status themselves from the positions of their companions. A group of men conscious of their status, power, and security differs in emotional tone from a [homeless] group in the [old New York] Bowery. Individuals possess self-respect or self-depreciation in terms of their group relationships and the status of their group. One of the functions of the initiation ceremonies is, in these terms, the insurance of "fit," or consonance, between the males already in a group and the newcomers to it. A group of men is pleased with itself and with its status and quality. To affirm to its members and to outsiders that recruits are worthy of membership, a process of initiation is contrived which involves stringent ordeals to test the courage and endurance of initiates. This proves or disproves their suitability and keenness to join. The initiation ceremony, then, is part of a male-male "courtship" pattern tied to a tendency for males to seek status among other males, to form groups with them, and to value highly the corporate "presentation-of-self" to the community at large. The implacable reality of this identification is suggested by the gangs in

West Side Story: "When you're a Jet you're a Jet all the way" runs the song; the commitment is almost like a marriage. . . . The musical . . . illustrates the dynamics of male bonding with vividness and understanding of the meaning of bonding for the men involved.

Initiation is a courtship in the same sense that privileged [heterosexual] men are more likely to marry equally desirable women. The superior male groups can attract the best candidates, can insist upon the most rigorous entrance ordeals, and can provide the greatest satisfaction and rewards for the membership. The *Alte Herren* of the elite German student dueling society, the Deutsche Burschenschaft, " . . . not only finance fraternities but are said to find jobs for members and generally operate as a closed society. To be expelled from a fraternity can still mean social ruin: to belong means life-long protection and obligation."[1]

A comparable process appears to occur in some North American fraternities. How potential members are selected by the various individual fraternities on a campus is of interest here. At a number of review sessions with candidates, sometimes called "ding" sessions, fraternities and potential initiates seek to match each other. There are variations in membership fees, standards of living, dress, entertainment, etc., between fraternities, which complicate the process of "fit" between initiates' socio-economic position and the fraternities. "Fit" is generally achieved, though there are individual cases of upward mobility involving persons who work part-time to maintain those standards that are informally but firmly applied to all members of each fraternity. Welcoming entertainments mixed with hazing activities occupy initiates until the final initiation takes place. By this time both parties are more or less committed to the bonding.

The initiations themselves frequently involve partial or complete nudity of initiates, and in many there are homo-erotic implications of greater or lesser clarity.[2] One fraternity in the U.S. evidently brands its members. Another conducts this ceremony as the pledges are stripped and stand in front of an open fire in which several branding irons are conspicuously heating. Pledges are then blindfolded and asked questions such as, "Do you really want to join the fraternity? Why do you? Are you worthy? Are you willing to be hurt for the fraternity?" It is rare for an individual to withdraw his candidacy at this point. Then the candidate is told he is to be branded. The branding irons are withdrawn from the fire and plunged into a bucket of cold water to create a hissing noise at the same time as a cold iron is jabbed against the buttock of the member. He is then a member (pending a final formal initiation). Another fraternity strips pledges and ties bricks to their penises. After being blindfolded the pledges are asked to pick up and throw the bricks without knowing that the strings attached to their penises have been cut. In Montreal, I once encountered a group of about ten men wearing dinner jackets and looking drunk but exhilarated. They were carrying another of their number whom they were pummeling as they dragged him along the sidewalk at the busy corner of Peel and Sherbrooke streets, near McGill University. A good [citizen], I looked more closely and noticed he was bleeding from the face and tried to stop them from hitting him any more. The pledge protested my action, saying, "Leave me alone, I'm being initiated," and one of his tormentors said, "It's nothing, it's just fun." Suddenly a car appeared and all eleven men pushed their way into it and veered through a red light. Interestingly, when pledges are finally received into the group, they may don a fraternity ring, usually worn on the third finger of the left hand (which is either unconsciously symbolic or a capricious tradition of no significance).

A professional colleague has described to me the following initiation he experienced in a fraternity at Cornell University. It is almost a parody of the symbolizations implicit in many initiations. Before the ceremony, pledges are required to find a variety of objects with sexual connotations. These are brought to the ceremony. Included are a five-inch nail and a jar of Vaseline. Pledges are arranged in a circle facing in. Behind each pledge is a senior member of the fraternity. In a progression articulated with various vows and statements, the pledges remove all their clothes. They are handed their nails and Vaseline and told to grease the nails and pass the nails back to the seniors behind them. The room is now dark. Then they are told to bend over, in effect presenting their buttocks to the seniors. The right hand is placed on the right buttock and the left extended back to the senior, to receive the nail, but a can of beer is placed in the hand, the lights come on, the pledges dress, and a drinking party begins. It is difficult to avoid mentioning the superficial parallel between this ceremony and the pattern, among some primates, of dominant males briefly mounting subdominants; this appears to define or redefine status. By contrast, a female of the same university described a sorority initiation during which pledges wear white floor-length garments and vow to be true to the sorority and to the ideals of virtue—in particular, chastity.

These are, of course, relatively mild ordeals. Military ones may be far more severe. For example, the training of novice U.S. Marines at one point in the 1950s culminated in a number of deaths through fatigue, over-exposure, and illness. Entrants to certain military academies will have their heads shaved and will be subjected to an elaborate hazing and fagging [servitude] process by their seniors and by instructors. In one situation, entrants are required to stand stiffly at attention while any senior can punch the entrants' stomachs as hard and often as he wishes. Webster believes puberty rites and comparable rituals are not merely sadistic. "It is more likely that in many cases what we regard as merely tests of courage and endurance were once of deeper significance and were imposed originally for [religious] or magical purposes."

... The lists of punishments and humiliations suffered by candidates for initiation into societies around the world is an immense catalog of ingenious perversities, rigorous ordeals, and bizarre demonstrations of subordination.[3] This is largely a male phenomenon. The initiations of females are generally less violent. ... In comparison with the grim ceremonies of male fraternities, sorority initiations are more socially than individually oriented and involve considerably less harsh demands on pledges. For example, in a Canadian sorority, the initiation consisted in gathering a list of names, addresses, and telephone numbers of twenty-five male students. In another, as they walked around the campus, pledges were required to wear halos about their heads and large signboards giving their name, course [of study], and telephone number. This is not to say that clitoridectomy and scarification where they occur [in some female societies] are not painful and harrowing to individual females. [*Ed. note:* Since this essay was written in 1969, the number of deaths and serious injuries of female pledges in sorority initiations have continued to significantly trail similar numbers in male fraternities. However, instances of female physical hazing (branding, coerced drinking, degradation, shoving) were reported more often in the 1990s and early 2000s.]

. . . This chapter cannot conclude without my comment that I do not know what kind of biological mechanisms would operate should there in fact be a biological basis for secret societies, initiations, clubs, and so on. It is difficult to specify the central constituent of the bonding process. This is, of course, the critical gap in the argument. . . . I have [elsewhere in his book] already referred to suggestions that cortical-amygdaloid evolution was associated with pertinent patterns of hierarchy formation and the inhibition of intra-group aggression. Closely associated with this is the apparently general association of relatively intense emotional experience during initiations, in secret societies, and between members of formalized male bonds. It is a finding of ethology that strong emotion tends to occur during behaviors of biological importance: that is, behaviors which are basic to the nervous systems of the animals concerned and thus which in the logic of evolution reflect early and crucial adaptations. Another clue may be the primarily male and generally unisexual character of the organizational forms with which I have been dealing. This need not only result from biological propensity but from the obvious need in any culture to differentiate the sexes, if only to surround the process of reproduction with reliable structural supports.

Another clue . . . is the curious association of bonding with a concern for blood initiations, with nudity . . . , and (particularly in Euro-American cultures) with the drinking of alcohol. All these phenomena may connect with the hunting history of man and with the relationship between male bonding and hunting behavior. [Anthropologist] Raymond Dart has suggested that Australopithicines may have drunk the blood of the animals or conspecifics they killed.[4] I [note] the symbolic importance of mugs to fraternity members . . . and the considerable role of drinking in men's groups in many cultures. While it is very much a suggestion, is there some relationship between human hunting history and contemporary drinking behavior—particularly of the "clubby" and "hail-fellow-well-met" variety? In the military, "drinking level" is an important mode of social control of drinking and of establishing group norms. It is part of folklore that persons who drink alone are especially prone to alcoholism. Is it possible that group drinking facilitates male bonding among inhibited individuals (who also believe that alcohol eases the often complex process of heterosexual liaison)?

But these various factors, singly or together, do not combine to provide specific information about the specific mechanism of bonding. We do not know if the "morale" of a group of fighting, working, or drinking men is reducible to mechanisms similar to sexual attraction between males and females. We cannot say if successful leaders stimulate "followership" behavior in essentially the same way that attractive females evoke sexual interest among males.

Notes

1. Adam Corinna, "Duels and Jobs for the Boys," *New Statesman,* June 18, 1965, 952. It is still necessary to receive a scar in dueling to validate membership, though now it may be a tiny scar which nonetheless retains its symbolic value.
2. The author thanks Stanford Lyman for information and discussion on fraternity affairs.
3. See Harold Garfinkle, "Conditions of Successful Degradation Ceremonies," *American Journal of Sociology* 61, no. 5 (March 1956).
4. Raymond Dart, "The Minimal Bone-Brecia Content of Makapansgat and the Australopithicine Predatory Habit," *American Anthropologist* 60, no. 5 (October 1958).

3   Groupthink

Irving L. Janis

Editor's note: *In 1977 and 1978, I researched and wrote an essay on fraternity hazing deaths for* Human Behavior *magazine. My sources included Yale University psychology professor Irving L. Janis, now deceased, who in conversation with me warmed to the idea of my applying his "groupthink" theories to in-group fraternity chapters that chose to haze pledges. Eventually, in my 1999 book* Wrongs of Passage, *I adapted the term "groupthink" to become "Greekthink," a reference to the less common, but more dangerous, fraternal groups that indulge in reckless behaviors and pledging rituals, display near-delusional feelings of invincibility, fail to heed an individual member's or their national executive's moral qualms in the interest of group unanimity, put a newcomer in harm's way, and demonstrate post-incident denial in the face of clear-cut evidence that they have erred. Likewise, the theory helps explain why pledges will risk death for esteem, backslapping, and bonding with a fraternal chapter. "All of us are very hungry for that sort of thing," Janis said back then to me. "None of us can get enough of it."*

The excerpt from Groupthink *that follows is Janis's raw theory of groupthink.*

Year after year newscasts and newspapers inform us of collective miscalculations—companies that have unexpectedly gone bankrupt because of misjudging their market, federal agencies that have mistakenly authorized the use of chemical insecticides that poison our environment, and White House executive committees that have made ill-conceived foreign policy decisions that inadvertently bring the major powers to the brink of war. Most people, when they hear about such fiascoes, simply remind themselves that, after all, "Organizations are run by human beings," "To err is human," and "Nobody is perfect." But platitudinous thoughts about human nature do not help us to understand how and why avoidable miscalculations are made.

Fiasco watchers who are unwilling to set the problem aside in this easy fashion will find that contemporary psychology has something to say (unfortunately not very much) about distortions of thinking and other sources of human error. The deficiencies about which we know the most pertain to disturbances in the behavior of each individual in a decision-making group—temporary states of elation, fear, or anger that reduce a person's mental efficiency; chronic blind spots arising from a person's social prejudices; shortcomings in information-processing that prevent a person from comprehending the complex consequences of a seemingly simple policy decision.

One psychologist has suggested that because the information-processing capabilities of every individual are limited, no responsible leader of a large organization ought to make a policy decision without using a computer that is programmed to spell out all the probable benefits and costs of each alternative under consideration. The usual way of trying to counteract the limitations of individuals' mental functioning, however, is to relegate important decisions to groups.

Imperfections of Group Decisions

Groups, like individuals, have shortcomings. Groups can bring out the worst as well as the best in man. Nietzsche went so far as to say that madness is the exception in individuals but the rule in groups. A considerable amount of social science literature shows that in circumstances of extreme crisis, group contagion occasionally gives rise to collective panic, violent acts of scapegoating, and other forms of what could be called group madness.

Much more frequent, however, are instances of mindless conformity and collective misjudgment of serious risks, which are collectively laughed off in a clubby atmosphere of relaxed conviviality. Consider what happened a few days before disaster struck the small mining town of Pitcher, Oklahoma, in 1950. The local mining engineer had warned the inhabitants to leave at once because the town had been accidentally undermined and might cave in at any moment. At a Lion's Club meeting of leading citizens, the day after the warning was issued, the members joked about the warning and laughed uproariously when someone arrived wearing a parachute. What the club members were communicating to each other by their collective laughter was that "sensible people like us know better than to take seriously those disaster warnings; we know it can't happen here, to our fine little town." Within a few days, the collective complacency cost some of these men and their families their lives.

Lack of vigilance and excessive risk-taking are forms of temporary group derangement to which decision-making groups made up of responsible executives are not at all immune. Sometimes the main trouble is that the chief executive manipulates his advisors to rubber-stamp his own ill-conceived proposals. In this [chapter], however, I shall be dealing mainly with a different source of defective decision-making, which often involves a much more subtle form of faulty leadership. During the group's deliberations, the leader does not deliberately try to get the group to tell him what he wants to hear but is quite sincere in asking for honest opinions. The group members are not transformed into sycophants. They are not afraid to speak their minds. Nevertheless, subtle constraints, which the leader may reinforce inadvertently, prevent a member from fully exercising his critical powers and from openly expressing doubts when most others in the group appear to have reached a consensus. In order to take account of what is known about the causes and consequences of such constraints we must briefly review some of the main findings of research on group dynamics.

Effects of Group Cohesiveness

In applying the concepts of group dynamics to recent historic policy decisions, I am extending the work of some pioneering social scientists. The power of a face-to-face group to set norms that influence members was emphasized by two leading sociologists early in the twentieth century—Charles Horton Cooley and George Herbert Mead. During that same time period, William Graham Sumner postulated that in-group solidarity increases when clashes arise with out-groups.

Kurt Lewin, the social psychologist who began using empirical methods to study group dynamics during the 1940s, called attention to the prerequisites for effective group decisions. He described the typical dilemmas faced by executive committees, including wartime groups of military planners who select bomb targets and peacetime groups of policymakers who try to improve relations between nations. Lewin emphasized the need for fact-finding and objective appraisal of alternatives to determine whether the chosen means will achieve a group's goals. He warned that the lack of objective standards for evaluating goal achievement allows many opportunities for error of judgment and faulty decisions. Lewin's analysis of the behavior of small groups also emphasized the importance of group cohesiveness—that is, members' positive valuation of the group and their motivation to continue to belong to it. When group cohesiveness is high, all the members express solidarity, mutual liking, and positive feelings about attending meetings and carrying out the routine tasks of the group. Lewin was most interested in the positive effects of group cohesiveness and did not investigate instances when members of cohesive groups make gross errors and fail to correct their shared misjudgments.

The potential detrimental effects of group cohesiveness were emphasized by another theorist, Wilfred Bion, an eminent group therapist. Bion described how the efficiency of all working groups can be adversely affected by the preconscious myths and misconceptions that tend to preserve the group without regard for the work at hand.

Under the influence of Kurt Lewin's pioneering work, Leon Festinger, Harrold Kelley, Stanley Schachter, and other social psychologists have carried out experiments and field investigations on the consequence of group cohesiveness. Summarizing a large body of research findings that had accumulated during the

1950s and 1960s on the ways members of cohesive groups influence each other, Dorwin Cartwright (1968) concluded that the evidence converges on three main types of effects:

> Other effects being equal, as cohesiveness increases there is an increase in a group's capacity to retain members and in the degree of participation by members in group activities. The greater a group's cohesiveness the more power it has to bring about conformity to its norms and to gain acceptance of its goals and assignments to tasks and roles. Finally, highly cohesive groups provide a source of security for members, which serve to reduce anxiety and to heighten self-esteem. (92)

Also under investigation are the causes of group cohesiveness—how and why group identification and feelings of solidarity develop. It has long been known that group solidarity increases markedly whenever a collection of individuals faces a common source of external stress, such as the threat of being injured or killed in military combat. Some researchers are beginning to consider the effects on group solidarity of subtler sources of stress.

Conformity to Group Norms

In studies of social clubs and other small groups, conformity pressures have frequently been observed. Whenever a member says something that sounds out of line with the group's norms, the other members at first increase their communication with the deviant. Attempts to influence the nonconformist member to revise or tone down his dissident ideas continue as long as most members of the group feel hopeful about talking him into changing his mind. But if they fail after repeated attempts, the amount of communication they direct toward the deviant decreases markedly. The members begin to exclude him, often quite subtly at first and later more obviously, in order to restore the unity of the group.

A social psychological experiment conducted by Stanley Schachter with avocational clubs in an American university—and replicated by Schachter and his collaborators in seven European countries—showed that the more cohesive the group and the more relevant the issue to the goals of the group, the greater is the inclination of the members to reject a nonconformist. Just as the members insulate themselves from outside critics who threaten to disrupt the unity and esprit de corps of their group, they take steps, often without being aware of it, to counteract the disruptive influence of inside critics who are attacking the group's norms.

The norms to which the members of a cohesive group adhere do not always have a positive effect on the quality of the group's performance. Studies in industrial organizations indicate that while the norms of some work groups foster conscientiousness and high productivity, the norms of other, similar work groups foster slowdowns and socializing activities that reduce productivity. The same type of variation in norms that facilitates or interferes with the group's work objectives may be found among policy-making groups in large organizations.

Much of the current research on group dynamics is an effort to pinpoint the causes of the crucial differences in group norms that make for good or poor performance on group tasks, especially tasks pertaining to decision-making. Among the phenomena that have been intensively investigated are two detrimental tendencies arising under certain conditions not yet adequately understood—the tendency of groups to develop stereotyped images that dehumanize out-groups against whom they are engaged in competitive struggles and the tendency for the collective judgments arising out of group discussions to become polarized, sometimes shifting toward extreme conservatism and sometimes toward riskier courses of action than the individual members would otherwise be prepared to take.

Group dynamics is still in the early stages of scientific development. A framework developed by Graham T. Allison grows largely out of the work of Herbert Simon, James March, and their collaborators. The organizational process model emphasizes factors that limit rationality in decision-making by individuals and organizations. These factors include the limitations of man's capacity to process information, constraints on attempts to obtain the information necessary for calculating maximal gains, and the tendency to find a course of action that will satisfy the most minimal goals instead of seeking for the action with the best consequences. This approach takes account of "organizational rigidities" such as routines and procedures of bureaucratic organizations that grind out platitudes about what can be done to attain objectives.

What Is Groupthink?

The group dynamics approach is based on the working assumption that the members of policy-making groups . . . are subjected to the pressures widely observed in groups of ordinary citizens. In my research on group dynamics, I was impressed by repeated manifestations of the effects—both unfavorable and favorable—of the social pressures that typically develop in cohesive groups—in infantry platoons, aircrews, etc. In all these groups, members tend to evolve informal norms to preserve friendly intragroup relations and these become part of the hidden agenda at their meetings. When conducting research on groups of heavy smokers at a clinic set up to help people stop smoking, I noticed a seemingly irrational tendency for the members to exert pressure on each other to increase their smoking as the time for the final meeting approached. This appeared to be a collusive effort to display mutual dependence and resistance to the termination of the group's sessions.

Sometimes, even long before members become concerned about the final separation, clear-cut signs of pressures toward uniformity subvert the fundamental purpose of group meetings. At the second meeting of one group of smokers, consisting of twelve middle-class American men and women, two of the most dominant members took the position that heavy smoking was an almost incurable addiction. The majority of the others soon agreed that no one could be expected to cut down drastically. One heavy smoker, a middle-aged business executive, took issue with this consensus, arguing that by using will power he had stopped smoking since joining the group and that everyone else could do the same.

His declaration was followed by heated discussion. Most ganged up against the man who was deviating from the group consensus. Then, at the beginning of the next meeting, the deviant announced that he had made an important decision. " . . . I have gone back to smoking two packs a day and I will not make any effort to stop smoking until after the last meeting."

Whereupon, the other members beamed at him and applauded enthusiastically, welcoming him back to the fold. No one commented on the fact that the whole point of the meetings was to help each individual to cut down on smoking as rapidly as possible. As a psychological consultant to the group, I tried to call this to the members' attention, and so did my collaborator, Michael Kahn. But during that meeting the members managed to ignore our comments and reiterated their consensus that heavy smoking was an addiction from which no one would be cured except by cutting down very gradually over a long period of time.

This episode—an extreme form of groupthink—was only one manifestation of a general pattern that the group displayed. At every meeting, the members were amiable, reasserted their warm feelings of solidarity, and sought complete concurrence on every important topic, with no reappearance of the unpleasant bickering that would spoil the cozy atmosphere. The concurrence-seeking tendency could be maintained, however, only at the expense of ignoring realistic challenges (like those posed by the psychological consultants) and distorting members' observations of individual differences that would call into question the shared assumption that everyone in the group had the same type of addiction problem. It seemed that in this smoking group I was observing another instance of the groupthink pattern I had encountered in observations of widely contrasting groups whose members came from diverse sectors of society and were meeting together for social, educational, vocational, or other purpose. Just like the group in the smoking clinic, all these different types of groups had shown signs of high cohesiveness and of an accompanying concurrence-seeking tendency that interfered with critical thinking—the central features of groupthink.

I use the term "groupthink" as a quick and easy way to refer to a mode of thinking that people engage in when they are deeply involved in a cohesive ingroup, when the members' striving for unanimity override their motivation to realistically appraise alternative courses of action. "Groupthink" is a term of the same order as the words in the newspeak vocabulary George Orwell presents in his dismaying 1984—a vocabulary with terms such as "doublethink" and "crimethink." By putting groupthink with those Orwellian words, I realize that groupthink takes on an invidious connotation. The invidiousness is intentional:

Groupthink refers to a mental deterioration of mental efficiency, reality testing, and moral judgment that results from group pressures.

Fiascoes

At least seven major defects in decision-making contribute to failures to solve problems adequately.

First, the group's discussions are limited to a few alternative course of action (often only two) without a full survey of the range of alternatives.

Second, the group does not survey the objectives to be fulfilled and the values implicated by the choice.

Third, the group fails to reexamine the course of action initially preferred by the majority of members from the standpoint of nonobvious risks and drawbacks that had not been considered when it was originally evaluated.

Fourth, the members neglect courses of action initially evaluated as unsatisfactory by the majority of the group. They spend little or no time discussing whether they have overlooked nonobvious gains or whether there are ways of reducing the seemingly prohibitive costs that had made the alternatives seem undesirable.

Fifth, the members make little or no attempt to obtain information from experts who can supply sound estimates of losses and gains to be expected from alternative courses of action.

Sixth, selective bias is shown in the way the group reacts to factual information and relevant judgments from experts, the mass media, and outside critics. The members show interest in facts and opinions that support their initially preferred policy and take up time in their meetings to discuss them, but they tend to ignore facts and opinions that do not support their initially preferred policy.

Seventh, the members spend little time deliberating about how the chosen policy might be hindered by bureaucratic inertia, sabotaged by political opponents, or temporarily derailed by the common accidents that happen to the best of well-laid plans. Consequently, they fail to work out contingency plans to cope with foreseeable setbacks that could endanger the overall success of the chosen course of action.

I assume that these seven defects and some related features of inadequate decision-making result from groupthink. But each of the seven can arise from other common causes of human stupidity as well—erroneous intelligence, information overload, fatigue, blinding prejudice, and ignorance. Whether produced by groupthink or by other causes, a decision suffering from most of these defeats has relatively little chance of success.

Hardhearted Actions by Softheaded Groups

Groupthink is conducive to errors in decision-making, and such errors increase the likelihood of a poor outcome. At first I was surprised by the extent to which groups adhere to group norms and pressures toward uniformity. A dominant characteristic appears to be remaining loyal to the group by sticking with the decisions to which the group has committed itself, even when the policy is working badly and has unintended consequences that disturb the conscience of the members. In a sense, members consider loyalty to the group the highest form of morality. That loyalty requires each member to avoid raising controversial issues, questioning weak arguments, or calling a halt to softheaded thinking.

Paradoxically, softheaded groups are likely to be extremely hardhearted toward out-groups and enemies. In dealing with a rival nation, policy-makers comprising amiable groups find it relatively easy to authorize dehumanizing solutions such as large-scale bombings. An affable group of government officials is unlikely to pursue the difficult and controversial issues that arise when alternatives to a harsh military solution come up for discussion. Nor are the members inclined to raise ethical issues that imply that this "fine group of ours, with its humanitarianism and its high-minded principles, might be capable of adopting a course of action that is inhumane and immoral."

The concept of groupthink pinpoints an entirely different source of trouble, residing neither in the individual nor in the organizational setting. Over and beyond all the familiar sources of human error is a powerful source of defective judgment that arises in cohesive groups—the concurrence-seeking tendency, which fosters overoptimism, lack of vigilance, and sloganistic thinking about the weakness and immorality of out-groups.

I do not mean to imply that all cohesive groups suffer from groupthink, though all may display its symptoms from time to time. Nor should we infer from the term "groupthink" that group decisions are typically inefficient or harmful. On the contrary, a group whose members have properly defined roles, with traditions and standard operating procedures that facilitate critical inquiry, is probably capable of making better decisions than any individual in the group who works on the problem alone.

And yet the advantages of having decisions made by groups are often lost because of psychological pressures that arise when the members work closely together, share the same values, and above all face a crisis in which everyone is subjected to stresses that generate a strong need for affiliation. In these circumstances, as conformity pressures begin to dominate, groupthink and the attendant deterioration of decision-making set in.

The central theme of my analysis can be summarized in this generalization, which I offer in the spirit of Parkinson's laws: *The more amiability and esprit de corps among the members of a policy-making in-group, the greater is the danger that the independent critical thinking will be replaced by groupthink, which is likely to result in irrational and dehumanizing actions directed against out-groups.*

4   Cult-like Hazing

Hank Nuwer

Editor's note: *The following essay was published in* Wrongs of Passage *in 1999 and then gained additional scrutiny in it reprinting in the* Chronicle of Higher Education. *The attempt here is to offer an alternative for administrators contemplating the elimination of their Greek organizations after one or more chapters find themselves in hot water for hazing. I try to do this by identifying chapters that have a history of deliberate problematic behaviors that put these chapters in to a category I refer to as cult-like groups. Rather than eliminate all fraternities and sororities for the wrongdoing of a few chapters on campus, administrators might be advised instead to yank the charters of the problematic chapters whose pledging rituals show them as more likely to one day experience a death or serious injury. The chapter ends with a previously unpublished interview with a pledge dropout who was seriously injured during a beating routinely administered by his chapter.*

Part One

The term "cult" conjures up images of the burning of David Koresh's Branch Davidian settlement and the mass suicide of Jim Jones's Peoples Temple devotees. Most of us believe that cult members are misfits who live in remote places; we take comfort in the fact that their influences are far removed from our daily lives.

Yet, in fact, many students, faculty members, and administrators regularly confront—and even participate in—cult-like behavior. The most prevalent cult-like groups among us are the numerous fraternity and sorority chapters that engage in abusive hazing practices on campuses, large and small, all across the United States.

No one has a firm count of how many members of fraternities and sororities engage in at least some form of cult-like activities. None of the national organizations that represent Greek organizations on various campuses have conducted formal surveys. But based on my research of the topic since 1978, I believe that the percentage of Greeks, mainly male, who perform cult-like acts of hazing is probably at least as high as the 20 percent of athletes who admitted in a national survey [conducted by Norm Pollard and Nadine Hoover in 1999] that they had been severely hazed.

Examining the cult-like aspects of hazing in Greek organizations can help us all understand why the practice is so difficult to stamp out. It also reinforces the urgent need to find new strategies to prevent the pledging-related injuries and deaths that have occurred for decades, despite strong efforts to eradicate them.

The latest attempt to discourage hazing is the Massachusetts Institute of Technology's decision to revoke the diploma of a graduate who was accused of serving alcohol at an event where a freshman pledge drank himself to death. MIT president Charles Vest offered the family of that pledge, Scott Krueger, $6 million as a settlement. However well-meaning, MIT's gestures seemed only to make the graduate a scapegoat and, more important, did not come to grips with the complex influences that produce hazing behavior. If we recognize that the abnormal behaviors found in Greek organizations are similar to, and as deeply rooted as, those found in cults, we will take a first step toward developing a broader, more systematic approach to the problem.

In *Cults in Our Midst,* author Margaret Thaler Singer (1995), a former adjunct professor of psychology at the University of California at Berkeley, identifies many traits characteristic of cults; traits that, I believe, are shared by fraternities and sororities that practice hazing. I do not apply the term "cult-like" to the many Greek groups that operate legally without hazing, only to those that use, in Singer's words about cults, "systematic" manipulation and coercion to effect "psychological and social influence."

For instance, the control and isolation of newcomers is a technique used both by cults and by fraternities and sororities that engage in hazing. Some Greek groups order pledges to limit or suspend communication and intimacy with parents, classmates, and others outside the chapter. Members pressure pledges to give their waking hours to the chapter and deprive them of sleep to get maximum involvement. Members of some fraternities order pledges to avoid speaking to nonmembers. The members shave pledges' heads, forbid them to take showers or change clothes, and mandate the wearing of strange apparel.

Cut off from the day-to-day life of the college, fraternity and sorority recruits develop, in Singer's words about cults in general, an "enforced dependency." Just as cults convince recruits that membership brings with it the one true answer, so, too, hazers reassure tired, spirit-numbed pledges that the reasons for abuse will become apparent after initiation. So, too, do they claim to be able to satisfy all needs and wants.

Members of hazing fraternities and sororities, like those of some cults, emphasize the notion of "family." They appeal to recruits who consider themselves in need of friends and potential dating partners or who find themselves under stress in a new environment. And, just as in cults, members of hazing fraternities and sororities believe that pledges are not part of the brotherhood or sisterhood until they have endured an ordeal or have successfully made it through an initiation ceremony.

Researcher James C. Arnold (1992) has examined the alcohol addiction prevalent in white college fraternities; his writings convince me that both cults and hazing fraternities fall into the category of addictive organizations. Many fraternities, especially those made up predominantly of white males, have alcohol problems. Reports of alcohol-related injuries and deaths in fraternities are so frequent as to be almost commonplace. Predominantly African-American hazing groups have fewer problems with alcohol. But activist leaders of those groups, such as John Williams [in an interview with me on April 16, 1998], founder of the Center for the Study of Pan-Hellenic Issues, argue nonetheless that the quest of many black pledges to complete physical ordeals in order to become members can be an obsession that is tantamount to an addiction.

Members of cults and of hazing Greek groups alike are extremists who try to justify actions outside the range of normal human behavior. Members of the one true family—be they Greeks or cultists—veer away from conventional moral standards; they tolerate members who perform illicit and even illegal acts behind closed doors. Like cults, many Greek groups encourage near-delusional feelings of invincibility, fail to heed an individual member's moral qualms in the interest of group unanimity, put a newcomer in harm's way with seeming disregard for that person's well-being, and, after a dangerous or fatal incident, deny that they have erred, even in the face of clear evidence to the contrary.

One difference between a cult and a Greek organization that engages in hazing is that the latter lacks a quasi-deity, such as a David Koresh or a Jim Jones. Nevertheless, at the local level, chapters that haze have gung-ho pledge-class presidents or members who act as "pledge educators." Those individuals pressure newcomers to accept a collective identity and to put the chapter ahead of self-interest. They resemble charismatic military and corporate leaders who jump-start the stalled resolve of others, calm fears, and renew fighting spirit. As scholars in the behavioral sciences know full well, a group not only reflects the values of such a leader but can, under his or her influence, suppress members' common sense and rational thought.

Finally, just as cults make it hard for their members to leave, fraternities and sororities make it difficult for a pledge to quit. When pledges in a high-intensity hazing fraternity or sorority decide not to join after all, they can experience the same kind of post-traumatic stress, disconnectedness, and angst that experts have associated with cult members who opt to leave their group.

National Greek organizations, confederations, colleges, and foundations have poured time, dollars, and soul into trying to eliminate hazing behaviors. Yet those behaviors seem always to repeat themselves, leaving everyone frustrated and wondering if the problem will ever be solved.

Simply abolishing fraternities and sororities is not only impractical but also unfair to those Greeks who do not haze and who support the passage of anti-hazing legislation at the state level. It also is unrealistic for national fraternities to say that once-sodden houses will be "dry" by 2000, as executive directors of a number of national fraternities envisioned several years ago. Only about nine national fraternities were able to persuade their undergraduate delegates to vote for no-alcohol rules by 2000, and even those reformists have no power to stop students from returning stumbling-drunk to their "dry" houses after imbibing to intoxication at local pubs.

Nonetheless, I think that reforms can occur if we recognize the cult-like influences that prevail in many Greek groups and develop specific strategies to deal with them.

My solution is to abolish—with no second chance to recolonize—all hazing chapters that exhibit dangerous cult-like behaviors. Colleges and universities must identify clearly the rituals and acts that are illegal or that have led to deaths, injuries, and incidents of post-traumatic stress and must publish those definitions widely in anti-hazing policy statements.

Forty-three states have their own laws governing what constitutes illegal hazing; colleges and universities can educate their students about the laws that apply to them. In addition, institutions should clarify which activities are dangerous, manipulative, or inconsiderate of a pledge's human rights, and then communicate those characterizations often. Those steps would significantly strengthen the general but often ineffectual institutional bans on hazing. We must put an end to decades of passivity, during which institutional leaders have been able to ignore the problem because its definition has been so vague as to be meaningless.

College administrators must expel students who engage in illegal or dangerous hazing practices. Away from the pressures of a group identity, those hazers may finally examine their own thought processes and the consequences of their actions. Since seven states lack any anti-hazing laws, the Association of Fraternity Advisors could specify which practices merit suspension or expulsion.

Campus leaders should employ trained counselors to help end destructive patterns of behavior in student organizations. Too often during rush weeks, advisors to Greek organizations heartily greet pledges but never inform them that others like them have died or been injured during pledging at institutions across the country. Instead, an expert in abnormal behavior could describe examples of cult-like activities during hazing and could tell pledges that they have an ethical responsibility to report any such activities. Counselors should routinely interview students who voluntarily resign or are blackballed by the chapter to ascertain whether hazing has occurred.

Senior administrators should designate specific offices on their campuses where victims of hazing can receive counseling. Many institutions now provide support services for people who believe that they have suffered sexual abuse. Hazing victims, however, have no similar resources when they are feeling stunned, bewildered, lost, or psychologically distressed (unless the hazing was sexual in nature).

When pledges have been treated for alcohol overdoses or have participated in dangerous hazing rituals, administrators should enroll them in mandatory counseling and alcohol-awareness classes.

The magnitude of the problem is great, and other strategies should be adopted as well. Among them:

- Whenever a fraternity or sorority, or one of its members, is convicted of hazing in a criminal court or in a student judicial procedure, campus administrators should keep a record of it and then publish those records each time rush is held. National fraternal organizations should commission surveys on cult-like and hazing behaviors to ascertain the extent and severity of the problem. When asked informally, individuals have often been unwilling to admit to being hazed—but they have given positive responses when asked questions about specific hazing activities, such as whether they have ever been forced to drink excessive amounts of alcohol or eat contaminated food. By assessing the specific ordeals that pledges have undergone, researchers could begin to get an accurate picture of how prevalent and severe hazing is in fraternities and sororities.
- We should put responsible adults in Greek living units. Colleges, with support and guidance from national fraternity and sorority headquarters, should hire trustworthy people and train them in aspects of Greek life, notably how to deal with cult-like practices and hazing.
- National Greek organizations must expel fraternity alumni who cannot accept positive change or who themselves participate in hazing activities that could result in death or injury. While many alumni serve the fraternity or sorority system as mentors, financial supporters, and moral consciences, a few others have been present during initiations that have caused injuries or deaths. College presidents should inform participating alumni that they have a duty to report hazing and that they must refrain from encouraging it.
- Courts, not student judicial groups, should handle those actions that meet the definition of criminal hazing as determined by each state's laws. Often, student judicial groups—whether they consist of students alone or administrators and faculty members as well—view pledges as willing participants rather than susceptible victims of cult-like groups; as a result, they punish hazers too lightly. College administrators should encourage every state to enact harsh legal penalties for hazing and hand over to legal authorities any cases that appear to involve criminal behavior.
- Finally, if college presidents cannot get results, Congress should mandate hearings on the alcohol and hazing problems in our institutions.

After decades of failed efforts, the message is clear: We must all work together to attack the problem of hazing with specific strategies aimed at causing social change. College and university presidents, student-affairs and other administrators, faculty members, alumni, psychologists, substance-abuse counselors, anti-hazing and anti-substance-abuse activists, legislators, and the many non-hazing fraternities and sororities should all contribute to the effort. Only then will we break the seductive, powerful grip of the cult-like subcultures found in fraternal groups on too many campuses.

Part Two

Because no national survey on hazing practices has ever been attempted, no researcher knows precisely how many national or local male fraternity chapters can be lumped into the category of "cult-like" groups, the minority of chapters that conduct dangerous or even criminal hazing acts. But civil suits following a death or injury make it clear that chapters that do haze their pledges severely often sanction paddling or beatings, underage drinking and some drug use, assemblies in unpleasant house rooms in which lined-up pledges experience verbal abuse, restrictions on pledge movements, isolation of pledges from nonchapter entities on campus other than sports teams, servitude, and encouraging pledges to deceive advisors, national fraternity representatives, and school officials. What follows is an interview by the editor of this book with a former pledge who endured serious abuse in a cult-like chapter at a private university and was rejected for admission into the fraternity after he reported a head injury he received to school officials. The young man was treated by a neurobiologist for headaches and mood swings. The fraternity member who allegedly delivered a blow to the pledge's head is now an employee of another college, and neither he nor the president of his school responded to requests for interviews to get a second side of the story. Neither would the school where the pledge was injured accede to a request for an interview with the vice president who disciplined the fraternity only after months of badgering and the threat of a lawsuit. The advisor of the chapter left the school and is now a coach at another school; he too failed to respond to a request for his insights and recollections. Nonetheless, the chapter's long history of transgressions has caused its charter to be yanked by the school and its international fraternity, albeit not without protest from the latter. The following interview with a victim of cult-like chapter hazing was conducted late the night of September 10, 2001, and concluded in the early morning hours of September 11. The conversation took place in the home of the victim's parents. I have removed the name of the victim from the interview, along with information that would identify his chapter and school, because at the time of this chapter's publication, the victim has made a fresh start for himself in a new athletic endeavor and has accepted a cash settlement from the fraternity. The persons accused of being hazers, unfortunately, are also protected. I regret this circumstance.

Nuwer: In looking over the transcript [of a deposition made by the pledge] . . . it seemed as if the chapter was determined to break rules from the beginning . . .

Pledge: You got your bid and then there was about a three-day period where you didn't have to be at the house, and you didn't have any duties. During those three days, every day there would be everyday beer slides, parties, and all the fun. The brothers gave you the understanding that come the end of the third day it was over with. The fun you had was gone and it's time to get down to pledging, which was the most important thing to them. In those three days you got into the house when you wanted. They showed you around the house. They gave you all the free beer you wanted. Generally, they were partying a lot of the time.

Nuwer: [Anthropologist] Lionel Tiger calls it "males courting males."

Pledge: That's what they did. In hindsight, maybe I should have taken better notes. (*Laughter.*)

Nuwer: Often the hazers act as a designated group. They get a kind of status from what they do. It helps the brothers that don't haze assuage their conscience or consciences. . . .

Pledge: We got into our hazing. . . . There were brothers who were just, you know, assholes. Whether they were hazing or not, they had a chip on their shoulder. But there were people like the number-one pin, which I'll explain in a minute, when he walked into that [hazing] room in the basement, he wasn't [himself], he was the number-one pin. You could tell by the way he carried himself. He was a little guy, about half my size. When he came down, I remember the first time we saw him, he came flying down the stairs like a gorilla, screaming. All the other times when there was hazing, he would just walk around and he would be fearless, walking up and down the rows screaming at people. I talked to him several times when we weren't in the basement and he was just a very different person. There was an authority about him, but it was greatly [changed] from when he wasn't in the room.

Nuwer: Is this theater or sadism?

Pledge: It was a lot of theater. In hindsight, every time I talked to him outside the room, I always thought he was kind of scared of me. I was 21, just actually four months younger than he was . . . but some of the mystique he had wasn't there when we weren't in the room.

Nuwer: He was like an actor getting ready to come onstage . . . or an athlete before a ballgame?

Pledge: Definitely. I was told that before he came downstairs he would be in his room drinking or whatever, and a lot of the brothers would come in to fire him up. They'd get him all riled up, saying we weren't respecting the house. They would just provoke him, or maybe they'd just get him angry, or a little drunk. He'd come in and, like I said, he'd be this different person. . . . They were getting him hyped up, jacked up, ready to go.

Nuwer: Did you have alums there getting involved?

Pledge: I had alums there the last night I got hit down in the basement. The alums were there for the weekend, but they came in Thursday night. It was very uncomfortable having alums there because they still felt they owned the house. But the brothers in the house, they ran the house. . . . It was tension, when the alumni came back and they acted like they owned the place. . . . The night I got hit there were two alums in the basement. I know there was one standing right next to me, because he kicked me during the night. Normally, if it's a hazing night and they're in the basement, they're the ones in the basement running things.

Nuwer: One problem is the NIC [National Interfraternity Conference] and the national fraternities don't have a way to police alums. There's not much they can do to them.

Pledge: No, it's the whole older-person mentality. You leave middle school and you go to high school [and] when you walk around the middle school you're king of the valley. They [alums] have that same mentality. We're not in college anymore; we're in the real world. We're not going to take any crap from some college boy. . . . I did meet a lot of alums who very nice to me. They didn't haze me, and they didn't like the hazing.

Nuwer: With undergraduates it's supposed to be your [chapter] experience in the house, and yet one of the reasons for hazing [supposedly] is that the house changes very little over time. There's no way anyone can do that. One pledge class can change the house dynamics—

Pledge: —Yeah, there were people who graduated a year or two before and they were revered in the house. Beyond that, the names got hazy. You didn't know anyone else. So it's like you said, yeah, trying to keep the legacy of the house, trying to keep the house the same.

Nuwer: . . . Did you think the hazing was a sort of profane [deviation] from the sacred [values] the fraternity holds dear?

Pledge: That's a hard question. The hazing I went through, there were some sacred cows, if you will, that you had to do. First, you had to respect the brotherhood at all costs. We were told this several times— "Protect the brotherhood at all costs." Just behind that was this: you had to know the pin number. You *had* to know it. These were like biblical numbers[,] the pin numbers.

Nuwer: Can you explain this? I never went through anything like this [in my fraternity].

Pledge: When you were pledging, you wanted to be the number-one pin, meaning at the end of pledging, you wanted to be assigned number-one pin. The number-one pin, when he was a senior, he would lead the hazing. He would be in charge of hazing; he ran it, the whole show. It would never be the president, because if he got hit, caught, or in trouble, it would take down the whole fraternity. So it was deliberately separated. But he [the number-one pin] ran the house. The president had to run the ideas through him, the top dog. If the number-one pin couldn't do something, the number-two pin took over, the number-three pin, and so on down the line. The top ten pins in the house got single rooms. Everyone else below, you had to live in a double.

Nuwer: Did you feel that anytime there'd be music playing from *The Godfather?*—

Pledge: —Yeah, it was bizarre. During the week you had to do favors for the brothers. A favor could be anything like just going to the store for some bread, or some beer, or some fast food. You had to get at least one favor done for all the brothers in a week. But if I was doing a favor for someone whose pin number was twelve, and a pin number of anything higher than twelve called, I had to leave that guy and go.

Nuwer: How did he feel about it?

Pledge: The twelve? He wouldn't get mad at the other person. Occasionally, someone would take it out on you, like "You left me and I didn't have this." Then he'd make you do pushups and stuff. Now that never actually happened to me, but it happened to other pledges.

Nuwer: Did you ever find yourself caught up, where you thought, *I want to be number-one pin or number-four pin?*

Pledge: Yeah.

Nuwer: You did?

Pledge: You're brainwashed in a sense. I had a lot of time since this [injury] happened to think about it. You know it's not right. Something about it isn't right, but it's like you convince yourself that it's not that wrong. Then you get into this whole mentality, not of right or wrong, but like: *Well, they can't break me.* It was like, whether I agree with the hazing or not, you will not break me. I knew because of a [prior] concussion I had from wrestling that I couldn't be the number-one pin, because I couldn't do the heads [headstands for a prolonged time], so to compensate for that I was always around the house. I was 21, so I went out and bought all the other brothers beer, the ones who were 21 or not. So yeah, you got into it. You wanted to be the top pin at the end.

Nuwer: Interesting, so you had to do servitude in order to get status. It would be like bootlicking if you were in the military.

Pledge: You're basically their slave. You have to run around and do all kinds of favors for them—some being very easy, some being very hard. It just depended what mood the brother was [in]. I can't speak for all the other pledges, but I couldn't stand it. That's the thing I hated. I didn't mind the physical stuff. To me, I could always turn it off. I didn't mind people in my face yelling, especially [name of number-one pin], because he's yelling and he's half my size. I knew if it was an open street fight, I would kill him. But to go get a guy a drink who is like two doors away from a fridge, or to sweep out his room, that always bothered me. I know it bothered a lot of pledges to be someone's servant. I don't know whether anyone else did this, because I had to keep this quiet and to myself, but when they would send me to get drinks, I would spit in them. That was my little way to rebel against it. If I had to get ice, I rubbed my hand on the ground before I got the ice. If you were a brother and you were rude to me, most likely I spit in something you had. But you're so proud that you spit in someone's drink, you forget you just walked down four flights of stairs, because you're kind of brainwashed and you're into it.

Nuwer: Did you notice pledges change from the first day?

Pledge: Yeah.

Nuwer: What did you notice? Utter obeisance? Rebellion?

Pledge: No one rebelled, no one rebelled. . . . My close friends ask, what's the one thing you wish you could have done in that situation? Well, when that first kid got hit, not me, I should have walked out, and I should have told someone. That's something I've got to live with, the fact that I was a coward. My biggest regret is that I didn't rebel. How it affected the pledge class a sociologist would go crazy for. Out of my two closest friends at the school, one went headlong nuts into it, just fanatical. I don't know how he stayed in college because he never studied. I would be going to class and he'd be there [in the house] studying the pin numbers. You'd be given a list [to figure out pin rankings]. The first brother's name was correct; the others were all clues and mysteries. He was basically the first to decode it, because he spent all his time doing it. He spent more time in the house than I did, and I was usually there a lot to do favors.

Nuwer: Did some members treat him with contempt?

Pledge: No, the brothers liked it. To his face, they hated him. They'd yell at him, they'd make him do pushups until he'd be almost crying. This was during the day when no one really would get hit. But they'd make him stand on his head until he'd fall over and get sick. They'd yell at him, and he'd be just taking it and being all proud, like *I can take anything you dish out because I want to be a brother.* As soon as he walked out, the brotherhood would—

Nuwer: —Think, we've got a good one here.

Pledge: Yeah, there was a buzz about. It gives you a sense of pride. There was one weekend, alumni weekend, in which I think I slept seven hours in three days. Your spirits get crushed, and you're always someone's—I don't have a real good [term]—someone's bitch. All the time, you got to do this and you got to do that. Then someone would come up and say, "The brotherhood"—they never said "they," just "the brotherhood"—"The brotherhood's really impressed that you're here all the time. It's been taken note of." I can't lie; it made me feel good. I felt I was a part of it. The other end of the spectrum [was] kids that just couldn't take it, although when I was there no one quit. Basically, I didn't really quit. They forced me out when I stopped showing up because I was sick. I still remember this little redhead; he was skinny and couldn't do more than four pushups. He was terrified every time we went down to the basement to begin our hazing. I used to sleep or try to get some sleep in my big brother's room before it started, and one night [name of pledge] crashed on his couch, and I woke up and there was [name of pledge], just crying—terrified almost. Everyone fell between the two extremes: my one friend who went hog-wild into it to the kid who was breaking mentally. Everyone [else] fell in between. [The brotherhood] wanted you to be more toward the breaking, so [it was] not that [name of pledge] was not the norm, because they wanted you breaking.

Nuwer: It sounds like a concentration camp—

Pledge: I wouldn't say that, but like a prison. The minute you walked into the house, and the minute your foot crossed that door, you were in a prison, you were theirs. On campus, you belonged to them, but it was more open because people were watching. Always, the brothers and pledges were always very tight on campus. You couldn't tell a pledge from a brother walking on campus, I mean when they interacted. Everything that was [done] in the house stayed in the house. When you were walking to classes you talked to the brothers like you would talk to your friends.

Nuwer: What was they psychology here? Why did they do this?

Pledge: They told us. They wanted everyone else to think that [all was run as the school and national headquarters wanted things run]. Yet everyone knew [that this chapter at this school] had the worst hazing. Everyone knew it, but no one ever said it. They wanted to keep the illusion up.

Nuwer: That's deception. How did they feel about the deceiving?

Pledge: The brothers? Well, to them it wasn't deceiving. To them, it was protecting the brotherhood—that's what I'm trying to say. That was the main thing you had to do.

Nuwer: So loyalty was more important than any moral qualms [they might have]?

Pledge: Yeah. They put on this big happy front for all the sororities, for all the administration, for everyone to see. The reason is that so no one would suspect all the horrible things they did once you walked into that house. It was a masquerade and it wasn't a masquerade, because many, many brothers really wanted you to be there. Hazing was something you really, really had to go through, because they went through it too. That was the reasoning. And if I was a pledge on campus and someone [outside the chapter] who was disrespecting the house started a fight with me, the whole brotherhood would come. They stressed the mentality of all for one and one for all. If I had a problem throwing [an obnoxious guest] out of the house, they were all there. But that was a front, trying to make everyone believe that we were once cohesive unit. But when you walked into that house and there was no one in there but brothers, you were in for a world of pain. . . . But you couldn't talk to anyone about the hazing outside the fraternity—outside your pledge class—if anyone knew, and this was a small campus, that was it.

Nuwer: But this [cohesiveness] is also a foreshadowing to the pledges of what life will be like once [you're] in as a member.

Pledge: Yes, exactly. It's going to be good times all around.

Nuwer: Were they trying to humiliate you when they had you get beer for them, or what?

Pledge: We were sluts—we were told that. One night there was a meeting while I was out of town coaching at a high school and everyone had to repeat the mantra, "Women are sluts." One pledge [and a fellow pledges were] told [by a member], "My mother is a slut, your mothers are sluts. Women are sluts."

Nuwer: So this is hearsay?

Pledge: Yeah, it's hearsay in that I wasn't at the meeting where they said this, but I heard it enough [from other pledges] in other conversations. The women were nothing. Women were nothing to the brotherhood. A girlfriend, you gave her respect, and if she wanted a beer you got one to be polite, but other than that, women were just a commodity. I worked the door [at numerous parties]. All I had to do was let in young freshmen or sophomore girls, or sorority girls—basically if they were hot they came in. The whole task of being the doorman was keeping the highest number of girls and the lowest number of guys. Women might have thought [the brotherhood] paid special attention to one sorority or another, but they didn't care. To them, they said, they were nothing more than whores.

Nuwer: This is not acting—they actually believed this?

Pledge: Yeah. Women were nothing, and to prove a point, I threw out one of the pledges' girlfriends out of the house because she was acting very drunk and very rude while I was the doorman. I said, "It's time to go." I kicked her out. He got mad, with reason, since someone just kicked his girlfriend out of his supposed house, but the brotherhood didn't care. [Someone said,] "You made the right decision, because she was a stupid slut." Now the same guys who would say this would then go and cuddle with their own girlfriends. And sometimes, in the basement in the middle of hazing, they would just tell funny sex stories. You always got the feeling that women meant nothing.

Nuwer: Did they call you feminine names?

Pledge: They called you a faggot; they called you a homo, pussy, things like that, but nothing to make you feel like a woman. It was brothers, pledges, everyone else.

Nuwer: Are they actually anti-homosexual, or was that acting or satiric?

Pledge: They were anti-homosexual in the fact that you got a houseful of thirty-five or forty homophobic guys. The word faggot and homo was thrown around a lot, but not with a connotation. I don't think anyone ever sat around and thought, "This means homosexual." But there never would be a gay pledge or a gay brother—I'm pretty sure of that. They would never allow that. But I never saw them kick anyone [visitor] out of the house for being gay, and I never saw them targeting [gays].

Nuwer: Anti-black?

Pledge: As for race, there were no black guys. A lot of brothers used the word "nigger," but they also never went out of their way looking for trouble with black people.

Nuwer: Did they get into fights with other fraternities?

Pledge: There were two feuds going on when I was there. We hated [name of fraternity] for some reason. I was never sure—Apparently a couple years ago someone started a fight. Did I personally hate [name of fraternity]? No, a couple guys I lived with [their] pledges. We were told at the beginning that [name of fraternity] was our biggest rival, and that you were to hate [them] no matter what. We were told the opening night of pledging that a pledge is lower than whale shit, but higher than the [name of fraternity] president. . . . We had a running thing. They kicked us out of their parties, and we kicked them out of our parties. But no one ever actually fought, because if I threw a punch, I could be expelled. The feuds really were just a lot of talk. I've had time to think about [the pledge hazing sessions]. If I had turned around and dropped the president [with a punch] or the number-one pin, I don't think anyone would have done anything. . . . They would do all this violence against the pledges, but the minute they got into a real-world situation where someone could fight back, you'd never see it. They were cowards in the sense that they fought [the pledges] in numbers, too.

Nuwer: Did you have sorority little sisters?

Pledge: No, but sororities would bring their pledges over.

Nuwer: Did [your chapter] haze their pledges?

Pledge: We watched them get hazed.

Nuwer: What was the [hazing] behavior?

Pledge: They'd maybe get forced into a line, yelled at, but it was mostly things like having to do silly dance moves. You weren't embarrassed for them. You'd think, "Great, I go down into a basement and get the shit beat out of me, and they have to dance to Ricky Martin—This isn't quite fair." I don't know what they did when they weren't here, but they'd haze them for about twenty minutes while we were there watching, and then it would be, "OK, party!" Our connection with the sororities was this: You never offended a sorority too bad because you wanted to have sex with them. That was the whole mentality. You could have a girlfriend, and be in love with a girlfriend, but you never ever chose a girlfriend over a brother. . . . And in our fraternity, Ecstasy was a huge drug, huge drug, taken with alcohol all the time. You'd take it to get through hazing. . . . You knew which brothers had access to certain drugs. It wasn't just fraternities but sororities [on campus]. The sororities were actually bigger on Ecstasy than the male fraternities.

Nuwer: What about you not getting into the group? Did they consider you to be deviant even though they were the ones doing criminal-like behaviors? In my book *Wrongs of Passage,* there is a passage on rites of passage: you pass through liminal space or a portal from where you are a nonmember to where you [go through pledging rituals and] become a full member. But you suddenly dropped in the middle so that you are no longer on the side you started, nor on the other side with the brotherhood [where you wanted to be]. You can't go exactly back to your parents but you can't be with the brotherhood either.

Pledge: Yeah, yeah. One thing you learn right away as a pledge is that you will never be right whether you are right or not right. You run around in this great wrong area. I never felt like a deviant, I just figured that whatever I say, I'm going to be wrong. But when my scenario ended, I was really adrift. I don't talk about this. The only time I've told the whole story was with my parents at a deposition the first time, and they actually heard everything. The hardest thing, what I couldn't believe, was when I got done, that these guys, who I looked up to, who I had hung out with—I couldn't believe that they would sell me out that quickly. I didn't want to get most of the brothers in trouble. I just wanted to get in trouble the brothers who hit me or who allowed it to happen. Two of the pledges were my best friends on campus, and there were three others I hung out with. They were all 18 or 19, and I was 21. I was kind of a surrogate big brother who always bought the beer. I was shocked, and I don't think I've ever gotten over the fact that these kids, and not only did I pledge with the two, but I wrestled [on wrestling team] with them before we even thought about pledging. That had always been a sacred bond with me. Whether you liked them or not there would always be respect. The minute I got sick with my concussions and I couldn't go to the meetings because I was sick, I don't think anyone would have spit on me if I was on fire. Total separation—they just left me. I was shocked, and for the longest time I couldn't believe it. Even five months after the whole thing happened, I was just mentally blown away. I was actually more pissed off at my pledge brothers than the brothers. These guys, at the drop of a hat, betrayed me.

Nuwer: Do you replay this in your mind?

Pledge: Oh, when [name of number-one pin] hit me in the head I've seen it a million times. I don't think I'll ever forget the "getting hit" part. It was just that—after I got hit and came back, and I started getting the concussion symptoms, I was talking to one of my friends, the wrestler, and he said, "Pledge, don't turn this in to the school." I never told anyone I was thinking of turning in anything to the school, even though I'd been thinking of it. Even then it was a foreign idea to me but I said, "I have a headache every day—and I have dizzy spells," and I go, "What if I drop out?—If I drop out I am never going to be allowed in anywhere." He said, "Pledge, don't worry, when you're a senior we'll let you in." Like, that would make up for everything.

Nuwer: How did you feel when you were not a member any longer?

Pledge: I missed the camaraderie. You really do. I never missed the yelling, the being hit. But it was a sense of friendship that you miss, and my older brother was in a fraternity at school and my father was in a fraternity. So when I was pledging I called them up and talked to them, though [I] wouldn't tell them what we were doing. They would just give me words of encouragement—stick to it. Afterwards, when I finally explained what [the brotherhood] was doing, they were astounded. Even now, I don't think my parents know how bad it was. . . . I don't think even my [biological] brothers know how deeply [I felt] affected by this. I was adrift from the brotherhood, but I knew I didn't want to be like that. That realization came over a period of time. For the longest time, I actually felt guilty about turning them in.

Nuwer: How did you do that?

Pledge: I went to the dean's office. I asked them, I said, "Listen I don't want to get anybody in trouble—these guys are my friends—but if you could just pay for some of the medical tests." Or if they could just cut me some slack. I was sick, I had headaches, I couldn't go to class, I was falling over. I'd be sitting places, and I couldn't even remember how I got there. These were all symptoms of post-concussion syndrome. I just asked them for certain courtesies—they laughed at me. My dad told me, "I called the dean." I said, "Dad, this is my life—you can't do that," and so, to a certain extent, they forced my hand. . . . I knew that was the right thing to do, but you see, that's the thing no one ever tells you when you're a kid. They always tell you it's good to stand up and do the right thing, but they never tell you how painful it actually can be, or how many times you actually regret it. I turned them in, and for a time, I felt bad about it. I felt bad that I was going to punish my friends at that school. The main turning point that pushed me away from the brotherhood was another wrestler friend, not one that I was super-tight with or anything, but we lived in the same eight-man quad. He came up to me one day and he said, I know you're turning in the fraternity. I hadn't told anybody, but he knew. If someone wants information, there is no way of stopping it. Secretaries saw me walking in and out [to register a complaint at the school], and half of them were students who knew I had an appointment there. He said, "Pledge, if I had all the concussions you've had, and they'd done the same thing to me, I'd do the same thing you're doing. I don't hold anything against you." When I look back now, I can't believe he actually said that. That took a lot of guts to say that. He said there were two of his best friends and another guy in the house who [would] basically make [my] life a living hell. I was shocked. He said, "Sorry, I wouldn't do anything." I cleaned out all my stuff, and I left. I came back over Thanksgiving to pick the rest of my stuff up. On the other hand I couldn't go back to my family. They had no understanding of what it was like. . . . Yes, the fraternity did get kicked off, but other than that, nothing has happened, no apologies. . . . I feel like I haven't gotten any justice over this. . . . I know my dad felt bad for recommending [fraternities] to me. . . . I was adrift. I couldn't go back to my family. . . . And so I transferred . . . and now once a week at least I think, I'm at a school I hate because of the brotherhood. . . . Because of this fraternity, I lost the school I liked going to, and professors who were well known in philosophy for which I wanted to go to grad school, I sacrificed that. I had one great professor, and if I was there I'd be his right-hand man now. I lost that. I lost two best friends in the house and we'd gone fishing—fishing!—That's a bond. (*Laughs ironically.*) . . . If you talk to my parents, they'll tell you that somewhere along the way I lost my compassion for other people. . . . It's changed the way I view people. Before, I always thought there was something good in people. Now I tend to think there is something wrong with people.

Nuwer: This is speculative, but have you envisioned what you might be like had you gotten in? Would you have hazed somebody else?

Pledge: You know, I would love to say that I wouldn't have done this to someone else. You always want to be the bigger man. The truth is, I couldn't tell you. When it was happening to me, I thought, *This is wrong, and I hate it, and if it was me, I wouldn't do it.* Of course, I know on the other hand that it's this huge adrenaline rush to be feared—to have people quiver under you. In wrestling, I was ranked in the state and it's kind of a rush, and I can see that going to people's heads.

Nuwer: What I wonder is whether something actually changes in a person that goes through the hazing so he . . . then it becomes [likely that he reciprocates].

Pledge: Yeah. Something does change in you. It's like when you're running a mile or any distance, it really hurts when you're doing it, but then when you're done, you don't remember it. When people go through hazing, it's the same: They hate it, they hate it, they hate it. There are two camps I saw . . . with nobody in the middle. They either go all the way and be Super Hazing Man or they're not going to do anything. That's how they picture themselves when they're [pledging], but when they are out, I tell you, it's a flip of the coin as to who is doing it and who isn't. . . . At my new school, you find out [who the hazing groups are]. If you want to find something out [about who the hazers are on campus or anything else], you can—you must be observant and listen. I told [some Greeks], "Hey, I'm not coming to this school for any trouble. I had a bad incident with a fraternity, and I just ask you respect the pledges—the song and dance every one of them all gives—and never send a pledge over to me [doing favors or other acts of servitude] to ask, "What are you doing tonight?" I told them, "Never do that to me." A girl at school who had a crush on me actually sent her sorority pledges to me, and I went to talk to her. I realize that I have a lot of anger because I set out to lay it all out analytically, and before I knew it, these words were coming out of my mouth: "If you ever send over a pledge, guy or girl, I will beat the shit out of you." And . . . I've said to pledges . . . in passing, "You're a human being. Nobody has the right to make you their slave." I mean, it's so culturally accepted that I've got to watch this being put in my face.

Nuwer: From what you're saying it seems to be that hazing which is cult-like is the worst—

Pledge: —It is. It's such a cult, and it's accepted. It's accepted by the people in it. It's accepted by the people around it—other college students, it's accepted by the administration, it's accepted by the community, and on the whole, it's accepted in the United States. That's what it runs on. No one ever steps up to say no.

Nuwer: It's like the tacit approval that used to be given date rape, it—

Pledge: —It is to an extent. People who went through it will say after, "Oh, it really wasn't all that bad." It's so accepted and you get so brainwashed into a way of thinking, even if you fight it and spit into a cup as a rebellion, eventually you go along and man, this goes and gets you, too. You get sucked into it—it *is* a cult.

Nuwer: I hope people reading this finds that what you say demystifies [hazing]. You have a certain credibility because you've gone through this.

I think it helps people in Greek organizations who say hazing isn't so bad because their [own] chapters didn't haze.

Pledge: Yeah. My friend [name withheld] goes to the University of Virginia, and he's in a fraternity. . . . I'm kind of a big guy, and he told his friends, "Don't bring up fraternity [hazing] in front of him because he gets angry . . . " I see that basement [where I was hit] in my mind sometimes, and it makes me angry. I lost a lot, and I lost it as you say, because I got sucked into a cult[-like] mentality. . . . You don't ever want to be cynical, and you hope it will change, and I hope, I hope the fact that I got the fraternity closed down means someone there won't [need to] get closed in the future. That's the thing that won't ever change—that cult status. The only people I think who can stop this is the school administration. But they protect themselves. The [hazing] at [my old university] could have been ended a long time ago. And, while I don't know this for a fact, I think [hazing] could end at any other college if the administration there would only take another approach to it. It's like drugs. It's like [underage] drinking. Everyone knows it's there, but nobody says anything. If [the administration] wants to find it, they can find it, but no one ever does anything or disciplines people. It's the same thing with fraternity [hazing]—it's on the same level.

Nuwer: If a college professor ever treated students the way a fraternity treats students, he'd be out of a job [as an abuser].

Pledge: Yeah, but because it's a fraternity. . . . it is a mystery, and you [as a student] want to be involved in it so you get sucked into it.

Nuwer: [A cult-like group] is a sort of self-indulgent little kingdom.

Pledge: Yes it is. It is the crown jewel of hedonism. This is the same house where I watched brothers drink until they pass out and vomit on themselves, and then I had to clean up the bathroom half the time. The old-timers who went through the Greek system . . . ? They love it now because they think it's the same [as it once was], but it's not.

Nuwer: I [see] a need for realistic [quantifiable] research surveys of hazing to determine how many people actually haze—

Pledge: —Yes, I know that in the house I was in, it's "protect the brotherhood at all costs."

Nuwer: What about the national headquarters? Didn't—

Pledge: —They had an advisor there. Now the pledges were told by the brothers that the advisor didn't know what was going on. Well, if so, I've come to the conclusion that he is retarded, or he chose to look the other way. They had the advisor *there* because incidents had been reported before. . . . There was no way he couldn't know what was going on—no way.

Nuwer: Did he see underage people drink?

Pledge: Yeah, he'd come into a room, and we'd be having a beer. Everyone would be having a beer. It was more like a "walk by and scoping of everything out."

Nuwer: The one argument for keeping fraternal groups going is community building, but [cult-like groups] are anti-community. It's really in the Greek system's best interest to get rid of criminal behavior.

Pledge: Yeah, but the mentality is that if you're ratting on one fraternity, you're ratting on all of them. I wish I had thought of "cult-like group" myself to describe it, because it's perfect, because everyone wants to be in on that little mystery that no one else knows about. . . . It's the fact that you're involved in something that no one else knows about—it might be a little counterculture because you're not a conformist. Then here you go over to this fraternity with the biggest conformists.

Nuwer: At DePauw there was a sorority where the pledges were given brands on the inner thigh, . . . and [the larger sorority chapter] was broken into families. They had family secrets, family words. At IUPUI, I was part of a program where African-American fraternity members invited in gang members and they compared rituals. Some were pretty similar—

Pledge: —Yeah, when I was in it, your pledge brothers *were* your brothers. Until you became a full-fledged brother your pledge brothers were your family. You dealt with your problems internally, and in it there were leaders and followers.

Nuwer: You were a wrestler, and now we're seeing hazing with sodomy . . . and sexual stuff [initiations], but you want close bonds with your teammates and—

Pledge: Yeah, but our wrestling coach never allowed any hazing, and he openly said one time, "If I see you harassing a freshman, you're off the team." He said, "Beat . . . him when you're wrestling if you want to show you're better than him." He was adamant about no hazing, and there was a strict no-hazing policy on the wrestling team. But because you wrestled, and took turns with some of these guys who were freshmen, you sweated in the same room and there was that bond. It was the same bond they tried to bring about in the fraternity through beatings. It was mind games, and even the beatings played into the mind games.

Nuwer: Can you reform a group like this? If you have a problematic group like this, you simply have to do away with it.

Pledge: You have to. You can't put an advisor in there; you can't give a slap on the wrist. You have to get rid of them. . . . If anything, you have to understand the idea of "Protect the brotherhood at all costs." It was stressed over and over again: "Protect the brotherhood at all costs. . . . " I compromised the brotherhood and they all turned on me.

Nuwer: In the black fraternities, you can either be a "paper member" who gets in with the [legitimate] rituals imposed by national headquarters, or a so-called "devil" member who goes through hazing to get secret sounds, words, and poems. If you don't go though hazing you're not a real member.

Pledge: You're taught that all the other fraternities on campus are powder puffs.

Nuwer: One thing I wondered is if an initiation done in Georgia by a national is the same as an initiation done by a chapter in Pennsylvania. Is the ritual pervasive in a single fraternity or not?

Pledge: Fraternities differ from campus to campus. It's hard to know where these more violent ones spring up. . . . At [name] College, anyone who wears a [name of fraternity] shirt is basically a coward thug. He fought in numbers and was a half-step away from being a date rapist. . . . Their sense of loyalty and what is right are now so skewed. I'm not saying that these people are going to go out and commit mass murder, but their views on what is good loyalty and bad loyalty [are] now skewed.

Nuwer: Were you asked as a cult-like group to sleep in small rooms all together?

Pledge: On certain nights we all had to sleep in the house. We didn't have to sleep [together] in a big room, but you had to sleep in your big brother's room. If it was after a hazing or a party, you usually slept with two or three pledge brothers in your big brother's room on the floor or on the couch. After parties you couldn't leave unless you had a good, viable excuse.

Nuwer: But if it was with your big brother, was that to isolate you?

Pledge: Yes, we were isolated in that we were forced to stay in the house. We couldn't leave the house at certain times—like the night of a party or during hazing. We were stuck in the house, isolated from everyone else. . . . You feel different from half the campus. You can't tell Joe Blow sitting next to you on campus who asks what you did last weekend, "Well, I went down to a basement and got the shit beat out of me. Then I had to do all these pushups and calisthenics and then I got beat up again. And then I had to clean an entire house." All that doesn't lend itself to talk, and so you do get isolated.

Nuwer: What about alcohol and the addictive side of fraternities?

Pledge: The funny thing is that before I pledged I'd been told, "When you pledge, don't drink." About the addiction, we as pledges weren't allowed to drink. We had to stay alert. But people still did. I remember the first night of hazing that three kids ran out, throwing up. [Name of veteran member] told us, "As a pledge I wasn't allowed to drink. You guys aren't allowed to drink. But I know some of you are going to drink. Just be sure you can handle it. If you have to run out to throw up, you're going to [have to] do more stuff." I decided not to drink [to intoxication] because I didn't want to throw up. The most I had to drink was that an alumni brother made me chug one beer—that was it. But a lot of brothers did drink and a couple of pledge brothers were doing Ecstasy. But on the whole, the not-drinking thing kind of bound us a little. We knew we were going to have a few drinks to "bond" us together, but you would think making us drink would bond us, but not making us drink was a hardship and that brought us closer together. The addiction part was still there because I was 21 and older than half the brothers. Who do you think went out and bought all the beer? It was addiction in the sense that I and another kid with fake ID when we went out, we'd get like $500 worth.

Nuwer: But if someone were to die, you would be liable.

Pledge: I would be so liable. That's why they sent me to do it. When I said we didn't have to drink, it's not like alcohol wasn't the most impor-tant thing. It still was. You just weren't allowed to drink unless you could handle it. It was huge there. You always had to keep the beer cold. You always had to have a pack of cigarettes on you in case somebody wanted one. It had to be the right brand. Everyone in the house either smoked Camel Lights or Marlboro Lights, and then it got decided that all pledges would walk around with Marlboro Lights.

Nuwer: Did you have to know "pert" [pertinent information] like their favorite drinks?

Pledge: Not really. You had to know their pin number, their name, where they lived, and their major. But they would lie to you. They wouldn't give you the right answer. So you'd get into more trouble. They wanted you to get to know the brothers and to have one-on-ones with the brothers.

Nuwer: Were there kidnappings . . . ?

Pledge: We were sent on missions. The day after I got hit I was assigned [to go] but I was allowed not to go. They would call you up in the middle of the night and you had to run out to some location and run back. And if you could steal anything from another fraternity house or sorority house, that was gold. You were to break in any way you could and steal, but don't get caught.

Nuwer: Did you have to keep pledge books? [Pledge books are forbidden by most or all fraternity headquarters.]

Pledge: Yeah. In it you had to have the names, the history. The best book to get was [name of member who hit him], the [former] number-one pin, because his pledge book had everything.

Nuwer: Did you have demerits?

Pledge: No, but if one screwed up, everyone screwed up. That was the mentality. If you were the [pledge-class] president and someone screwed up, you got it the worst and then everyone else got it. He got hit more than anyone else.

Nuwer: How did you choose the [pledge] president?

Pledge: It was the first day. It was like an initiation ritual. We've got to sit down and pick people. I got the idea right away that they were eyeing us. I got the feeling right away, *There's something hidden here.* This is not a prestige thing. So for the president, everyone voted while we sitting around a table. I was like, "Who do you think should be president?" A couple would raise their hands. "Him or him—OK, it's good." And that's how our [president] was picked.

Nuwer: How is the chapter president picked?

Pledge: By voting. The number-one pin, though, can never be the [chapter] president, because there is too much liability.

Nuwer: Did any faculty member ever come to the house?

Pledge: Not when I was there. It had a bad reputation when I was there. It was one of those things, that everyone knew something was there.

Nuwer: I've been to the campus. Didn't anyone ever hear [outside] what was going on in the house?

Pledge: Oh, you couldn't hear what was going on in the basement. They were clever little shits. They know what they're doing to get away with it. They knew every trick in the book to make sure we wouldn't get caught.

Nuwer: Supposedly [headquarters] thinks you are learning fraternity values, but you're learning about deception, brutality and—

Pledge: —Brutality! What I learned was rebellion. None of them ever said you couldn't cheat—on anything. So I used to cheat on anything. You're supposed to go down to the basement in a T-shirt and shorts for hazing. I always went down in a sweatshirt—why? For the padding on the elbows. There were things you could get by with like that. Or if a brother had his pledge book lying around in his room, I'd take it and copy everything down I could. When I went to bed I was prepared, for rest assured, [chances were] I'd be woken up that night.

Nuwer: If you were on this side of the microphone, what questions would you be asking? What am I missing?

Pledge: I think you hit most of the questions [but] the one thing— Remember, [you] talked about how hard it is for people [school administrators, Greek advisors, headquarters liaisons] to get in on the inside of fraternities? I have a different view of that, I really do. I could go to any strange fraternity and find out any information. I'd tell anyone, this is my recommendation, don't take [your charges of hazing] to the school—take it to the cops. Schools will hide it. The best thing is going to the cops. When I walked into my judicials [school judicial hearings], they [the members charged] were all cool as could be, but I knew they were terrified of me, because I knew what they did. I was right, and they were wrong. Those kids, if you get them as a whole roomful, they'll sit there and they'll deny everything. Except like the president [names him] who got expelled, the core group would lie on its own. You take those two wrestlers I was talking about. Yeah, maybe the one was hardcore [and would deny everything], but the other? You couldn't sit in a room with him for twenty minutes before he'd tell you everything I was saying was correct. Like I said, they are cowards. . . . They fight en masse, they hide en masse. You make the right one understand that there are consequences if he lies, and you've got them [all]. There are, as I say, the hardcore guys, so you've got to root around.

Nuwer: The word "depraved" comes to mind . . . In so many of the fraternities where there were deaths, they did something stupid and inane—like they exchanged bottles [between big brothers and pledges] and a kid would drink the whole thing. It's almost like I can understand it, though not tolerate it, but such people can be educated. I think you can teach them what happens if you drink two bottles of alcohol, and they can understand [the danger] and change. But this is calculated, barbaric, unethical as can be, and all within an educational system. This is anathema to an educational system. I am not making light of a death, and they bother me an awful lot, but this bothers me more because I don't know how to stop—

Pledge: —It isn't just one [national] fraternity. Every campus I have ever been to, it's always a little different. At my school, [his former fraternity] may be the jocks, and at another school it might be the chess team. I've heard about animal abuse [at chapter houses], but I never really sat around and thought about it.

Nuwer: [A pledge] raised a hamster [at a northern Maryland university] and then squashed it [on the order of members].

Pledge: This is all like a badge of courage—how much can you take? There are the physical beatings along with the mind games that they play, and you get sucked into it because you don't want to lose. It's the randomness too. A pledge on one side of the room gets asked a question and answers it wrong, nothing happens. A pledge on the other side gets it wrong and he gets punched in the mouth. The whole thing gets into your head—the violence, the air of violence. A lot of the brothers, I can't say all, did it because it had been done to them. We had paddles, you and your big brother, but they were never used [for paddling] because they were symbolic. [The statement trumpeted by members] "We don't paddle" was supposed to be a huge advancement.

Nuwer: It was another form of justification. What we are doing must be okay.

Pledge: Yeah.

5 Hazing and Alcohol in a College Fraternity

James C. Arnold

Editor's note: *Iota Nu Sigma (INS) is the pseudonym for the fraternity chapter whose members James C. ("Jim") Arnold observed, studied, and spent years interviewing. He promised anonymity in exchange for access. Members are identified by nicknames only. Arnold's research is valuable for describing the "group as addict" concept and for illustrating how the fraternity lies to both itself and outsiders about its abuse of alcohol. This study also demonstrates how such organizations consider hazing-dominated pledgeships to be an integral, even inviolate, part of a fraternity's identity. In other words, these groups believe they practice "responsible" drinking and hazing even as they operate in an absolutely irresponsible fashion. Finally, his observations and interviews with chapter members make it clear that fraternities believe that their hazing may help new members cope with life's problems. The latter is a medieval way of thinking that recalls Martin Luther's insistence in 1539 that each new Wittenberg student be hazed in order to be able to bear "heavier vexations" later in life.*

Part One: Rush and Pre-Pledgeship

An addictive organization possesses and exhibits the characteristics of an individual who is addicted to a substance such as alcohol or narcotics—or to a process taken to obsession such as gambling, religion, or sex. The literature on addictions has demonstrated that individual characteristics of addicts are quite consistent, regardless of the type of addiction, according to the work of Anne Wilson Schaef and Diane Fassel (1988). Schaef and Fassel (60) define a "system"—in this study, a college fraternity—as a group made up of "content (ideas, roles, and definitions) and processes (ways of doing things)." It is essential to that definition that the fraternity has a past and future life distinct from the lives of members. Barring factors such as expulsion, that organization will continue operating in the future. A dysfunctional family unit (e.g., a family or group with an alcoholic member) is a prototypical example of a small system that itself exhibits the characteristics of addiction, according to the work of Sharon Wegscheider-Cruse (1981). My argument is that a fraternal chapter such as Iota Nu Sigma (INS) can be depicted in much the same manner.

Some characteristics of addiction noted by Schaef and Fassel include:
(1) *Denial*—not acknowledging the existence of a problem
(2) *Confusion*—no one knows what will happen next
(3) *Self-centeredness*—the self is perceived as central to everything that happens
(4) *Dishonesty*—lying to oneself and others
(5) *Perfectionism*—an obsession with never being good enough or performing well enough
(6) *Control*—members try to manipulate others in the group
(7) *Ethical deterioration*—a lifestyle centered on addiction separates the addict from his or her spiritual base.

Schaef and Fassel listed "underlying processes" indicative of an addictive organization. Two to be considered in the case of INS are the *process of the promise,* in which individuals tend to focus on the future and an expected reward rather than staying tuned to present thoughts, feelings and experiences, and *the process of external referencing,* in which one's success in the world is based on the perceptions of others, not self-perceptions. As the story of INS unfolds in this study, the manner in which some of these characteristics and processes are manifested in this organization will become quite apparent.

INS Rush

No one joins a fraternal organization by accident. The process by which Iota Nu Sigma recruits potential members who are likely to preserve its values is intentional in design and implementation. The two main phases of the socialization process for this (or any traditional) fraternity chapter are "rush" and "pledgeship," activities well known to anyone connected with fraternities.

"Rush" is the selection process whereby a chapter first identifies individuals that the group deems worthy of consideration for membership. These are considered rushees. After screening and culling, the chapter gives those who are chosen a written invitation to join the group called a "bid," which is subsequently signed by a rushee to signify that he accepts the invitation to become a "pledge." Pledgeship occurs over a period of time in a fraternity, completion of which signifies the individual's readiness for—and worthiness of—membership. At the conclusion of the process, the ceremonial ritual called "initiation" is the culmination of the entire experience.

Rush Dynamics

Two active members, called the "rush chairs," are elected by the entire membership and put in charge of rush. The process they facilitate extends from the time of initial contact with prospective members until the time some are invited to join. I was repeatedly assured by INS interviewees that rush and pledgeship were "dry," that is, alcohol free. A source named Wolfman, an officer of the INS fraternity, stated this:

> During [the time I was here for] rush I was very pleased and impressed that we didn't have to drink or do anything of that nature. There is no drinking during rush by the [rushees] and there shouldn't be. [Containers of] alcohol are not to be seen by [those] rushing here and there are heavy fines for people who do [have alcohol out in the open].

However, it was to become evident over time to me that what INS members *say* they do and what they *do* are sometimes contradictory. The term "dry" is loosely, if not falsely or inaccurately, defined, since alcohol plays a role in this chapter's rush and pledgeship. The rush process may start with designated members contacting a high school senior or a college freshman (or, less often, the occasional sophomore or upperclassman). In addition, some undergraduate males may contact a member or attend an informational meeting to express interest. A prospective pledge that notes a family member who is an initiated member of the fraternity is given a special status; he is known as a "legacy."

Rush is a very purposive effort on the part of INS to recruit and select individuals that fit the fraternity's self-perceived mold and values. They have a well-coordinated effort to contact and solicit nominations from INS alumni and others who know what the house stands for. They have a weekend experience that most of the rushees attend which is virtually identical from year to year and a selection process that thoroughly examines the academic and athletic record and personal presentation skills of every potential member. When examining the record of each rushee, INS members focus on past behavior and achievement as a predictor of future success and on whether or not these individuals possess the appropriate values for INS membership.

Rush Weekend

Two or three weekends are designated rush weekends to get to know these prospective members. Seniors in the house may take part, but they generally are not as involved as the freshmen, sophomores, and juniors. The member Spock pronounced the event alcohol free for rushees and members from Friday at noon until Sunday at noon. Embedded in Spock's admonition that the event was free of alcohol were themes and apparent values pervasive in all my interactions with INS members, namely the "four corners" of INS: scholarship, brotherhood, campus activities, and intramural (IM) sports. These terms are part of every INS member's normal vocabulary. Also evident was the message that partying and getting to know campus females are part of the INS experience, but during rush, there is a partitioning of the priorities, and rush weekend is alcohol free and a time for getting to know the members—which is serious business here.

When a rushee arrives at the chapter house he is met by his "rush host," an active member who has been assigned to him. The identity of the rush host has been disclosed to the rushee prior to the weekend by a handwritten letter. The host ushers the rushee to a meeting where he is given an overview of the weekend, including the information that it is dry, and then lunch is served. After the meal downstairs in the dining room, rushees and many members spend the afternoon playing basketball to show off individual athletic ability and to socialize. This group then returns to the INS house for about an hour of unstructured time. Dinner is held downstairs in the dining room.

After dinner comes time for the "rush entertainment." Typically this begins with the INS slide show, but the first time that I observed this event a university sports team was playing on television, preempting the slide show. Instead, self-serve pizza and soft drinks were available. Although no alcohol was available to rushees, alcohol was not entirely absent. Upon my arrival at the house, I met Wolfman, who had just driven up, in the driveway. He walked me into the house while carrying an open can of Coors and the rest of an unopened six-pack of beer.

During halftime of the game, one member distributed handouts, indicating the previous semester's all-house and pledge-class grade point averages of the fraternities on campus, to the sixteen rushees present. The fact that INS was first in both was noted as an indication of the importance of academics in this chapter.

INS's school won the big playoff game on TV, and active members in the room huddled in front of the screen and sang the school's fight song. There was an obvious division of participants (the members) and observers (the rushees and me). After the fight song, we all went outside on the lawn to celebrate the victory. The rushees and I, of course, merely followed along. One member urinated at the side of the house—with his back turned but in full view of passersby and all of us on the street. Finally, after a spontaneous basketball game involving just members, everyone headed back down into the basement, where it was time to have dessert. Attractive young women served ice cream while members watched part of a second game on TV. At halftime, the TV was turned off and we all moved into the dining room to view the entertainment.

A makeshift curtain fashioned from shower curtains had been hung from pipes that ran across the room, just beneath the ceiling. Many of us sat in chairs that were placed atop tables so that we looked down upon the "stage." About 100 of us were in the room. A few more females had joined the group, in addition to the ones that had been serving us ice cream.

As additional evidence that alcohol was present, during the skits, I observed one female drinking a bottle of Miller Lite®. Further, I had heard Wolfman say that some members were allowed drink, namely the ones that were involved in putting on the skits, "so they're not so nervous." The Rush Entertainment Committee members are a "select" group for this weekend, said Wolfman, and "they sort of enjoy having the chance to do that [drink together]."

There were about eight or ten skits. During one of them, two members, portraying "cool" fraternity males, talked between themselves about what being in a fraternity is like. For example, one asked the other what happened after the party the other night, with the reply, "Hey, I got laid, sucked, and fucked. It's a given!"

That set the tone for the remainder of this skit. Women were referred to as "bitches" consistently throughout the dialogue, and females were usually yelled at with an order to do something or to perform some act. For example, two vocabulary words that were repeatedly used were "leave" and "cram," and each was explained and used in an appropriate context. "Leave" was illustrated in a number of shouted sentences such as "Bitch, leave your clothes over there!" and "Bitch, you better leave—I can hear your boyfriend honking outside." "Cram" was used in a sexual context. Much laughter accompanied almost every line of the skit. It appeared that everyone in the room thought this dialogue was very funny.

The few women in the room were laughing along with all the males. Here are the thoughts of Dawson, responding to my questions on the INS attitude toward women that I had observed in the skits:

> There are different skits we do, but that doesn't reflect the attitude of the house, necessarily. I mean, [in your writings] I noticed the thing about how the females are treated. That is what you would [find in] the typical "Animal House" fraternity. That's what we consider a "frat guy," a real face man, you know, the good looking, GQ guy; that's how they talk 'cause they think they're a badass, or they're real cool. And that [the skit during rush entertainment] was more the mocking of the "frat guy" impression more than the mocking of the guys in the house. So it wasn't that anybody that did the skit actually believes what they say, but it's more, like again, it's mocking somebody of that, that is the typical, generalized, stereotypical, frat guy.

Hoping to clarify what he was telling me, I asked, so "you're making fun of a *caricature* [of a fraternity member]?"

> Yeah, of a frat guy, of what everybody perceives this frat guy to be, you know? People on the outside, that's what they think, and when they watch *Animal House* sometimes that's . . . the idea they get, that, "Oh they're just a bunch of beer guzzlin' women chasers and they don't really respect [women]." But I mean [the skit's] just making fun of them. Really, it was a joke [and] really it was funny to watch, but it doesn't reflect the views of the majority, ninety percent of the guys in this house.

While noting Dawson's protestations, both times that I observed rush, the skits communicated similar negative messages regarding females. Dawson's assurances to the contrary, the insensitivity exhibited toward women in these skits, if displayed in a public forum, would produce pronounced condemnation.

In my view, messages regarding women during the rush process relegated them to the role of objects for males to use.

Two years after first experiencing the event described above, I attended another rush weekend to see the ritualistic slide show I'd missed because of the televised game. At one point during the setup for skits in the dining room, a member set three cases of beer on one of the tables. A rush chair noticed this infraction of rush rules and ordered the cases expeditiously removed. The carpet looked freshly vacuumed—and everything in the house seemed to be spotless and in place. A two-foot-tall trophy had been placed on top of the room's grand piano; the inscription on the award said: "IFC Academic Excellence Award Traveling Trophy."

About 6:15 P.M., right after dinner, twenty-five rushees, members, and a few female guests and I gathered in a darkened room in front of a screen. Some hooting and hollering from the members commenced as the first slide—an exterior view of the INS house—was shown. The next slide was a small group picture taken at one of the annual parties called the INS Luau. A later slide, representing INS's focus on academics, was a staged picture of a house member, partially in the nude, accepting a scholarship plaque.

Other photos depicted the Red Rose formal dance. The narrator observed that a lot of the members "tend to get very drunk at the Red Rose." Some of the members and dates in these shots appeared to have a difficult time standing. Additional slides with an alcohol focus depicted activities associated with the university's annual Spring Festival, which is touted as the "highlight of spring." Some pictures showed members consuming alcohol in milder climates during spring break.

A traditional, if reckless, activity associated with INS membership, as the slide show depicted, is the celebration of a member's 21st birthday with, apparently, the express intent of getting the celebrants very drunk. A few members were pictured in very sad shape. One member is caught as he's gesturing wildly to a group of members and, as a narrator says, "explaining the meaning of life."

The room erupted into cheers occasionally. In one slide, a member handed a bra to a female as the narrator said, "Here's Brother Smith returning an undergarment to the girl he shacked with last night." Often cheers greeted pictures of members, such as one shown on his side in a trash-filled hallway, passed out, with a large electric fan resting on his head.

The predominance of drinking and alcohol-related activity in these pictures brought loud and enthusiastic reactions from members. To me, the show seemed produced to communicate and illustrate to the new members a variety of the social dimensions of INS—that this was, after all, a *fraternity,* and that a significant part of what we do here is have fun. And to have fun, we *party.* And to *party,* we have alcohol. In all fairness, all of the various aspects of the house that are stressed at INS during rush and pledgeship *do* come up during the slide show—including academics, intramurals, campus activities, and brotherhood.

Not all who attend rush become members. Some decline bids. Others who want to join are excluded. Those newcomers offered a bid are selected during an often-raucous, sometimes-confrontational "hash" session in which the members decide whom they will accept as pledges and whom they leave out.

INS Pre-Pledgeship

Alcohol plays a large role at the INS house on any night the chapter hosts an informal, nondate party; that is, an event to which many males and females come unescorted. Gramps described what I would find just before I attended such an event, where other guests from campus fraternities and sororities are present.

> [W]e have one or two people working outside in the front or, of course, the driveway and you just check everybody who walks by; you know, if they start coming up the walk, you say, "Can I help you?" You ask them right away, before they even get close to the door. And then you have [them] go in through the back. Only one door is open that you can come in and out of; it would be the back door. And there are three people from our house and any other fraternity that would be partying with us; they would have people there also and that's how you check who is coming. It's mainly like, you know people in your house and they go in right away. Any girl is kind of like your choice, you know; if you want to let her in. And then there's also a list that you have; it's mainly the guy list, it's, you know, friends that you want to have and each house has their own separate list and you check off. So that's kind of pretty strict on how you get in, you know, and there's always, there's people manning all the stairwells, because there's no alcohol allowed except in the party room downstairs, so they keep it all down there and so anybody who tries to walk up you have to bring them back and make them put the beer down.

> I think there are only two stair[ways] you can get out, the back stairs and these main stairs here. There's [*sic*] also a couple "roamers." They roam around the house making sure there's no alcohol out and to make sure that, you know, if the dean would come up, I guess. I've never been one of these [a roamer]; I don't know exactly what their job is—they just kind of walk around and make sure everything's in control. You know, a guy out here in the trophy room who makes sure everything's in control out there, watches for people and then, I guess there's the servers, they're constant security, because they take care of the alcohol if anybody comes. But the way we have set it up is you have to walk up the stairs to second floor, around and back down two flights to the basement so you can't come in through just the front door or the back door and you can't directly go downstairs. All the main ways are all blocked off, so it's a real tedious process.

According to Gramps, an important part of security is the precaution that is taken lest campus authorities see too much.

> If the dean would come, they [security] would let us know and all the lights would come on and we'd cut all the taps, put away the equipment that we pour with, and then we have to bleach down the room [i.e., clean up the room's floor by dousing it with a dilute solution of bleach in water] where the beer's served and lightly

bleach down the party room, not too much so it really stinks, in case it's a false alarm, and then I guess they'd have to walk, I don't know how the dean would get there. I wouldn't think she'd [the dean would] walk all the way around the way that the kids walk, that would be kind of ridiculous, that would take forever. So I don't know how she would come in, but she would try to get us as fast as possible, I would think. And so hopefully by the time she got there, we'd have all the cups collected from everybody and it would be clean so she wouldn't see anything, but she really doesn't, because of our grades, you know, because of our standing in the college, they really don't try to come bust us. They may visit us on a couple, they visited the Luau that one time [but] didn't do a thing because we don't cause trouble and we're above the all-men's average on grades, so I guess that's why we don't get a big hassle from them. So I've never been here yet when they've, you know, had a problem.

The Spring Festival party is one such event where alcohol flows at the INS house and at many other campus events. I attended a party much like the one described by Gramps, including a variety of house security measures, a circuitous route to find the party room, and many partiers engaged in the consumption of beer. Standing at the head of the driveway was Dawson, the fraternity president, walkie-talkie in hand. As we chatted, I learned that the dean was out making her rounds tonight and had already made several stops at Greek houses to monitor heavy party activity. I also learned that this particular event was a "three-way": one other fraternity and one sorority were involved. [Similarly, a "two-way" event would involve INS and one sorority; a "four-way" would involve INS, one other fraternity chapter, and two sororities.]

I went around to the back of the house and partway up the back stairs to a landing, where three members seated at a table met me. These were the guys responsible for monitoring all those who entered the house and seeing to it that no alcohol-related items left the house. On the table were scraps of paper with names on them—the official party list. Presumably, only members of the three official houses—and their guests—were allowed inside. A few who did not qualify did not make it in, but most everyone who arrived negotiated their way past the greeters. No one left the building, however, with any beverage container in his or her hand. That particular rule appeared to be inviolable.

I finally went to the basement—and the party. I emerged downstairs at the entrance to the dining room, now transformed into party central. Virtually all of the furniture in the dining room and another large area called the Maple Room (a lounge adjacent to the dining room) had been removed, and the dining room was packed with bodies. To my right was the kitchen area, from which the beer was being served. Most of the people downstairs were on this side of the room, bunched together, cups in hand, waiting to be served a beverage. A live band was playing loudly; another group of partiers was crowded in that direction.

I located one of the rush chairs up on second floor and followed him around for a little bit, and we finally found one rushee (prospective member) down on the first floor. He appeared to be here with his girlfriend, who said she was in high school. I introduced myself and told him that I been studying this house for some time now (he recognized me from the rush weekend I had attended the previous week). He said that he had a brother in the house at the present time and that not really much of this life was new to him. He had been acquainted with Spring Festival parties and INS for a long time. I had hoped to get his first impressions of the campus, but it was much too late for that with this rushee, who already spoke in the jargon used by members. I asked him what he thought of the slide show the previous weekend. He said that what the slide show was about was "emphasizing the brotherhood—you can kinda see that—that's really important here."

Once again downstairs, I found that the band was taking a break, so it was much quieter. People still congregated around the beer-dispensing area. I went into the Maple Room and tried to decide where I might be able to be out of the way to observe, when a member waved me over to sit down on the sheet of plywood now protecting the pool table. This sophomore member was someone I had met before—the younger brother of Klinger, a past INS president. Mostly we chatted about me having known and interviewed his brother and how I have extensively interviewed three of the last four presidents for the purposes of this study. He also mentioned how just last week one of the student-affairs staff (an assistant dean) had been by to talk about alcohol use in Greek houses and had elaborated on three rules he used in dealing with the Greeks. These rules, as related to me by this sophomore, were 1) "Don't lie to me"; 2) "Get me through the house quickly"; and 3) "Don't put it in my face." Presumably, these rules guided this person's behavior when he was out visiting Greek houses (such as the visits by the dean's staff that night). This sophomore summarized his understanding of the dean's rules: "If you want to play this game, you have to play by my rules—and here they are. We'll all get along fine as long as long as you do this."

I tracked down three rushees in the Maple Room, who were led to me by Klinger's brother. These males, too, recognized me from rush weekend and were willing to talk a little bit—though they seemed pretty intent on partying. Their attention strayed as I tried to initiate a conversation and ask some questions, but none appeared to be so obviously drunk as to be out of control. One seemed to speak for this group when he indicated that he really appreciated the fact that rush weekend had been dry and that rushees and members could start to get to know each other "as they really are." He also offered that it was nice to be down here for Spring Festival weekend and to see that, basically, the INS members are the same in this environment, too. "The guys in this house are just great—really nice and personable, you know? When you come down here for Rush Weekend, you sort of suspect that they might be putting on a facade—but you come back for this weekend and they're just the same. Everybody's very friendly—and something that I really want to be a part of."

After this brief encounter, I called it a night for this Spring Festival event. By that time, it was about 1:00 A.M. and I had just learned that the beer had run out.

Rookie Week

One of the rituals at INS was called "rookie week." This time period consists of a few days (less than a full week, actually) in which incoming pledges, primarily new freshmen, stay at the house just before the beginning of the school year. For a few days, rushees experience this new environment, away from parents and things familiar to them, and begin the transition to college life. They move into a structure of approximately 100 other men, mostly strangers. Below is a quotation from the INS pledge-educator files regarding rookie week.

> The freshman class will be instructed to arrive at [the INS house] on the Wednesday immediately before classes are scheduled to begin. Upon the pledges' arrival, the freshman advisors will have the responsibility of greeting them and showing them to their assigned rooms. The active brothers will be instructed to act NATURAL toward the pledges upon their arrival. Any problems or questions the freshmen might have should be directed to the freshman advisors.

> The goal of "rookie week" is for the new pledge class to meet each other and to become accustomed to living together. There will be no rules as such placed on the pledges, but there will be activities, organized by the freshman class, [event names and locations are listed here as examples]. Something will be planned for every night.

Rookie week is not really thought of by the initiated members of the group as part of the pledgeship experience per se—although many or most of the pledges at the time seem to think that their pledgeship *has* started. "I was under the impression that we had started," said Klink.

Roberto, a veteran member, described rookie week in this manner:

> It's basically for them to just come down and they're from high school. They're green, they don't know what to expect. They think, "I'm in a frat house now" and [are unaware that] we never say "frat," [we say] it's a fraternity. They'll say, "Oh yeah, we're in a frat. Let's go get girls and get drunk," and that's basically it and then they do a lot of stupid things, and this year they went and stole a banner off of one of the sorority houses and hung it up in ours. Like "Welcome Back" it said on the sorority house and they ripped it down and brought it over. What was [*sic*] some of the other things that they did? Just very, very rude to the sorority girls that come over, just because they really don't know how to act, I suppose. I mean, most of them are intoxicated, but rookie week is traditionally a heavy drinking week for the freshmen.

From these comments it is evident that the members believe that the freshmen moving in are quite naive ("they're just green as hell"), which is a likely assumption. They are starting a totally new phase of their lives and have yet to learn how things really are done and their true place in the house. The pledges are furnished alcohol by the members and encouraged to "do stupid things." These "stupid things" are kept track of by the members in a logbook called the "bitch list" (in which the stupid things the pledges do during rookie week are called bitches). Of course, all of this is totally unknown to the pledges, who tell me they are leading what they presume are rather normal lives, though some found the week uneventful, even boring.

As it happens, four of the most important people in the lives of these pledges are waiting purposely in the wings, surreptitiously preparing to take center stage. The "pledge educators" (PEs)—the four active members who are in charge of their pledgeship experience—are intentionally making themselves invisible during this time, as they had during rush weekend. Dawson, who spent two years in the PE role, recalled this experience:

> I was just, kind of, just a background figure at rush. . . . I rarely met any of the pledges unless I knew them previously. And if I did meet them I would give them a false name. And so they don't remember me, I don't really remember them, except for the guys I knew. . . . I remember when I was a pledge I had no clue who the four PEs were. No clue. It's just [when pledgeship starts on Monday night that] they find these four guys [in their face]. . . . No one has a clue who they are, really. Where in the hell did they come from? Where have they been?

Part Two: Pledgeship

Iota Nu Pledgeship and Alcohol

Pledgeship continues the transition process into INS membership. Similar to rush, pledgeship is touted by INS as being alcohol free. This ban on alcohol is clearly stated in the official rules as set forth to pledges on the first night of pledgeship. However, this prohibition is often violated. Mercury told me in an interview that despite the no-alcohol rule for pledges, there were definite times where drinking is sanctioned by the chapter.

> We've got a party called the INS Luau that we have usually in late September or so, which is just like an island party, basically, and the pledges are allowed to go to that. They get dates and are allowed to drink during that. Let's see, also we have dad's weekend [which] usually falls during pledgeship and so we usually have a bar for the dads or kegs going. That's always a football weekend too, so we'll have kegs downstairs before the game and mixed drinks and then also, later that night, we'll have casino night with kegs and mixed drinks. The pledges, they're allowed to drink downstairs with us before the game with their dads and with their dads that night, too. And then also during pledgeship, the biggest thing is probably they get a little party that we call the pledge dance, which is just one night out of pledgeship, usually after it's been going on for a while, where they get their own party. They have a date party in the house and they just get just really, just butt wasted and the seniors bar tend. They get a couple of seniors to bar tend for them and it's just like a stress reliever. And those are probably the only times.

Mercury's recollection of the number of times when pledges are allowed to drink points out numerous violations of INS's own pledgeship rules. Even this list of drinking events is incomplete, however. I am reminded that it is useful to ask what the form and meanings of drink in a particular group tell us about that group. In a complex modern society, made up of many subgroups, the drinking patterns of each subgroup or class may reflect its special characteristics as well as the cultural frame of the whole society, as noted by anthropologist D. G. Mandelbaum (1965).

Pledge-Class Unity

The pledgeship program, which Wolfman said is "typically around ten weeks long," nonetheless can take as long as is necessary for the pledge class to "come together." This means that the length of time any particular pledge class remains in pledgeship depends on the class itself and the PE's assessment of their progress toward their primary goal of total group cohesiveness. The program is featured prominently in the international Iota Nu Sigma's glossy fourteen-page brochure that introduces the group to prospective members and interested others, such as parents of pledges. In part, the brochure describes the pledging process in these words:

> Our pledge education program has always reflected the philosophy of encouraging cooperation, mutual respect, and brotherhood among individuals having diverse personalities and interests.

> The primary responsibility of each freshman is to achieve the highest scholarship of which he is capable. Our study program includes a proctored study table five nights a week. This proves to be extremely beneficial in establishing good study habits.

> Pledges at [Iota Nu Sigma] are expected to become familiar with the history and organization of the college, the fraternity system and [INS]. They are also instructed in etiquette, table manners, and in the traditions and songs of the fraternity.

> The emphasis on scholarship, individuality, and overall excellence in [INS's] pledge classes leaves no room for paddling, hazing, or the legendary "Hell Week." Rather, a constructive effort is made to smooth the transition from high school to college. Each freshman has a Fraternity Father to help him with the problems of this transition, and may go to him whenever the occasion may arise.

> One of the most important aspects of pledge education is the strong feeling of closeness the pledge comes to feel for the rest of his pledge brothers. This tight bond of friendship stems from a common goal—the desire to integrate into [Iota Nu Sigma].

> We . . . feel that our progressive program of pledge education has had much to do with the success of individual brothers in college and later life, and with the chapter's outstanding record in the areas of scholarship, activities, athletics, and brotherhood. Pledgeship at [name of chapter] is a very rewarding experience, unmatched anywhere in its benefits for the college freshman.

In many ways, the story of INS pledgeship that follows corresponds to the one just advertised in the international fraternity's manual. In a variety of other ways, however, it can be perceived much differently—as may be demonstrated in this quotation from Wolfman, one-time president and two-time pledge educator, speaking about the INS pledgeship experience: "Obviously, anytime you want to indoctrinate somebody, the way you do it is to restrict their food, restrict their sleep, get them run down, and then really emotionally play with them."

As indicated, during rookie week many of the freshmen were under the impression that pledgeship had already begun. Because they were not exactly sure what pledgeship did entail, each came in with their own preconceptions and ideas of what this process was all about. When asked to recall what they initially expected of pledgeship, Santa, Batman, and Rhett responded thus:

Santa: I thought pledgeship was going to be duties and cleaning and just work kinds of things. I had no idea at all how stressful it is. And I don't like the word "hazing," but you know the pressure and the "us against them" kind of thing—I had no idea what that was like. I didn't expect that at all. I just thought it was work and duties and responsibilities.

Batman: I kind of came down here with the idea that it was going to be pretty bad, just because—and that may have been kind of naive—I really didn't have any idea of what it was truly like, because unless you go through it. . . . I mean, I had heard stories about other fraternities and things that they did and I really didn't know about [pledgeship here] because particularly with this fraternity it's something that's just not discussed, really, with other people and so, I mean, people really don't have much of an idea what goes on, but I came in here expecting that it was going to be pretty tough. I thought it was and I knew I was kind of prepared for "steam bath" [see below] just because someone had told me, another brother who was already in the house. He didn't tell me about it, he just said to be ready for Monday night because it's going to be kind of a shock. I mean, he didn't tell me, that was all he said, and that made me think I was ready for it. More so than maybe some of the other people that came down here. . . .

Rhett: . . . My older sisters who had gone through college, they were like, "Yeah you're going to have to do this"—trying to scare me and all this stuff—but they never convinced me that it would be anything more than cleaning or anything more than I could handle. I mean, I could sit here and tell somebody who's going to be a pledge next year, I could go down and tell him the program bit by bit, you know: you're up by a certain time, you got to clean at certain times, you got to do this, and you to do that, but I mean I could tell them word for word the pledgeship and how it's run, like and it would still . . . catch you by surprise.

Many INS members told me that they believe the essence of pledgeship—and indeed, the brotherhood of INS—stems from the concept of "pledge-class unity" (or PCU). It was a theme that I heard repeated many times. Roberto told me that PCU is

the biggest part of pledgeship, the most important. As graduates you look back and you remember your pledge class, you remember your pledgeship days, the best times of your life. I got a couple of pictures up in my room; after, whenever you're around the house, you can go look at [them]. One of them I blew into a poster and it's our pledge class on spring break skiing at Aspen, and we all have a picture of us hugging each other and other times during the Luau, you go out and get foliage and trees and leaves and so on and after it gets dark you decorate the place out here as a pledge class and it's about four in the morning and two people stand on guard all night, because everyone on campus knows we have this dance and a lot of houses don't like us, so they'll try to vandalize it. So we have two people guard until about four o'clock in the morning, about literally thirty-five degrees, and we're all just sitting out there having a great time, about six or seven of us, and it's those times. I just looked through pictures the other day of pledgeship and you remember your pledge brothers and to this day after chapter, the seniors who are still living in get together and we'll go down to [a bar down the street] or we'll sit in the senior den and just talk and this is most important thing—the pledge class. It's just—you can't describe it. You really can't. You get through this, not that it's that rigorous, especially physically it's not a rigorous program, but mentally you help each other through.

Related to the whole notion of PCU is the idea of the pledge class "coming together." I asked Roberto to elaborate on the meaning of these terms.

[Coming together is] helping each other through, living together, I mean you're all up in the cold dorm [a large room with bunks] together and you sit up there and talk. Anytime before you go to bed, I don't care if you're a freshman, sophomore, junior, or senior, you just talk before you go to bed, so you're talking to these guys. You play on the same intramural teams with them, you clean with them and it's not a forced thing at all, it's fun. I mean, anything you do, you do it with your pledge brothers whether playing practical jokes on a walkout* or whatever, you're doing things together. That's what's important about it.

Mercury also spoke about the process of the pledges "coming together" as a group.

Well, I mean that's why we're on top of everything is because everybody comes together as a pledge class, but in order to do that you can't just come down to school and move into a fraternity and . . . automatically be best friends with everybody. So in order to carry on the tradition, we feel that we have a pledge program that literally just molds everybody into the kind of person—we say "gentleman," a mature gentleman that you should be.

These views of PCU and the "coming together" of each pledge class appear to be completely consistent with the description of pledgeship in the international fraternity's brochure: "The most important aspect of pledge education is the strong feeling of closeness the pledge comes to feel for the rest of his pledge brothers. This tight bond of friendship stems from a common goal—the desire to integrate into [Iota Nu Sigma]." The description of pledgeship in the chapter's pledge education files begins by listing its purposes. Consistent with the

---

*A walkout at INS was an unauthorized major departure as a group from normal pledgeship activities.

brochure's account of the program, it is stated that INS pledge education is designed to "develop each pledge to his fullest capabilities. The objectives set for the pledge class have this purpose in mind."

In addition to chapter objectives, one of the most important components of pledgeship, the "pledge education committee," is described in the PE materials:

The committee shall be comprised of four active brothers whose character, activities, leadership, and commitment to the fraternity best exemplify our high standards. There shall be one sophomore, and three brothers selected from the junior and senior classes. Their role shall be to set an example for the pledges in daily conduct; they shall be respected by the pledges, not hated; they shall offer group-oriented constructive criticism; they shall not yell at the pledges nor call them derogatory names; they shall work in conjunction with the cabinet, the freshmen advisors, and the graduate advisor.

The selection of these four chapter members, the "PEs," is *the* crucial element in making pledgeship what it is from year to year. They are the ones that facilitate the pledgeship process and are responsible for ensuring that the pledge class develops PCU. For a member to be elected to the position of PE is to have elite status in the fraternity: much of the responsibility for the success of the house draws upon their success as PEs. Within the PE ranks, different roles are designated. For example, there is generally a senior who has one prior year of experience as a PE and is designated as the head PE. He is the one that can teach the job of PE to the others less experienced in the role.

During one of Dawson's interviews—when he was in the middle of his term as sophomore PE—he shared some of his thoughts of his general philosophy and approach to the job.

Well, as far as being a PE . . . , I mean, I take the job seriously. I think my job is really is to be . . . they call it the "bloody PE," because I'm the freshest one out of pledgeship. [The bloody PE is] the one who yells the most, the biggest cock. I'm the one who always bitches at the pledges for every little thing. I'm the one who notices the little screwups because I'm so fresh out of it [pledgeship]. I mean just the little things. I know when they're not doing something. I know when they're lying. I'm the one that can get about anything out of them and can make them tell on each other, because I won't say that the sophomore PE has the most power, but I think that I'm the one that can respond the best because I'm so close to the pledge-class program, just getting out of it a semester earlier. So I think that to be the "bloody" PE is accurate because the sophomores [in general] are generally considered "bloody" because they're generally like, "Oh, we're going to get these guys back"—you know, vindictiveness. But it's like once you get over that feeling of, "Oh, I'm going to screw these guys bad," and you get to that thing, well, it's not so much that I want to screw 'em, I'm going to yell at them for their screw ups so that they build it all up to that goal [of PCU] so they realize I'm the one that's going to teach them the goal and I've got to help them realize it.

In order to get as clear a picture as I could about the various roles the PEs played, I urged Dawson to keep talking about his job. I said, "So your PE philosophy is to be the toughest one?"

[Yeah, my job] is to be the harshest, is to be the one that is going to be the biggest cock. Yeah, it's just to be their worst nightmare. You know, they don't want to come down and sit at my table, you know, they're going to want to know my pert [short-hand for pertinent information about each member and pledge], they're not going to want to screw up my room, because I'll notice the little things. I mean, I'll notice the dust in the cracks.

I'll notice when they won't dust a small thing, I'll notice when they leave cleaning supplies, I'll notice when their PCU is bad, like at practices I'll see them not sitting together, stuff that [other] people don't look for and like you can see the cliques forming. You know where they're studying because you know where you went as a pledge. I mean, as a senior you can forget what you used to do. I know where they are on the weekend. I mean, I know the kinds of things they do on the weekends. I mean, everybody remembers the good things, but I remember the bad times too, when we all got separated, when people were ditching on [skipping out on the preparations for] the Luau.

In addition to the PEs, the chapter has freshman advisors. The identity and existence of freshmen advisors are not known to the pledges until the first night of pledgeship. One way of conceptualizing these contrasting roles is to define the PEs as the ones who *challenge* the pledges, individually and collectively, and the freshmen advisors as the ones who *support* the pledges. It is the primarily the job of the head PE to see that these two functions maintain some kind of balance.

It is during the first Monday night of pledgeship that the world of the pledges turns upside down as they embark on their symbolic journey, which is both real and symbolic. When he was interviewed not long after he finished pledgeship, Batman tried to sift through the meaning of the whole experience:

I think workwise, like I've done a lot more things that were more strenuous and whatnot—like actual physical work and stuff. But as far as like mental pressure and back to getting into the stuff that I didn't know I was going to get into, it was like by far the toughest thing that I've ever been through mentally, having so many people against you, I guess. I had never experienced that, and I know I've talked to several of my pledge brothers that were like "this is the toughest thing I've ever been through." And I just think it's awesome to look back and think that I made it, that I went through it. I think it's a real character builder, I think it really adds strength to your personality. It teaches you in the future that when you come into problems with people, you know how to stick through it and I just think it really makes you stronger. I really do. Knowing that I've went through that, it adds to my confidence as a person. Because for me it was really tough.

I mean, I've heard a lot of the brothers say that pledgeship was the best and the worst experience they had in their fraternity years . . . and I can already feel this and I think everyone in our class can; there's no other time where you're going to be as close to—[there are] twenty-seven guys in our class—as you are during pledgeship and you're just so close to everyone.

Steam Bath Ritual

Pledgeship per se begins on the first Monday of the fall semester, the evening of the first day of classes. The event that kicks it all off is called "steam bath." For pledges, the experience of steam bath takes place during one evening, and since they are never officially told of the event's existence, there is not necessarily any anticipation of the evening. However, the PEs have been preparing for this event, intellectually and emotionally, ever since their election to the post. Finally, the night before steam bath arrives and the four PEs get together to prepare the "script" for the lines they will soon deliver to a surprised pledge class which will inform them of the beginning of pledgeship. Dawson described that Sunday evening's script-writing meeting.

> Well, the four PEs went over to a hotel, [and] two of the PEs from the previous years came over. One had been the head pledge educator for the last two years and the other one was a sophomore pledge educator from a previous year. The four PEs of this year were all rookies so we had no idea—the script from the year before had been lost, and [since] you always pass it on, we had to start from scratch. We were there for four hours. We did the rules [see next section] and then we wrote the bitches, and we all knew who would be talking [when], so it was kind of like a play. You had your cue and then you had another one talk. It took us about three hours to write and we practiced it for about an hour. All we did, is the four of us, we started from the top, went through what we had to say, we said it all out loud, we didn't yell, then we did the bitches, [including] side comments at the same time, so we got a good feel for it.

The "bitches" just referred to are the items on the "bitch list" kept by the house membership during rookie week. Dawson elaborates on the use of these items during steam bath.

> You don't use them all, but you pick out [some], like each year sometimes during the bitches there will be a theme. Like my year, there was a guy and it was like Chapter 2 on such and then Chapter 3—it was on the same guy and there [were] five chapters of all his screw ups. And this year we had like Cock number 1, Cock number 2, and Cock number 3, because there are three guys that consistently thought they were INSs already and screwed up. So you don't pick everybody out. There's three or four guys that get really reamed hard and I'll tell you it was pretty intense doing the script. A lot of us got nervous and then you get excited and then you're really ready for that day to come, the next night. You're really excited to get down there and just go nuts on them.

Thus, at least part of the steam bath script is relegated to pointing out the shortcomings of members of the incoming pledge class. In the script that Dawson and his fellow PEs wrote, the kinds of things that attracted attention were:

> Telling brothers they could set them up with girls, acting like their room was your room. They got real drunk, obnoxious. I mean, yell at your friends, your girlfriends. They'd do stupid stuff like that. I mean, they would just act like they were seniors in the house. They just disrespected all members in the house. I mean,

just pretty much anything that, you know, anything that you wouldn't want to do when you went into an interview, that you wouldn't want to do to upset or turn someone the wrong way then they would do it because they thought they were badasses because they were pledges now.

Instead, the pledges learn that they are so lowly that the members pejoratively refer to them collectively as frogs. After all the waiting, anticipation, and some performance anxiety, the day of steam bath is upon the group of PEs. Dawson recalled this:

> God, it was just a day of intensity. Anybody who walked down the hall, I mean, everybody knows who the PEs are in the house. I mean, everybody knows everybody in the house, but when you pass a PE, everybody's giving high fives, smiles are all around, [and] you have . . . everybody . . . getting intense for this. The sophomore rooms are really going crazy, you know, coming up. One of their rooms got me a card and got me a big green frog, you know, and they all came in and wished me luck. And, you know, all my pledge brothers were wishing me luck and really felt like you're going into a state championship game.

Finally, the PEs start the first formal pledging assignments. As one last part of their personal ritual before meeting the pledges, the PEs all change into their good suits under the false assumption [contrived by chapter members] that the international fraternity has asked them to pose for photographs.

The pledges are put into a tiny room where the temperatures in August can reach 100 degrees. The windows are shut. The humidity is intense. The lights are off. Pledges are ordered to stay silent by the pledge educators, who assume the demeanor of drill sergeants.

Dawson stated that the purpose of the first night of pledgeship is to get the pledges' attention. Recalling the "wake-up call" nature of steam bath, which tended toward physical and mental abuse, he said this:

> I'd say the biggest purpose of steam bath would be to, it's such a—I don't want to say violent, but [for] lack of a better word, it's such a violent change from what they've been expecting or I guess what they've had from the past few days and I think it's something—it's more of an attention getter, because the honest truth about steam bath is the freshman really don't hear a word you say. All they remember is four guys bursting in the door yelling. I mean it sounds like a really awful night, and when you go through it it really is, but the real purpose is an attention getter. [We] introduce them to the four corners of the house and let them know that this is something that we take seriously and we expect [them] to [take it seriously also] and if you're not ready for the commitment then you need to evaluate where you really want to be. I mean it's not something to frighten them or scare them although it probably does a lot of people. Some people get through that night fine, some people are terrified, but it's the one night like it; there's no other night that they'll be that intimidated. A lot of people might say if they heard about that that there wasn't a purpose there, but it's really the only way to be able to start our program. I mean you can't ease into our program from [when] they come down for the first four or five days and have a good time with their brothers—you couldn't just come down to lunch one day [and say] "This is the way it's going to start."

It's just something, I think, that's symbolic of them starting together all at once, they're all down there and stuff. The first time they're all together, probably, well not the first time, but as far as pledges it's the first time. So I think that's the biggest purpose of it is to let them know this is the official start, this is the outline of what you're going to go through, because basically you tell them what's going to happen, you tell them the whole pledgeship, and if they, see, if people were smart enough to realize, "Hey look, these guys are laying down the whole or eight to twelve weeks, they're laying down the whole outline right here" and if they would pay attention they would know that, but the purpose is not for them to pay attention and hear that, the purpose is just for them to sit down and listen and realize that this is the kickoff, [and that] it's serious. It's something that, I mean, you know probably as well as any other outsider the traditions of this house, it's something that is taken quite seriously by 99 percent of everybody in here and they realize, "God, they're going to be serious," but they also realize at the same time, it's good we're yelling and whatnot, but I think they realize too that [we've] said, "No there's not going to be any bullshit, there's going to be a purpose" and that's something that when I was a pledge I didn't hear quite as much about, something that we said the last two years, always telling them there's a purpose and always let them know that no one's going to touch you, which is a big part of fraternities now people come in anticipating, Am I going to get this? Am I going to get that? and they want to know and we always tell people, we're not going to touch you because that's not part of the program and that doesn't do anything. But that's what steam bath is all about.

In spite of all the talk about purpose and no physical hazing, however, here too is dishonesty, deception, and denial. As will become apparent later in this report, INS pledging ends in a night where physical hazing and reckless striking out are rampant. Here is the recollection of the opening session from another past pledge educator:

So then they stay in here for that forty-five minutes or an hour, and they're pretty much exhausted just from heat and then they are taken downstairs (and I don't know if they're blindfolded or not—no, no they're not—there's other times in pledgeship where they are blindfolded, but not at this time). The pledge brothers are lined up in alphabetical order. . . . They're lined up, [and they] put their hands on the other guy's shoulder in front of them, each of them their left hand on the guy's shoulder in front of him—sort of a train—and then they walk downstairs.

After the pledges march downstairs, members light up cigars and go outside. One hundred or more members peek at the goings-on from the outside windows and blow cigar smoke into the room. The pledge educators, aware of the external audience, keep up their shouting at the silent lined-up pledge class.

Next come the room changes for pledges, which are meant to disorient them and to get them to understand they are being put in their proper place—a very small place. Pledges change rooms many times in order to meet the most brothers possible, but the first time typically is most unsettling. They are given two minutes to grab whatever personal items they can from their previously assigned space and relocate to another room.

"And then there again, they're encouraged, *very much encouraged* by loud screaming" and blaring music, according to a pledge educator's recollection. The pledges are encouraged to help one another out, and they are screamed at if they overlook this duty. The pledges assemble in a dorm-type room. Especially for a pledge, the living conditions in the fraternity house leave members little space to call their own. Wolfman said that "they [the pledges] don't get much space at all. They probably get . . . maybe a laundry bag's worth of space, a laundry sack. And there are 'frog boxes,' they have what's called frog boxes. I can show you one, they're just wooden boxes that have [space] for your stuff as a freshman, and if you get one of those, you're pretty stylin', because you've got, you've actually got some room."

After the room change, the freshman advisors talk to the class, playing the role of good cops to the pledge educators' bad cops, and they serve the newcomers cold and much-welcomed iced soda pop. The role of the freshman advisors is to calm the pledges down, listen to their concerns, and generally support them through the evening of steam bath and the weeks of pledgeship to come. Other than each other, the freshmen advisors, and eventually their fraternity dads (who will be described later), pledges have nowhere to turn for support. The exhausted pledges fall into bed, often without brushing their teeth or even going to the toilet. "Your eyes open up and you see you're not in the country club," said a member. A pledge educator concurred: "It is a wake-up call; it is."

Clearly, from the description above, much more happens during this evening than mere information sharing. Despite the admonition in the PE files that the pledges not be "intimidated or scared," during this time, most—if not all—certainly *are*. And the pledges feel the impact. For the most part, nothing in the experience of these raw recruits to this point had prepared them for steam bath. It is meant to be an awakening to what real life as a pledge will be like. The PEs are naturally quite aware that steam bath catches the pledges off guard. Despite their overtly aggressive behavior toward the pledges that evening, however, the PEs display anxiety as they await the outcome—how the pledges are coping with the experience—which they learn through reports from the freshmen advisors.

Some pledges are caught so much by surprise that they feel they will be unable to adjust to the rigors of the pledgeship that has been outlined for them during steam bath. The option that some individuals pursue, therefore, is to drop out of the pledgeship program—in short, they "depledge." Such was the case for Dawson's cousin and six others during his year as the bloody PE. "I think it was a group thing more than individual. I just think some people just didn't expect it and I think that if they would have stuck it out for the rest of the week, they would still be here today. I think they just got scared and just decided that they couldn't deal with it," recalled Dawson.

Roberto also had some observations about those who choose to leave INS after experiencing steam bath.

[For me, there's] always a concern of *what* will they tell [and] *who* will they tell. Obviously a lot of them are disillusioned with the house after steam bath and the ones who quit, I have a hard time thinking that somehow they're going to end up in the dean's office, . . . but a lot of them go to other houses. I'd say 60 or 70 percent move on to another house after they depledge ours. Then there's that 30 to 40 percent who [say] "Fraternities aren't for me." That's their line, "The fraternity is just not for me."

Most of the pledges that experience steam bath, however, stay with the program. If for no other reason than that they refuse to quit or that they think that future status as a member makes the temporary pain of pledging endurable or even attractive, they demonstrate that pledgeship with hazing apparently is worth the effort. However, to make it through pledgeship, they now have to live by an entirely different set of rules—rules that were literally screamed out to them by the PEs during steam bath. These rules are from the pledge educator files.

The Rules of Pledgeship

1. Pledges shall keep secret any fraternity traditions or customs not proper to be made known.
2. All pledges shall leave the house for class each morning by 9:00 A.M. and return by 3:30 P.M. Pledges are free to be in the Maple Room during this time. Entertainment of some sort will be provided (TV, stereo, ping-pong).
3. Pledges not in class, or not conducting necessary business, shall study together QUIETLY in the library.
4. Pledges shall acknowledge all actives at all times, using first names.
5. Pledges shall not be allowed to consume alcohol or any intoxicating drugs.
6. Pledges shall work together in the chapter house and are encouraged to spend their free time on campus together.
7. Pledges shall not display any INS letters.
8. Pledges shall not enter the senior den except to clean.
9. Pledges shall first fill in all corner seats next to the pledge educators, then fill in the remaining corner seats. Pledges may not sit at the President's table or at the head of any table.
10. Pledges shall say "pardon me" when being seated and "excuse me" when leaving the tables at the end of meals.
11. Pledges shall answer the house phone by stating, "[Iota Nu Sigma], may I help you?"
12. PLEDGES ARE REPRESENTING [IOTA NU SIGMA] AND ARE EXPECTED TO ACT ACCORDINGLY AT ALL TIMES. THIS INCLUDES TREATING OTHERS WITH RESPECT AND COURTESY, AND INTRODUCING THEMSELVES TO GUESTS.

The rules above are the standard ones which are listed in the PE files. PEs have the option of making up other rules when they are writing up the script— and it is not uncommon for them to add their own variations, which the pledge class will have to obey. However, it is over a period of the next few days that the rules really sink in as being "real." The pledges are so scared and intimidated when they hear them the first time that they are typically dismissed or forgotten. They have to be repeated again right away the night of steam bath by the freshmen advisors and repeated many more times by the PEs for the pledges to come to accept this as their life. As Falconer said about hearing the rules for the first time, "Really, when they started setting some rules down, I thought they were all a joke. I thought they were all a joke." INS pledges find out soon enough that *none* of this is intended as a joke by the PEs or the membership.

Nicknames

Each INS member has a nickname, usually assigned by pledge brothers during pledgeship. The nickname is an "everyday name" that each pledge and member is referred to by other pledges and fraternity brothers. Mercury expressed to me the belief that house nicknames are related to the INS emphasis on brotherhood and are indicative of the focus on PCU and "coming together" as a pledge class. "I mean the main thing that we stress is coming together as a class during pledgeship and that's just one of the things that brings a pledge class together and get[s] them to know everything about every other person, and it's just something that they can share within their own pledge class, why this guy got this nickname and I know him for this—this is what he's like."

Because nicknames were viewed with such seriousness, I was curious about how the pledges find out about nicknames and what is said to them about the process of picking a nickname. I said, "How do you communicate that to the pledges, that that's part of the process? What do you say to them?" Dawson replied,

> Well, they pretty much know that everybody has a nickname. Like at tables [being seated for a meal—a type of ritual to go over pert] we'll usually go, go around the table and [say] "Tell us everybody's nickname, all your pledge brothers." If they've got a stupid nickname for a stupid reason we'll say, "That's a dumb nickname." You know, nicknames are for respect, people *respect* these nicknames, you want your parents calling you this and you want to tell them why. I mean, a lot of nicknames come from very funny stories that people won't tell their parents but some nicknames are stupid and you get rid of them. It goes again with respect to the house.
>
> And it's also a thing of honor. It's just an honor to have a nickname. I mean it's an honor to wear the IM jersey with your nickname on it, just as it is to wear any IM jersey with someone's nickname on it in the house. You just feel [proud], yeah. I mean, you got your nickname and these great people call you by this. I mean, it's something that you're proud of. You're proud of your nickname, you're proud of the house. It's a way of saying, you know, to talk to people on campus and have them call you by your nickname shows, you know, I mean you're not afraid. I mean, everybody gets called their nickname out on campus. It's not something

just for the house, but it's a, I mean, if someone calls you by a nickname, everybody knows you're an INS. I mean, everybody knows that INSs have nicknames on campus. I think it's an honor within the house. It's something that definitely connects you with the group as a whole also, not just for the pledge class, but as a whole.

Meals and Pertinent Info about Members

During pledgeship newcomers learn to focus on the group rather than the individual. The pledges in INS are encouraged to, and find that they *have* to, put aside self and rely on each other. As John van Maanen (1984) has written about socialization, the process appears to involve self-destructing and reconstructing rather than self-enhancing—in my observations, at least.

This self-destructing/reconstructing pledgeship process, from the viewpoint of the organization, is one of intentional *control* over the individual, and control is one of the critical characteristics of addiction. Virtually every waking moment of a pledge's life is manipulated or regulated by the PEs. Once the real experience of pledgeship begins during steam bath, the pledges have no more freedom. They are told when they can be in their house and when they can't; their time in the house is controlled with the cleaning and other duties to which they are assigned; when they show up at meals, they must correctly recite pert or be ridiculed; they are told what room is theirs and for how long—and they must change room assignments at the PEs' whim; and they have regular, monitored study times. Additionally, these pledges are simultaneously undergoing their introduction to the academic part of university life, although their experiences with persons outside the pledge class and fraternity are limited by time and space.

Themes of denial and deception seemed to me to pervade the experience. Like rush, the pledgeship program was one that is supposedly "dry." However, the pledges were heavily involved in the production of the INS Luau, an occasion focused on alcohol use and abuse. Dawson observed this: "Everybody knows that the pledges are going to go away on the weekends and party and we accept it—we act like we don't know. And . . . in a way it makes them be more cautious because they know, 'Okay, we're not supposed to be drinking so let's be responsible when we drink.'" On the other hand, members readily admitted to telling pledges about a nearby cheap motel where the newcomers could drink by themselves or catch up on sleep or studying but mainly bond with other pledges without interference from the brotherhood. Wolfman also stressed that the PEs controlled the pledges even when they were away from the house, for if they were caught in the company of nonpledges on a weekend, the PEs would forcibly criticize the individual and the pledge class, question their solidarity, and threaten a longer pledge period.

Thus, pledgeship was not only quite different than many freshmen envisioned it when they agreed to a dry, non-hazing experience but it was also different from the way that the national fraternity's literature described the entry of newcomers into the group. Compared to the rather relaxed social experiences of rush weekend and rookie week, pledgeship was nightmarish at times.

During meals, the pledges were required to sit in corner seats at each table near the pledge educators, according to one of the rules of pledgeship. The PEs ask them to show their knowledge of pertinent (pert) assigned for that week. Pledges do get at least fifteen uninterrupted minutes to eat, or so the files mandate. When I asked the group consisting of Falconer, Penguin, and Rhett "What were some of the terrible times of pledgeship?" they replied, in unison, "Meals, by far."

In short, the PEs can make this quizzing a very uncomfortable time when they so desire, and according to recent pledges, that was their intent. It was only during meals that PEs actually talked to pledges, and they were there mainly as inquisitors to see what the pledges did and did not know about the brotherhood. After a meal, when the pledges were alone, they too put pressure on fellow pledges that had let down the group through ignorance or laziness by not knowing the called-for pert.

Batman concluded that the grilling was necessary to motivate the pledges to learn pert about all the active members and fellow pledges. He and others expressed the feeling that such knowledge helped a pledge feel pride in the organization.

> Even though you should want to know about other people in the house, if they just gave it to us and just said, you know, "Learn this about these brothers and we'll have a test on it," or whatever and didn't constantly remind us of that fact, I just don't think people would learn it as well. Because although you *want* to know it, I mean, there's . . . over 100 guys in the house right now, and you don't want to sit there and look at what exactly they've done their entire lives, just for the sake of doing it. You know, because obviously even though it's important it does get monotonous and there are times when, you know, you're really frustrated, you're like "Why am I doing this?" because I could be doing something else, I could be doing homework. Instead I'm wasting my time doing this, you know, but I think the pressure that they put on you to learn it is one of the things that keeps you going. . . . When you're going through you don't sit there and think about it, you just like *do it*. . . . I didn't really think about it that much; all I knew was I wanted to get done, you know. I didn't want to be the one to screw up and get yelled at [at] the table, you know, and so you learn it.

Here is what the chapter files require in terms of pledge education:

> Pledges will be required to learn about active brothers, their pledge brothers, house history, fraternity traditions, and the international fraternity. They will be required to pass a standard exam covering the international fraternity prior to initiation.

> ACTIVE BROTHERS—Pledges will be responsible for learning full names, home towns, majors, outstanding high school activities, campus activities, and house activities.

PLEDGE BROTHERS—Same as active brothers, with the addition of names of parents and siblings.

HOUSE HISTORY—This will be covered in their pledge manuals, which they will receive the night of steam bath.

FRATERNITY TRADITIONS AND INTERNATIONAL FRATERNITY—This material will be found in the [INS] Handbook, which they will receive the night of steam bath.

The pledge class shall receive the following pertinent schedule the night of steam bath:

WEEK 1: Pledge educators, cabinet, freshman advisors, [INS] Handbook chapters 1, 4, 9, 10.
WEEK 2: Senior class, pledge class.
WEEK 3: Junior class.
WEEK 4: Sophomore class.
WEEK 5: House history.
WEEK 6: Rest of the [INS] Handbook.
WEEK 7: AND BEYOND: Final testing.

The pledge class will follow this order until all areas are covered adequately.

The INS Luau

The INS Luau is a major theme party that occurs early every fall semester during the first half of pledgeship. The party has a Hawaiian Island motif—the house is decorated and partygoers are attired accordingly. This is the first event of pledgeship, and it is an example of a time when the no-alcohol rule for pledges is violated.

Bones shared a description of the luau:

INS Luau [is] like, everyone just gets back [to campus]. It's like the third week of school, [and] it's just for [INS]. It's the most fun, but people just don't last past 11:00 at night. Everyone's passed out by then, because . . . everyone like in the house will probably start drinking about, real early, and everyone comes [over] probably about 6:00 [P.M.], because you know, you want to make sure you get everything ready. So everyone's over here by about 6:00, get your dates, everybody's over here all dressed up, because there's no beer that night, nobody drinks beer. Everyone just gets whatever they want, . . . like fruity punch drinks [with Everclear® or rum], and everyone just gets hammered and is out rolling around in the sand. The band's playing and that is, that truly is just an all-out drunkfest, I mean people were just butt wasted that night. Everybody, girls, guys, it's just absolutely craziness. That's like a fraternity, I mean. We think of a crazy, out-of-control fraternity party, that's usually it, but I mean, everyone's within reason, but it just gets crazy and it's fun. I mean, that's a really fun dance.

One indicator of this event's significance is its inclusion in the pledge-educator files. It is an important part of pledgeship because pledges dedicate themselves for an entire week to luau-related activities. They are responsible for decorating the entire house and grounds for the event, including literally tons of sand, which they move into the parking lot; they also perform the cleanup the following day. The luau could not be put together in the manner it is without the pledges working virtually full-time to make the necessary preparations. The event is also significant because of the fact that pledges are allowed to drink, for the first time, in the presence of their PEs and other active members. Roberto, in his role of PE, talked about pledges being allowed to drink on this particular evening:

> [For the] INS Luau we have [the pledges] make out a alcohol list and of course they want three times what it would take them to get drunk, so we cut it down and they generally drink a pretty nasty Hairy Buffalo–type drink [vodka, tequila, Everclear®, and whiskey with pieces of fruit or orange peel] with their dates and pledge brothers. It's odd, but this is one of the times that I have to see them drink, so they, usually when they drink we don't see it happen, but this is one of them where we will.

Dawson described the pledge's experience preparing for the luau, the event itself, as well as its aftermath:

> It's a week of hell. This year the week was fairly hot; last year it was really hot. The first couple of days really suck. You're all sweaty, [but] you make all the effort to make yourself look good before you go to class, getting all the sweat off in the sand. By the end of the week, it's just like you don't care. You know, you've got classes with all your pledge brothers, [and] you just go in there all sweaty, sand all over you, come back and work some more. As the week goes on you realize, and the pledge educators have been telling you all week, this is a fun week if you make it. You can learn a lot this week, and you finally start to believe [that] at the end of the week Thursday and Friday when you're almost done. . . . The dance itself, as far as a freshman point of view, I didn't have that good of time; it didn't really do that much for me. The cleanup was just crazy. I mean, it was funny because you see everybody hung over and tired, but it's just an exhausting day.

The INS Luau is a party for both members and their dates, so nonmembers are always a part of the event. In order to more fully appreciate what this party was like, one September evening I spent the evening observing what it was all about. On the appointed night, I arrived at INS about 5:30 P.M. and approached the house just as a few members were arriving with their dates. I immediately walked downstairs. One significant feature of this event is a roasted pig, and I observed that it had been cooked by a hired food vendor and was ready to serve. As I sat down for a moment to further take in the scene, I saw that the doors to the Maple Room were open, revealing a patio area outside with a concrete floor and a few pieces of outdoor furniture. The pool table had been boarded over with plywood, and a large multicolored hand-printed sign that said "INS LUAU" was on the wall behind it. The whole floor was covered with a layer of sand a few inches deep. Two small empty wading pools, about five feet in diameter and eighteen inches high, were in the room. Large rocks had been placed around each of the pools, and leaves and branches hung from the ceiling tiles and the doors. There were a few green plants scattered about. On one side of the room was a makeshift lean-to: a sloping wooden roof coming out from high on the wall that was covered with straw and supported by two upright poles. Some wooden dining-room chairs had been scattered about the room, as well as a couple of black wrought-iron chairs, apparently brought in from the patio. The Maple Hallway, which leads from the Maple Room to a stairway, was also covered with sand, and there was another small wading pool—this one containing water, rocks, and long green leaves. Plants lined the side of the hall, and more branches and leaves were hung from the ceiling. Outside, the parking lot was covered with sand, and members of the band were unloading their equipment and setting it up under the window of a lounge area. The band's area was set apart in the corner of the parking lot by bales of straw, two bales high at points.

The back of the parking lot and the driveway had been blocked off with several suspended patched-together bed sheets. On the sheets were large hand-printed letters, approximately four feet high, which proclaimed "INS LUAU." A large painted head of an island "native," with a bone through the nose, was displayed to the right of the word "LUAU." Nearer the house itself, there is a similar display. At the top of these sheets "IWANALEIU" is printed in letters about eight to twelve inches high. There were lanterns on bamboo poles, which line the perimeter of the parking lot–turned–party area. A small pool had been built in one corner under the disguised basketball hoop. It was surrounded by rocks and was fed by a waterfall coming from the top of the backboard, which was camouflaged with branches and leaves. In another corner was what looked like a large tepee and a few palm trees. All the males appeared to be dressed in straw-colored or green grass skirts with a variety of athletic and other shorts underneath and had body paint on their bare chests, backs, and legs. The paint was applied in a variety of designs and sayings. One member who I recognized as a sophomore had "Fuck off Frogs" written across his back—a reference to his opinion of pledges. One member crossed a hallway wearing a straw skirt and a headband—also popular attire—kicking a large white plastic bone from room to room. Most of the women wore bikini tops and shorts with fabric wrapped around their midsections.

While strolling the hallways, I was invited into a room containing two INS juniors and their dates. On the floor, strategically placed in the middle of the room, was a 22-quart clear plastic container containing a mixture of Hawaiian Punch® and rum. In the syrupy, pink liquid floated a white Pizza Hut® plastic cup for dipping and dispensing. There appeared to be about a gallon or so in the container when I entered, and all the room's occupants had their large plastic cups filled. It was explained to me that these cups change color from year to year. This year's color was pinkish, almost magenta, and had a palm tree on it with the words "INS LUAU" in large letters with "iwanaleiu" in smaller scripted letters underneath.

While making small talk, they pointed out that the reggae of Jamaican singer Bob Marley was on the stereo. One member said, "We've got fifteen minutes before we eat. Let's do shots before we go down." One of them reached high on a shelf and pulled off a full fifth of rum, and while pointing out to me that drinking rum was consistent with the INS LUAU theme, he grabbed a handful of ice and deposited it in another plastic cup, then poured some of the rum over the ice. After a minute or so, he poured some of the chilled rum into a shot glass, which the other member chugged. Although they were invited to partake, the females declined to participate in this ritual. The males matched each other shot for shot. At one point, one said, "How many have we had now?" to which the second replied, "I've had three and you've had two. I'm ahead of you, as usual." The first member responded by offering an amused, though disgusted look— and a snort. They carefully took turns pouring out the shot for the other person and, with some degree of seriousness, explained to me, "You never pour your own shot. That's the sign of an alcoholic."

I imagine that a variety of explanations could be offered for this behavior, for instance, a simple display of machismo. However, to my eye, these practices seemed very alcoholic-like. The practice of making drinking a contest, drinking multiple straight shots in a very short period of time, and using language and behavior that minimized their behavior are all indicators to me that these men could be headed for lifelong alcohol problems. This behavior certainly qualifies as "binge drinking," according to the most recent Harvard School of Public Health definition of that term as applied to college students. Alcoholics are fa- mous for finding ways to engage in denial. They offer rationalizations such as: "I never touch a drop before dinner"; "I only drink beer"; "I only drink on week- ends"; or, in this case, "Only alcoholics pour their own shots." All of these state- ments are typical of people with drinking problems who are actively denying the seriousness of their issues with alcohol. Further, by directing their com- ments at me, they seemed to be engaging in some kind of attempt at impression management. They wanted to give me some kind of "spin" on what I was ob- serving so I would not get the wrong impression.

I headed back to the dining-room area again, just as the class of juniors started filtering in. My hosts from a few minutes ago entered and appeared to be a trifle wobbly and getting glassy-eyed. They noisily called out to one another in recognition as they decided where they were going to sit. After they had de- cided on a spot (they left their drink cups—mostly magenta-colored party cups, but one woman was drinking a wine cooler—to mark their place), they got into line for the food, still loudly calling out to one another and talking all the while.

One of the members approached me. Knowing that I was doing research on alcohol in this group, he told me that the Luau is a "very atypical event" for this group; a "once-a-year event." It was almost as if this member felt a need to deny the importance of the event, even though this Luau happens in pretty much the same way every year, and I have learned from my research that it is very much a part of "who and what this group is."

The meal consisted of roasted pig meat, fruit salad, and a roll or biscuit. The place was a mess after the juniors left. They left the room in general disarray for the next group. The area was littered with used paper plates, plastic utensils, cups, bottles, wet napkins, and food on the table and some on the floor. The next group was the freshman, though, and I assumed that they meant for the pledges to clean it up.

One member walked though with his date when just a few people remained in the room. Another member asked him, "Have you had anything to drink tonight?" To which he shrugged, shook his head, and replied, "I'm not. I'll talk to you later." It appeared that drinking was normal and expected at this event, so much so that a member was embarrassed when admitting that he was choosing not to drink. The drinking member didn't seem to apply any pressure on the other male, however.

Somebody yelled, "Frogs, you're next!" and the freshmen started filing in. When they saw the mess left on the tables, a few of the first to arrive start to clean. One pledge placed his arm from wrist to elbow along the table's width and physically scraped the debris off and into a waiting garbage can, strategically placed at one end. After all the tables had been superficially cleaned in this manner, the pledges and their dates saved their places at the tables, just as the members before them had done, with their drink cups and lined up for the food.

At 7:30, the seniors were about to eat. A member on the other side of the room hollered out, to no one in particular, "I'm so fucked up I'm going to be hung over for three days!"

I sat down at the same table I'd been at before, and the president of the house located me. He indicated that this party was costing about five to six thousand dollars—about half of what last year's party with hot tubs had cost. In time, one of the seniors yelled, "We've got some fucking frogs that are going to sing to us!" The pledges filed in as a group, without their dates, and stood along the edge of the tables where the seniors were seated, exactly where I had been minutes earlier. The group seemed quite disorganized. Some near the center had their arms around one another, but mostly the whole group stumbled around. Eventually, when they started singing, the seniors started throwing food at them; they were pelted with all sorts of material from the plates and tables, which rapidly escalated into whole cups of punch being thrown in their direction. Most of the accumulation of solid and liquid propellants (some of which were thrown very hard) did strike a target. Throughout the barrage the pledges kept singing, apparently determined to finish their song, but for self-protection some left.

Once again the pledges had been reminded that they did not have the full privileges of membership in this group.

By the time things had quieted down in the dining room, it was 8:00 P.M. and the band was prepared to start. It was dark outside and all the lanterns had been lit. Very shortly there were probably at least 100 people or so outside, many talking in small groups and listening to the band. Most everyone had a plastic cup in their hand; many of the members were also carrying pitchers of punch with them as they stood or walked around outside. Some of the females were consuming considerable amounts of alcohol.

Upstairs, a large group of seniors had congregated in a hallway around what must have been a 30-gallon plastic garbage can full of punch. The president spotted me and said, "Ah, I knew that I'd see you up here." One senior seemed to be in charge of preparing the mixture, the Hairy Buffalo, and stated that its composition was the following: "Four half-gallons of vodka, four half-gallons of rum, one half-gallon of Southern Comfort®, one half-gallon of Seagram's Seven®, another fifth of Southern Comfort®, a pint of a concoction similar to peppermint schnapps, one bottle of Boone's Farm Country Kwencher®, an additional fifth of vodka, and a variety of fruit (chunks), punches, and Kool-Aid®." This mixture practically filled the large garbage can. The senior who had given me the recipe winked and told me that "it's very easy to drink and everybody loves it; it's a real spread-your-legs potion."

One member suggested that I take a drink and I was offered a cup just about at my lips. I said, "No, thanks." Another *insisted* that I take a drink, and a number of members and dates were watching. I was feeling the pressure to consume. I resisted. A recovering alcoholic, I had been nine years without a drink.

A member that I had briefly talked to earlier in the evening came up to me and asked if I'd like to see the "effects of beer." Before I could respond, he banged his head against the wall several times, very hard. "I've got a hard fuckin' head," he said. The band finished a long Doors medley and left for a break. At about 10:25 P.M., I decided to go downstairs to the dining room to check out its condition. As I walked through the doors from the Maple Room, I saw a member vomiting into a large plastic garbage can on the opposite side of the room. A small group of members and dates were standing not far away, barely paying any attention to him at all. The tables appeared to be upright, but many of the chairs were overturned. The walls had been plastered with splotches of garbage here and there. From end to end, the room appeared to be demolished, to my eyes more the picture of "Animal House" than a "responsible fraternity."

Dad's Night

INS pledges are assigned a fraternity father or "dad" by the third week of pledging. The pledge-education committee tries to match member and pledge by interests and personality traits. The dad is supposed to be another ally, tracking his pledge's academic progress and serving as a primary support person. At some universities, dad's nights have led to alcohol-related deaths, but INS restricts its Dad's Night drinking to beer as a precautionary measure. Members offer this relationship as evidence of how the chapter supports its younger members. The custom of having a fraternity "dad" is quite common in fraternity chapters. The expressed intent of being a dad is to act as a big brother—a "confidant, friend, and mentor" to a pledge.

Nonetheless, even members such as Wolfman perceive that some outsiders might see Dad's Night as just another hazing event:

> Dad's Night is just a night where we do what they might consider hazing. I mean, you yell at the freshman, blindfold them, tell them how rotten they're doing and

things of that nature and then lead them downstairs, sit them down in the dining-room area, and at that time they're still yelled at and then after that part, their blindfolds are undone and their dads are usually the ones right there with the beer in their hands saying, "Would you like a beer?" "Have a beer." And then after that they'll drink plenty. It's amazing because a lot of them want to, and there again, there's a lot of different reasons why they drink, but they will. . . . People were just getting drunk. That's what people do. So then we go off and serenade [sing at sorority houses] after [we've] had plenty to drink.

Pledge Dance

Some time during the last half of pledgeship the freshmen are permitted to have their own party with dates. The party is held downstairs in the dining room and the Maple Room. The chapter furnishes alcohol, and two seniors selected by the pledge class serve as bartenders. Although many of the events described so far have ignored the pledges' no-alcohol rule, perhaps no event demonstrates the rule's inapplicability better than the pledge dance—which seems to be totally focused on out-of-control consumption of alcohol. Spock indicated this: "The pledge dance is ugly. It's, 'OK, this Thursday you guys got a pledge dance,' and like they just drink and drink and drink and drink. They just drink *amazing* amounts. . . . There's no reason to have a date at pledge dance, you just drink, and about 11:00 all the dates [are given rides home in cabs or from members], because all their dates are so drunk and obnoxious."

Penguin commented on the protective nature of the PEs during the pledge dance:

I mean, at the pledge dance, particularly in my case—because I got pretty sick at it, as far as alcohol goes—I remember one of the pledge educators taking care of me. . . . You then find out when you talk to this guy later, that one of the responsibilities is to take care of you, especially in those situations in the sense that, I wasn't close to death or anything, but he put me to bed and stuff like that. He didn't let anybody, you know, take advantage of me or marker all over me or do stupid stuff like that. You know what I mean? He [the PE] really, he was in charge of the program and really was in charge of protecting the pledges.

HP Night

The letters HP stand for "holiday party," which is so named because it generally occurs in the month of December. Batman explained the name "HP" this way:

It's the best holiday present they [the members] could give you. It got that name before they got into all these big anti-hazing rules and everything. The pledgeship was a lot tougher and a lot more physical from what I've heard. And it [pledgeship] lasted until about Christmas and usually right before they went home for Christmas is when they would have that.

The evening is characterized by much alcohol use, and this time it is the actives who are drinking. HP night is scheduled by the PEs when it is determined that the pledge class has finally come together. Like Dad's Night, the scheduling also takes into account the academic calendars of individuals in the pledge class, because any obligations the next day are likely to be missed. Interestingly, there was no description of this event in the pledge-education documents; this seemed to be consistent with members' prolonged reluctance to talk to me about this event. Now and again, members would make fleeting references to HP but offered no clarification until I had been around the group for quite awhile. Wolfman spoke of the event this way.

> OK, [HP is] a big night—a lot of planning goes into it and it's an emotional night. It takes a lot of time, but it's kind of fun, in a way, for the actives and the pledges. That night, it's like anything else in tradition, it changes slightly every year, but everything overall stays the same. [The pledges] will be in studying and as often happens, they'll be interrupted.

According to various members and recently inducted pledges, HP-night rituals start with a closing of the blinds, and, for the first time, pledges are rousted out one at a time. One pledge said that the class was unsettled by this: "We were like 'What the hell?' because they're calling us singly, you know. We're always told to stay together and now they're separating us! People were freaking out, I mean, I was so scared. So everybody [went out] one at a time—we didn't know what was going on. What they did was, we walk in and four guys say, 'Hey you're done with pledgeship, you know, you made it!' And they're trying to act like you're done and then they go, 'Just go ahead and go through those doors, somebody's got to talk to you'—so you go through there and then there's a couple of seniors in there just to give you all kinds of hell. I mean, there was hazing. Like it was bad."

Another recent pledged concurred, calling the ritual "old-school" hazing. It involved strenuous physical hazing such as pushups, and the members screamed and yelled. Part of the mental hazing was for pledges to realize that the "congratulations" they received were part of the mental hazing. Not only weren't they in; the hardest night of pledging was ahead of them. The PEs, dressed in military gear, force the pledges into a hallway. Other members are there, and the pledges must oink like pigs or sizzle like bacon or do other inane tasks, but the commands are delivered by members who seem angry and upset, as if the pledges have let down the brotherhood. In fact, more mental hazing follows as the pledges hear that their old pledge educators have so had it with them that new ones have been appointed. "You've completely embarrassed the house for the last ten weeks!" shout the members impersonating new PEs.

What is more than a little intimidating and potentially dangerous is that the members in the hallway are the biggest males in the fraternity. They have been drinking heavily, and they act in a violent manner, breaking bottles and screaming and slamming paddles into walls. One PE, Wolfman, compares the experience to a drunken father lashing out:

> So they're just running around this hallway doing this for about forty minutes or however long it takes them to get them out of that study table. Once that's done, then they get up and they quit acting like animals and they're in the hallway and they're lined up—then they go from acting like animals to lined up. And they're kind of tired, because if you're around on the ground acting like a [pig], I mean, [you're] kind of sweaty and tired. So now they're lined up and the new PEs come in and the lights are off, and then the new guys come in—and they're heavily garbed in military [clothes]; they've been drinking, they're pretty drunk probably. They are intimidating. I mean, they yell loud, scream loud, they punch holes—we have ceiling tiles and it's very easy to punch holes in them and once you punch a hole in them, the whole thing just disintegrates and comes down all over the place. They have beer bottles in their hands and they're clearly drunk, which, as a pledge, you never saw people really drunk. I mean, your PEs were never drunk, never, never, never, but now these guys are out of control, they're drunk. It's kind of like the father coming home drunk and you're worried now, because this is getting out of control and these guys, you don't know what they're going to do and they're throwing beer bottles against walls, smashing them, and they're smashing near you. I mean, it's pretty dangerous and it's intimidating. They're screaming right in your face, walking up and down the hallway. They're usually the more muscular guys in the fraternity [and] they're usually the big mouths also. Usually they're very bloody people, too. They really want to get on these guys and so they would garb in military, showing their muscles. [It's] pretty intimidating, just an intimidating environment, it really is. We've had, I remember—again it was my sophomore year and we did it, the new PEs made one guy faint. I mean he just fainted, and he had to be taken upstairs. It gets so hot and intense and that's happened before, too. I mean, that's not the first time it's happened, it happened the year before also, somebody fainted.

Some of the behavior was so bizarre that some of the pledges saw right through it, but the paddles crashing into walls gave them pause. "It made you think, are they going to hit [someone] with that?" said a recent pledge. Their doubts intensify when they're sent to a small room to sleep on beds without mattresses, just springs, and the fraternity president announces that things have gotten out of control—that members apparently want to go back to the old days of hazing that the pledges have heard so much about. One pledge had this recollection: "The president was there and he told us, 'Hey, it's out of control. We can't do anything. It's up to the seniors. Just try to get through this. This [the takeover of pledgeship and hell week] is totally illegal; you can't tell anybody about this.' We really thought it was serious."

At this point, frustrated and intimidated, some pledges often get teary-eyed. They're allowed enough time to just fall asleep on the springs, and then they are rousted again, allowed to wear only underwear, and taken to the cafeteria and sprayed with ice water and beer. Cold and wet, the pledges then are ordered to perform spontaneous skits by the original PEs, who appear on the scene again.

Five or six ice-cold spoons are placed in the mouths of the shivering pledges and breathing gets difficult for them, as the members are not only swilling beer but smoking cigars as well. "So finally the skits are over," recalled Wolfman. "A bunch of them have spoons in their mouth and, of course, by this time, they're very cold and very—it was funny when I went through it. I thought it was funny, but at the same time, you know, you're like 'This *sucks*!' But at the same time, it's really funny. Some of the skits are demeaning, they're certainly demeaning. . . . You're just like [thinking], '*God*!' You're cold, and you're laughed at, and people will throw beer at you and that hurts. I mean, they pour cold beer all over you."

Believing a hell week has started, the pledges are allowed to get dry and fall into bed. Minutes later, they are again forced out of bed with orders to put on their shoes. Wolfman recalls one such event:

And then they wake you up again and they have what's called "frog races" and that's around the warm dorm. There are usually a couple of guys in the house who play lacrosse, so you've got lacrosse shoulder pads and lacrosse helmets and then they'll have what's called frog races: you line up two freshman and they'll race around the bunk beds upstairs and they'll have bunk beds and mattresses placed in certain ways so you don't get hurt, but then you race with two guys. You go up over bunk beds, under bunk beds, and all sorts of things and then the loser of that race has to go down through what's kind of a "haunted house." I don't know if you'd call it a haunted house, I mean, that's sort of what it resembles which you would probably relate to, and the winner keeps going on until he loses. Until finally, you know, everybody's lost a race or there's one final ultimate winner. But you start going through from the cold dorm all the way down to each station— each big man room [larger than average-sized rooms], we have four big man rooms at the back of the house, two upstairs and two downstairs—and they'll have stations. Each bathroom has a station and you just do certain things to different freshman. I mean you do different things to them. One where we had them, like they had a trash can full of ice water, and you got in it and you went down all the way, got your head wet, and then got out and you're just freezing when you get out of it, and you'll move off to the next station. One was "space invaders," where you'd go like this back and forth, you know like this, you're supposed to go like this back and forth, you know like this [attempting to imitate a video game character], you're supposed to go like this back and forth and then they'd throw, I can't remember what, oh, I think they'd get wet toilet paper and just throw it at you until you got hit and they'd stand back at a certain distance and if you got hit, you were dead, [and] you had to go on to the next station.

And then there's one where they had you on a table like this and one of them would grab you. This table was coated with just oily, messy—the worst stuff in the world. One guy would grab a hold of your feet and then you had to shoot down a plane and he'd run you around the table and just grab on your legs and run you around the table and you're trying to shoot down these planes and this time you're just getting absolutely filthy, messy. But anybody comes out of it just says it's kind of fun. I mean, it's just like going to an amusement park except it's kind of like going through a haunted house only it's even neater because people are actually . . . I mean you're really getting abused, but you're not getting hurt and, of course, it's dangerous, because some people do get hurt, like their foot will get cut. One guy our freshman year got his foot cut on glass and had to [stop]; it was pretty much over for him. But you'll go through it and most people don't ever get hurt and then you come downstairs.

... [And] we'll make them touch stuff that you'd think was gross, but nothing that was ever *real* though. . . . I mean, you'd make them believe it was something bad. Or they'd fill a bota bag up with hot water and spray it on them and tell them that they're pissing on them. Really not good stuff, but of course, they are blindfolded at this time though, throughout the whole thing they're *blindfolded,* I forgot to mention that—which is pretty major thing.

Yeah, I think they're even blindfolded when they do the space invaders thing. They may take them, at certain stages they may take off a blindfold. Of course, there again, it depends, you know, if the people decide to do it, at a station take off their blindfold. Yeah, actually, as a matter of fact they do, because I remember being able to see certain stations. So, yeah, yeah. (Of course when you're on the other side of it, you always, you don't remember if they took off their blindfold or not, because you've seen both sides of it, so you always have the mental image. If I had never seen it from a sophomore or junior side, I probably would just remember, if I didn't get the blindfold taken off all I could remember is my blindfold on, but I do, I think you do get your blindfold taken off.) I remember seeing, there's a station down here, we had a fireplace and you say, oh you had to write, you had to sign a book [or] something, I can't remember what you had to do; you had to sign some sort of book saying that you were committed to being an INS or something. I don't remember what it was; they just make up this stuff the night of the thing and it's nothing [permanent]. Every year it changes a little bit and you try to remember. There's always people who remember real well what stations were their freshman year and what they liked, and so they'll do those usually and other people make up some new stuff and do it. There's nothing really rigid about it, but it's sort of an obstacle course every year.

At this point, each weary pledge is taken to the dining room by an upperclassman. The ritual is about the same each year at this point, according to the recollections of pledges and Wolfman.

"What are you?" scream the members.

"Shit!"

"Do you really want to be an INS?"

"Yes."

"What do you want to be?"

"An INS!"

"Do you really want to be an INS?"

"Yes."

"So be it."

The blindfold comes off.

"OK, you're done!"

Each pledge receives a sweatshirt with Greek letters. The emotions of members run high, and the abuse stops—totally. A keg of beer is waiting, as are congratulations from the members. Batman recalled the experience:

Yeah, it's just a great feeling when you finish because everyone's there, congratulating you and everything, patting you on the back and it's just a good feeling. It's hard to explain that night because it was probably the toughest night, one of the toughest nights I've ever had really. And I can remember, after I finished with it I just started crying and it wasn't even just because I was upset really, but it was just like, I couldn't believe that it was over. And I was so, like you get ready, when you know something's coming, you kind of get ready for it to happen, you know, and obviously get like a really big rush before.

There are times, now that I look back on it, and I think, I've heard a lot of the brothers say that pledgeship was the best and the worst experience they had in their fraternity years, and I can already feel this and I think everyone in our class can, there's no other time where you're going to be as close to . . . twenty-seven guys in our class as you are during pledgeship, and you're just so close to everyone and, you know, I kind of miss that in some ways.

Part Three

The long proving-ground journey pledges must take in order to become full members is nearly concluded. All pledging has ended, except for the formal initiation with reading of rituals prescribed by the international that goes back to the days of the founder.

Because of the range of activities described, and because all are of them are fundamental to the INS pledgeship experience, it is difficult to imagine an INS pledge actually experiencing what might reasonably be termed a "dry pledgeship." Despite protestations to the contrary, alcohol use is pervasive in the INS pledge program. One merely needs to recall the pledge dance, where the pledges "just drink *amazing* amounts," or HP Night, where the active members are "guys out of control" as they are smashing beer bottles against the wall, to catch on to the idea that virtually all members and pledges participate in extremely dangerous or potentially dangerous drinking behavior at one time or another. The rigidity of the program itself—the manner in which pledges' lives are continually regulated and manipulated—is evidence for the addictive characteristic of control.

Linking Socialization and Organizational Theory

How is it possible to offer an analysis on the organizational level given that just one facet of INS—its socialization process—has been investigated? That is, in this case, is INS pledgeship really equivalent to the organization itself?

It is not at all unreasonable to make statements about INS as an organization based on a study of its socialization, for it is during this process, in ethnographer and sociologist John van Maanen's (1984) words, that the "cultural learning" of a group takes place. When newcomers are processed into the organization, their socialization experiences teach them what the organization *is*. Further, an intense indoctrination process such as that of INS creates almost total conformity to group norms and adherence to it assumptions—a "custodial orientation," according to Schein's (1990) framework. Because recruits learn about the organization during their socialization into the group, we should be able to learn about the group by engaging in a study such as this.

To corroborate my viewpoint that INS pledgeship and the organization are pretty much equivalent, in an interview with Wolfman I said, "Someone here said that 'It's the pledge program that makes this house.' That's a paraphrase, but that's what I remember. Do you agree with that?"

> Absolutely, absolutely, I do. And I think it not only makes your house, but it will destroy your house at the same time and I think that's what's happened to a lot of houses across the country when pledgeships become silly. I look at them and just laugh; it's silly, stupid, [they] have no purpose, but I think ours does have a purpose. It's tough, but I think it's tougher than those other programs that are silly, but yeah, I think it definitely makes the house. It could also break our house, too. We also say that too—it will break our house if it doesn't get done responsibly.

During the time I spent observing INS members and interviewing them about their drinking and socialization practices, much was made of the notion that everything related to pledgeship had an underlying *purpose*. Members were eager to point this out to me because they believed that there were important, nonfrivolous justifications for all their actions. They were attempting to communicate that INS pledgeship was not like the pledgeship programs of other fraternities with "nonsensical" or "silly" rules and practices but that everything in INS was done with a goal in mind. The goal most often mentioned with respect to this program was that of "pledge-class unity."

Wolfman talked about how the intensity of the program had lessons built into it to help members cope better with other life problems, including the relationship to authority figures.

> A lot of times the people who cope the least [well] are the ones that are the cockiest or are the so-called studs. They are the ones that get broken down the most, have the most stress—because they've got this big ego to try to keep inflating, or to try to keep up. And they're the ones that get broken down very quickly and that's why you have a situation where pretty soon they start respecting a guy who maybe doesn't have as big a ego; he's a little pipsqueak or whatever, but they both encourage each other and both continue on encouraging each other before the meals and helping each other out with pert. That's exactly what we want, we want that to happen.
>
> I feel like having a pledgeship like this, I think you learn that authority isn't as big a deal as it once [was]. During the pledgeship you really think [the PEs are] authoritative. After pledgeship, you realize the pledge educators aren't as serious as you thought they were. So you begin to realize that in a class when a teacher says, "If there's any cheating going on, well, I'm going to have to do this." While he's doing that to threaten the people, but he knows damn well he's kind of scared to do it himself, because there's a long process he's got to go through to prosecute that student. So he's going to sound tough, and that's just a small example. You're a camp counselor and you learn how to be a better counselor as a result of being

on both sides of the program, and as a fraternity, you're on both sides, you're on the pledge side, where you think everything's serious, you're on the other side. So you learn, I think your coping skills are actually improved because you learn how things really work, how people threaten to make people do things and then you learn how to, if you're the one threatened, how to really to learn that a lot of threats aren't true, just a lot of neat aspects of this. I think actually in the end, it helps your coping skills in college. So I think it's a real positive experience. I think it makes you a stronger person. You get it done by having somebody come up to you in your face and start screaming. You can take it and you can fire right back at them or you can do things that you need to do, whereas I think before this, some people are very timid. I think when you get done, you're not timid at all. Kind of like [a basketball coach where] the guy yells and screams and causes a lot of problems for his players, but when you get into the final few minutes of the game, that pressure that they had is not nearly what it is during practices or during other parts of the season, and I really think that's why that's successful. I think the same's true with our program here. During pledgeship is probably your worst as far as getting yelled and screamed at. Later on, when you've got alums, I get a lot of pressure as a president, tons of pressure from our alums, you know, "How are you doing gradewise, how is this going, how is that going?" and they're not going to yell and scream at me like a pledge educator is, but they're doing the same sort of mental thing, putting a lot of pressure on me. I can handle it; I have no problem handling it. I've gone through a pledgeship where day after day, week after week, I was subjected to it twenty-four hours a day; it's nothing for me, it really isn't. I've learned a lot about how to cope as a result of going through this program.

Dawson discussed the purpose of the no-alcohol rule for pledges. He expressed the belief that although the rule is broken regularly, it helps to promote "responsible drinking" by pledges and members.

Really, the rule of no alcohol is just a rule that is there to be said. . . . I was always thinking, "They don't want us drinking," but the whole house knows we're out drinking. [For] INS Luau, we just make the exception. I think the pledgeship tries to promote responsible drinking. . . . I think it gets them away from thinking that college is just drinking and partying. It makes them think that you've got to study while you're down here and hopefully that will overlap into the future years that they won't go out to the bars every night when they're juniors and seniors, that they'll study like Sunday through Wednesday or Thursday and then they'll enjoy the weekends. . . . The house buys their alcohol on weekends typically, so I don't think it's there to prohibit them from drinking, but instead to be responsible. I think it's the same thing as with the fraternity systems, with the deans. They say no drinking on campus.

I think that a dean just says it so people will be aware about security, so that the dean is trying to really promote responsible drinking. If he finds responsible drinking, then he leaves you alone. And I think it's the same thing . . . we try to promote the same thing with the pledges, . . . to be responsible with your drinking. Know when drinking is okay. Yeah, you shouldn't be drinking the night before a test, I think that's the whole thing. It's just to get this into their heads that college isn't about getting drunk every night and about going out with girls and partying, but it's about academics and they'll have plenty of time to party. I think you're trying to balance the two; you're trying to give them the balance.

The pledgeship process of Iota Nu Sigma can be viewed in several ways, of course. Wolfman, another member who had served the chapter as president, revealed that he understands pledgeship the way a drill sergeant understands basic training—the program exists to mold raw recruits into marines. The program is about breaking them (in this case, the pledges) down and building them back up again into a cohesive group—a *unified* force. And the mechanism that works best for accomplishing that goal is hazing; "responsible hazing," according to Wolfman—or "fun hazing," according to Roberto.

There is no shortage of opinions regarding what the various elements of pledgeship are about. But these opinions, either directly or indirectly, refer to the overarching purpose of *everything* that INS members do: to achieve pledge-class unity. If there was any one element was mentioned more than any other about the goals of pledgeship, PCU was it. Perhaps the purpose of steam bath is to get the attention of the pledges and the purpose of the no-drinking rule is to communicate responsible drinking, but, taken as a whole, the purpose of pledgeship, as stated in their brochure and echoed many times over by individual members, is to promote the cohesiveness of the pledge class. "Coming together," "pledge-class unity," and "PCU" are the watchwords of this group. The various purposes illustrated in this section seem to serve the function of providing continuing justification for methods of achieving group cohesiveness —methods that they are convinced must be utilized anyway. Experience has taught them that these methods work to achieve their primary objective of pledge-class unity.

A Metaphor for Understanding INS Socialization

A number of individuals expressed justifications for a variety of aspects of INS pledgeship. In this section, the focus shifts from rationalizing to conceptualizing. An incumbent president, Klinger, verbalized what it means to be a member of Iota Nu Sigma. Klinger outlined the process of "pledgeship as a book."

During my interview with Klinger, we were discussing the first rule of pledgeship—that is, secrecy—and how participating in this research study had violated that rule. Members who were interviewed for this report did so by violating the first tenet they learned as an INS pledge. It was at this point when he chose to offer this rambling conceptualization of pledgeship as a "book."

[INS is] the most airtight, secretive organization on campus. I sit down with the pledges the first night after steam bath and tell them about secrecy, about what pledgeship is. I tell them that pledgeship is like a book. [And] it's a rather lengthy book. It's a big book. When our pledge parents come down, this is the exact same thing I tell them; what I say is [pledgeship is] a rather lengthy book. [It's] small type, single-spaced, long. And I'll tell you what, for a pledge who doesn't know how long it's supposed to go, every time you turn a page it seems like you're not going anywhere. For him, it could be infinitely long, but we [the members] know *exactly* how long that book is. And as a matter of fact, as a fraternity, we write the book, and somebody would argue you write the book as you go along, but . . . we know exactly how many chapters there are in this book. We know . . . the purpose of each chapter, and we know that it's going to lead you in a certain way. So I tell the pledges, "If you leave pledgeship now and walk away from it, for whatever reason, and some reasons are better than others, we hold nothing against you. I feel a little sorry for you if you walk away from it now." They've only seen Chapter 1, right?

. . . Where secrecy comes into play is [this]: I know your girlfriend's a great girl, you love her, whoever she is, she might still be high school, she may be here on campus, you may love her and all, you may tell her everything, but you don't tell her about pledgeship. And it's not because we feel what we're doing in pledgeship is wrong. What I feel we do in pledgeship is very right. Everything has a purpose; there's not hazing for the sake of hazing. It's not like it was before with the lineups, just to yell and get your point across. It wasn't paddling; you don't need that to get your point across. The whole point of secrecy is you love your mom and your dad, you love your best friend, but do you have to share something with them? OK, if you share this with them, you are giving them a piece of the book. You are giving them something that they didn't pay for. You're loaning the book, this book that you worked [for]. I mean, it took you a semester . . . to get the money to afford to buy this book. And now you're just going to give it away? Here, take it. That's like . . . working all summer [on] a paper route to buy a bike and just giving it to your brother, just giving it away. No one in their right mind's going to do that. To give that piece away, you'd be crazy to give away your bike, OK? The thing is, if you don't tell the pledges up front about this right away, they may learn that later on when they're in Chapter 18 of the book, they may learn, "Shit! why am I telling these people this? This is important to the house!" But their gut instinct at first is the next time they talk to their mom or dad . . . [about] how's pledgeship going? "Oh my god, mom, you can't believe what happened, listen to this, OK?" And it goes back to things getting out, you won't believe who knows who and it getting back to the university or to nationals or whatever. So what you've got to sell them on is, "Have some trust in us."

. . . I mean, you call someone a brother, I mean, that is an experience. I mean, I have a younger brother and I have pledge brothers. My younger brother I have lived with now, he's 19 years old, I've lived with him for nineteen years. You are trying to condense nineteen years of knowing someone down into several weeks, and yet you're going to place that label of brother upon them. Well, we hope you actually know him that well. We actually do hope that when you're cleaning you'll be talking, "Geez where did you go to high school, what did you do?" You'll want to learn about that guy because he's going to be your best friend for the rest of your life.

[Secrecy] does separate you from the rest of the campus, and people think we have the hardest pledgeship because they don't know anything and they assume, since no one knows anything, that you've got to be hazing the shit out of people so they won't say anything, right? But it's just the opposite. You don't have to haze as much because you trust the guys, that they're not going to say anything. So that is how pledgeship is set up and it is like a book, and it is hopefully a book that has a purpose and has a meaning. Like any book, you're just setting it up right now [at steam bath], and just introducing the characters, and setting, and kind of who the main characters are, you know. Where as the book goes along and you see there's a lot of relationships with drinking, with studies, with intramurals, with the university, with your parents, with the graduates. It's a very complex book . . . and it's a book in a series. That's year one or semester one, but then you become social chairman, I mean there's a whole new book for social chairman, there's a whole new book for rush chairman, for being president, I could copyright a series myself for being president. Because you have no idea, every time you take a chairmanship, what's it's like.

I think everybody knows what the book's about, it's about growing up. I think it's about learning how to survive a college. It's learning that grades aren't everything, relationships are. It's learning that what you take away from college is more than a number.

We always say here, you get out of the fraternity what you put into it. Use it like a whore. Meaning as much effort as you put towards meeting the people in your house, getting to know the brothers in your house, helping out with chairmanships, helping out with the graduate relations, the more you put into those programs the more you try to be the best chairman, the best president you can be, the more you're going to get out of it and take away from this experience, you know? If you just read the book, great, but if you highlight and underline and put notes in the margins while you're doing it, it will be more meaningful to you. A little more hand-eye coordination, you got to recognize and retain more. There's more to the house than just pledgeship, do you know what I'm saying? There's more to the house than just drinking. There's more to the house than that.

The Metaphor of the Organization as Addict

As an outsider to Iota Nu Sigma, I have not undergone the indoctrination process that everyone there has. Consequently, I believe that I have the ability to offer insights from a different perspective. Much of what I have to offer in the way of interpretation and analysis stems directly from my personal and professional experience with alcohol use and abuse. My ability to connect INS with the literature and the conceptualization of organizations as addicts would likely not have come about had I not encountered problems with alcohol myself, sought to educate myself in the field of addictions, and had the opportunity to participate in Alcoholics Anonymous (AA) and an alcohol treatment program. It is this subjectivity regarding addictive behaviors and characteristics that leads me to the analysis below, though I rely heavily on existing literature as a basis for portraying INS as an addictive organization. The interpretation outlined here integrates drinking behaviors and attitudes with the socialization process of the group. I attempt to merge concepts from organizational socialization theory, the addictions field, addictive-systems theory, and a social organization such as Iota Nu Sigma. Schaef (1987) has previously taken a similar approach with Western society, and Schaef and Fassel (1988) have done so with work groups. It is my extension of addictive-organization theory to a *social* group (rather than a work group) in this study that is the primary contribution toward the refinement of this conceptual framework.

I begin with the concept of pledge-class unity (PCU), an element which seems to be overwhelmingly central to everything that INS says it is attempting to accomplish. What pledgeship is about, according to virtually everyone in the chapter I talked to, is achieving group cohesiveness through "PCU." Schein (1990) labeled conformity of this sort a "custodial orientation" of members, whereby members learn and obey group norms and adhere completely to its assumptions. This type of processing in newcomers is one that is built on a model of *control*. Individual addicts and alcoholics, dysfunctional families, and addictive organizations are all examples of entities that rely heavily on control, according to Schaef and Fassel.

As I noticed that control, in the form of rigid conformity, was a dominant theme in the world of INS, I gradually became aware of other characteristics of addiction in the ways that INS does things. For example, I saw how denial, dishonesty, self-centeredness, confusion, and perfectionism are also operative. Collectively, this set of INS characteristics suggested a fit to the model of the addictive organization described by Schaef and Fassel. I hypothesized that the theory of addictive organizations that grew out of the study of work groups could be reconstructed to fit nonwork (social) groups. The remainder of this section illustrates how Iota Nu Sigma may fit into that model of the organization as addict.

The Characteristics of Addiction and Iota Nu Sigma

The model of the addictive system previously described by Schaef and Fassel is based on the hypothesis that an organization may exhibit the characteristics of an individual addict or alcoholic. The terms "addict" and "alcoholic," both of which carry strong negative connotations, suggest that this model for organizations portrays INS extremely negatively, or even as "bad." I do not see INS as inherently bad any more than I would characterize anyone with an addiction as inherently bad. If we choose the disease concept of alcoholism and drug addiction, upon which most treatment centers and twelve-step programs such as AA rely, then individuals or groups that have issues involving an addiction are more aptly characterized as "unhealthy." "Individuals [or groups] are not their disease," as the AA saying goes.

I indicated above that once I began to view the INS goal of pledge-class unity as essentially a process of *control*, several other characteristics of addiction soon became evident. Although addicts and alcoholics are known to exhibit a spectrum of psychological and behavioral characteristics, there is no general agreement in the addictions field on a definitive list of such attributes. The discussion below addresses some of the more common characteristics of addicts and addictions.

Schaef and Fassel state that a "major preoccupation of the addictive system is *control*, or more accurately, *the illusion of control*" (1988, 65). An addict or alcoholic, and his or her family, "are constantly preoccupied with controlling one another," note Schaef and Fassel. This control is labeled an "illusion" because, ultimately, human beings cannot really control each other. In Iota Nu Sigma, the pledgeship process is a regulated process that dominates virtually every aspect of the lives of pledges. For example, practically every waking hour is scheduled for them for a period of weeks, and they are often screamed at when they are not meeting the PEs' expectations. For the duration of pledgeship, it may be that the fraternity can exercise just as much, or more, control than a family can exercise over a member because the fraternity has a specific reward to offer or withhold: membership. The goal of every pledge is to attain that status. Further, the aim of individual and group control is to create a unified pledge class—one that will conform to group beliefs and norms for behavior and is easily integrated into the larger organization. The objective is to control each individual so that the outcome for each is a custodial orientation such that the identity or "personality" of the group remains virtually unchanged generation after generation—a particularly relevant condition given pressures by college administrators and national organizations to force local chapters to change certain behaviors. In many ways, "control" in INS is more than just an "illusion." Control exists because members believe in it and pledges submit themselves to it.

However, control, even here, is an illusion. The organization cannot control those individuals who choose to leave pledgeship. Although they may try to shape the ex-pledge's perceptions by staying in touch or inviting him to parties, they cannot control what an individual says and does after leaving the group. And INS cannot control every minute of every pledge's time, despite all efforts to do so. Even the "bloody PE," who is closest to pledgeship and is the harshest in his treatment of the pledges, cannot get the group to obey or conform all the time (though he tries, by attending to the smallest of details). The PEs cannot control how swiftly the individuals in the pledge class learn their pert despite the fact that much pressure is exerted on the class so that peers insist that everyone learn their pert. It is a task that is ultimately beyond the control of the PEs. What they have to offer in exchange for learning pert and the group "coming together" is the promise of the end of the ordeal of pledgeship. Finally, the organization does not have control over the no-drinking rule that they say they impose on the pledge class.

Another characteristic common to addicts/alcoholics is that of *denial.* Schaef and Fassel (1988, 62) label this "the major defense mechanism of the addictive system [for] if something does not exist, it simply does not have to be considered. Corporations frequently say, 'We have a minor problem, but certainly not a major one. We are having a sales slump, but it is only temporary.' The alcoholic says, 'I am not an alcoholic. I may have a small drinking problem, and I may overdo it a bit on weekends or under stress, but I do not have a severe problem.'" Similarly, members of Iota Nu Sigma say, "Yes, we drink, but since we have a no-drinking rule for pledges, we are doing so responsibly." They also deny the seriousness of their hazing practices by indicating, "Sure, we haze, but what we do is 'responsible hazing.' What we do isn't really hazing because it's only 'mental' [not physical, even when HP activities clearly include physical abuse]." For both alcohol use and hazing—unlawful activities for the group—denial is a primary coping mechanism. The effect of such denial, according to Schaef and Fassell is to "prevent us from coming to terms what is going on before our very eyes. When we will not let ourselves see or know what is happening, we perpetuate a dishonest system" (1998, 62).

The characteristic of denial naturally leads to the inherent *dishonesty* associated with the system. In behavioral terms, Schaef (1987) points out that practicing addicts or alcoholics are "consummate liars. They lie about how much, when, where, with whom, and whether. Frequent and habitual lying is one of the more evident signs of [addiction]," pointed out Schaef (1987, 50). Associated with this propensity to be dishonest are three levels: lying to oneself, lying to other people, and lying to the world at large, according to Schaef and Fassel (1988). Lying to oneself is evident in the discussion above. Members are being dishonest with themselves, for example, when they justify hazing as "fun" or "responsible" behavior. Wolfman admitted that this phrase "responsible hazing" is an oxymoron. I believe that members such as Wolfman and Roberto have convinced themselves that the hazing they do is "mild," "responsible," or "really not hazing at all." Although I'm inclined to agree that abusive behavior labeled as hazing can lie along a continuum from mild to harsh, my assessment of such occasions as steam bath or HP Night is that they constitute rather significant hazing experiences. INS members, virtually uniformly, report feeling fearful, intimidated, and/or degraded on such evenings. Additionally, INS members are also lying to themselves when they say that both rush and pledgeship are "dry." The numerous examples of alcohol use during both rush and pledgeship indicate that they clearly are *not*.

INS is well practiced in the art of lying to the world at large. Their expertise at this is demonstrated by the fact that this group was originally referred to me by an administrator as the "responsible" group of the campus with regard to alcohol use. They apparently have earned this reputation through expert impression-management techniques. By having a variety of chapter members who are high-profile campus leaders, by achieving a quite high house grade point average, and by being very successful in intramural athletics, they have developed and sustained the image of a chapter that *must* be responsible. They are fully aware of this and use it to their advantage in their alcohol use and hazing practices. They believe, justifiably so, that their image protects them from intrusive visits from "the dean." Finally, INS lies to the parents of pledges. When parents are invited to the house for freshmen parents' weekend, they are given a very carefully developed and articulated story of what INS pledgeship entails. The message seems to be that virtually anything is allowable in order to produce pledge-class unity.

Another characteristic of an addict or alcoholic is *self-centeredness*. The term means "making the self the center of the universe," note Schaef and Fassell. In part, this can be explained "because getting a 'fix' becomes the center of the addict's life, everything that happens is seen as either as an assault or an affirmation of the self" (1988, 63). In the case of INS, the goal of pledge-class unity is achieved by making the pledge class the center of the universe. Pledgeship is more important than parents, female friends, sleeping, or eating. It can even be interpreted to mean more than academics, since studying is just one aspect of pledgeship itself. It is so central that even when the pledges are "off" on weekends, the group is encouraged, and expected, to stay together. Although individual pledges theoretically have permission to go their own way and engage in activities which are *not* house related during weekends, the tacit message is that those who do not stay with the rest of the pledge class are somehow in betrayal—in essence, assaulting the very idea of what pledgeship is.

And the pledgeship process is not only central to pledges; it consumes the attention of the entire house every fall semester. From the time of steam bath to HP Night, the focus is on the pledge class. Wolfman agrees that "pledgeship is what makes this house" is the message that is communicated—and considerable time of the actives is devoted to supporting the pledgeship experience. Consider that almost every mealtime for almost half a year is preoccupied with the pledges and their progress in learning pert. Truly, pledges and pledgeship are the "center of the universe" for INS. They believe that without this focus they could not perpetuate themselves.

In the world of the addict or alcoholic, one of the watchwords is *confusion,* where "everyone spends inordinate amounts of time trying to figure out what is going on" (Schaef and Fassel 1988, 62). A dysfunctional family is always trying to guess what will happen next in their attempt to control the addict. Confusion "keeps us ignorant of what is really going on; it keeps us busy trying to figure out what is happening" (ibid.). In the socialization scheme proposed by van Maanen, the term that applies here is "variable"—pledges are always kept guessing what will come their way next in a process that is seen by them as wholly unpredictable. In INS pledgeship, the pledges rarely know what is going to happen from day to day; they are unaware of *what* will happen or *when* it will happen. Virtually from the moment they are subjected to the steam bath experience, they are perpetually off balance. When the end does come, it also comes unexpectedly and only after pledges experience what many fraternity chapters call Hell Night, the most intense hazing of the whole socialization experience.

Finally, *perfectionism* is one of the characteristics of addiction. Addicts "are obsessed with not being good enough, not doing enough, and not being able to be perfect as the system defines" (Schaef and Fassel 1988, 64). Perfectionism in INS is characterized by the term "success," a word that comes up often in the way that INS members describe themselves and their group. They state that they not only do well in such things as academic achievement (in terms of house grade point average), competition in intramural sports, and involvement in campus activities but that they also strive to be number one in all of these areas.

In INS, perfectionism seems to match addictive behavior less well than some of the other characteristics of addiction addressed above. Schaef and Fassel indicate that perfectionism in an addictive system "means always knowing the answers, being first with the solution, and never making a mistake" (1988, 64). I am not totally certain that the high aspirations of INS members are exactly what Schaef and Fassel mean, since they are speaking of perfectionists as "always experiencing themselves as failures" (65). INS members, in my experience, do not see themselves this way. However, if for some reason the group were to encounter decreased academic and athletic performance relative to the rest of the campus for any significant period of time, or if they were caught hazing and were suspended or had their charter revoked, I believe they would be very self-critical, given their tradition of success. In this sense, the characteristic of perfectionism does apply to INS.

The INS Chapter as Addict

An important concept in understanding the "organization as addict" metaphor is seeing an organization as a hologram. This concept stems from yet another metaphor, G. Morgan's analysis of organizations as "brains." To begin to comprehend the usefulness of this thinking, it helps to understand a particular characteristic of the animal brain as determined by the psychologist Karl Lashley (noted in the writings of G. Morgan and M. Talbot). Under laboratory conditions, Lashley trained rats to do a variety of tasks, including negotiating a maze. Then, progressively, parts of the rats' brains were taken out surgically and he observed their subsequent ability to run the maze. Quite to his surprise, he discovered that he could not destroy a rat's memory by removing various parts of the brain; the rats always retained the ability to run the maze (i.e., they kept their memory).

This result suggested that memories were, apparently, not located in specific parts of the brain but were delocalized throughout. From this, eventually, came the thinking that brains were like holograms, noted Talbot (1991, 55). Holograms, in essence, are photographic images produced by a split laser beam projected onto a photographic plate. An important property of a hologram is that if a section of holographic film is cut or broken into pieces and one of the pieces is then subjected to a laser beam, the entire original image will still be reproduced. As Morgan observes, "Holography demonstrates in a very concrete way that it is possible to create processes where the whole can be encoded in all the parts, so that each and every part represents the whole" (1988, 80).

Morgan, a student of organizations, suggests that we view organizations as brains *and* holograms. This means that characteristics of the whole reside in (or are the same as) the parts (i.e., individual members of the organization), and characteristics of the individual reside in (or are the same as) the whole (i.e., the organization). Schaef and Fassel theorize that in the addictive-organization model, "the addictive system is the same as the individual addict, and the individual addict is the same as the addictive system" (1988, 61).

Schaef and Fassel describe four different ways for addictive organizations to come about. The first is where a powerful or "key" individual in the organization is an addict or alcoholic. The second is where the group is formed from a collection of "codependents" who replicate their dysfunctional, addictive behaviors in the workplace. The third model is when the organization becomes the focus of one's addiction, defined as "workaholism." Finally, the fourth model is the one described here, where the group or organization itself functions as, or *is*, the addict. In this scheme, the entire group is seen as having the characteristics of an individual who is addicted to a substance or a process.

This conceptualization of INS as an addict, if it is indeed valid, suggests that each member of the group may function as an addict—that the group and its constituent parts are the same. One way this might be so is the centrality of alcohol, an addictive substance, in the lives of these fraternity members. I contend that just as an addict's or alcoholic's life revolves around a substance (getting "the fix"), the role of alcohol is pervasive and central to the life of INS and its members. A myriad of examples exist to support this hypothesis: 1) the statement by the group to rushees that INS rush is "dry," suggesting that no function can occur without addressing the role alcohol will play; 2) the role of alcohol in having the pledges do "stupid things" during rookie week; 3) the no-drinking rule of pledgeship, again addressing the role of alcohol, whether present or absent; 4) the central role of alcohol in pledges' weekend experiences and on walkout; 5) the focus on alcohol and its sanctioned use for pledges at such events as the INS Luau, Dad's Night, and the pledge dance; and 6) the out-of-control, drunken behavior of INS active members during HP Night.

In listing these examples I do not mean to imply that INS members are alcoholics. Nor do I believe that INS members would necessarily agree with this hypothesis; indeed, I'm certain that if the question were posed, many or most would unequivocally deny that alcohol is a central element to their group's existence. I merely suggest that it seems as if members are almost always dependent on having alcohol around or on addressing its role if alcohol is absent. It is central to the existence of the group, and this dependence may help to define the "addict-like" behavior of the group. And, as alcohol is central to the group, so it is central to its individual members. Both individuals and the group are focused on having alcohol as an integral part of fraternity life. Hence, in this model of organizations, the holographic nature of organizations leads to the belief that the organization and its members are one. Which, of course, in and of itself, is remarkably reminiscent of the "oneness" of the group suggested in the concept of pledge-class unity. At a number of junctures during my experience at INS, I noted how often the members seemed to speak "as one." The choice of words and similarities in the description of experiences all tended to support and confirm each another.

Schaef and Fassel claim that *seduction* is a process that can be aptly applied to organizations which are behaving as addicts. Expanding on the sexual connotation of this term, they state that seduction operates when "people are lured away from their own perceptions and to know what is right for them. [Further, it is operative when] people feel the expectation to do things they do not want to do, or are pulled into activities with which they feel uncomfortable. The organization supports seductive behavior by having no norm by which a person can test the appropriateness of these activities" (1988, 161). That is, an employee may feel pulled or compelled to participate in certain activities that ultimately do not "feel right." A specific example may be the suggestion that he or she "volunteer" for a committee assignment since such participation will not take much time from other duties and will lead to enhanced status within the organization. The employee subsequently discovers that the assignment takes an inordinate amount of time and is embroiled in so much controversy that there will likely be negative personal consequences.

Although the practices of INS may not precisely fit this definition of seduction, INS operates in a similar manner when recruiting members. They focus almost exclusively on high school seniors and first-year students, who have little or no prior experience on a college campus, and offer them part of something much larger than themselves. They are offered a part of that "success" that everyone at INS speaks of. The rushees and pledges are shown one side of the group during rush weekend, during Spring Festival, and then again during rookie week. They have been seduced into one image of the group, and then (as has been described), WHAM! The evening of steam bath hits and they are left saying, "Huh?" Those who are most unwilling or unable to cope with this seduction (and perhaps perceived betrayal) leave the group. Those who stay are willing to buy into (or at least live with) the seduction scheme and believe the story they are given. Hence, it is not unreasonable to apply the term *seduction* to this part of the indoctrination process.

One of the ways that this seduction is generally so successful is *the process of the promise,* in the words of Schaef and Fassel. The "promise" of addictive organizations "directs [them] toward the future, to some hoped-for reward, while keeping [them] out of touch with the present" (1988, 68). In the case of an addict or alcoholic, their family perpetually lives with the hope or expectation that things will turn around. Someday, the thinking goes, the substance abuser will stop using and things will be okay again. In the case of INS, pledges are always focused on the hoped-for reward of their ordeal; that is, the attainment of the status of full member in the organization. It is possible that the communicated promise that "this will all be worth it" keeps pledges disconnected from the reality of their everyday lives. I contend that the promise of a better (and privileged) existence post-pledgeship keeps pledges doing what they're doing and continuing to endure the regimentation, intimidation, and humiliation of the process.

Another critical feature of addictive organizations is their propensity to keep *secrets.* Schaef and Fassel note that "there are many secrets in addictive organizations. Secrets are usually 'for their [employees'] own good.' Decisions about money, salary, and personnel are often secret" (1988, 141). Furthermore, families of addicts or alcoholics are generally inclined to lives of secrecy, perpetually attempting to hide the habits of their addicted member. One of the "rules" of families with an addict or alcoholic member seems to be that "no one may discuss what is really going on in the family, either with one another, or with outsiders," as Wegscheider-Cruse observes (1981, 83). In the case of Iota Nu Sigma, secrecy is the number-one rule during pledgeship, although in this case the rule is intended to apply to outsiders. What they do, who they are, and how they are doing it are all things that need to be kept from the outside world. This rule is of such primary importance to the group that it was literally screamed at pledges during the evening of steam bath and was a primary topic of conversation with the president very shortly thereafter.

A normal part of the way that addictive organizations operate is that often participants are set up to *take sides*. Members "have to be for one or the other person, idea or product [because] it is very seductive to take a side. It engenders an identity and a feeling of belonging. The organizational norm is to join" (Schaef and Fassel 1988, 162). In INS, pledgeship is designed as an "us [the pledge class] against them [the active members]" scenario. Santa described this when he said, regarding the learning of pert:

> Just the idea of like the pressure thing, [it's] us against them. You know we could sit down every night and just study it and they could have us recite it every night, but this way, it gets you mad at them and it's us against them, that all just adds to the brotherhood. I mean, it really does; there are other ways you could learn it, but in combination with the way guys are and how that affects and adds to the brotherhood, I really don't think that there would be a better way.

The process of taking sides in an organization is a reflection of a group characteristic of *dualistic thinking*. In this mode of operating, very few options for an issue are recognized or considered. A course may be pursued because it is "right" and all others "wrong," for example. Wolfman's statement that "we do pledgeship this way because it works" seems to be a form of dualistic thinking. "This is the right way; there is no other way as right" seems to be the message.

Schaef and Fassel indicate that a fundamental process of an addictive system is that of *external referencing*. "Success" in such an organization is defined "by how other people perceive us. We become adept at learning what pleases others, and we get busy doing those things" (1988, 70). The process of external referencing is related to lying to the outside world, or at least spending a great deal of time managing the impression that others have. Denying that a problem exists and keeping the group's secrets are other forms of external referencing. Just as Wegscheider-Cruse found that a family of an addict or alcoholic tends to put up a front to the outside to world in order to hide the family's secret, an addictive organization puts up a front, too. Schaef and Fassel explain that "the addictive organization wants to control how it is seen by others—and believes it can" (1988, 168). In the case of INS, much time is spent portraying the image of themselves to the world as the "responsible," "successful" group. INS members are campus leaders, they are successful in athletics, and they achieve good grades. INS is "successful" because that is traditionally how they see themselves but, just as important, "success" shows a side of the organization to everyone that effectively shields them from visits from "the dean" or a national organization field representative who may discover their alcohol abuse or physical hazing practices—their secrets.

In addictive organizations, much time and effort is spent focusing on the *structure* of the group. In essence, there tends to be a preoccupation with "the form" of the organization, so that they impress people outside the group. The external referencing process just described falls under what Schaef and Fassel termed "structural preoccupation." In organizations that function addictively, "there is a firm conviction that when [a variety of] structures can be perfected, the people inside them can be adequately controlled" (Schaef and Fassel 1988, 172). In INS, pledgeship is the structure, and the organization is always attempting new things to get the process just right. As Schaef and Fassel have noted, "the form of control" in such groups "puts power in the hands of a few manipulators, and coping with it wastes energy that could otherwise be spent making the organization more effective" (1988, 169). In INS, pledgeship is a highly regulated process that is controlled by a "few manipulators"—the pledge educators. The considerable time and energy put into this process could be put to some kind of other use that would be more beneficial for the group, and its members, in the long run. A focus on activities that are more congruent with the goals of the academy, for example, studying and learning material from courses, would seem more appropriate than the considerable effort put forth in learning trivia—pert.

Forgetfulness is also a characteristic of this type of organization. For individual addicts, an often-repeated maxim is that "they cannot learn from their behavior because they have no memory[,] [and] addictive organizations have the same problem" (Schaef and Fassel 1988, 145). Addicts, alcoholics, and members of their families tend to "repress" painful memories by "burying them somewhere deep in the subconscious" (Wegscheider-Cruse 1981, 66) or by turning off their feelings by continuing to abuse substances. When work organizations function as addicts, they manifest this characteristic by forgetting important deadlines or projects which should be attended to, not learning from past mistakes, proposing organizational restructuring schemes that haven't worked before, and losing touch with their overall mission (Schaef and Fassel 1988). In the case of INS, forgetfulness is manifested by pledges when they conclude pledgeship. All of the negative experiences are immediately forgotten, says Batman.

> Well, it's amazing how much like after it's all over, how much you forget the things that people did to you. Like I remember that after HP Night, I went out to eat with three or four of my pledge brothers and two of our pledge educators at 4:00 in the morning. [We were] just talking and laughing and having a good time, and it just seemed so, I mean, you'd think you'd hold a grudge, and we know guys who were assholes during pledgeship, but you just don't think about that at all, you know, it

doesn't really bother you that much anymore. I mean, just because you just assume it's part of it, really.

INS pledges make that transition into membership by blocking out the memories of the more traumatic times associated with pledgeship. They have reached their goal, and that is all that is important to them. Thus, they are unlikely to step forward as members and say that changes to the house regarding hazing and alcohol need to be made.

Summary of the INS Organization as Addict

Central to this entire discussion of INS as an addictive organization is the characteristic of *control*, the attribute which Schaef and Fassel (1988) label the "prime characteristic" of this kind of organization. Iota Nu Sigma attempts to control all aspects of its existence. The organization's primary stated objective of pledgeship is pledge-class unity, which is achieved through a highly controlling socialization mechanism that produces a "custodial orientation" of its members. Every aspect of a pledge's existence is regulated for a period of weeks in order to achieve the desired group cohesion, much as Marine Corps basic training does. The process is in the hand of a select few "manipulators," the designated pledge educators, who call virtually all the shots in the house during this period of time. Once the pledges are appropriately molded, they are elevated to the status of full members. It is not overstating the case to say that they are "clones" of the class members that preceded them. Control has been exercised to ensure that this is so.

Alcohol use and hazing are integral parts of the pledgeship process. Even if these activities are not as controlled as internal or external policies outwardly call for, the *thinking* about them is. The no-drinking rule becomes one that is "there just to be said" or is there to promote "responsible drinking." Hazing is "nonexistent," "mild," "only mental," "fun," or "responsible." The house controls, through its tacit definitions of these terms, what is acceptable and what is not. The ability of INS to engage in denial controls what happens with regard to alcohol use and hazing practices.

The house is also masterful at controlling, or attempting to control, its image on campus. Their focus on campus activities, intramurals, and academics is such a tradition because, at least in part, "success" in those areas keeps them protected from scrutiny by "the dean." By controlling their collective image they keep the administration at bay—and they ultimately control, on campus, the latitude of behaviors that is permitted within the confines of its structure.

A final note on control has to do with attitudes toward women exhibited by INS members. In various portions of the narrative, I have included references to the treatment of women (e.g., rush weekend, INS Luau, pledge dance). I believe that the demeaning comments made about females in this group are yet another aspect of their need (or at least their desire) to control. While, as Dawson says, "that's just how males talk," this behavior can be taken to reflect an attitude that places women in "one down" positions. They are objects to be used, manipulated, and controlled, which is consistent with the fraternity's focus on control in other spheres. Women are referred to as "bitches," they exist to "shack" with, and, in one instance, the pledge dance, their presence was specifically stated to be merely "symbolic." All of this turns out to be quite consistent with other arguments made regarding the addictive system. Schaef states that what she calls the addictive system and the "white male system" are one and the same, "because the power and influence in it are held by white males and are perpetuated by white males" (1988, 7). Hence, in a wide spectrum of its existence, including its treatment of females, INS exhibits a propensity to control. This characteristic is a significant piece of evidence that identifies this chapter as an addictive system.

Implications of This Study

A codependent is generally defined as one who has a significant relationship with an addict or alcoholic, such as a spouse or other family member (Beattie 1989; Mellody 1989; Schaef 1987; and Weinhold and Weinhold 1989). Another descriptor historically associated with this term is that of *enabler* because of the supporting role that person plays in the life of the addict (Wegscheider-Cruse 1981). A codependent may be looked upon as a co-conspirator in the disease process. College administrators, national headquarters executives, and others are in significant relationship with INS as an addictive organization and, I contend, tend to participate together in perpetuating this unhealthy system, thus keeping it intact. That is, in the analytical model that identifies the fraternity as an addictive system, these individuals and entities are the codependents. Thus, the individuals most likely to be interested in a study such as this are other higher education researchers or those charged with oversight responsibilities for fraternities on campuses today such as administrators and national fraternity executives.

Consider, for example, a letter preserved in the pledge-educator files. The letter was from the student-affairs office; it was addressed to an INS president and commented on the proposed revised pledge program, which the INS chapter had submitted to them in writing (essentially the pledge program that has been described in this chapter). The letter from the student-affairs officer offered the following comments:

> I would hope that leadership in all Greek organizations would be mature, thoughtful, kind and understanding. In the past, I feel that your chapter's pledge education program has disregarded several of these items. As an example, I would remind you that every student at the University has basic rights such as the right to travel wherever he wants to, the right to come and go as he pleases, the right to study when he wants to, and the right to live at the location he is paying room and board to at all times. These are the general overall concerns I have with the pledge education programs in the past at your chapter. I believe that in the past the INS chapter

has assumed that they give certain rights to men who pledge their chapter. However, I am in total disagreement with this entire philosophy. Every student has inherent rights in a variety of areas. Pledging a fraternity does not supersede any of those rights.

The letter also provided point-by-point commentary on various aspects of the pledge program. Virtually all of the areas of pledgeship outlined in this study were addressed, with the notable exception of HP Night (the inference is that INS neglected to inform them in any way about this event). I found some of the comments surprisingly positive, presumably because the person who wrote the letter was going by a written description rather than the event as it truly exists. For example, regarding room changes: "I think if this is done in the proper manner it is a good idea. It is a wonderful way for each of the pledges to get to know the other men in the chapter." Regarding fraternity fathers: "This is a terrific idea. *This* is the kind of thing that should be taught in the fraternity." Regarding pertinent: "I like the fact that you state exactly which areas all new members will be responsible for learning. . . . I do not think this is hazing per se." However, some comments are fairly critical of specific current practices. For example, regarding rookie week: "I don't like the name of this week. I think it shows a whole attitude we are trying to get away from." Regarding steam bath: "The whole concept of calling it 'steam bath' is against what I believe in." Regarding meals: "I am against quizzing pledges or any members of the chapter during their meal time. As you recall, this is one of the areas that has caused a lot of problems in the past. I believe there is no way to do this without people getting out of hand."

The letter concludes with an admonition:

I want to warn you that we will not tolerate any further problems with the pledge education program in this chapter this year. In the past, I have tried to deal with this in a very educational and constructive manner. My patience is wearing thin, though. I think we should both know where each other stands.

This letter illustrates the views of at least one student-affairs administrator regarding the kinds of activities in which INS engages. It is obviously quite strict in tone and implies that sanctions will be applied to the group if the negative aspects of their pledge program continue. The pledge-educator files also contain letters from INS fraternity executives sternly reminding the group that an anti-hazing agreement had been signed by the chapter president. Information regarding hazing practices at INS occasionally reaches the office of the international, which prompts such contact with the local group.

Despite such warnings from on-campus and off-campus officials, INS pledgeship and its traditional indoctrination of pledges continues, in almost the same way, year after year. What can this really mean other than everybody knows what is going on but no one is doing anything about it? Before 1987, the INS chapter responded to some of the objections to its pledgeship by getting rid of some of its "sillier rules," but so many aspects of the program remain the same that some "legacies" can enter the fraternity with a fair amount of knowledge of what pledgeship at INS is going to entail. Could this system be perpetuated in its present form if the administrators and fraternity executives responsible for this group did not tacitly approve?

It seems reasonable to conclude that they either approve of what is going on or have developed incredibly effective denial mechanisms. In either case, those responsible for INS oversight seem to be supporting the very kinds of behaviors that they (at least publicly) purport to be against. I contend that neither a group such as INS, nor Greek systems more generally, will change without some major motivation to do so. In the world of the alcoholic, the motivation to change comes from "hitting bottom," a place in life that becomes so terrible that the individual becomes motivated to seek help. In this vein, sociologist Rich Sigal, who is quoted in *Broken Pledges: The Deadly Rite of Hazing,* believes that only a wide-scale societal crisis will be enough impetus for change in the fraternity world. This is not a cheerful or optimistic picture. But in speaking about the relationship of society at large to fraternities, Hank Nuwer offers the following observations:

> The Greek system, like any other bureaucracy, has only the law and order that it as a group gives its members. The influence for good or evil is powerful. Moreover, when values break down and individuals in various institutions—college administrators, faculty, fraternity executives, politicians, you name it—no longer work together for mutual interdependence, this can be disastrous in a society such as ours.
>
> Fraternities, for example, assemble to feel that satisfying wholeness we as human beings get when many are one. The difference today is that the symbols of this collective oneness no longer have the same meaning for many of today's Greeks. (Nuwer 1990, 226)

Hence, because of "mutual interdependence," Nuwer sees that there is hope for change in the fraternities. But in issuing this call, Nuwer expressed the hope that "adult leaders of the fraternity world" will step forth and "help their younger brethren get their acts together" (226). I am not so sure that this is going to happen. My opinion is that adult leaders in the fraternity world are not invested in changing things. They are part of the addictive system and they themselves are locked into processes that rely on denial and control. (The control that they exercise comes from becoming involved with these issues as merely an exercise in "risk management.") Many on-campus Greek advisors and all fraternity executives connected with Greek life on campuses are fraternity members themselves. These adults contribute to the status quo, to the perpetuation of alcohol use and hazing practices. These persons, who are now in positions of responsibility, likely remember with great fondness their undergraduate affiliation with Greek organizations and believe that far-reaching change is not necessarily desirable. Perhaps when administrators and fraternity executives themselves experience their own wake-up call, things will start changing. It is hard to imagine that members of a group such as INS will initiate change on their own. What they have been doing has been working, and working well from their point of view, for far too long for them to change too much too fast. Somewhere, somehow, they must hit bottom before they will change. That bottom could be perhaps be reached more readily if what campus administrators and fraternity executives did not support the status quo.

This all comes down to a moral question: How ought we (as campus administrators, fraternity executives, and others) to be in relationship to a fraternity? It stands to reason that we should not continue our roles as codependents and maintain this addictive system; instead, we need to move to change this unhealthy relationship. An often-noted phenomenon for me, in my profession as a counselor, is that when one party in a relationship begins to change, the other party is left with choices: They can change or lose the relationship. If those in relationship with a fraternity take responsibility for themselves and move toward change, then perhaps they can turn away from a model of control and continued participation in an unhealthy system and through their actions demonstrate a healthier way of being.

At best, whatever optimism I have is tempered by a healthy amount of skepticism. Maybe the healthiest stance would be to give up on models of control that rely on policymaking, alcohol-education programs, and risk-management strategies. Perhaps the healthiest posture is one of surrender: to realize that no change is really possible.

6 Pledging and Hazing in African-American Fraternities and Sororities*

D. Jason DeSousa, Michael V. W. Gordon, and Walter M. Kimbrough

Editor's note: *During the 1990s and 2000s, few members of African-American fraternities were more outspoken than these three chapter authors about the need to end abusive hazing practices in NPHC groups. In addition, Michael V. W. Gordon and Walter M. Kimbrough were major participates in a national Black Issues in Higher Education Conference that called for an end to hazing practices in historically African-American Greek groups.*

In February of 1990, eight international presidents of historically African-American fraternities and sororities gathered in St. Louis, Missouri, with an ominous task before them. They had to do something about the increasingly serious injuries incurred by college students who were seeking admittance into the fraternities and sororities they presided over. They were especially keeping in mind recent deaths to students who were seeking membership through pledging. Moreover, in an increasing litigious American society, parents and loved ones were seeking relief through the courts. The settlements and awards were becoming larger and larger, sometimes resulting in hundreds of thousands of dollars, maybe even millions. The continued existence of these organizations was even at risk.

"Pledging" a fraternity once meant pledging to the ideals of the fraternity set forth by their founders; the prospective members attended meetings and were assigned "tasks" to "prove" their worthiness to become members. On almost every college campus there were overly enthusiastic active members who extracted activities that went beyond what any civil person would cast as within

---

*The authors originally titled this essay, "Unintended Consequences: A Critical Review of African-American Fraternities and Sororities Status of Pledging or Non-Pledging on American College Campuses."

the dignity of an adult seeking membership into a reputable organization. Sometimes these activities amounted to servitude; other times they included extortion of money or favors. Brutal physical punishment sometimes resulted in injury, and sometimes deaths occurred.

The fraternity and sorority presidents met and decided that it was in the best interest of the continued existence of these cultural hallmarks of African-American society to end pledging as a condition for entrance into their organizations. They reasoned that over the years, pledging in undergraduate African-American culture had really become synonymous with hazing. It had become common for an undergraduate to ask of another, "How hard did you pledge?" What was assumed by that question was "How much physical hazing did you endure?" The presidents decided to approach the membership in convention later that year and the following year with a proposal to create an "intake procedure" as a substitute for pledging.

Each of the eight organizations met in national conventions and ratified plans to initiate the intake procedure. This would generally consist of initiating aspirants after a short period of application for membership, followed by a weekend of activities during which the prospective members had a crash course in the history and customs of the organization. More details on how to be an effective member were designed to be given systematically after initiation. The sacred and secret rituals would then be preserved and conducted by high-level and trustworthy elders of each organization. Variations of each plan have evolved over the ensuing years. But each organization clings doggedly to the idea that pledging has ended and that the solution for all the hazing, injuries, deaths, lawsuits, and threats to their existence has been found and implemented.

Yet recent news accounts demonstrate that neither the idea nor the practice of pledging has ended. At Louisiana State University, a student received a gash in his buttocks over seven inches in length and a half-inch deep due to paddling. At Old Dominion, another male student sought medical treatment for asthma and was subsequently treated for wounds to his hands and buttocks that he said were due to a fall. At the Ohio State University, a student required major dental work following injuries sustained during the no-pledge intake program.

Quite frankly, one of the worst-kept "secrets" in the history of American higher education is the underground pledging of African-American fraternities and sororities. Everyone—high school students, parents, faculty members, even casual visitors to just about any student union building on any campus where there are African-American fraternities and sororities—can ask three succinct questions of just about any student, black or white, and find out surprising details about how the activities take place; Where does pledging occur? To what extent does "hard pledging" take place? and Which organizations are most notorious for such activities? When an injury or death occurs, it is amazing how everyone involved runs for cover. The students involved have often been shown to lie immediately about everything that took place. Even the victim, if still alive, often tries to protect the perpetrators.

Despite the obvious signs of pledging, there is no acknowledgement of a problem by the national organizations.

Not long ago, a severe hazing put a fraternity chapter and its headquarters under scrutiny. The investigation of the fraternity prompted an e-mail reply from its international president that threatened a lawsuit against anyone who persisted in insisting that a young victim of hazing was trying to pledge the fraternity. The president stated that his fraternity had ended pledging, so therefore, according to his logic, no one could accuse his fraternity of culpability. [*Ed. note:* The case in question is in civil courts and the name was withheld for privacy reasons in fairness to the plaintiff and defendants.]

Any university that allows or supports the idea that fraternities and sororities contribute to or augment its academic mission and looks the other way injury after injury, death after death is as naked as the emperor who thinks he is clothed in the finest attire. These fraternities and sororities have national and regional conventions that display enormous financial, intellectual, and cultural resources. These conventions are held in the finest hotels in America and the Caribbean. Limousines and hotel suites abound. But nowhere on the agenda of any of these organizations is there an honest look at the new monster created by an act of eight presidents eleven years ago but never reexamined, evaluated, or revised since.

The vast majority of the undergraduates of the nine organizations that now compose the National Panhellenic Council are in a rebellious mood! Using e-mails, chat rooms, proposals, and even attempts at international conventions of their respective organizations, they have expressed a desire to have a voice in formulating a plan to deal with these issues. Many of these undergraduates are disingenuous; there is no doubt about that. Their call for a return to pledging is not just that belief in a rite of passage that they feel is missing. Instead, many want a return to organized hazing.

Many young people on hundreds of American campuses have thrown themselves into flagrant violations of the intent and letter of the Intake Procedures [Membership Intake Program] to the detriment of their reputations, the grades of the "pledges," and the actives (active members) themselves and have risked outright expulsions from these organizations. And there have been many expulsions and removals of charters of undergraduate chapters who have violated international fraternity or sorority policies. Many who haze have stated they feel that they are upholding the "true nature" and traditions of their organizations.

Many responsible leaders in the African-American fraternity/sorority world applaud the decision that their international presidents made in discontinuing organized pledging in favor of the intake procedures. By their actions at that time, they averted the kind of lawsuits that could have removed all the physical property of one or more such organizations and awarded such property to grieving parents of students whose lives were lost during procedures that seemed to be part of what it took to become a member of such a fraternity or sorority.

That leads us to today. In 2001 alone, news reports of at least five injuries and one death have made headlines. Two deaths of sorority members in California have been disputed by sorority leaders, but a civil suit has been launched by the family of victim Kristin High nonetheless. The national organizations should consider the issue of pledging to be a crisis, but they appear satisfied with their public nakedness on this issue.

This essay serves as a clarion call to the national academic community to engage in dialogue to form solutions to stop the disgraceful brutalities that result from totally unsupervised acts by undergraduates to create of rites of passage for prospective members of historically African-American fraternities and sororities. The authors call for a national conference to address these problems.

The issues to be pursued include these conclusions:

1. The welfare of students in the African-American fraternity and sorority system should be the primary concern and driving force behind any reform movement.
2. Neither international presidents nor their membership bodies alone can provide solutions to the problem of undesirable student-culture activities. The academic community, especially student-affairs professionals, needs to come together.
3. The ultimate responsibility for what happens as far as campus life is concerned is really in the hands of college officials. National fraternity leaders apparently believe they can wash their hands of responsibility by declaring that they have outlawed pledging. Yet everyone, including national officials, knows that pledging has gone underground.
4. The international presidents need to call for some kind of review or evaluation to examine the monumental decision to end pledging made in 1990.
5. Some sort of recognized pledge program which national fraternity/ sorority leaders can subscribe to under the watchful eye of university officials should be thoroughly discussed.
6. The universities should develop a plan for cooperation with national fraternities and sororities. A yearly review of excellence should be used to determine whether fraternities and sororities on college campuses should continue.

7 Examining Violence in Black Fraternity Pledging

Ricky L. Jones

Editor's note: *A lecture on hazing that I delivered at the University of Louisville many years ago brought me into contact with a then-junior faculty member named Ricky L. Jones, who described his fascinating work in progress on hazing in African-American Greek organizations. Later, as he began publishing his work, I read his prescient ideas with interest and admiration. His chapter in this book is a work of scholarship with practical use for all who work with African-American fraternities and sororities. Jones's research is impeccable. Kate Babbitt, the copy editor for* The Hazing Reader, *said Jones connects ancient and modern culture in a "deeply profound" way while also addressing "the issues of loss of memory and anomie."*

Since the late 1980s, and especially after the death of a Southeast Missouri State University student in 1994, the pledge/initiation process of black Greek-letter fraternities (BGFs) has come under intense scrutiny.[1] The tragedy in Missouri was not the result of anomalous violent behavior in BGFs. Unfortunately, physical abuse is often encountered in the BGF initiation process and has led to the hospitalization or death of a number of young black males. The belief that violence in these groups is not isolated is further supported by the near-death of a University of Louisville student in 1997,[2] two additional incidents at the University of Maryland, Baltimore County and Kansas State University in 1998, and injuries to students at Grambling State, Mississippi State, and Georgia State Universities in only the first quarter of 1999. The perseverance of hazing continues to baffle college and university administrators, BGF officials, and an increasingly concerned community at large. The fraternities have been taken to task by these institutions and communities, but hazing incidents continue and remedies remain elusive.

In this examination, I contend that if solutions to the destructive behavior which sometimes manifests itself in these organizations are to be found, we must begin to take different approaches to understanding the impetus which lies at the heart of the pledge process. I do not wish to frame my approach in such a way as to view it as a directionless anthropological aberration of black men who wish to impose violent behavior upon one another. On the contrary, it must be approached as an activity which has been historically viewed as functional. The fact that injured pledges are victims of violent physical aggression is indisputable. However, I will not focus my attention on these injured individuals; rather, I focus on the fact that the modern pledge process is an operation of historical social import as well as a powerful aspect of black fraternity legend and lore. It is important to understand that, contrary to the beliefs of many BGF members, the BGF pledge process is not unique in and of itself. The modern BGF pledge process is a form of sacrificial ritual, and such rites (whether or not they are fatal) cannot be explained intellectually unless one can locate some basis for them in historical and contemporary social reality.[3]

Violence Vehicles: Rituals as Social Stabilizers

As long as we insist on interpreting the violence of initiation rituals in purely individual psychological terms, we can only assume that BGF members are dysfunctional sociopaths. This view must consequently suggest that members seek some sort of moral justification for their acts after the pledge process is completed by showering the newly initiated neophyte with "love" in the form of verbal and social acceptance or gifts. Upon initial observation, it would appear that the pledge is simultaneously disdained and coveted, because such quick movement from a position of loathing to one of love seems implausible. Pledges are often told by their deans of pledges (members who are primarily responsible for the progress and well-being of potential initiates), "None of the brothers like you. You have nobody but each other and me." Beyond this creation of an illusion of aloneness and adversity, the reality must be that the pledge is somehow loved all along (whether this type of love is pure or healthy is arguable)—even when he is the object of violence from his future fraternity brothers. This love/loathe ambivalence would seem to be, on its face, nonsensical. When examined more closely, however, it can indeed be explained.

It must be clear that fraternities are filled with rituals. These rituals, written or not, are nothing more than forms of behavior or interaction that are repeated again and again so the fraternal vehicle can function in a particular way. For example, ritualistic processes are often employed at the beginning and end of fraternity meetings, others at weddings of members, and others still at the funerals of members. Many of these are not considered mandatory in that there is no threat of dissolution of the group if members neglect to perform them. The fraternal pledge process, however, is unique in two ways. First, it stands alone as the ritual perceived by many fraternity men as mandatory. There exists the belief that if the pledge process is tampered with too extensively or eradicated, the very fabric of the organization will certainly unravel.[4] The pledge process alone is viewed as that which has the power to inevitably determine the course of the group because it is seen as having an inordinate impact on what the neophyte *is*. The second reason the pledge ritual is unique directly relates to the first. It is the only rite in fraternities that does not ask for, but demands, sacrifice. This is not necessarily sacrifice of the altruistic type; it is the kind of sacrifice that places the pledge in positions which threaten him emotionally and physically at levels and which are, in many cases, unequaled in intensity and largely unacceptable in the larger society. The fact that the pledge process falls into this category of sacrifice moves it to a very different place from which it must be engaged.

Most supporters of the ritualized pledge process defend it as central to the purposes of fraternities. Whether this is true or not does not invalidate the fact that, in one sense, fraternity rituals have the same purposes as rituals found in everyday life. These include religious ceremonies ranging from marriage, baptism, and weekly worship to modern rites of passage such as graduations. Rituals, while often containing some emotive messages, exist to define the traditions of an organization. When paired with ceremonies unique to particular groups of people, a standard formula for the organization's activities and teachings is forged. When taken together, ritual and tradition form almost impenetrable barriers which determine whether a person is accepted into the bond or denied access. Bonding rests on the supposition that every member participates in the same ceremony, hears the same words, and lives the same experience. If successful, this common experience gives the organization continuity and structure. Through this continuity, a fraternity brother from one part of the world should be able to meet a brother from anywhere else and instantly have a connection. This is central to fraternities' notion of brotherhood. Consequently, rituals which seek to achieve this connection are strongly functional. Fraternity initiation rituals (of which the pledge process is only a part) are meant to bring about solid, concrete results. If the functional nature of this operation is not realized, the moorings of this historic phenomenon will remain misunderstood and the particular type of violence which has become a part of it will never be resolved.

Initiation rituals and rites of passage, anthropologically, go far beyond strictly drawn lines of individual racial and social disfranchisement. Even though it is often veiled, all rituals of this type have a sociopolitical component in one way or another. In fact, common threads run through this variety of sacrifice which bind participants regardless of their religious, political, or fraternal affiliation. Sacrificial ritual, according to Rene Girard, is always social whether or not this fact is realized. In *Violence and the Sacred* (1989), Girard advances a hypothesis for the development of ritual and culture which posits that ritual arose from what he calls "mimetic desire and ritualized scapegoating" to prevent universal violence. He sees violence, in one form or another, as inevitable. There is, however, good or legitimate violence and bad or unacceptable violence. The task of societies, therefore, is to choose through which vehicle they will allow violence to manifest itself:

> Fieldwork and subsequent theoretical speculation lead us back to the hypothesis of substitution as the basis for the practice of sacrifice. This notion pervades ancient

literature on the subject—which may be one reason, in fact, why many modern theorists reject the concept out of hand or give it only scant attention. Hubert and Mauss, for instance, view the idea with suspicion, undoubtedly because they feel that it introduces into the discussion religious and moral values that are incompatible with true scientific inquiry.[5] And to be sure, Joseph de Maistre takes the view that the ritual victim is an "innocent" creature who pays a debt for the "guilty" party. I propose an hypothesis that does away with this moral distinction. As I see it, the relationship between the potential victim and the actual victim cannot be defined in terms of innocence or guilt. There is no question of "expiation." Rather, society is seeking to deflect upon a relatively indifferent victim, a "sacrificeable" victim, the violence that would otherwise be vented on its own members, the people it most desires to protect.

The qualities that lend violence its particular terror—its blind brutality, the fundamental absurdity of its manifestations—have a reverse side. With these qualities goes the strange propensity to seize upon surrogate victims, to actually conspire with the enemy and at the right moment toss him a morsel that will serve to satisfy his raging hunger . . . *Violence is not to be denied, but it can be diverted to another object, something it can sink its teeth into.* (1989, 3–4, Jones's italics)

This supposed link between violence and ritual will certainly seem implausible to some. The notion that all sacrificial rites are more similar than different at their cores will breed even more debate. A cursory glance at rituals located in different cultures, however, illustrates that the pledge process belongs to a historical ritualistic genre which is not unique to BGFs.

Some scholars, directly or indirectly, posit that what we today regard as fraternity ritual has its roots in freemasonry, which can be traced back to ancient Africa. Various Afrocentrists assert that ancient Egyptians, specifically, developed a complex religious system called the Egyptian Mystery System.[6] According to the Afrocentrists, the Mystery System was the first system whose structure was geared toward the achievement of salvation. George G. M. James notes that this system regarded the human body as a "prison house of the soul," which could be liberated from its "bodily impediments" through the disciplines of Arts and Sciences and advanced from the level of a mortal to that of a god (1989, 27).[7]

The belief that structured initiation rituals have their roots in Africa is certainly disputed. The dispute, however, is not necessarily over ritual, but over a more central and pressing Afrocentric claim. That claim is that modern western society is based on the faulty assumption that Greek tradition is at the heart of what we presently know as religion, the arts and sciences, and, maybe most disturbing of all, philosophy. The current anti-Afrocentric attack is led by Wellesley professor Mary Leftkowitz in her work *Not Out of Africa* (1996).[8] Whether or not one accepts the Afrocentric stance, examination of the work of James (1989), Molefi Asante (1988), James Brunson (1991), Maulana Karenga (1984, 1990, 1993), and others provides us one place in which we may locate other ritualistic processes of the type with which we are concerned. We also find other locations where rituals have historical and social significance.

There are a number of instances where ritualized initiation appeared outside of Africa. The origins of these rituals are not known in all cases. The Eleusinian and Orphic orders in the Greco-Roman tradition, for example, included mysteries systems in their traditions.[9] Eleusinian mysteries include four particular elements: purification, communication with the mystics, exposition of holy objects and symbols, and investiture by crowning with a garland. People are said to have traveled from around the Roman Empire to take part in these rituals. The most important part of the festival included a play based on the Greek myth about the abduction of Persephone, daughter of the goddess Demeter, by Hades, the god of the underworld. The events that unfold in the myth serve as an explanation for why seasons change. The theme of death and rebirth was central to the Eleusinian initiation.

The Orphic mysteries were performed by ancient Dionysian cults.[10] In these rituals, Dionysus represented both productivity and destruction, the sacrificed and the sacrificer. These cults continuously sought to affirm that true individuation could not be achieved without interaction between the individual and the collective. Only the initiate who was able to move beyond the individual self to an affirmation of Dionysus was able to achieve a transformation which illuminates the transitive interaction between the individual and society.[11] The Dionysus mysteries aimed to restructure the individual so that he was no longer tied to the minimal "I" but was tied to a larger community. This commitment to a larger cause falls neatly in line with Girard's hypothesis, because this commitment may indeed call for individual sacrifice in order to maintain the well-being of the whole.

Mithraism provides yet another example of ancient ritual that ties into our study. This cult, which worshiped the Persian god Mithras, had a wide following across Europe and parts of Africa. This is evident in the numerous temples of Mithras excavated in Germany, the United Kingdom, Algeria, and Italy.[12] In this ritualized system, the initiate went through seven degrees representing the seven spheres through which the soul passes on its way to perfection. Much like modern freemasonry, the neophyte was considered a "servant" until the third degree was completed.[13]

Despite their different geographic locations, all of these rituals display commonalities which have been passed to today's fraternal world in one way or another. These include: *purification* of the neophyte; some type of *symbolic journey* which includes symbols, objects, or other means of identifying initiates (these may include a crown, tattoo or scar, jewelry, etc.); *inspiration* through lectures on the expectations of future behavior based on the values presented in the initiation; and *degrees or multiple levels of initiation* which usually call for some waiting period. These ancient and modern rituals illustrate that the themes of death, rebirth, and perfection are quite common. These themes hit closer to home in the west when we consider rituals in Christianity which survive today. The symbolism of death and rebirth is quite clear in the Christian ritual of baptism in water. Ceremonies still exist which mark the attainment of different levels of achievement in the church; the ordination of priests, deacons, confirmations, for example. Ritual in the sacred as well as the secular shows that ritual participants are, in one way or another, past-oriented and continue to long for a sense of enlightenment and community through the completion of prescribed rites.

The Commonalities of Modern Fraternity Ritual

Modern fraternity initiation rituals are no different than ancient ones in that they also seek to maintain some form of stability within organizations. They are not unique; they are syntheses of materials from a number of sources, including historical rituals from other civilizations (especially Africa, Asia [or what in less-informed times was called "the Orient"], and Greece); freemasonry; other adult lodge groups such as the Knights of Pythias, Knights of Columbus, Order of Odd Fellows, and the Knights Templar; and religious books and liturgies. Some Greek organizations also developed commonalities because men in one fraternity assisted men who were starting new fraternities. Kappa Alpha Psi historian William Crump (1991) recounts that the founders of Kappa Alpha Psi, a historically black fraternity, found that white Greeks at Indiana University were quite willing to help them in certain fraternal endeavors when they began to feel that the new black organization was no threat to them.

Bobby McMinn (1979) summarizes modern fraternity rituals as having five basic ritualistic precepts and seven common components. The precepts include: *character* (honor, leadership, morality, truth, and loyalty); *scholarship* (academics, intellectual development, and the pursuit of knowledge); *fellowship* (brotherhood, group unity, shared values); *service* (to the less fortunate and/or to a particular profession); and *religion* (respect for a higher authority, sometimes a particular denomination's views). Without divulging the particulars of any surviving fraternity's initiation ritual, the work of McMinn illustrates that most fraternities use some or all of these precepts as part of the themes of their initiation ceremonies.

McMinn posits that initiation rituals usually progress in a very deliberate manner. The following steps may occur at different points in different rituals, but they are almost always present. The first step is the *preparation of the candidates and a procedure for admitting them into the initiation room.* Usually this consists of dressing the neophyte in a robe, often blindfolding him. He is then led to a door by an already initiated guide, where there are knocks on the door and an exchange of dialogue and sometimes an exchange of signs, grips, or passwords that gain the neophyte and the guide entrance. Next, there is *the administration of an initiation oath.* In most groups, the chapter president administers the oath. The neophytes are often standing but may be kneeling and may have their right hand raised. Some of the items included in the oath may be to keep the secrets of the fraternity, to promote the interests of the fraternity, to obey orders from superiors, to strive to improve oneself in areas of the precepts of the fraternity, to not join any other college social/service fraternity, and to promote the interests of the host institution (when applicable).

Third, the neophyte is *taught the secrets and symbols of the fraternity.* These usually include passwords, a motto, recognition signs, symbolism of the coat of arms, significance of titles of officers, and interpretation of the fraternity flag, flower, whistle or call, song, and so forth. Fourth, there is the *investiture of the badge/pin,* which is usually done by the big brother sponsor or president. If a more prominent fraternity officer (national or regional) is present, he may assume this duty. Fifth comes the *charge of responsibility.* Often, a charge of responsibility is read to the new initiate(s). This, again, is usually done by the president. These charges may include encouraging the initiate to fulfill the ideals of the fraternity, complete his college education to the best of his ability, pursue lifelong learning, strive for unity, and serve the fraternity in the future. Most fraternities make use of a *prayer* at some point in their ritual. Finally, and most important to our study, is the practice of requiring the neophyte to undertake a *symbolic journey.* The symbolic journey carries with it two important purposes. It is designed to teach the neophyte the ideals and virtues of the fraternity through the use of personification and sound and sight effects. It is also designed to afford him the opportunity to prove his allegiance to the organization by presenting him with situations in which he must sacrifice himself for the good of others and/or the fraternity. This ordeal ideally determines whether the neophyte is prepared for membership in the fraternity and impresses upon him the necessity of guarding its secrets. It is here, within the symbolic journey, that we locate hazing's lair.

The Symbolic Journey and Hazing

It is important to understand that the pledge process of fraternities is what McMinn calls the symbolic journey and is nothing more than another dramatization of the death and rebirth theme which comes to us from the ancients. The completion of this ordeal symbolically represents the replacing of a life of hopelessness, selfishness, and solitude with one full of hope, light, and fraternal love. All of these aspects, along with the desire to attain and affirm manhood, serve as the carrots dangled by secret orders to attract men. One examiner of initiation ritual, Mark Carnes (1989), sees the initiation rites of fraternal orders as a distinct product of Victorian American culture and society. While this assertion is debatable, Carnes does provide valuable information on specific events which take place in fraternity initiation rituals that attract men. He opines that while thousands of rituals were written for different orders, "probably no more than twenty were successful." These particular rituals, which struck a responsive chord in members, "were shamelessly pirated or slightly modified by rival orders, and certain themes reappeared in scores of ceremonies" (39). The purpose of all these rituals was not only to establish a fraternal identity but also to forge a vision of a complete self to help men take their places in society.

To elucidate this point, Carnes examines the attempt by the Improved Order of Red Men to attract members in the mid-nineteenth century. The Order of Red Men was initially established in 1834 by former freemasons. Its original initiation ritual included little more than the initiation oath and charge-of-responsibility components of ritual. Absent from this ritual was anything resembling the symbolic journey. After quick initial growth, the order began to falter and by 1850 had little more than 3,000 members. During the following two decades, the fraternity concentrated primarily on developing a ritual that would be effective in attracting and retaining members. The Red Men finally settled on the Adoption Degree of 1868 as the initiation ritual, and fraternity officials credited it with the order's renewed success. Carnes feels that "the question as to why earlier rituals failed to elicit 'general approbation' while the Adoption Degree of 1868 gave 'excellent satisfaction' is ultimately unanswerable" (Carnes 1989, 40). On the contrary, I feel that this question is very answerable. First, however, it would be useful for us to recount the Adoption Degree, which was published verbatim by the National Christian Association, an organization which sought to destroy the appeal of secret ritual by making it public. The major difference in this ceremony from that of Greek-letter orders is the fact that the characters, who have symbolic opponents, are "Red Men" and "palefaces" instead of "Greeks." Carnes summarizes the initiation ceremony as follows:

It began with an invocation by a sachem, who prayed to the "Great Spirit of the Universe" to bring harmony to the tribe, to preserve the Indians' homes, and to "shed Thy boundaries upon all Red Men of the forest." Despite these hopes, however, the ritual's main theme was death. The sachem called upon the Great Spirit to give each Red Man the "holy courage" to paddle his canoe safely to "that undiscovered country from whose bourne no traveler returns." During the invocation he returned to the subject of death:

Teach us the trail we must follow while we live in this forest, and when it is Thy will that we shall cross the river of death, take us to Thyself, where Thy council fire of love and glory burneth forever in righteousness.

Then the council fire was kindled; in the preparation room the candidate—a "paleface"—removed his shirt and shoes and put on moccasins. A scout rapped at the "inner wicket" and motioned for the candidate to follow. They padded silently around the lodge room, avoiding a group of Indians who were "sleeping" at the far end. Then the scout tripped over one of the sleeping Indians. The awakened Indian shouted, "Spies! Traitors in our Camp!" and the group captured the candidate; the scout escaped. The Indian "hunters" then conferred around a fire:

First Brave: This paleface is of a hated nation: let us put him to torture!
Second Brave: He is a squaw, and cannot bear the torture!
Third Brave: He fears a Warrior's death!
Fourth Brave: Let us burn him at the stake!

The discussion continued in a similar fashion. At last the initiate was informed that he would indeed be consumed by fire.

They proceeded to the opposite end of the lodge, where they were led to a tepee. Just after they had been admitted, another Indian rushed at the candidate with an uplifted knife, only to be intercepted by a hunter, who assured him that "paleface" [quotes the editor's] would soon be tortured. "Then let us proceed, paleface, and unless some Chief interposes, you perish at the stake. . . . Why do you tempt your fate? Or is it your wish to become a Red Man?" The candidate was prompted to answer yes. The hunter warned: "Know, then, that Red Men are men without fear, and none but such can be adopted by our tribe." After more questions the hunter demanded proof of the candidate's courage: "The honest and brave man meets death with a smile—the *guilty* trembles at the very thought."

The initiate was bound to the stake, and the hunters were encouraged to prepare their scalping knives and war clubs. The Indians commenced a scalp dance and fagots were lit. Another Indian ran to summon the prophet. The prophet, however, emerged from the tent, halted the execution, berated the hunters for their impulsiveness, and pronounced the candidate a "man without fear." The prophet then lectured the candidate on the family of Red Men, explaining that they held property in common and were dedicated to their "brothers," the "children of the forest." However, he warned the candidate that the final decision about his adoption rested with the sachem. The prophet gave the candidate an eagle's feather as proof of his courage.

After more speeches and a pledge of secrecy, the candidate was led to another tepee in the far corner of the lodge. As he approached, the sachem threw open the flap and upbraided his guards for sleeping on duty, thereby allowing a paleface to come in his presence. The warriors did not immediately respond and the sachem started to throw a tomahawk at the initiate. One of the hunters then grasped the sachem's arm. "No, Sachem, no! Thy children when on duty never sleep!" The hunter added that the initiate had passed the ordeal and been endorsed by the prophet. He produced the eagle's feather as proof. The sachem, realizing his error, tossed his tomahawk aside and shook hands with the candidate: "Then you are welcome to our bosom." The sachem delivers a welcoming speech stressing the protection that the order afforded members of the tribe, much as "the eagle shieldeth her young and tender brood." (Carnes 1989, 41–42)

The common threads of fraternity ritual covered by McMinn are clearly evident in the Adoption Degree of 1868, which differed from the group's other proposed ceremonies in two important ways. First of all, it had a symbolic journey. Second, the symbolic journey incorporated the motifs of sacrificial death and rebirth, just as we found with the ancients. It is this ritual death that moves the initiation to a zone of speciality.

The ritualistic rebirth of the initiate marks not only his entrance into the fraternal order but also the birth of a new self. The symbolic threats of death are not easily overlooked in the Red Men initiation ritual, as they should not be in all sacrificial rites, for it is the threat of death that gives the rites their appeal. This fact answers Carnes's earlier query about what made the Adoption Degree of 1868 particularly successful. In the Red Men case, while the neophyte is twice spared from execution at the hands of his brothers-to-be, he experiences a metaphorical death. His former self does not really survive the ritualistic symbolic journey. His previous life course has been shown to be flawed. With the help of the ritual and the guidance of the Red Men, he has chosen an alternate route. Simply put, the life of the paleface had come to an end and the life of a new Red Man had begun. The attraction of the death motif can be clearly linked to Girard's hypothesis, which sees sacrifice as utilitarian because it is a necessary act for the good of the community. In the Girardian sense, the fraternity is not the community but a symbol of the community. Social and fraternal rituals, however, ideally serve the same purpose—they maintain order, continuity, and goodness. Through the trials of the ritual, the new initiate becomes able to contribute to the maintenance of order and the continuous survival of the fraternal community. This is so because he supposedly moves from his place of individualistic egoism to one of altruistic sacrifice and bonding with his brothers. Only in this way can brotherhood and the vitality of the whole be kept alive.

The purpose of initiation ritual is not to reform the initiate but to *remake him entirely*. It is no wonder then that BGF members often refer to their date of initiation as the day they were "made" and that members who initiated other members will say "I made him" or "I made you." In the case of the Red Men, Carnes remarks, "Though apprehended for the crime of trespass, he [the initiate] was to be put to death for a failing of character: He was a 'paleface' and a 'squaw' who 'could not bear torture.' He was excluded from the tribe which consisted of 'men without fear,' because he was unfit. Through the transformative power of the ritual, the initiate's courage was confirmed" (1989, 44). This is not only a confirmation of his fitness for membership in the fraternity but, more deeply, a confirmation of his manhood and fitness to undertake greater endeavors in life. Ultimately, the reborn neophyte is expected and expects to be quite different from the candidate who began the process. In most cases, just as the journey in this ordeal is symbolic, the tests and threats which are embedded in it are also symbolic. Modern hazing, however, is the phenomenon of members taking tests out of the realm of symbolism and catapulting them into reality. Instead of the initiate being *threatened* with torture to prove his fraternal worth and manliness, he is actually tortured. Specific hazing tactics are nothing more than creative variations deployed by individual fraternity members to push initiates to their limits in a supposed effort to establish worthiness.

Seeking Liminality: The Ritualistic Remaking of the Self

Whether or not the past-oriented ritualistic initiation process truly holds transformative power is debatable. While the majority of members do not seem to openly endorse the hazing which often comes along with the BGF pledge process, many strongly support the process itself. In the black instance, hazing practices certainly take on a different face during the symbolic journey because they are often intensified through the use of physical violence. The physical violence involved in the BGF pledge process is the element which, to many BGF members, positions the ordeal as particularly sacrificial and even legitimate.

Outside of the vehicles of hazing, however, there is a unity of purpose in most fraternal initiatory rituals—black, white, or other.

Sacrificial rites of passage for all Greeks, whether the acts during the symbolic journey are threatened or real, have to do with the acquisition of new status for the initiate and stability for the organization. These rites are designed as processes which confer upon new initiates the privilege of full admission to the fraternal community. That this process is political should not be doubted. Just as accepted avenues to achievement in the larger society exist—attending the "right" schools, obtaining the "right" degrees, and living in the "right" neighborhood—avenues of entrance into BGFs which are considered more legitimate and respectable than others also exist. What has been missed, however, is the possibility that such sacrificial processes are political not only on the individual or organizational levels but also the societal level. In our society, which is less and less based on the notion of community, individual passage from one status to another always presents problems of adaptation, but these are thought to be limited to the individuals directly involved in the process. This belief is one which potentially serves to limit the modern scope of inquiry into problems of violence. While we, in the postmodern west, tend to largely detach individual existence from that of the society, many earlier societies made no such separation. Girard remarks, "In primitive societies . . . the slightest change in the status of an isolated individual was treated as if it carried the potential to create a major [societal] crisis" (Girard 1989, 281).

To be sure, thinkers such as Girard, Feldman, and Roberto Calasso (1991) embrace ritual violence and sacrifice as that which maintains the stability of a community.[14] In Calasso's view, sacrificial ritual in more civilized societies eventually gives way to less violent, more worldly devices such as romantic stories of adventurous exploits, fantastic journeys, and amazing encounters of love. These fantasies are all very seductive and make for impressive cinema, but they teach nothing about human loss. Ultimately, Calasso sees the societal loss of sacrifice as the root of people succumbing to a material life empty of true ceremonial content. Modern people are therefore left with a great, aching absence. Hence, nothing seems legitimate and nothing can be made legitimate once they lose touch with sacrifice—be it physical or emotional. This nebulousness is what is commonly referred to as anomie. When a society changes rapidly, there no longer exists a cohesive set of values that are accepted by the majority of people. This is so, Calasso believes, because it is the primordial act of sacrifice which defines human limits and balances social relations. Only ceremonies of loss and death can teach people how to *live* together. It is the deficiency of legitimacy, brotherhood, and community that Greeks and other groups which employ sacrificial rites seek to eradicate or avoid altogether.

Most criticisms of these groups do not center on the intended ends of the pledge process; instead, they center on its means. That is, the methods involved in the pledge journey are considered abhorrent. But the methods endure because just as they are horribly sick to some, they are sacred to others. Again, central to the pledge process is the fact that it is concerned with a change in individual status or, as Arnold van Gennep (1909) called it, liminality. Liminality is involved in all rites of passage and has two distinct stages. In the first stage, the initiate loses his previous status, and in the second stage he acquires his new one. The gap between the stages is the void which the pledge process must fill. To members, the process is one which moves the initiate from the place of a disconnected individual to that of a connected, metamorphosed fraternity man. At the outset, the initiate is seen as different from his brothers-to-be. The pledge process, like all sacrificial rites, is intended to eradicate this difference. This eradication, however, becomes troubling if Girard is right, "for if all violence involves a loss of difference, all losses of difference also involve violence" (1989, 281). While Girard's conversion may be a bit coy, it certainly seems to apply in this particular case. The violence used to eradicate difference can often be extreme, for difference is considered contagious. This stance is not disturbing to Girardians because they agree that "perfectly innocent phenomena can provoke fear, but that fear cannot dismiss it as mere fantasy; there is nothing fantastical about its impact or its results" (ibid.).

The love/loathe ambivalence of the pledge introduced at the outset of this study can now be explained. The pledge "in passage" is not hated; rather, the difference he represents is disdained. He, therefore, must be regarded in the same light as a criminal or infected individual who could potentially infect the entire fraternal body with his difference. His presence alone mandates violence in an attempt to destroy the contagion of difference which, if not treated, can destroy the body. Only through the completion of the process can he be "cured" and subsequently embraced. If we conceive of contagion in terms of microbiology, we miss the point. In this case, the fraternity is the body and the individual is the virus. This, to be sure, is a shift in—or more appropriately a minimization of—Girard and Calasso's community. Fraternity members are, in the main, not conscious of community in the Girardian or Calasson sense, for the fraternity (all too often) *is* their community and the differentiated individual must be altered or decontaminated before he is allowed entrance. Logically then, the first step is to isolate the infected victim, forbidding all contact between him and the "healthy" members. He is placed on the periphery of the society—in a different, almost surreal, isolated realm where the violence of undifferentiation reigns.

As in other rituals of this type, the initiate is quite often "stripped of his name, his history, and his family connections; he is reduced to a state of anonymity" (Girard 1989, 282). Violence is the tool which determines the result of this endeavor. The pledge must submit to the violence, but never with full knowledge of the outcome of the process. Because much of fraternity life is esoteric, the pledge knows what he is losing but can conceptualize only a vague silhouette of what he will gain. The mysticism of the process is precisely what affords the pledge journey its appeal. It is this mystery and the promise of rebirth it brings that aligns the pledge process with ancient sacrificial rites of passage:

Although the prospect of the passage may appear terrifying to the primitive mind, it also offers hope. After all, it was by way of a general outbreak of violence and universal loss of difference—that is, by way of sacrificial crisis—that the community achieved a differentiated order in former times. And it can be hoped that this crisis will achieve the same results. Differences will be restored or established; specifically, the neophyte will gain his new coveted status. A happy outcome must depend on the good will of supreme violence, but the community believes it can influence this outcome by channeling the "bad" energy into prearranged outlets. In order for the final results to match those of the original action, however, every possible precaution must be taken to follow the original model. The neophytes must adhere to the rules laid down by tradition; they must try to shape the new event in the mold of the old one. For only if the ritual reiterates the original crisis is there hope that the outcome will be the same.

Such is the reasoning behind these rites of passage. . . . Instead of avoiding the crisis, the neophyte must advance to meet it, as his ancestors did before him. Instead of fleeing the most painful and terrifying aspects of reciprocal violence, he must submit to each and every one of them in proper sequence. The postulate must endure hardship, hunger, even torture, because these ordeals were part of the original experience. . . . [The] celebrants in certain festivals are required to perform a number of actions that are normally forbidden: real or symbolic acts of sexual aggression, stealing, the eating of proscribed foods. (Girard 1989, 283)

While never referencing BGFs or Greek-letter fraternities of any kind, Girard describes the psychology, recognized or not, behind the pledge process perfectly —it is one which ultimately seeks stability through the liminality of the initiate. Even in the Afrocentric case, the process reappears. Echoing George G. M. James, James Brunson sees initiation ritual as one which is intended to "teach the candidate the secret of making one's self a perfection of God" (1991, 86). To accomplish this task, the initiate must endure seven major trials: seclusion, beatings, exposure to cold, thirst, eating of unsavory foods, punishment, and threat of death. While Brunson makes it clear that he does not necessarily condone the current BGF pledge process, he does use Asa Hilliard's (1985) study of African initiation systems to draw comparisons between them and the BGF pledge process. When compared to our earlier citations of ritual and their components, Brunson's list illustrates clearly that geographic boundaries do not neatly separate such rites:

1. The initiates were physically segregated from the regular of daily life.

The "pledge line" is formed. These individuals are required to interact, learn as much about each other as possible, work together, and depend upon each other with as little assistance as possible from any outside sources, except, of course, their deans.

2. They retreated from their familiar environment to an environment that enabled them to get more directly in touch with nature. This symbolized a move from the infantile situation into a situation which would allow for more maturity.

The pledge(s) are put into pressured situations that often require them to get in touch with the psychological "inner self" and intellect and utilize their individual and group creativity and resourcefulness toward goals of self-actualization.

3. The initiate joined with other initiates of the same age and shared their lives in common, since a common living experience was also a common learning experience.

The pledge(s) at times are required to eat, sleep, and live together; study together; visit their "big brothers"; and review required learning materials together. They get to know each other as one would know a blood brother or sister.

4. The initiates were separated from their parents in addition to being separated from the large community.

The pledge(s) may be put into situations known as "social probation" where they are denied social interaction with anyone outside the classroom or pledge line. They are not allowed to talk, socially interact with, or engage in any form of interaction that calls into question the dynamic of ostracism.

5. The initiates had to renounce all that recalls the past existence.

The pledge(s) state(s) an allegiance to the tenets of the organization that they are being initiated into. They are given specific expectations that also demand a fuller respect for humanity.

6. The initiates were then taught by the old men and women of the village or town.

The pledge(s) are taught the philosophic and pragmatic aspects of the organization as well as its ideologies inherent to Greek-lettered organizations. They learn fraternity and chapter history, poems, information regarding other chapters, myths of the organization, the Greek alphabet, etc.

7. The initiates frequently went nude or wore clothes made of grass to symbolize the clothes of the first men or women.

Pledge(s) is/are expected to wear uniforms or outfits signifying their status as an initiate as outlined by that organization. The attire may mandate dresses [for females in sororities] every day or a specific day, shirts and ties, army jackets and boots, beanie caps or hats, shaving one's head or facial hair, etc.

8. The initiates underwent purification baths.

In a symbolic ritual called "crossing the burning sands," initiates often undergo a series of trials designed to bring them from "darkness into the light."

9. During the course of initiation a number of tests of audacity, courage, fasting, flogging, hazing, mutilations, and scarifications were conducted. The purpose was to give the opportunity for the initiate to demonstrate a refusal to take life as it is given as a way of opening the mind to beauty, joy, and ecstasy.

Initiates are sent through a variety of trials during a week-long ordeal, referred to as Hell Week, that are supposed to test their desire to be a member of the organization.

10. Initiate learned a new and secret language.

Neophytes are given the passwords, grips, and signs designed for that specific organization.

11. Initiates were given new names.

During Hell Week, the candidates are given preliminary names such as "dog" and "probate" [and] line and number names that are subsequently transformed after the initiation.

12. The initiation process symbolized a rebirth.

After the "crossing of the burning sands," initiated members become "neophytes" (new in the light) of their organization.

13. The initiation process included a number of exercises and things to be learned such as physical and military training, songs, and dances and how to handle sacred things such as math and tools.

Pledges learn rituals, songs, poems, history, and Greek literature perceived as relevant to the sustaining and perpetuation of the organizations' existence. These ideas are passed on from one pledge class or line to another. (Brunson 1991, 93–96)

By this point, my hypothesis should be undeniable that there is nothing distinct about the origins or the aims of the BGF pledge processes that explains why violence has become such an integral part of them. This is not to say that BGF pledge processes have no distinct characteristics. Clearly, the personas many members of Kappa Alpha Psi have taken on with cane-twirling and the "pretty boy" image distinguish them in an exteriorized way from Omegas and the infatuation of some with the "Que Dog" moniker and all its trappings: dog collars, boots, and barking.[15] The emphasis placed on these differences by the members of each organization is the sole factor which gives each fraternity its particular initiatory quality. Beyond these cleavages, however, there is little difference between Alphas, Kappas, Omegas, or Sigmas. Ironically, it is these cosmetic differences that many members seem to desire and covet to the point that they will hold on to them feverishly, even if the most fundamental ritualistic practices and ideals of the organizations fall into neglect or disappear from their lives completely.

The reason why many Kappas cling to their canes and many Omegas bark, even if they are no longer active in their groups, is not really the primary philosophical question here. Our concern lies in locating the unity of sacrificial rites and the link between violence and ritual and understanding that, while it may not be realized, this ritualized violence originally served a societal purpose. In modern times, ritual violence has been lowered from its societal status and therefore minimized, abused, and rightfully disdained in the main. At the outset, ritual sacrifice was not about the victim or guilt at all; it was concerned with the preservation of a particular social order. Clearly, the stance that violence is inevitable and that the wise society constructs ways to channel and confine it brings the age-old debate over human nature to bear. It is unfortunate for humanists who prefer to see the world through rose-colored glasses that history (to this point at least) has proven that Hobbes was more right than wrong when he said that men were little more than brutes. Girard must have had this in mind when he opined that "violence is not to be denied" (4).

Conclusion and Recommendations

This study has examined the pledge processes of BGFs as attempts to recreate ancient sacrificial crises and subsequently maintain community (organizational) stability through the use of ritualized violence. Clearly, the fact that BGF physical violence has risen to inordinate levels relative to other Greek-letter fraternities is cause for distress. While this violence certainly deserves concern, at its core, it is nothing more than the use of different tactics during an initiate's symbolic journey to achieve liminality. The very real threat to black life which comes along with these tactics, however, mandates that we not only understand BGF violence but also seek to curb it. Curbing hazing in BGFs will be no easy task, but a few steps can be taken to begin movement toward this goal.

As we seek solutions to hazing, we must be clear that the pledge ritual is perceived by many BGF members as an overwhelmingly important force in the preservation of black fraternal orders. To many black Greeks, physical hardships speak much more thunderously than intellectual challenge, for these hardships are thought to instill fraternal love and serve as mechanisms which supposedly afford the pledge opportunities to prove his worth. These ordeals make the establishment of the fraternities' hierarchies of respect (those who pledged as compared to those who did not) appear to be an extraordinary blessing to members who were "made right." Be it conscious or not, the violence of the pledge process has evolved into a staunch political device for keeping certain members "in their places" so that adherence to the process and the domination it brings will not die.[16] Ritual violence can only be killed slowly—if it can be killed at all. The possibility that violent initiation practices are immortal is quite real, and this realization moves us to the issue of memory engaged by the Dionysus cults so long ago. Ritual and the steady march of time present the potentiality that many members may not know why they do what they do anymore. As Dr. Walter Kimbrough, a member of Alpha Phi Alpha and an administrator at Albany State University noted, "There are a number of members who have defended pledging as a construct of black culture that cannot be understood by outsiders. Many others, however, are not interested enough in historical and cultural knowledge concerning BGFs to effectively make such arguments."[17]

The reality of the situation is that, in many instances, pledge ritual today is random, aimless, and degenerative. This could be so because of a loss of memory (or complete absence of knowledge) by members. As we have seen, the purpose of sacrificial ritual was, and is, to channel the uncertainty of violence down avenues of certainty to achieve particular results. With regular repetition and perceptions of success, though, these rites are gradually transformed into simple tests or trials which become increasingly symbolic and formalistic. In this progression, the sacrificial nature of the process tends to become obscured until finally it is hard to say what the symbols are intended to symbolize. What members often do not understand is the fact that they participate in a process which has historical roots and that its purpose has been to channel otherwise random violence into controllable, purposeful directions. Educational institutions and fraternity national offices need to work diligently at designing mandatory seminars and workshops on every campus where BGF chapters exist which address this reality and challenge members to critically examine why they participate in the violence of modern black fraternal activities.

Those concerned with constructing correctives which will enhance the quality of black Greek life must insist that the long practice of ignoring BGF violence by college and university administrators cease. Not only has this neglect added to hazing's intensity because of few (or no) institutional checks on black fraternal organizations (especially at predominantly white universities), it has also augmented the feeling among many undergraduates that what they do to their pledges is "nobody's business." The general neglect of some institutions where the problems of BGFs are concerned can possibly be examined from a societal perspective. If it is possible that an individual can be collectivized, then it is also possible that groups can be individuated. That is, members of the dominant American core group who believe that many (or even most) black males resemble the stereotypical violent, thuggish, underachieving black man will have little problem with the presence of violence within this "sacrificeable" group as long as it does not spill over into the core. In actuality, spillover has not affected educational institutions; the particular violence found in BGFs has not "infected" white groups. More disturbingly for the institutions, the violence has begun to bring legal concerns of liability to the fore; there is, after all, "a direct correlation between the elimination of sacrificial practices and the establishment of a judicial system" (Girard 1989, 297).

When issues of violent hazing and injuries present themselves, educational institutions usually mete out suspensions and expulsions of students and chapters rather than make serious attempts to study, understand, and prevent the occurrences. This reliance on punishment instead of prevention must be eradicated. One way to move toward prevention is for administrators to stop neglecting the problem. While this reality does not absolve members of responsibility for their behavior, universities would be wise to employ minority administrators with knowledge of, and memberships in, BGFs whose primary job is to guide the activities of these organizations. These individuals could work to construct and enforce regulations which consider the unique make-up of black Greek-letter fraternities. While such personnel (who usually hold the status of assistant dean of students or its equivalent) are usually in place for historically white organizations, black fraternities and sororities are often managed by part-timers or graduate students. This is an easily correctable institutional error which must be addressed.[18]

Finally, further serious study of the histories and purposes of BGFs needs to be conducted by scholars. I can hope that such studies will contribute to realistic strategies which emphasize prevention instead of punishment after injuries and deaths. These strategies will need to be jointly constructed by concerned intellectuals, fraternity national officers, fraternity general memberships, and college and university administrators. The failure of the Membership Intake Program (MIP) (a BGF alternative to pledging), which was launched without the input of most brothers in the early 1990s, illustrates that initiatives enforced without member evaluation will more than likely fail.[19] It should be noted that every injury and death mentioned at the outset of this study happened *after* the MIP was introduced. Initiates and members continue to be drawn to ritualized pledging and hazing and the acceptance they bring. Since the pull of the pledge ritual is so strong, it would seem that a logical place to begin for those concerned with the future of these organizations is the study and understanding of the ties to BGFs to sacrificial ritual. Until such an understanding is established and the historical and social dynamics of such rituals are taken into account by fraternity members, fraternity officials, and college and university administrators, they will continue to be plagued by member and student defiance and injuries and deaths in their organizations and on their campuses.

Notes

1. The fraternity pledge process and the hazing which usually accompanies it are not new phenomena. For a fine historical documentation of "reported" hazing incidents, injuries, and deaths see Hank Nuwer, *Broken Pledges: The Deadly Rite of Hazing* (Marietta, Ga.: Longstreet Press, 1990). Concern over the brutality of the BGF pledge process, however, became quite public in 1989 after Morehouse College student Joel Harris was killed while attempting to join Alpha Phi Alpha. This concern was intensified in 1994 when Michael Davis was beaten to death by members of Kappa Alpha Psi at Southeast Missouri State University. For an account of the Davis case, see William Cox, "Joining a Fraternity Should Not Result in Death," *Black Issues in Higher Education* (1 March 1994): 88. The finest account of the Davis case was probably written by J. P. Olsen in "Blood Brothers," *Swing,* February 1995, 49–53.
2. The student injured in this case sued the Omega Psi Phi Fraternity. The case ended in August of 1999 with the student being awarded over $950,000 for damages.
3. A number of works seek to explain ritualistic ordeal by placing them into a social context. Notable among these works are Boudervijnse's edited volume, *Current Studies in Rituals: Perspectives for the Psychology of Religion* (Atlanta: Rodopi, 1990); and M. Edem, *Confused Values in Nigerian Context: Rituals Reveal Mythology* (Lagos: Jeromelaiho & Associates, 1993). This essay primarily engages Rene Girard, *Violence and the Sacred* (Baltimore: Johns Hopkins University Press, 1989).
4. The reluctance of BGFs to cease participation in activities which they regard as "traditional" is examined to a degree in P. Applebome, "Lawsuit Shatters Code of Silence over Hazing at Black Fraternities," *New York Times,* 21 December 1994, B8, B15; and Eleena DeLisser, "Violent Hazing Threatens Black Fraternities," *The Wall Street Journal,* 18 November 1994, B1, B2.

5. Girard has no such self-imposed limitation where the incorporation of reli-
    gious values are concerned. His work, in fact, revolves around religion in
    that he uses religious parables and myths from numerous societies. Ulti-
    mately, he goes so far as to assert that we find the roots of ritual in religion.

6. Various Afrocentric texts assert that African secret societies are the true
    sources of similar orders found in the western world. Among these works
    are Ra Un Nefer Amen, *Metu Neter* (Bronx: Khamit Corporation, 1990);
    James Brunson, *Frat and Soror: The African Origins of Greek Lettered Organi-
    zations* (Southfield, Mich.: Cleage Group, 1991); and George G. M. James,
    Stolen Legacy (Newport News, Va.: United Brothers Communications Sys-
    tems, 1989).

7. An in-depth (though highly disputed) account of the Egyptian Mysteries
    System and the grades of initiation can be found in Chapter 3 of *Stolen
    Legacy.*

8. Even though Leftkowitz denies the very existence of the Egyptian Mysteries
    System, she does assert that the *myth* of the Mysteries System among Euro-
    peans was integral in the formation of freemasonry. Certainly one must ask
    a number of questions here: Why would Europeans create a myth of an
    African-dominated Mysteries System? Even if this system is, in fact, a myth,
    does not the fact that the myth *exists* and has had such heavy historical con-
    sequences mandate that we examine it as historically important?

9. An outstanding condensation of commonalities among fraternal and histori-
    cal ritualistic systems can be found in Bobby McMinn, "A Content Analysis
    of the Esoteric Ritual Manuals of National College Social Fraternities"
    (Ph.D. diss., University of Mississippi, 1979). Even though McMinn does
    not adequately deal with BGFs in his work, the sections of this chapter
    which address the commonalities of fraternity ritual borrow heavily
    from him.

10. Many representations of the Greek god Dionysus suggest a fusion or confu-
    sion of the sexes. He is also associated with newborn or youthful things,
    vegetation, the phallus, and masks. A very important element of Dionysus is
    that he calls for abandonment of the ego. According to Greek myth, Diony-
    sus appears among the mortals of Thebes and eventually causes the death
    of the ruler Pentheus because the Thebans, egotistically, do not acknowl-
    edge Dionysus's divinity. Pentheus is induced with amnesia and is subse-
    quently led through a series of identity crises by Dionysus. The power of for-
    getfulness is induced among the citizens of Thebes by wine and
    enchantment from Dionysus and they eventually kill Pentheus without real-
    izing what they are doing. Some see this story as an examination of ego and
    identity by making use of the concept of memory. The theme of forgetful-
    ness or memory is found extensively in literature. Two examples of engage-
    ments of such a theme are Robert Luyster, "Dionysus: The Masks of Mad-
    ness," *Parabola* 20, no. 4 (Winter 1995); and Alexander Tulin, "A Note On
    Euripides' *Bacchae,*" *Mnemosyne* 47, no. 2 (April 1994).

11. A transitive interaction is an exchange between individuals and/or groups
    during any process in which all parties involved actually participate and
    contribute to the outcome (even if one seems to be the agent and the other
    a passive victim) and are changed by it.

12. For more readings on the spread of Mithraism, see Oliver Nicholson, "The End of Mithraism," *Antiquity* 69, no. 263 (June 1995): 358; and Alan Schofield, "The Search for Iconographic Variation in Roman Mithraism," *Religion* 25, no. 1 (January 1995): 51.

13. For readings on freemason ritual see the freemason publication *Ceremonials for the Use of the W. M. Grand Lodge of Ancient, Free, and Accepted Masons of the State of Illinois and Its Constituent Lodges* (Bloomington, Ill.: Panograph Printing & Stationery Co., 1931).

14. Roberto Calasso's *The Ruin of Kasch* (Cambridge, Mass.: Belknap Press of Harvard University, 1994) supports the stance on the historical importance of ritual which Girard presents in *Violence and the Sacred*.

15. It should be noted that Omega Psi Phi's International Headquarters does not, nor has it ever, condoned the use of canine references by members of the organization. While the use of the reference is not universal among members of the fraternity, it is widespread.

16. See Ricky L. Jones, "The Hegemonic Struggle and Domination in Black Greek-letter Fraternities," *Challenge: A Journal of Research on African American Men* 10, no. 1 (1999).

17. Walter Kimbrough, interview with the author, December 2, 1995.

18. The University of Louisville, for example, has changed very little in its policies or personnel relative to BGFs since the 1997 incident mentioned at the beginning of this chapter. It did, however, immediately suspend its chapter of Omega Psi Phi from campus activity for an unprecedented ten years.

19. For an in-depth analysis of the failure of the Membership Intake Program, see Jones, "The Hegemonic Struggle and Domination in Black Greek-letter Fraternities."

8 Troubled Times in a New England University's Fraternity System

Jonathan R. Farr

Editor's note: *Jonathan Farr documents the troublesome events surrounding the fraternity system at a New England university from 1956 to 2002. Farr establishes a pattern of repeated mistakes and offers an analysis of what he sees from his own perspective as a student-affairs professional. Farr's intent is to examine one school's history of problems with many of its fraternities. While not all of his article deals with hazing offenses, Farr's study shows that hazing is part of a general pattern of fraternity-life problems. The university's identity is withheld and the Greek groups and names of administrators he uses are pseudonyms.*

This chapter presents the results of an investigation that explores events that have plagued one school's fraternity system over nearly five decades. This investigation may shed light on why reforms ultimately fail so often. Instead of organizations learning from their mistakes, a constant four-year cycle of students attending the university means that the culture is young and vulnerable to repeated mistakes. This inexperience has manifested itself through similar poor judgment exercised time and again. Incidents, some of which are criminal, have differing details, but they occur like variations on a theme.

This study concentrates on fraternities that own or rent chapter houses near the university. I did not find evidence that sororities here were involved in any behavior problems close to what the fraternities experienced.

The incidents in this study do not represent every shameful act that happened in the past four decades on the selected campus. I have selected those incidents that show best the historical state of the university's fraternity system. My hope is that through re-exposure to these stories, those in authority at other schools may see parallels with their own counterproductive chapters and plan appropriate responses.

The following exploration presents enough of this fraternity system's closeted skeletons to precipitate a most negative image. Having said that, I must disclose my personal view that there are fraternities and sororities that are productive, supportive, and contributing entities. Much evidence of beneficial and commendable community service performed at this campus and others can be documented. Other chapters may not contribute volunteerism but stay out of trouble and serve a social function.

Nonetheless, too many chapters at this university are counterproductive or destructive to the campus community, and their drawbacks detract from any service they perform. No amount of daffodil planting, litter collecting, or fundraising can offset one fraternal death, rape, or criminal hazing.

The Evidence

Though this study deals principally with the past forty years through 2002, premonitions of trouble predate 1962. The fraternities' more positive image that campus-life expert H. L. Horowitz observed from the 1920s to the 1950s was about to end. At the New England institution of which I write, an October 1956 letter to all fraternity presidents from Dean of Men Walter Jacobs recognized that newly initiated members were given copious amounts of alcohol:

> This has resulted in overloading the freshman capacity and subsequent violent though temporary illness of the freshmen who overindulge.
>
> The purpose of this note is to ask you if you can't think of some other way of celebrating the advent of new pledges. It seems to me that you could do better than having a beer bust for the freshmen. The fact that some of them may say that they are expecting it cuts little ice in my opinion[,] and I think that you could certainly have some kind of celebration that was less likely to cause a disturbance and a mess in the student dormitories.

Four years later, in March 1959, the university president made a candid and direct statement of the status of fraternities in a statement that appeared in the student newspaper:

> The fraternities by their own activities and history of operations are their own worst enemy in terms of progress. By and large . . . the majority of Fraternities (not Sororities) have operated at the universities for two main purposes, contradictory to what they say in local and national charters as their reason for existence.
>   1. As a center for drinking parties on weekends . . .
>   2. As sub-standard, poorly managed, overcrowded, unsanitary, and unsafe housing quarters in competition with the university dormitory system.
> These two characteristics haven't changed much in the past five years, even though the administration has repeatedly discussed them with the fraternities.
>
> I am sure that if a committee composed of the Board of Trustee members, disinterested citizens, *not* from the town, and fire inspectors were to tour the fraternity houses tomorrow, they would recommend closing all but three or four of them immediately . . .
>
> Almost unanimously the fraternities on this campus have demonstrated a com-

plete and continuing inability to control their parties or maintain either order or a semblance of decency in handling the alcohol problem.

The preceding analysis by the president succinctly sums up the problems that the university's fraternities encountered back then, perhaps demonstrating why it is so difficult to reform a culture that was so long in the making. I obtained a greater understanding of this culture as the result of a candid interview with former dean of students Bradley Farrell.

Dean Farrell began working here in 1951, serving as university dean from 1961 to 1988. He points to a number of factors occurring during the 1950s and 1960s that helped create such a culture. First, the enrollment of the university exploded as soldiers returned from World War II. In addition, the university president stressed that the doors of the university should open to all who thought they could handle college. After this drastic change in admissions policy was implemented, the influential fraternity system at this university began to evaporate. This information is corroborated by enrollment data from 1953 to 1965. Figures show a steady rising growth of male students at the university, while the percentage of fraternity membership decreases. As one newspaper article writer put it ten years later, "The campus grew and the Greek system didn't."

By the end of the 1960s, many students had rejected the Greek system because the "do your own thing" attitude prevailed on campus. Anti-establishment sentiment was prominent on campuses across the country, and the ultra-conservative Greek system was a target, according to Horowitz's *Campus Life* (1987). A shift in the economy "that continued to create more well-paying . . . jobs," plus the reality of the wartime draft for males, whose failing grades while pledging could mean a loss of a student deferment, resulted in a shift in students' agendas. "Scenes of students in laboratories and libraries were replacing those of goldfish swallowing," noted Horowitz (220–221).

Yet many in fraternities at the university failed to change their behavior for the better. In the 1960s, the neighbors of fraternity houses complained officially about noise, trash, and aggressive brothers. Many fraternity males flunked out even while other students kept their grades high. A May 1967 memo from Director of Fraternities Jerome Sullivan to Dean Farrell documents the status of fraternities at that time—summing up the state of the system at the end of the decade.

A year ago when we discussed the status of fraternities, we determined that the system, as a whole, was in a critical state. The chapters had been operating for over a year as "social clubs" and major reasons for joining were parties and drinking. Members lived for the present with no regard for those who would replace them in the future. "Social" hours and open sale of liquor led to investigations by the . . . local police. Members were unable to pay their chapter fees and accounts receivable led to accounts payable. . . . Most advisers were in name only. . . . Scholarship was not stressed as a chapter obligation to the University. . . . Over 15 per cent of the total membership flunked out in June, 1966. Upperclassmen were deserting the houses for apartments; there was little loyalty to the group. . . . We discussed closing every chapter for a year and then starting over again, but this solution was economically unfeasible since the house corporations could not finance empty houses.

Additionally, in the 1960s, hazing was just one of many categories of incidents that contributed to doubt about the value of fraternities.

The first hazing incident of the 1960s at the university concerned a sick fraternity pledge who went to the infirmary in May of 1961 complaining of "severe diarrhea and abdominal cramps," according to a memo from a school physician. After the doctor discovered that the pledge had been forced to drink several bottles of citrate of magnesia as part of a hazing ritual, he sent a memorandum to Dean of Men Jacobs registering his displeasure. Jacobs followed with another memo to fraternity presidents, referring to a pledge who had recently died in California. "Please assure yourselves and me that this kind of thing will not happen again," he wrote.

His request fell on deaf ears. Two years later, another chapter was suspended for a prank that involved two of their pledges who were dropped off in the country by members and who fabricated a story for the police who picked them up for hitchhiking. Three fraternities also were placed on social probation for violating university drinking restrictions.

As the 1970s arrived, the same problems remained from the previous decade. In 1971, the position of Greek Area Coordinator was established, with Robert Mansfield as its first appointee. His annual report of that year documents the same critical state that Sullivan spoke of. Mansfield expressed hope for the future, citing examples of initiatives that could be undertaken to boost membership, image, and morale. By the mid-1970s, fraternities were experiencing higher membership and renewed interest. University officials, in one newspaper account, asserted that the organizations were returning to their founders' values.

Dean Farrell, however, disagrees with that conclusion. "It was a resurgence of illegal bars," he says. The state drinking age during most of the 1970s was 18, so beer was free-flowing not only at the fraternities but also in university dormitories. As the end of the decade approached, the state raised the drinking age to 20—prohibiting roughly half of the university's students from drinking in the residence halls—and the popularity of the fraternity bars increased. Now, not only were they unlicensed but many houses served minors.

In 1978, a Greek Area Coordinator took action on this issue. She placed limitations on who could acquire liquor licenses and when—only on weekends, and then only one chapter at a time could obtain them. Other university officials cited "a drink-and-destroy image" held by the fraternities and claimed that the liquor-license restrictions would help.

More Hazing Problems

In the mid-1970s, hazing, according to one administrator interviewed in a newspaper, was a "thing of the past." That was before an anonymous letter to the editor of the student newspaper documented horrifying sounds coming from the Chi Alpha Tau house. The author, a member of a university sorority, knew that the sounds were pledges screaming during a hazing ceremony prior to initiation.

In the 1980s, more hazing came back to light for the university community. In November 1988, the county paper reported that fourteen pledges of Chi Alpha Tau were doused in cold water as they slept and were sodomized with carrots as part of their initiation. The vice president of student affairs closed the fraternity for two years. Ironically, the state had just passed anti-hazing legislation at the beginning of the year, which stated that any "method of initiation that 'willfully or recklessly endangers the physical or mental health of any student'" was illegal.

Nationwide, a growing number of pledging-related deaths occurred in the late 1980s.

Zoning Changes

Around this same time, the town took an action that indicated that the patience they had with the fraternity system had worn thin. On November 14, 1988, the town voted to rezone the campus residence district containing fraternity row into a general residence area. Once a house was sold, the bylaw said it could no longer be reinstated as a chapter house. Existing houses could remain, but the law's passage meant a reduction in the number of houses in that area over time.

A Problematic Chapter

The file marked "Eta Xi Rho" in the cabinets of the university's Greek Affairs Office details a chapter that required high maintenance with little evidence that members took reform seriously. In March 1989, a letter from Dean of Students Martin Donovan informed the members of Eta Xi Rho that their recognition had been terminated for a large number of alcohol violations and illegal party citations. Even communication from the chapter's alumni did not effect positive change among the fraternity members. An August 1988 letter from a member of Eta Xi Rho's Eta Corporation (their local alumni group) expressed protest and severe disappointment about the condition of the house, the financial devastation of the chapter, and the attitudes of the fraternity's leadership.

In spite of a bad track record, in 1990, Eta Xi Rho was once again granted recognition. The fraternity reverted back to its old ways a few years later. In October 1997, the county newspaper describes activities at Eta Xi Rho's address that violated school regulations or the law. Students inside and outside the structure were seen to be sick, incapacitated, or both. Reports charged that those under the drinking age of 21 appeared to be in the majority. The reporters witnessed no efforts on the part of the fraternity members to actively ensure the safety of those attending the party; none were checking identification or providing any other type of control. In 1999, citing repeated violations of policies and a fight which had recently occurred at the house, the charter of Eta Xi Rho was once again pulled by the university.

The chapter was readmitted in 2002.

Sexual Assaults

In 1996, two fraternity houses endured accusations of sexual assaults that had allegedly occurred in their houses. The Lambda Psi Beta house was accused of two rapes in one month. Police eventually did not file charges against anyone, but the house self-destructed. Members trashed the house when they left.

Also in 1996, a 20-year-old university student filed a lawsuit against Phi Omicron Zeta, claiming that she was sexually assaulted in the basement of the house. The lawsuit claimed the fraternity had been negligent, citing failure on its part to provide "protection and security when she attended the party." In September of that year, the fraternity and the woman's attorney reached an out-of-court settlement totaling $200,000. Shortly thereafter, the university chapter of Phi Omicron Zeta closed its doors, reorganized, and reopened the chapter three years later.

Chapter House Fire

In October of 2001, the Xi Chi Beta chapter house at the university was destroyed by a fast-moving fire. The cause was an unattended candle which had been placed too close to bedding, and twenty-three brothers lost their residence. I was there as one of the first university officials on the scene. A police captain told me that I should be glad that this happened at 2 P.M. and not twelve hours later that Friday night. "The way this house has been going, I don't know how many dead people we'd be pulling out of there," he told me. The fire-detection equipment had been disabled, perhaps to keep cigarette smoke from setting off the alarm. At a meeting the following week, the town fire chief told members of Greek organizations that if the detection equipment had been operating properly, the house might have been saved. Also, when town fire officials conducted surprise inspections of the other houses the day after the Xi Chi Beta fire, they found detection equipment similarly covered up in two other houses—though tampering with fire-detection equipment is a federal criminal offense.

No Real Power

One chapter cannot be singled out as the biggest troublemaker. A town police officer says that "it seems like every semester they take turns." One semester, the officer informed Interfraternity Council members that they should expect undercover officers to be visiting chapter houses to enforce, among other things, the legal drinking age. The following weekend, officers with a search warrant confiscated beer and $1,500 in party profits from a fraternity house. "They didn't listen," he said. "Instead of 'How can we make these problems stop?' it was 'How can we get around the rules; how can we keep from getting caught?'"

The officer, who asked that his name be withheld, criticized the way the university administration handled the discipline of the fraternities. Greek Affairs directors often give a chapter "social probation," theoretically limiting its ability to have gatherings with alcohol. But "it doesn't mean anything," the officer said. Dean Farrell agreed, offering that assigning *responsibility* over the fraternities—as the Greek Affairs director is given—has nothing to do with exerting *control* over people.

In the fall of 2001, as a staff member of the Greek Affairs Office, I accompanied the town building inspector and fire chief as the office made its semiannual inspections. I found the sorority facilities to be livable. The fraternities, however, were far below minimum standards. While I respected the right of students to live however they wanted, it was clear that few men had made any effort to make their places look respectable—or in any way congruent to their purported values.

My research leads me to conclude that the university's administrators, national-level Greek officials, and local alumni would be well advised to devise more effective strategies to deal with problematic students and their chapters. To use a metaphor employed by a fraternity official in Hank Nuwer's *Wrongs of Passage* (1999), social probation for fraternities is like "trying to place a Band-Aid on something that [needs] heart surgery."

My exploration here tells me that the university's fraternity system also needs heart surgery.

9 A Sorority Executive's Perspective on Hazing: A Conversation with Holiday Hart McKiernan

Conducted by Hank Nuwer

Editor's note: *Holiday Hart McKiernan is an attorney and past executive director of Alpha Chi Omega [female] fraternity. She speaks frequently on ways of addressing alcohol and hazing in student groups.*

Nuwer: The number of deaths from sorority hazing is low and in National Panhellenic Conference (NPC) groups but one person, albeit one too many, has died in a hazing. True, since 1988, the number of reported hazing cases is higher than the number of reported cases prior to 1988, but then again, the education programs put on by many national sororities are far more sophisticated and prevalent in the 2000s. Is there still cause for national sorority and female fraternity executives to promote education and to remain vigilant?

McKiernan: Although tragedies from sorority hazing are not reported, it does appear that women participating in inappropriate new-member activities is continuing, if not increasing. I find this quite troubling. A new member should be engaged in the Greek experience through affirming activities. Anything that demeans or belittles a woman is not acceptable.

I firmly believe national organizations must promote the value of the Greek experience—hazing has no place in that experience. Unfortunately, the use of alcohol limits the ability of women to exercise wise judgment when planning and executing new-member activities. We must continue to facilitate the conversation about the Greek experience and challenge undergraduates to use their skills to create a positive community.

Nuwer: Certainly hazing in male groups has been characterized by unintended deaths, particularly where alcohol or physical mishandling of pledges has occurred, but what does your research tell you the characteristics of hazing in female groups tend to be?

McKiernan: Our experience is that alcohol misuse is frequently at the heart of the hazing activity. Hazing takes two basic forms. First, members challenge new members to participate in high-risk drinking, for example drinking numerous shots. This high-risk drinking may result in alcohol poisoning and health risks. The second form of hazing, which is linked to the first, is that new members are encouraged to participate in at best foolish and at worst humiliating conduct.

This conduct often includes activities that demean women with respect to men. Frankly, these activities are appalling—especially in 2003. I have not seen hazing that is physically challenging. What crosses my desk is embarrassing and humiliating conduct.

Nuwer: Studies by Alfred University have produced thousands of questionnaires filled out by male and female college and high school athletes that show a troubling frequency of hazing in athletic groups. Since some sorority women are varsity athletes, have you seen any connection between the two that seems to merit a heads-up as sororities educate their members?

McKiernan: The comparison to athletes is an intriguing one. I believe there is value in athletic organizations and Greek organizations pooling their talents to address shared issues. Currently, I do not have data that would suggest that as more women are involved in athletics there has been an increase in hazing within Alpha Chi Omega.

Nuwer: Hazing has long been a presence on campuses, but current awareness programs, hazing policies, and tougher sanctions for incidents can be seen as a more recent phenomenon. What remains to be done from your point of view?

McKiernan: It is interesting that the education efforts have been increased and yet there still remains an issue as to undergraduates appreciating why hazing has no place within the Greek experience. College students want to find a community, a part of the campus environment to which they can belong. They want a community that provides the support needed. It seems that changing a culture is challenging when those [who are] part of the culture fail to see the value in that change. Students do not want anyone to be hurt. That is valued. But when traditions are seen as part of the culture, a culture they value, students find it difficult to either disregard or change those traditions. I believe that our efforts need to be redirected away from policies and enforcement to engaging undergraduates in describing what they could form as an organization if they were creating that today.

But even more important than changing traditions and a hazing culture is the need to change the high-risk alcohol culture. As hazing and alcohol are so intertwined, I suggest that by addressing the high-risk alcohol culture and truly working to change that paradigm, the hazing culture would also change.

Nuwer: Financially, does the cost of insurance reflect the potential high costs to a sorority if a settlement or trial loss occurs because of hazing or related risk-taking behavior?

McKiernan: Insurance is an issue for all businesses—Greek organizations are no exception. Alpha Chi Omega's insurance costs have been driven most recently more by the market conditions that have been created following September 11th [2001] than by claims experience.

Nuwer: Since sorority houses are dry by mandate, when a sorority or female fraternity does haze with alcohol, does this strike you as particularly problematic? How so?

McKiernan: Alcohol and hazing. The two, in my opinion, go together. Rarely do we have a hazing problem that does not also include alcohol. Interestingly, hazing rarely occurs within the chapter house. Hazing most often is off site, but I don't believe that is because the chapter house is a substance-free environment.

What I find very troubling is that a high-risk alcohol culture has manifested itself in Greek life—a culture that the national leadership does not value. This high-risk alcohol culture leads to a multitude of harmful outcomes, including hazing and sexual assault. I suggest that part of the way to address hazing is to address the high-risk alcohol culture. Changing that culture requires a commitment from the institution, from the Greek organizations, and from the students. The entire higher education community must see the high-risk alcohol culture as undermining not only the Greek experience but higher education as well.

Nuwer: A small but troubling number of incidents has occurred among female athletes and female fraternity members where males have gotten involved in the actual hazing. From a safety and ethical standpoint, should this cause concern to those who oversee such groups?

McKiernan: Men being involved in hazing women. This is troubling for several reasons. First, including men where there is alcohol and peer pressure to be accepted by a group provides a context that is not safe. But what is perhaps even more disturbing about a scenario as has been outlined is that women would place other women in such a position. The culture of Greek life needs to focus less on the social interaction between the men and women's groups and more on what each of the groups and their members need to succeed. Clearly the fraternity and sorority experience is a social experience. But by what social means needs to be considered from the perspective of the founding of Greek organizations.

Nuwer: The numbers of scholarly studies that examine only female hazing are small at this time. From any discipline, where would you see strong possibilities for relevant research in the area of hazing?

McKiernan: Data on female hazing would be very helpful. It would be helpful to learn the context in which the hazing takes place as well as why the individual participated in the hazing. We need to learn how to empower women, women who want to be accepted, to refuse to participate in activities that are demeaning and humiliating. I would suggest that research be conducted on campuses that are rich in tradition—[on] campuses that have a history of Greek life.

Nuwer: More so than hazing, the number of deaths of sorority members from alcohol-related accidents (traffic, falls in male fraternity houses, drug-related OD at party) is a concern for those who supervise Greeks. The annual studies from the Harvard School of Public Health and other surveys show little evidence of a reverse of risky behaviors. What do you suggest be done?

McKiernan: The high-risk alcohol environment is truly harming Greek life. Greek life must be a complement to the academic mission of the host institution—there must a value to the institution in having a Greek community. Today, on many campuses, administrators would be challenged to articulate the value that Greek organizations add to the institution. It is time to change the culture. The report of the National Institute on Alcohol Abuse and Alcoholism (NIAAA) has put Greek organizations and higher education on notice. Greeks are a high-risk population. Strategies must be adopted that will change this culture. But it will take more than just the Greek organizations—this effort needs to include the entire campus community, and the leadership needs to begin with the president of the institution. The institution must have mechanisms that hold the undergraduate chapters accountable.

The NIAAA report suggests strategies that have been successful. Together we must strive to change the college drinking culture. This change needs to begin now.

10 Military Hazing

Hank Nuwer

Editor's note: *In the late 1980s, my interest in hazing in frater-nal groups expanded to an interest in why and how military organizations engage in hazing and initiations. By 2003, I had interviewed current and/or past members of military groups who condoned hazing in U.S., East German, and Czech units. I have written about military hazing in my book* Broken Pledges *and for* American Legion *magazine. As a disclosure, I am a dues-paying member of the Sons of the American Legion.*

Hazing. The word itself gives a commanding officer the shakes, conjuring up inquiries from Congress, visits from reporters, long-distance calls from mothers. Precisely what military hazing *is*, however, defies definition. One recruit's hazing is another recruit's "shape up" exercises. Most civilian definitions of hazing fail to take account of its varied meanings in military life. Then there are the wide number of ways hazing can be applied to rituals in the military: The term is used to describe a good-natured punch on the stripes when someone is pro-moted, horseplay, or, rarely, criminal assaults during equator or Great Lakes crossings and harsh boot camp activities when superiors or peers say they must try to transform a balky recruit into a trustworthy team player. There also are degrees of hazing and degrees of people in the military who are crossing lines that shouldn't be crossed.

Of course, over time a Black Forest of paper pulp has been devoted to con-gressional investigations into hazing—called "dibbling" as a slang term at West Point in the nineteenth century—at the military service academies. Although national hazing scandals occurred at West Point in 1881, 1900–1901, 1907, 1917, 1973, 1976, 1979, and 1990, none caught a shocked nation's attention so much as a congressional inquiry ordered by President William McKinley after the death of plebe Oscar Booz. Following evasive testimony by cadet Douglas MacArthur and others, the committee uncovered brutal beatings and even tor-ture, and though it concluded that Booz had been savagely abused, his death was health related, not hazing related. The family of Booz disagreed with that assessment.

Of course, not only the U.S. military hazes. Hazing in Canadian, Czech, and

Russian armed forces is widespread. In former East Germany, veteran soldiers in the army used to beat newcomers on the back with a strap and demand types of servitude, according to former soldier Uwe Zenner, who spoke in a conversation with me in Dresden in January 2003. In Russia, many first-year soldiers die at the hands of their superiors, whom they call "grandfathers." While no verifiable numbers have been published, published claims say that deaths from hazing, killings by recruits to revenge hazing, and accidents occurring as the result of hazing may reach the thousands, and they arguably served to destroy morale and discipline in the former Soviet and current Russian military. In addition to whippings, some recruits endure sadistic acts such as the demand to lick a toilet bowl clean, says Charles Moskos, a Northwestern University sociology professor and chairman of the Inter-University Seminar on Armed Forces and Society.

Significantly, hazing experts such as Charles Moskos and Lionel Tiger make some significant distinctions between military hazing and, for example, fraternity hazing. The purpose and end result of military hazing—keeping troops alive—doesn't apply to Greeks bearing paddles. Nonetheless, many fraternity members in trouble with a dean for hazing point to military practices in a losing effort to justify their own illicit actions.

Although the first scandals involving hazing in U.S. service academies began over a century ago, the general public heard little about hazing in the military branches until 1956. That year all training procedures went under a microscope following the drowning deaths of marine recruits at Parris Island. Demands that military hazing stop escalated in the late 1960s after one national magazine exposed unusually vigorous artillery Officer Candidate School (OCS) hazing conducted by Vietnam returnees.

Today stories about hazing in the military are commonplace. Following inquiries by Senators Richard Lugar and Dan Quayle of Indiana, details emerged of the savage hazing and sodomizing with carrots dipped in axle grease of young coast guard enlistee Joe Branson aboard the *CGC Mesquite* during a Great Lakes crossing on November 11, 1986. In addition, three marines were charged with miscellaneous offenses in 1999 on Okinawa, Japan, after an initiation allegedly injured the hand of a marine. A 1998 scandal occurred at Fort Knox after a recruit's marine classmates beat him during a ritual-like "love session." Video recordings of marine paratroopers involved in so-called blood-pinning rituals filled the airwaves from 1991 to 1997. In 2002, a military court found Lt. Cmdr. Jeffrey B. Martin of Virginia's Oceana Naval Air Station guilty of hazing and other crimes, sentencing him to five days in jail and a $10,000 fine. On June 5, 2002, *The Virginian-Pilot* of Norfolk, Virginia, noted that Martin could have received a sentence of up to 37½ years "for hazing, theft and dereliction of duty." The paper noted one witness statement that Martin had "tacked on the crows"; that is, that he pierced skin with a subordinate's promotion pin.

Like Martin, dozens of hazers were disciplined in military justice courts during the 1990s and 2000s for miscellaneous offenses. Julian Neiser, a former drill instructor, worked at Parris Island and saw the careers of men he considered honorable self-destruct. "I've seen guys who were excellent marines, combat veterans, guys who were extremely qualified, do something stupid to a recruit," says Neiser. "Before they knew it their career was ruined. They were wearing an orange jumpsuit and picking up trash on the side of the road."

What's responsible for today's furor over hazing? Joe Jansen, a former marine sergeant from Indianapolis, points to instantaneous communication on the Internet and on CNN. In particular, witnesses to hazing use video cameras to capture secretive rituals on tape and give or sell them to media producers, who can count on a quick ratings shot in the arm, he says.

The result is public outrage. "I don't think that society has a natural aversion to rites of passage and ritual," says Jansen. "But I think that society does have an aversion to senseless brutality."

Ironically, some hazing activities continue in spite of the U.S. press's scrutiny. Richard (Rich) Sigal, a New Jersey sociologist who gives public seminars on hazing, says press scrutiny fails to check all but the most severe hazing, driving it underground and causing officials to give lip service to eliminating it.

Then too, because hazing is perceived by many soldiers to build trust, to continue tradition, and to instill discipline, it shows little evidence of disappearing altogether. While the U.S. Navy has declared hazing verboten, some clandestine, if subdued, vestiges remain of old "Order of Neptune" initiations when a "pollywog" or "landlubber" crosses the equator for the first time and is initiated by veteran "seafarers" or "shellbacks." At its least harmful aspect, the initiation involves noncriminal donning of silly apparel.

More seriously, the hazing scandal at Fort Knox, in particular, has caused a domino effect. Late-night barracks inspections are far more frequent in recent years. Why keep hazing around at all, considering the risks to career and reputation? For one thing, not much time has passed since expressions such as "this man's army" were common. A well-known sociologist, Lionel Tiger of Rutgers University, says the public's zeroing in on hazing in the military is part of a general process of what he terms "feminization in community."

What's happening in society is that women increasingly have been assuming previously male roles and responsibilities in the military, workplace, and even at home—many are rearing children without a male's presence. "The norms of female behavior are increasingly and successfully applied to male behavior," says Tiger, author of *The Decline of Males* and a Pentagon consultant.

That means that hazing has been increasingly frowned upon by the society Tiger describes. Though some 1990s women have begun to haze, perhaps to attract tough men or to display toughness themselves, the practice essentially has been a guy thing, says Tiger, whose research made the term "male bonding" a household term. As a consequence, navy chiefs who make a new chief wear a dress as part of an acceptance stunt may not get into trouble for criminal hazing, but they do risk censure from feminists should word leak out about their activities, says Tiger.

Experts suspect it's not the actual hazing that superglues young recruits together but the sharing of experiences that try their souls and give a feeling of satisfaction if endured. "Going through shared misery is what bonds people, not hazing per se," Moskos says. The troops get tighter as a unit when they can laugh about their troubles.

After lights go out during basic training, jokesters usually start a running banter. They good-naturedly make fun of the system and the drill sergeants that tell them they are tearing them down to put them back together. Recruits that were dressed down and humiliated that day can re-invent their experiences in a humorous light by seeing how things looked through the eyes of their fellow soldiers. Often they laugh until the tears come, says Moskos, then hop to their tasks the next morning with new resolve.

Maj. John Jansen, a marine stationed in a California unit of the Airwings, says a matter of degree separates activities that constitute an acceptable military rite of passage and unacceptable behavior that rightfully gets perpetrators in trouble with the Uniform Code of Military Justice.

For Maj. Jansen (brother of Joe Jansen), a nonobjectionable and perhaps necessary rite of passage would be a symbolic gesture to acknowledge a soldier's new rank, so long as that might involve nothing more than a nonhurtful, symbolic blow. As an example, he notes that when a lance corporal becomes a corporal and noncommissioned officer, his peers and sometimes his superiors will punch him on the "blood stripe" on the outside of his dress blue trousers. No nudity or any suffering more than momentary stinging pain is involved. Yet I have talked with a female former marine who did not object aloud at the time to being punched at promotion time but thought the ritual moronic.

Jansen sees no justification in the marine paratrooper blood-pinning rituals that have been shown in gruesome detail on television and Internet news programs. In various videotapes that surfaced between 1991 and 1997, marines were shown ramming symbolic gold-winged pins into the chests of those who had fulfilled a ten-jump requirement. "That was so wrong it wasn't funny," says Maj. Jansen. "The guys looked like captives, screaming, yelling, and gnashing their teeth. . . . This kind of hazing, no question, is wrong and the Marine Corps doesn't countenance that kind of behavior."

In fact, in 1997, both U.S. defense secretary William S. Cohen and Marine Commandant Gen. Charles Krulak deplored such pinning. Subsequent investigations resulted in a flurry of punishments and demotions for those judged guilty.

Consider military rites of passage that cause neither injuries nor lasting pain and aren't taken to dangerous extremes by sadists or negligent individuals. At least one expert thinks they should be tolerated within reason, seeing value over a long period of time in the tribal initiations that signify and shape a child's entrance into adulthood. "You can't have a rite of passage without some hazing," says Moskos, who vigorously condemns hazing taken to an extreme. "A zero tolerance for hazing is counterproductive."

Sociology and psychology are still academic infants compared to some other disciplines. No reputable scholar has spent time fully studying the pro and con effects of rites of passage in a military setting, although several have written about pollywog ceremonies for scholarly journals interested in folklore.

What investigations into behavior during initiations per se that have been done are old and in need of reassessment. An oft-cited 1958 study, financed by the National Science Foundation, tried to assess the effect of severity of initiation on liking for a group. The research, performed by researchers Elliot Aronson and Judson Mills (the latter then with the U.S. Army Leadership Human Research Unit, HumRRO), determined that a severe initiation did make individuals like a group more. Curiously, in that experiment the test subjects were all women, and the "severe" initiation was the reading of obscene text or words. These two conditions, given Tiger's observation that males and females view hazing differently, may quite possibly signify that a new study of severe military initiations might show males responding in a negative fashion to their outfits.

Certainly Tom Hohan, now a New Orleans businessman, outright rejects any suggestion that the intense physical hazing he endured to complete OCS training in the late 1960s made him like his artillery outfit more. "I hated it," he says.

Nor did he bond with his fellow recruits, all of whom were competing with him for officer slots. "Out of the 74 or 76 who graduated I'd be surprised if 10 percent would differ from me about hating it."

Drafted out of a Pennsylvania steel mill in 1968, Hohan joined 140 other males in artillery Officer Candidate School at Fort Sill. A mere 40 percent graduated, including Hohan, one of only two non-college men to do so.

Hazing—or a combination of hazing and discipline building—claimed the rest, says Hohan, who since has become a University of South Carolina graduate. "Hazing during OCS was legendary and the POW camp you had to experience if [you were] caught during an escape-and-evasion exercise was pure hell."

Hohan has vivid recollections of the two years, ten months, and three days he spent in the military. He recalls asking permission to swallow bites of food half the size of a thumbnail. He recalls saluting a goldfish and waiting for it to swim around and face him before he was allowed to shower. Mostly he recalls a torturous prisoner-of-war simulation that seemed more real to him than an exercise. Hardened veterans back from Vietnam had the OCS candidates lift telephone poles, endure long periods in stocks, and maneuver through mud laced with traces of fecal material.

All that would make Hohan a firm opponent of hazing then—right? Wrong. "It helped me survive," says Hohan, who says the hazing gave him the mental toughness to survive in Vietnam and to survive punishing deadlines in the real world after his mustering out. "OCS and all the hazing steeled me, taught me how to react and function. . . . It was a very intense part of my training and it taught me I could survive."

Neiser, now living in Pittsburgh and attending law school, agrees with that assessment. He cautions that turning out sloppy soldiers who can't be counted on in wartime is no solution to the hazing problem. Every day that Neiser exited through the rear hatch of the school at Parris Island he reread a sign that bore into his very core. "Let no man's ghost say, 'If only your training program had done its job.'"

On the other hand, hazing practices internationally—most seriously in Russian and former-Soviet-bloc military organizations—have led to the deaths of thousands of soldiers over time. In 2002 alone, Russia admitted that more than 2,000 hazing reports had been documented. One has to wonder, what might all those ghosts say if they could speak?

11 Rites of Passage and Group Bonding in the Canadian Airborne

Donna Winslow

Editor's note: *Author Donna Winslow has earned an interna-tional reputation for her research documenting Canadian Air-borne Regiment initiation rituals.*

In January 1995, the Canadian public was shocked by videotaped scenes of hu-miliating and, at times, disgusting initiation rites in One Commando of the Canadian Airborne Regiment (CAR). It may seem incomprehensible to an out-sider that the initiates actually participated voluntarily in these rites. Yet the im-portance of the ritual is, in part, a reflection of the nature of unit requirements at this stage. Initiates are strangers to each other and to the Airborne, and the bonding of the initiation pulls them together in a very short period of time.

The impact of this extreme form of initiation was noted as early as the 1950s, when Aronson and Mills remarked that an initiate who endures severe hazing is likely to find membership in a group all the more appealing, because in these rituals soldiers prove their readiness to participate in the group regardless of personal cost and thus gain peer-group acceptance.[1] As one soldier put it: "I am proud to have done it; it proves to myself and others that as a member of the Canadian Airborne Regiment, I will face and overpass any challenge or tasking given to me."

Unit Cohesion

This chapter speaks directly to the issue of primary-group bonding and unconventional methods for promoting unit cohesion. Conventional army training intensifies the power of group pressure within its ranks by teaching recruits the need for teamwork. Teamwork, or cohesion, is one of the ways in which the army can marshal the capabilities of each individual member for the pursuit of a common goal. In the words of one Canadian soldier:

> You have a bond. You have a bond that's so thick that it is unbelievable! . . . It's the pull, it's the team, the work as a team, the team spirit! I don't think that ever leaves a guy. That is exactly what basic training is supposed to do. It's supposed to weed

out those who aren't willing to work that way. . . . And that's the whole motivation, that when somebody says we want you to do something then you'll do it. You'll do it because of the team, for the team, with the team and because the team has the same focus.[2]

In the Airborne, group bonding is particularly intense because the men must depend upon each other each time they jump. A member of the team will make sure that they exit the aircraft in a secure spot and another member of the team will perform the safety check on their equipment. In fact, some authors have likened the jump experience itself to a rite of passage,[3] and the discussion below shows how the Canadian Airborne Regiment's initiation rites parody the exercises of the Airborne Indoctrination Course (Airborne basic training) and the trust necessary for the parachute jump experience. Thus, both formal and informal experience promote the dependence of the individual on the group.[4]

The discussion begins with a brief description of the Canadian Airborne Regiment, formal initiation into the Regiment (the Airborne Indoctrination Course), and informal initiation rites. One Commando's initiation rites are presented in detail using models developed in anthropology to describe rites of passage in traditional societies, which occur in three stages.

The first occurs when the initiates' former identities are stripped away and they are set apart and made like one another. They are leveled into a homogeneous group in an effort to suppress individuality, thus encouraging an investment in the group.

Initiates then enter the liminal phase of the rite, in which events become parodies and inversions of real life and group bonding is reinforced as the initiates undergo similar processes of testing and humiliation.

In the final stage, initiates are reincorporated into the group as members of the Regiment. After this discussion of One Commando's rites I look at hazing and rites of passage in the other two commando units of the Canadian Airborne Regiment and conclude with a discussion of the use of extreme initiation in primary-group bonding.

Research Background

Research for this chapter was carried out in 1995–1997 during preparation of a study of Airborne culture for the Commission of Inquiry into the Deployment of Canadian Forces to Somalia.[5] Its interpretations and analysis were based on over fifty in-depth interviews in addition to several focus groups held with military personnel from a variety of ranks and with some of their families. Interviewees were selected randomly, through word of mouth, and were conducted almost exclusively with former Airborne soldiers and military personnel who were deployed to Somalia, although several were carried out with people who had been involved with the Airborne but not deployed to Somalia. The names and identity of my interviewees have been disguised so that they are all referred to in this text as "Canadian Airborne soldier."[6]

I have also drawn upon testimony to the Commission of Inquiry itself. The soldiers and officers who testified are identified in the public transcripts and therefore here as well. I also viewed the footage of three videotapes that were taken during the initiation rites that were entered in the public record of the Commission of Inquiry and military police reports of investigations of these videos.

Brief Background on Paratroops in Canada

The Canadian Airborne Regiment was formed in 1968.[7] The aim was to create a light, highly mobile mini-formation capable of small-unit or light-formation operations in virtually any climate or geographic region in the world. It was to specialize in northern operations and maintain a high state of readiness for peacekeeping commitments. From 1968 to 1977, the 900-man CAR was based in Edmonton. According to the Regiment's last commanding officer:

> The Regiment's trademark for tough, fast-paced and challenging training was firmly established in the initial years. An array of exercises was conducted embracing Canada's West Coast, a variety of locations in the Canadian Arctic, Alaska, and Jamaica as well as schools in unarmed combat, mountaineering and skiing.[8]

In the early 1970s, due to pressure for equal representation, the Airborne acquired a Francophone commando unit; thus, the CAR was constituted of men and officers sent from each of the three Canadian army regiments. The Canadian army has regimental divisions reflecting geographic and linguistic divisions in Canada; for example, western Anglophone (PPCLI, Princess Patricia's Canadian Light Infantry), central and eastern Anglophone (the RCR, The Royal Canadian Regiment), and central Francophone (Royal 22e Regiment, known as the "Van Doos" in English). These territorial divisions define areas of recruitment, training, and residence for regimental members.

In the 1970s all members of the Airborne, even the Van Doos, worked and mingled together in western Canada in a base near the large urban area of Edmonton. The 1970 October Crisis [in which separatists kidnapped Quebec's labor minister] was the first test of the Canadian Airborne Regiment in operation. The unit performed a number of internal security missions in Montreal. At that same time, the CAR was a UN standby unit. They mobilized in thirty-six hours to go to the Middle East but were not sent. However, in 1974, One Commando was sent on a rotation to Cyprus and after the Turkish invasion, the rest of the unit joined One Commando on tour. This earned the unit two Stars of Courage and six Medals of Bravery, but the price was over thirty casualties and two deaths. In 1976, the CAR was again deployed to Montreal, this time as security for the Olympic games.

In 1977, the unit was moved to a more remote base in Ontario, Canadian Forces Base Petawawa, near the Quebec border. According to Kenward, the last commanding officer of the Airborne Regiment, this was a watershed event, during which significant structural changes occurred, including a reduction in strength and loss of independent formation status.[9] Our interviewees also felt there had been a significant change: "When the Airborne moved to Petawawa it really hurt their pride. A lot of people said that they wouldn't go to Petawawa" (Canadian Airborne soldier). Further change was imposed with the creation of three separate exclusive rifle commandos around the three parent regiments, the RCR, PPCLI, and R122eR. One Airborne Headquarters and Signal Squadron and One Airborne Service Commando were also created.

> Up [until] 1977, two commandos represented the Airborne's infantry component—Commando, which was manned by R22eR (Van Doos), and Two Commando, which was manned by the PPCLI and RCR. From 1977 on, the regiment had three commandos—One Commando, Two Commando (made up of PPCLI only), and a new Three Commando (made up of RCR). (Canadian Airborne soldier)

The Airborne reflected the linguistic and geographic divisions in the Canadian Army—Two Commando (western Anglophone and PPCLI), Three Commando (central and eastern Anglophone and RCR), and One Commando (central Francophone and R22eR, the "Van Doos"). Soldiers and officers were encouraged to rotate in and out of the unit in order to gain jump and command experience. Some of our interviewees felt that the purpose of having the three commandos was to enable regiments to track their own people and thus control promotion and performance evaluations.

> When the commandos moved to Petawawa, Two Commando had just Delta Company and Echo Company, and their Echo Company became Three Commando. They would try to post all RCRs into Three Commando and all the Patricias into Two Commando. But the Patricias serving in Echo Company remained in Three Commando and the RCRs in Two Commando remained as well, until it was their turn to be posted out. One reason is that it's easier for the career managers to man and deal with their own regiment within One Commando. (Canadian Airborne soldier)

The result of this administrative change was that commando units no longer mixed with each other regularly; they lived on base in separate barracks and did not mingle with each other socially. In particular, the Francophones and Anglophones remained separate. Each began to develop its own particular subculture; that is, its own way of doing things and an associated identity. One Commando from the R22eR was French and sported the fleur-de-lis flag of the Province of Quebec in their barracks. Two Commando, drawn from the PPCLI, began to adopt the rebel flag, and Three Commando from the RCR became known as quiet professionals with the motto of "never pass a fault" (a slogan that means that Canadian Airborne Regiment members pay close attention to detail and offer full accountability). What is important for our research is the separateness of the commandos; little teamwork occurred outside each specific group. Thus, each commando began to develop its own practices for indoctrinating new members into the group.

In 1981 and 1986, the CAR did two more tours in Cyprus. In 1991, the regiment prepared for a UN deployment in the Western Sahara but did not go. A year later the regiment was again downsized, this time to a battalion structure of 665. The commanding officer went from being a full colonel to a lieutenant colonel, and the officers commanding—who were majors—were reduced to company commanders under the authority of the commanding officer:

> The command structure of the Canadian Airborne Regiment changed in the summer of 1992. It went from being commanded by a full Colonel, with the powers of a commanding officer, to being downgraded to a subunit commanded by a Lieutenant Colonel. Each of the Commandos, in the summer of 1992, was commanded by a Commanding Officer, a Lieutenant Colonel. In the summer of 1992 they became Officers Commanding. They were Majors and had no powers of punishment. There is a difference between being a Lieutenant Colonel, Commanding Officer or being an Officer Commanding as a Major.[10]

This represented a considerable loss in power and prestige for the unit, as the following quotation demonstrates:

> I suspect that the downsizing affected the Airborne. They downsized it by reducing the number of commanding personnel. So does it have an effect? Sure, anytime you take away a position of status and power, the influence you have and the prestige that you carry are similarly reduced. It has to be. And that's because we have an organization built on visible hierarchy. (Canadian Airborne soldier)

The Disbanding of the Airborne: A Summary

Immediately after downsizing began, the CAR went on its last mission to Somalia.[11] Following incidents during the Somalia mission where Somali citizens lost their lives and shocking videos were released to the media—one filmed in Somalia containing racist behavior among members of Two Commando and another of initiation/hazing rites in One Commando[12]—the CAR was disbanded in January 1995.

What is important to note from the above discussion is that by the 1980s, the Airborne was a constituted regiment; it was made up of members drawn from the three other army regiments in Canada. Although Airborne soldiers were "three time volunteers" (volunteering to be in the military, the army, and then the Airborne), the Regiment still needed to meld the men into a fighting unit quickly. In this way the initiation rites served to create bonds among a group of men whose primary loyalties had previously been to their parent regiment, not the Airborne Regiment or its commando units.

Airborne Rituals

Culture is a social force that controls patterns of organizational behavior. It shapes members' cognition and perceptions of meanings and realities. It provides affective energy for mobilization and identifies who belongs to the group and who does not.[13] As in the other army regiments, the Airborne had its own distinctive subculture, in which abstract ideals of brotherhood and harmony, love and union, sacrifice and cooperation, loyalty and discipline, were translated and formulated into concrete aspects of style. They were manifested through a variety of symbols and symbolic patterns and created a definitive and specific pattern of work and life.[14]

A soldier or officer joined the Airborne Regiment by first applying to take a jump course. After training, the soldier or officer received his jump wings and returned to his parent regiment. He then applied to join the Airborne Regiment and, in one of the next posting seasons, his parent regiment sent him to the Airborne. It is important to note that postings in the Airborne were intended to last only a couple of years, but in practice many men, particularly non-commissioned members, requested to stay on in the Airborne. Thus, in practice, officers tended to rotate in and out of the regiment while the men stayed on.

New members learned airborne history during the Airborne Indoctrination Course (AIC, one of the Regiment's socialization mechanisms). Soldiers were taught a sense of duty and that they had a debt to the past, to those who had fought and died in previous wars.

> When you hear about Airborne, it's the pride that strikes you. It goes back to World War II, Normandy and all that. They land and they're already upon the enemy and fighting. You never know what's going to happen. It's really something when you get to thinking about it, just jumping out of a plane, you know you've been there. (Canadian Airborne soldier)

The AIC was run either by the Regiment or the commandos. When the AIC was run by the Regiment, it was a method for ensuring that all newly arriving members were trained to one common standard. Once the commandos began organizing their own AIC, there was some variety in the way the course was run. The AIC was essentially a review of military and parachute skills (weapons handling, shooting, first aid, demolition, unarmed combat, rappelling, etc.). Because of the emphasis on physical fitness in the Airborne, the AIC had fitness tests (swimming, running) and drills that met a higher standard than that of regular army units. The AIC was an opportunity for a soldier and an officer to show that he could be a trustworthy member of the group.

> For the young guys, it's a question of gaining confidence and showing the others that they can do it. For the older guys, it's like they check out the younger guys to see who they feel they can trust. You have to be able to trust the guys you're jumping with. Anybody in your group can be checking your equipment, so you have to be able to trust everyone. (Canadian Airborne soldier)

> You're always being tested and if you screw up on the AIC it will come back to haunt you. Because even if it was just a small gang in the woods, news would come and go. They'd know. So for an officer, it was an important time, they'd be testing you, to see what you're made of. If you made it through that week, you'd be okay

for the rest of the time, so long as you didn't screw up. So it's a very important week for an officer. He's got to be on his toes. (Canadian Airborne soldier)

Earning the Coin

At the end of the AIC, there would be a ceremony where new members would receive their Airborne coin—an important symbol of group membership. If someone dropped out of the AIC because of an injury, he did not receive his Airborne coin.

> In the 1970s, they created a kind of coin with the Airborne Regiment crest on one side. And anytime you were going to some place, anywhere in the world; somebody could challenge you to prove you were in the Airborne. You had to show your coin. If you weren't Airborne, you didn't even know the coin existed. It was a pact, a secret code. If you were in danger you could show the coin and people would help you. It was like a secret code we had for the Airborne. (Canadian Airborne soldier)

For the remainder of his life, an Airborne soldier is subject to being challenged—"coined"—by anyone else who has passed the Airborne Indoctrination Course. If he does not immediately display the coin, which he should be proudly carrying at all times, then he is obligated to buy a round of drinks for all the Airborne members who are there. Thus, every member carries his coin with him at all times.

The Camouflage Crayon Ritual

All new members of the Regiment (regardless of rank) would be "cammed" on their first jump with the Regiment. I was told that camming began in the 1980s, a tradition picked up from the Americans, which entailed covering the person's face, head, and hands (all exposed body parts) with camouflage crayon. The other members of the group carded out the crayoning. It was somewhat painful, although not intolerable; however, it was somewhat annoying since the camouflage crayon was hard to wash off afterward. The camming would take place just before the jump when fellow jumpers who had already passed through the experience would grab the initiate(s). The "war paint" would be worn throughout the jump and could afterward be removed.

> The first jump you do with a unit is what they call a cherry jump. The type of things you do for a cherry jump is, you're the only jumper to wear a red helmet. And you're usually camouflage painted by members. Everybody will go through and they will cam you. You usually have to stand there with your hands behind your back or at your side. But you're not allowed to interfere with the camming procedure that's going on. Some of that camming will go hard on your face. You know it's rubbed in. It's scrubbed in. In the ears, in the nose. Cam paint is slapped on very generously and that's a ritual that is still practiced to this day. (Canadian Airborne soldier)

I was body cammed on my first jump with the Airborne. Again, that was tradition —nobody got hurt—all you had to do was take a little bit longer shower. (Canadian Airborne soldier)

If you arrive before the Airborne Indoctrination Course and do your first jump with the Regiment, then you'll get "caromed" from head to toe, everywhere, on your stomach, in your hair, whatever. And anyone can do it to you, whoever thinks of it first. But if you do your first jump while you're on the AIC, count yourself lucky 'cause you won't be cammed, because the AIC jump is an exercise jump and you're already painted anyway, but a lot less than if you were cammed. You won't have it in your hair and all that. (Canadian Airborne soldier)

Booze, Buddies, and Behavior

The Airborne regarded overconsumption of alcohol to be an important part of its initiation rites. It is also important to note that alcohol consumption was generally encouraged in the Airborne.[15]

Oh yeah, the maroon berets are show-offs: "I'm a real man. A man's man. I wear my wings and my maroon beret." When you get older things change. But in the beginning it's fights all the time, women, drugs. Lots of booze. Initiations. You drink and drink. (Canadian Airborne soldier)

Alcohol was very present in the initiations seen in the One Commando videos. Drinking is an important aspect of masculine identity. It can also be an important part of group bonding. As Ingraham has noted in his study of life in an American army barracks, "Soldiering and alcohol have been almost synonymous since the invention of armies."[16] Drinking in the Airborne took the form of sanctioned events that are "beer calls," when an officer would invite the men for a drink. In this case, alcohol was used to mark a regimental event or to mark the end of a workweek. For example, a beer call was always held at the end of the AIC and sometimes on a Friday afternoon.

After a week's work, the group'll get together some place and have a beer call. That's where we can really talk, we've always got something to say to one another. It's a place where we can all relax, because no matter how you look at it, the friction builds up in this work. Here, we can say anything and not worry about who's listening, we don't have to be in uniform. It does us good. (Canadian Airborne soldier)

Drinking allowed men and officers to get together and contributed to a sense of bonding. (Canadian Airborne soldier)

Like, the last time, it was a major who got the beer call going. He bought a case of beer, 'cause when you're new or when you change a group that's what you do. Everybody likes to have a beer when the major's buying a round. It creates an atmosphere where like, I could talk to the major, make a joke, still respecting him, and it would be all right. It's open. It's not like we're working, or doing something serious. It's like we're buddies, not just private, sergeant, and corporal, but buddies. (Canadian Airborne soldier)

Sometimes unsanctioned drinking binges would begin with sanctioned drinking and continue on in the men's quarters after the sanctioned event. In this case, someone would have to drive into town to purchase the cases of beer and bring them back to the base. At other times, the men would continue their drinking on the base in the non-commissioned members' club or in town at the favorite local watering hole. Drinking was at times purely recreational; that is, friends going for a drink. At other times it was affirmational; that is, when the focal activity is alcohol consumption itself.[17] This might mean a bunch of men getting "hammered" on base or it might take the form of bar-hopping. This form of heavy drinking carried with it the danger of reckless driving and bar fights. In 1985, the Hewson Report[18] on discipline problems in the Airborne Regiment found twice the number of assault cases among the Canadian Airborne Regiment than in any other unit and noted that drinking was high in Petawawa. Our interviewees agreed: "I think alcohol is a big problem, a big issue within Canadian Forces Base Petawawa. Drinking and driving were a serious problem on the base" (Canadian Airborne soldier).

The 1993 Military Board of Inquiry into the Airborne's comportment in Somalia suggested a relationship between heavy use of alcohol and incidents of insubordination by members of Two Commando. Private Grant testified to the Military Board of Inquiry that soldiers in Two Commando lost control due to the consumption of alcohol. One of our interviewees agreed.

I think it's just—like when it happens is because a lot of stress in the job, when we drink we kind of drink hard, and that some of the guys go a little overboard—when the guys release, they kind of go all out. (Testimony of Private Grant to the Board of Inquiry, transcripts, vol. V, 1142)

A lot of guys, once alcohol is consumed, lose their self-discipline a lot. And myself included, yes; I'll say pretty much the majority of the commando drank. (Canadian Airborne soldier)

In some cases alcohol was used ceremonially to mark an event. These ceremonies brought together a larger group of men than recreational and affirmational drinking, which was an activity restricted to a small group of friends or a clique.[19]

At the end of that exercise people had post-exercise drills in which we turned our weapons in and did those things which we perceive as normal in the combat arms; turn your weapons in, make sure your kit is all in order to be able to start training the next time the next day. We then met at a designated place, it may have been the . . . It was a place where all ranks could go, probably the top floor of the Junior Ranks Club, where everybody had a beer, or in some cases it could be a mixed drink in a helmet where you, you sort of had a sip of it, pass it to the next guy, signifying that you had passed and completed the requisite training and were now a full-fledged member. (Testimony of Major Martel to the Board of Inquiry)

Initiation Rites

In the initiation rites described below, the consumption of alcohol is an integral part of the ceremony.

Much has been made of One Commando initiation rites in the Canadian media. Very briefly, the videos were of initiation rites, not hazing. Hazing is technically continual abuse over an initial entry period into an organization, such as the first year of cadet school or the few first weeks or months of membership in a college fraternity.[20] [*Ed. note:* Prohibitions against hazing in U.S. and Russian military organizations have a far broader definition of hazing that includes ritual abuse or initiations such as those of navy chiefs.]

Hazing has a long tradition in military academies. The U.S. Secretary of War Board of Inquiry into hazing at West Point in 1908 noted that the practice had been going on since the 1860s.[21]

Interestingly, a study by Aronson and Mills showed that the more severe the rite of initiation, the greater the bonding to the group.[22] It is not surprising that members of One Commando were unwilling to talk about their initiation to authorities. For example, Corporal Robin, a "black" initiate, was reluctant to tell Somalia Inquiry commissioners anything that might incriminate or cast a bad light on other members of One Commando. Similarly, he testified that he was willing to put up with having "KKK" written on his back in order to be accepted by the group.[23] As Jones points out, severe initiation to a group promotes increased loyalty and devotion to the group.[24]

Hazing and initiation occur around the world and in countless organizations, from groups of medical student to football teams to military academies.[25] Many interviewees were quick to say that the One Commando ceremonies were not so bad and, besides, "everyone else does it too."

> Why do fraternities and universities have hazing? Why do hockey teams have hazing? You know. Hazing is something that has been a part of not only the military but a lot of different social groups. I think the timing was very bad for it to be seen on TV . . . for the Airborne Regiment. Very bad timing. (Canadian Airborne soldier)

> Soccer team parties at university are a lot worse than what's on those videos. I don't see what the big problem is. It's pretty bad when the Canadian government has so little spine that we lose a whole regiment 'cause of a few stupid parties. (Canadian Airborne soldier)

U.S. forces are known for hazing and initiation rites such as the infamous Neptune ceremony during which sailors (pollywogs) first crossing the equator are initiated by veterans known as "seafarers." The pollywogs dress up—sometimes in drag, eat inedible food, perform silly or demeaning tasks, and crawl on a deck covered in repulsive substances.[26]

Some American marines perform blood-wing ceremonies where pins are pounded into the pectoral muscles of the initiates.[27] They also capture recruits and tie them up with duct tape and put bootblack on their testicles. Army soldiers posted overseas drink disgusting concoctions. As suggested, there are countless stories and many tragic deaths associated with initiations.[28]

One Commando Initiation

One initiation rite took place in August 1992 at Canadian Forces Base Petawawa. I am also aware of other initiation rites and viewed the videotape of one that occurred in 1994. Although soldiers reported to military police investigators that initiations were a regular occurrence in One Commando, no one seemed to be able to recall when the practice started.

The videos and descriptions of these rites show that they follow the same pattern as the August 1992 rite with small variations. For example, in addition to the regular games, the initiates in 1994 had to run large metal spikes across a board, thus receiving what appears to be a sizeable electric shock. The closer the soldier got to one end of the board, the greater the electric shock. All One Commando initiations occurred in an isolated patio area behind One Commando's barracks, and, as Colonel Holmes testified to the Commission of Inquiry:

Q. And this particular event took place again, as we understand it, in the patio area of the first commando barracks. Is it reasonable to you that this could have taken place without other individuals on the base realizing that it was happening?

A. There is no doubt about it. The one commando barracks had an enclosed patio at the back of the barracks. If you like, a patio wall of substantial size and made of wood. So anyone on the outside who may have been passing by and looking in conceivably wouldn't know what's going on there.

I would also add that the military base after four or five P.M. on a normal workday is like a ghost town. If this particular activity took place after duty hours, very few people would have been around to see. Once the door is closed on the facilities, essentially the only people left on the base are the single soldiers, and the road that the One Commando quarters is on is not a major access route through the base.[29]

Initiates were thus physically separated from other members of the Airborne, which is the first step in an initiation rite. The actual initiation lasted several hours, although only one hour is on tape. The new members—troopers and corporals—of One Commando were initiated by the corporals and master corporals (called godfathers), who were initiates in the previous year's ceremony and who now directed the activities for the new initiates. The rituals were activities of the junior ranks, and no senior NCOs or officers were present during the entire ceremony. Sometimes officers and senior NCOs were present at the beginning of the rite but left shortly after consuming a beer or two. Thus, the "men" were left to themselves.

In August of 1992, about fifteen to twenty initiates were told by the older members that there would be a "get-together" at the end of the day. The initiates each contributed approximately $20 to buy beer for the party. What follows is a brief account of the August 1992 video of One Commando initiation:

- Approximately fifteen men (initiates) are lined up by the One Commando barrack block in Petawawa. They are passing a piece of bread to each other, on which they vomit and urinate prior to placing it in their mouths and chewing.
- Three initiates are doing push-ups on a piece of cardboard with feces splattered on it, while one initiate is pushed down chest first onto the cardboard by an initiator.
- A black initiate, with "I love KKK" written on his back, is in the push-up position with other initiates; an initiator also urinates on the black initiate's back.
- The black initiate is tied to a tree and one initiator says, "This is the real nature of a black." Later white powder is thrown on the black initiate and beer is poured down his shorts.
- An initiate is shown on all fours.
- The black initiate is on all fours with a dog leash wrapped around his shoulders being led around by an initiator who is holding the leash.
- An initiate fakes sodomy of the black initiate while the black initiate simultaneously fakes fellatio with another initiate.
- Two initiates are close-dancing on a picnic table; one is naked with his pants down around his ankles.
- One initiate with a mop wig on his head and a gun-tape dress kisses another male believed to be his initiator or "godfather."
- During the entire time, initiates are encouraged to binge drink beer and participate in "games" such as turning around a stick [until they get dizzy], carrying water, doing push-ups, and jumping from a table blindfolded.

The video of the One Commando ritual clearly establishes these activities as rites of initiation with the associated three classic phases of separation, liminal inversion, and reintegration. The separation phase is the moment when all initiates are "leveled"; that is, made alike. Their hair is shaved, they are all in the same maroon Airborne T-shirt. (No initiators are dressed this way.) As the initiates become progressively dirtier, their initiators remain immaculately clean, so that the initiates are separate and yet the same. It is the initiators, called godfathers, who direct the activities during the rite.

After separation occurs, initiates in rites of passage are often ritually "killed." In the Airborne case, this did not happen as it often does in other cultures' rites; rather, they were dead drunk and if not falling down from drinking, they were doing so from dizziness after turning around and around on a stick. They were also encouraged to vomit by their initiators—a ritual poisoning and purge, accomplished primarily by the passing of a wad of bread from initiate to initiate. But between initiates the "boulette" is vomited and urinated on, thus turning it into a method for provoking vomiting in the initiate, who must next chew it. Eliade describes similar events in Mayombe, Africa, where initiates' heads are shaven and they drink a narcotic potion and are spun around until they fall to the ground.[30]

Without too much exaggeration, the passing of the "boulette" is a ritual vaguely reminiscent of the communion ceremony during which one must eat sacred bread—the symbol of Christ. Certainly there are Christian ceremonies where initiates drink a secret liquid (e.g., wine) as a birth symbol. At this party, initiates drank copious amounts of bottled beer—a male drink in French-Canadian culture. Also, at the party, the priest or chaplain came and blessed the St. Michael's Mainz, a good-luck charm for soldiers who are Airborne.

> The priest or chaplain came and blessed the St. Michael's Mainz. Which is sort of a charm for soldiers who are Airborne. Then we give it to the new people. The soldiers, they line up, and we have a little prayer and then they get their St. Michael's medals. (Canadian Airborne soldier)

The ritual killing is followed by a series of acts designed to humiliate and further reduce the collective of initiates. As Nuwer has noted, the unpleasantness and ordeals of these rites of passage are not negative sanctions (sadism or punishment) but a test of loyalty and self-control, which are highly valued characteristics in a combat soldier.[31] One interviewee stated:

> I can't say that I am proud to see myself on national television, but I can say that I am proud to have done it, to prove to myself and to others that as a member of the Airborne Regiment I will face and overpass any challenges or taskings given to me. (Canadian Airborne soldier)

In One Commando's ritual, soldiers prove their readiness to participate in the group regardless of the personal cost. Keesing notes similar motivations during initiations of young men in the South Pacific:

> Boys become men, not through a natural process of maturation, but through a cultural process of creation: growth and physical strength, bravery and manliness are achieved through sequences of isolation and ordeal. . . . Unless boys undergo the rigors of initiation they will remain soft and weak.[32]

It is interesting to note that the soldier who would obviously stand out and not be like the others—the black initiate—was singled out for special treatment. This is consistent with other reports of similar initiations where there is extreme pressure to "level" all participants. While the black initiate was doused in flour, some of his white associates were rolled in mud. Again the inversion and parody of this liminal period are highlighted—black becomes white and white becomes black.

> It's the pride of belonging to a group, like in schools and universities, a rite of passage, but no one makes you do it. No one gets beaten or shaken up. What happens is that they'll pick on some personal characteristic. Like if you're black, they'll paint you white, but being black is not the problem. (Canadian Airborne soldier)

During this liminal phase, the initiates are "betwixt and between," no longer new members to the Airborne but not yet part of the group. Van Gennep, in his comparative work on rites of passage, remarked that in this gap between ordered worlds, almost anything can happen, including acts involving urine and feces.[33] Soldiers dance erotically with each other, men are in drag, and men perform mock sodomy acts. Here we see a parody of the military's emphasis on masculinity, particularly in an all-male society such as the Airborne. Thus the initiation rite touches upon homosexual impulses that surely are evoked in such an all-male climate.[34] Furthermore, Turner tells us that in the interim of liminality, the possibility exists not only of standing aside from one's social position but of stepping away from all social positions and formulating a potentially unlimited series of alternative social arrangements.[35] By mocking homoerotic behavior, initiates are formulating what is normally considered a totally unacceptable social arrangement for the Airborne. The following quotes concerning homosexuality reflect just how strongly the Airborne felt about gay men in their midst.

I remember in the old days, if we discovered that the guy living in the barracks was homosexual, we didn't beat him. We would bring him to the shower room, take mops, take everything we had, and we would wash him—without beating him. He was so scared he had to get out. (Canadian Airborne soldier)

At one point, someone made me realize that there was homosexual behavior among the men. But we're so homophobic that when we get free time, we go out and get ourselves a woman, just to prove that we're not homosexual. When we go out, the woman becomes a machine, an object that we'd use as much as possible and talk about as much as possible because afterwards there won't be any women around. When you're working two or three or even six months with guys and you don't even see any women, well sure you get some different behavior, jokes and stuff. It's acceptable to some point, but it's all borderline. So once you get the chance, you have to prove that you want a woman. If you have this borderline behavior and don't go out and get a woman, someone will start a rumor. If they start a rumor, you find yourself with broken legs. Really physically broken. (Canadian Airborne soldier)

We can't accept homosexuality because it represents weakness. We've still got the old 1950s values, when it wasn't acceptable. To me, if a homosexual keeps it to himself, it's his own business. If he does his job well, I can deal with it. It's like that in the civilian world, but in the army if you have any particular behavior, you'll get harassed. I've heard of guys getting dragged off to the toilets and getting their kneecaps and wrists broken by banging them on toilet doors. One guy got his leg broken, boot-kicked, just so he would leave. (Canadian Airborne soldier)

El Guidi has noted during the liminal period in the initiation ritual, neophytes are not yet classified, which is often expressed in symbols modeled on the process of gestation where neophytes are likened to or treated as newborn infants.[36] In the Airborne, initiates' heads are shaved, and some eventually end up wearing little or no clothes like newborns. They cannot feed themselves and are fed beer and alcohol like babies—only instead of being fed from the bottle, Airborne initiates are fed from plastic guns.

There is also an abdication of personal responsibility to the initiators, who are like family (godfathers). The initiates do what the initiators ask, trusting them with their personal safety like children. For example, initiates stand blind-folded on a table. The table is raised and shaken by four initiators. The initiate then jumps off, believing he is quite some distance from the ground (when ac-tually he is only one or two inches off the ground). In this way the young initi-ates practice and reenact in parody the abdication of responsibility to superiors which takes place in the military.

In the Airborne, soldiers will be asked to do the bidding of their superiors without question even when it puts their personal safety at risk. They will be asked to leap from airplanes, trusting in their superiors to let them out of the plane at a safe altitude and to spot them in the right drop zone. This trust is reinforced by initiators' statements, such as "We take care of you; nowhere else will people take care of you the way we do." Corporal Robin, the black initiate, testified to the Somalia Commission of Inquiry that he was cared for by his initiators; for example, he said that glass was taken away so he would not be hurt when walked on the ground like a dog and ropes were loosened so as not to bind his hands too tightly to a tree.[37]

It may seem incomprehensible to an outsider that the initiates actually par-ticipated voluntarily in all this. The importance of the ritual is in part a reflec-tion of the nature of the unit at this stage. Initiates are strangers to each other and to the Airborne and the bonding of the initiation pulls them together in a very short period of time. Perhaps the initiations were more severe in One Commando because of their marginal position as a French unit in a predomi-nantly English base such as Petawawa, but whatever the reasons, recruits emerge from the ordeal as new beings: members of One Commando. The passage is consummated. In essence they have been reborn as Airborne.

The Zulu Warrior

One Commando was not the only commando with initiation rites. Two Commando practiced the "Zulu warrior," which I was told came from the British.

The Brits picked it up the Zulu warrior thing in the Boer War in the 1900s in South Africa. They adopted this dance they called the Zulu warrior. (Canadian Airborne soldier)

Now the Zulu warrior, our soldiers picked that up from the Brits. That was going on for a while. At the end of battle we'd get together, the Canadians and the Brits in a big party. You'd always see the Brits by the end of the night doing the Zulu warrior on top of a table. He'd challenge the Americans, What can you do to beat that? Then the Canadian would come out, and say: This is soldiering. This is what soldiers do. But it's not hazing or all the rest of that. I never heard of that going on. (Canadian Airborne soldier)

The Zulu warrior ritual happened spontaneously during a party or after an AIC. My interviewees were convinced that someone who did not want to participate would not be ostracized; however, one wonders if participation was not encouraged in order to prove daring and gain prestige and acceptance.

> The Zulu warrior thing was spontaneous. For whatever occasion, they'd go down and buy some beer and they'd put it in the shack and the troops would start drinking it. That beer would go pretty quickly, two-three cases of beer and 110 guys don't last very long. So we'd pass a hat and collect more money and get the guys that weren't drinking to drive down to the liquor store. So then we got over thirty cases of beer. So they start drinking and about halfway through someone would say: Hey, let's get the new guys—they're gonna do the Zulu warrior. And that's basically how it ended up going on. It wasn't a formal thing. I remember one guy who wouldn't do it. No one thought any less of him for it. It wasn't like you have to do it or be ostracized. (Canadian Airborne soldier)

> Each unit after they have their AIC, they have a party, each unit had something different. Like Two Commando had a canoe party or porch party. They found an old canoe in the Ottawa River—filled it with ice and everybody that came brought a case of beer or whatever. They'd play out the Zulu warrior thing tradition every now and then. But each unit sat and drank beer and basically had a normal party. But as for all those hazings and all that, I spent many years there and I never saw somebody get razzed if they didn't want to do something. You get the normal name-calling when it first happened but the next day it was all forgotten. (Canadian Airborne soldier)

The "Zulu warrior" consisted of dropping one's pants, standing on a chair, and having a length of toilet paper inserted between the buttocks. The paper was then ignited and one had to down a beer and pull out the paper before it scorched his bottom. There were various versions of this rite, some involving two men on chairs and one piece of paper joining them. The middle of the paper was ignited, and may the best man down his beer first. [This involved] danger (fire), heights (Airborne), alcohol (a real man), and anal fascination (mock homoerotic behavior).

> They'll jump up on the table to some music or whatever. All of a sudden toward the end of the night, someone would say: "I have the nerve now, I'll jump up on the table and do the Zulu warrior." Whether there is mixed company or not, I've seen them do it. And just start dancing on the table and start taking their clothes off, and then end up with someone giving them a piece of toilet paper or something. And they'd end up with this piece of toilet paper attached to them somehow, and of course somebody would light it on fire while they were dancing around on the table. And everybody would sing the song, Zulu warrior. There's a song. It goes like, "Haul him down, you Zulu warrior, haul him down, you Zulu chief, Haul him down, you Zulu warrior." I think they repeat that twice. "Haul him down, you Zulu chief," and then everybody starts yelling, "chief, chief, chief" together and then somebody lights the thing on fire. Usually there are two of them. So there are two guys dancing and the thing is that this toilet paper is burning, and it's supposed to be who pulls it out first sort of thing, before they get burned. Who's got the most nerve? Everybody's standing around clapping or singing a song. Two guys try to outdo each other usually. And then somebody usually lights the toilet paper up higher, and a hand will come out of the audience or

something and light it up higher and watch this guy burn so. So the next day the guy wakes up not only with a hangover but he's got a burnt butt to deal with too. (Canadian Airborne soldier)

Kyle Brown wrote, in his autobiographical account of events in Somalia, that the Zulu warrior was "a smoker or initiation ritual at which we demonstrated to our peers that we new guys were enthusiastic and anxious to be part of the unit. . . . We all felt closer-knit and united after it . . . "[38]

Hazing Rituals

New men were also subjected to a kind of "cold-shoulder treatment" during the first six months of their stay in Two Commando. According to Private Grant, the NCOs and officers had nothing to do with this form of hazing. It was something the troops did to "welcome" a newcomer.

See, when you come to the Commando, you're not a new guy, you are a fucking new guy, that's how you are treated for six months. No one talks to you, no one is your friend, you do what you are told and you carry on. You're told to do this, by whoever, you do it. Now, if people want to get in, what they generally do, in any circumstance, they try their best to please. (Testimony of Private Grant to the Board of Inquiry, transcripts, vol. V, 864–889)

Private Gilbert described hazing behavior in One Commando to the Military Board of Inquiry.

A: Private GILBERT: When you arrive at the Regiment you're a "pouf."

Q: Major General de FAYE: What's a "pouf"?

A: Private GILBERT: They call us FNGs; Fucking New Guys.

Q: Major General de FAYE: D'accord, je comprends ça. Okay, anything else?

A: Private GILBERT: All this summer employment that arrived at the Regiment, it's the new one that does the job for approximately one year when new ones arrive after us.

Q: Major General de FAYE: This "pouf" designation, since tasks are assigned to personnel in this category, are they assigned by the chain of command?

A: Private GILBERT: No, it's when we had an O Group, they ask for volunteers, but you are volunteered. (Testimony of Private Gilbert to the Board of Inquiry)

Private Bass testified to the Board of Inquiry that a few guys from Three Commando would get drunk and burst into a FNG's room and wave guns around to scare the hell out of him. Three Commando seemed to have other forms of bonding. For example, in Rwanda, following Somalia, members of Three Commando had to be hospitalized for cutting their wrists too deeply in a blood-brother ritual.

A platoon, I believe, from the Three Commando was sent to Rwanda to provide security. It was a defensive security platoon, which is essentially guarding a certain perimeter. They were not deployed as a unit, just a platoon, thirty men under a captain. And two events took place. First one is one of the members of that platoon committed suicide while, I believe, on Christmas night, of all times. I believe there was drinking involved, while I'm not sure. But anyway he was a member of that platoon. Also there was a shooting incident, in that members of the platoon, while guarding a nunnery, were drinking and decided to shoot off their weapons into the air. I think it's at that event too, that they decided to do a blood-brother ceremony. Where, if you like someone very much, he becomes your blood brother, kind of an Indian ceremony where you slash your wrists and mix your blood. Now you have to put things in context. You have to remember all the horror of Rwanda, general lawlessness, who's right, who's wrong. Difficult living conditions because a lot of things did not work or were shocking, that kind of stuff. But again the disturbing part is the presence of alcohol. (Canadian Airborne soldier)

Rampage Initiation Rites

On the evening of October 2, military pyrotechnics were exploded illegally at a party at the junior ranks' mess at Canadian Forces Base Petawawa. In the early morning of October 3, a vehicle was set on fire that belonged to Two Commando's duty officer, who had reportedly called the military police following the disturbances at the mess. Later that night, various members of Two Commando (and perhaps others) held another party, this time in nearby Algonquin Park, at which they set off more pyrotechnics and ammunition.

It could be postulated that the weekend of the pyrotechnics display in October 1992, when soldiers set off thunderflashes [explosive devices similar to firecrackers], smoke grenades, and a flare on the base in Petawawa and then went on to party with stolen thunderflashes and personal weapons in Algonquin Park, was a form of rampage initiation rite. Alves describes rampage initiation rites as a form of "improv" initiation rites where antisocial behavior is used to express one's marginal condition.[39] Alves described how gang members prove their daring to each other in Los Angeles by committing crime and recounting heroic tales of their daring to their comrades afterward.

Thus, the Airborne who participated in these events could reinforce their "rebel" identity. It is important to remember that members of Two Commando called themselves the "rebels" and openly displayed the rebel Confederate flag in their quarters. This group had a reputation of challenging authority to the extent of being accused of burning an officer's car. Also, the pyrotechnics and other events such as car burning took place on a weekend of extensive binge drinking.

Conclusions

The Canadian Airborne considered themselves to be Canada's combat elite. As early as 1945, Grinker and Spiegel noted that the combat personality becomes more mature in self-discipline, self-sacrifice, and cooperation, but from another standpoint the combat personality becomes more dependent. "For what he has given up, he receives constant care and affection from his group as long as he plays his part properly."[40] In the Airborne, pressure was on to be part of the group, but the rewards were great.

> Most regiments are tight, but the Airborne was more so. Even disbanded they were a family. They really took care of you. They were out for their men. (Canadian Airborne soldier)

> We were very tight knit. You always have to cover your buddy; your buddy covers you. You have to look after each other no matter what. Even if you are partying downtown, if he gets out of line or gets in trouble it's your job to get him out. (Canadian Airborne soldier)

> Camaraderie was so close it wasn't funny. It was almost like you'd been working with those guys for years, because you would see them day in, day out. It kind of made things easier because you didn't have to explain what you wanted because three-quarters of the time he already knows what you want and it will get done. There was also a lot of peer pressure to spend our free time together. Say a sergeant would want to go shooting, he would take his entire section with him. He'd say "Screw the wives," but I didn't like that. Come Friday I said, "See you on Monday. I'm on my own time." But in a few instances it wasn't looked upon that lightly. If you didn't go to the platoon smokers (parties) it was frowned on. If a guy did all that they wanted, he got all he wanted, promotions, the courses he wanted, but he was never home. He went partying with them constantly, fishing, whatever. (Canadian Airborne soldier)

Soldiers who were not able to meld into the Airborne group identity were excluded. Corporal Purnelle testified that when he joined One Commando in 1990, he had not participated in the initiation and suffered some ostracism as a result.[41] To the ordinary civilian, ostracism may not seem such a horrible fate. "So if you get kicked out of one group, you can just join another," may be the reaction. But remember that a member of the military is not free just to join another group.[42] Although they come from a civilian society that elevates the individual, initiates are in a world where the value of the group is supreme.[43] Ambrose tells us that the result of these shared experiences is a "closeness unknown to all outsiders. Comrades are closer than friends are, closer than brothers. Their relationship is different from that of lovers. Their trust in, and knowledge of, each other is total."[44]

According to McCoy, "bonding" occurs as a lasting form of group identity brought about through an experience of shared suffering.[45] Studies of male group behavior, whether it is the Wehrmacht in World War II[46] or West Point cadets in the 1960s, have emphasized the importance of "bonding" or "binding" as a defining aspect of military organizations. Thus, initiation rituals give an outward and visible form to an inward and conceptual process.

It is important to note that although group loyalty and bonding is important during battle, small-group bonding can foster and maintain inappropriate norms. According to Janowitz, primary groups that are highly cohesive can impede the goals of military organization because they are informal networks.[47] Group bonding can pose a threat to legitimate authority or undermine discipline when the group becomes more important than anything else, including the army.

A strong group can also foster and maintain inappropriate norms. In addition, by assuring anonymity through norms of the group, it can facilitate acts of subversion and defiance, since the group will "circle the wagon" to protect individual members from military or civilian authority.[48] For example, prior to deployment to Somalia, Airborne soldiers would not "give up" the comrades who had been responsible for the burning of an officer's car. Investigations only encountered a wall of silence concerning a serious breach of discipline. Small-group loyalty thus became more important than good order and discipline. Similarly, members of One Commando had difficulty "remembering" details concerning the events of the initiation ceremony. Another example is that even when Corporal Robin reviewed the video, he still did not want to hurt the good name of the Airborne Regiment and was reluctant to criticize.[49] Severe initiation ceremonies such as those carried out by the Canadian Airborne Regiment promote increased loyalty and devotion to the group. But this group bonding is a double-edged sword: What can be functional unit bonding for war can quickly become dysfunctional in an army at peace.[50]

Notes

1.   E. Aronson and J. Mills, "The Effect of Severity of Initiation on Liking For a Group," *Journal of Abnormal and Social Psychology* 59 (1959): 177–181.

2.   Canadian soldier quoted in D. Harrison and L. Laliberte, *No Life Like It: Military Wives in Canada* (Toronto: James Lorimer, 1994), 28.

3.   See G. Aran, "Parachuting," *American Journal of Sociology* 80 (1974): 124–152; W. C. Cockerham, "Selective Socialization: Airborne Training as Status Passage," *Journal of Political and Military Sociology* 1 (1973): 215–229.

4.   W. Axkin and L. R. Dobrofsky, "Military Socialization and Masculinity," *Journal of Social Issues* 34 (1978): 163.

5.   See Donna Winslow, "The Canadian Airborne in Somalia: A Socio-cultural Inquiry," study prepared for the Commission of Inquiry into the Deployment of Canadian Forces to Somalia (Ottawa: Public Works and Government Services, 1997).

6.   The soldiers and officers who testified are identified in the public transcripts and therefore here as well. I also viewed the footage of three videotapes that were taken during the initiation rites that were entered in the public record of the Commission of Inquiry and military police reports of investigations of these videos. I have chosen not to identify any officers, since the initiation rites concerned only non-commissioned members; that is, corporals being initiated by master corporals who had gone through the initiation rite the

previous year. The few officers who were present at the beginning of the initiation rites could be easily identified if I were to refer to them as "officer."

7. Canada's paratrooping history actually began in 1942 with the formation of the First Canadian Parachute Battalion, which became part of the British Sixth Airborne Division and fought with it in Northwest Europe during World War II. At the same time a joint Canadian–U.S. unit, the First Special Service Force, or Devil's Brigade, was formed. This unit fought mainly in Italy and Southern France. Disbanded in 1944, the paratroopers from the First Canadian Special Service Battalion became reinforcements for the First Canadian Parachute Battalion, which, in turn, was disbanded at the end of the war. Paratrooping was revived in the Canadian Forces in 1949 with the formation of the Mobile Strike Force. It consisted of battalions from three Canadian Army Regiments: The Royal Canadian Regiment (RCR), Princess Patricia's Canadian Light Infantry (PPCLI), and the Royal 22e Regiment (R22eR) (Van Doos) plus support elements. This brigade was tasked with Canadian defense, particularly in the north. In 1958, the Mobile Strike Force was drastically reduced, but ten years later, in 1968, it was revitalized and the Canadian Airborne Regiment (CAR) was born.

8. Col. P. G. Kenward, "The Way We Were: Canadian Airborne Regiment 1968–1995," mimeograph at Petawawa, Ontario, 1995, 1.

9. Ibid., 2.

10. General Boyle, meeting with Judge Advocate General, Ottawa, 20 April 1995. Note that at the time General Boyle gave this presentation, he was a member of the General Staff. He subsequently went on to be the Chief of the Defence Staff.

11. When the unit was deployed to Somalia, it had to be augmented with additional personnel (such as medics and engineers), so it became the Canadian Airborne Battle Group. The commanding officer of the Battle Group was the commanding officer of the Airborne Regiment.

12. The decision to disband the Canadian Airborne Regiment was taken on January 23, 1995, more than nineteen months after the return of the troops from Somalia. The decision to disband followed the showing on television of two videos, one depicting a commando-unit hazing ritual and the other filmed during the regiment's tour of duty in Somalia. In his press release, the Minister of Defense wrote:

> [T]he incidents in Somalia last fall, which were subsequently investigated by the Chief of Defense Staff, and in combination with these two videos, demand action. I recognize that many changes in personnel and procedures in the Airborne have been made over the past year and that the people now serving are by and large dedicated professionals, however, I believe the problems of the regiment are systemic. (Speaking notes for the Honorable David Collenette, P.C., MP, Minister of National Defence, Press Conference, 23 January 1995, 10–11)

13. J. S. Ott, *The Organizational Culture Perspective* (Chicago: Dorsey Press, 1995), 27.

14. L. Parmar, *Society, Culture and Military System* (Jaipur: Rawat Publications, 1994), 152.

15. The role of alcohol in other Airborne units has been described by S. E. Am-

brose, *Band of Brothers: E Company, 506th Regiment, 101st Airborne—From Normandy to Hitler's Eagle's Nest* (New York: Simon & Schuster, 1992), 19.

16. L. H. Ingraham, *Boys in the Barracks: Observations on American Military Life* (Philadelphia: Institute for the Study of Human Issues, 1985), 91.

17. Ibid., 113.

18. C. W. Hewson, "Mobile Command Study: A Report on Disciplinary Infractions and Antisocial Behavior within FMC with Particular Reference to the Special Service Force and the Canadian Airborne Regiment (Hewson Report)" (Ottawa: Department of National Defense, September 1985), Annex H, 20.

19. See Ingraham, *Boys in the Barracks,* 119.

20. The much-publicized beating death of a young Somali named Shidane Arone occurred in 1993. He was slammed in the head and burned while in the vicinity of other Regiment members, who apparently failed to act to save Arone. The chief of defence convened a military Board of Inquiry under the direction of a major general in 1993. Because there were military police investigations going on at that time, this inquiry was unable to investigate the death of Shidane Arone. The absence of "independent" outside investigators further aroused suspicion. This military Board of Inquiry released a report on July 19, 1993, chaired by Major General Tom de Faye, saying essentially that discipline had broken down in the Airborne Regiment and that proper training had been lacking in preparing the unit for the mission in Somalia.

In Canada, the main political effort to uncover the truth of what happened in Somalia was the government-sponsored independent Commission of Inquiry into the Deployment of Canadian Forces to Somalia. By far this was the largest investigation ever into the Canadian military. The Commission of Inquiry into the Deployment of Canadian Forces to Somalia began work in March 1995. The Commission's mandate was broad, allowing it to investigate nearly all aspects of the events in Somalia.

21. United States War Department, *Hazing at the United States Military Academy: Letter From the Secretary of War, Transmitting a Response to the Inquiry of the House in Relation to Hazing at the United States Military Academy* (Washington, D.C.: G.P.O., 1909), 63.

22. Aronson and Mills, "The Effect of Severity of Initiation on Liking for a Group," 157–158.

23. Perhaps the best example of how difficult it can be for those in authority to get to the bottom of what goes on in hazing is the case of Douglas MacArthur. When he was a "plebe" at West Point at the turn of the century, MacArthur found himself in a hazing controversy and was commanded to testify at a congressional court of inquiry following the death of a cadet in a hazing incident. MacArthur "steadfastly refused to name the upperclassmen who had hazed him, yet he tried to appease the select committee by giving them the names of several men who had already quit West Point for one reason or another." See H. Nuwer, *Broken Pledges: The Deadly Rite of Hazing* (Atlanta: Longstreet Press, 1990) for details. [*Ed. note:* Since this essay was written, the following book has become available: P. W. Leon, *Bullies and Cowards: The West Point Hazing Scandal: 1898–1901* [Westport, Conn.: Greenwood], 1999).]

24. F. E. Jones, "The Socialisation of the Infantry Recruit," in *Canadian Society: Sociological Perspectives,* ed. B. R. Blishen, Frank E. Jones, Kaspar D. Naegele, and John Porter (Toronto: Macmillan of Canada, 1968), 167.

25. Annual hazing at the Ecole Nationale Supérieure d'Arts et Métiers, a mechanical engineering school in Bordeaux, is called "Bizutage." It was conceived to establish a lifelong "esprit de corps" among students. Students are forced to dunk their heads in dirty toilets, handle animal entrails and excrement, and strip and perform sexual acts. Second-year students carry out the victimizing or are victims once again if they refuse. While school administrators argue that hazing is not mandatory, students say that peer pressure and fear of retaliation make it an unavoidable rite of passage. See Marilyn August, *Montreal Gazette,* 12 December 1993.

26. Nuwer, *Broken Pledges,* 201–202.

27. This tradition was also practiced by German paratroopers, who recognized different levels: bronze wings, novice; silver, advanced; gold, expert. The highlight of the German wings ceremony was "blood wings"—the sergeant major pinning the wings through the soldier's tunic into flesh. See Peter Worthington and Kyle Brown, *Scapegoat: How the Army Betrayed Kyle Brown* (Toronto: Seal Books, 1997), 51.

28. See Nuwer, *Broken Pledges,* 286–324; A. W. McCoy, "Same Banana: Hazing and Honor at the Philippine Military Academy," *The Journal of Asian Studies* 54 (1995): 689–726; United States General Accounting Office, *DOD Service Academies: More Changes Needed to Eliminate Hazing: Report to Congressional Requesters* (Washington, D.C.: The General Accounting Office, March 1992).

29. "Testimony of Colonel Holmes to the Commission of Inquiry into the Activities of the Canadian Airborne Battlegroup in Somalia," Transcripts, vol. 4, 632–633.

30. Mircea Eliade, *Rites and Symbols of Initiation: The Mysteries of Birth and Rebirth* (New York: Harper Torchbooks, 1965), 76.

31. Nuwer *Broken Pledges,* 116.

32. Roger M. Keesing, "Introduction," in *Rituals of Manhood: Male Initiation in Papua New Guinea,* ed. Gilbert Herdt (Berkeley: University of California Press, 1982), 8.

33. Arnold van Gennep, *Rites of Passage* (Paris: É. Nourry, 1909).

34. R. Lopez-Reyes, *Power and Immortality: Essays on Strategy, War Psychology, and War Control* (New York: Exposition Press, 1971), 189.

35. Victor Turner, *Dramas, Fields, and Metaphors: Symbolic Action in Human Society* (New York: Cornell University Press, 1974), 14.

36. Fadwa El Guindi, *Religion in Culture* (Dubuque: W. C. Brown Co., 1977), 40.

37. "Testimony of Corporal Christopher Robin to the Commission of Inquiry into the Activities of the Canadian Airborne Battlegroup in Somalia," Transcripts, vol. 6, 8.

38. Worthington and Brown, *Scapegoat,* 56.

39. J. Alves, "Transgressions and Transformations: Initiation Rites among Urban Portuguese Boys," *American Anthropologist* 95 (1993): 897.

40. R. R. Grinker and J. W. Spiegel, *Men Under Stress* (Philadelphia: Blakiston, 1945), 123.

41. Corporal Prunelle, Testimony to the Commission of Inquiry into the Activi-

ties of the Canadian Airborne Battle Group in Somalia, Transcripts, vol. 35, 6822–6823.

42. M. S. Peck, *People of the Lie: The Hope for Healing Human Evil* (New York: Simon & Schuster, 1983), 219.

43. T. E. Ricks, "Separation Anxiety: 'New' Marines Illustrate Growing Gap between Military and Society," *The Wall Street Journal*, 27 July 1995, A1, A4.

44. Ambrose, *Band of Brothers*, 20.

45. See McCoy, "Same Banana," 695.

46. Edward Shils and Morris Janowitz, "Cohesion and Disintegration in the Wehrmacht in World War II," *Public Opinion Quarterly* 12 (1948): 280–315.

47. M. Janowitz, *Sociology and the Military Establishment* (Beverly Hills: Sage Publications, 1974), 9.

48. See Lt. Col. K. W. J. Wenek, "Behavioural and Psychological Dimensions of Recent Peacekeeping Missions," *Forum: Journal of the Conference of Defence Associations Institute* 8 (December 1993): 20.

49. "Testimony of Corporal Robin to the Commission of Inquiry into the Activities of the Canadian Airborne Battlegroup in Somalia," Transcripts, vol. 6, 1075.

50. The author wishes to thank the members of the Commission of Inquiry into the Department of Canadian Forces to Somalia for their assistance with and support for this research.

12 Traumatic Injuries Caused by Hazing

Michelle A. Finkel, M.D.

Editor's note: *Emergency room physicians routinely look for physical evidence of child or domestic abuse when examining patients under their care. In this chapter, Dr. Finkel, an emergency room physician herself, recommends that her colleagues keep watch for signs of abuse when students are brought in for treatment of certain injuries or an alcohol overdose. Many of her suggestions also have value for doctors and nurses working in college health centers and for collegiate athletic trainers.*

Hazing practices have become increasingly prevalent in schools within fraternities and sororities and athletic teams as well as in nonacademic settings, including the military, professional sports organizations, and street gangs. Hazing can be defined as committing acts against an individual or forcing an individual to commit an act in order for the individual to be initiated into or affiliated with an organization. Some of these acts can put the individual at risk for injury. Hazing victims have suffered severe traumatic injuries, including irreversible intracranial damage, blunt intraabdominal organ damage, third-degree burns, heat stroke, suffocation, aspiration, sexual assault, and death, making the topic pertinent to emergency physicians. These patients have distinct issues that are similar to issues of domestic violence patients, since hazing can be a violent practice that affects individuals on a physical, psychiatric, and social basis and can lead to victims' feelings of shame and the consequent potential for concealment. This chapter reviews the history of hazing, provides statistics regarding its prevalence, presents information on the victims of specific hazing practices and their traumatic injuries, and assesses alcohol's influence on hazing. It also offers recommendations on how to recognize victims of hazing in the emergency department and proposes guidelines for the treatment of these patients. Current legislation and information on the prevention of traumatic injuries from hazing are discussed.

Methods of Data Acquisition

Research for this article included a literature search of journal articles on the medical and forensic aspects of hazing; newspaper, news magazine, and news Web site reports detailing hazing incidents; reference texts on hazing; a nationwide survey of athletes regarding hazing practices; and social science journal articles on the precipitants and consequences of hazing.

History of Hazing

Hazing has been practiced for ages; it existed in ancient and medieval schools in Greece, North Africa, and Western Europe. At that time it was called "pennalism," and during the 1600s it became a requirement for graduation. University administrators and upperclassmen believed that underclassmen were uncivilized and had to be properly groomed. The pennalism requirement, however, was abolished in the 1700s because of serious injuries and deaths caused by the practice.[1] In the eighteenth and nineteenth centuries, English secondary schools reported problems with "fagging," the practice of upperclassmen coercing underclassmen to act as servants for their senior colleagues.[2] Some lethal incidents of hazing were reported in the late nineteenth century, including a well-documented hazing incident of a freshman trying to find his way home through the woods at night after his fraternity brothers abandoned him, and was killed after he fell into a gorge. Several more hazing incidents were reported in the late nineteenth century.[3]

In the early twentieth century, hazing was again accepted by students and school administrators as a way for newcomers to learn respect for a school organization. In 1916, a first-year university student was twice seriously harmed by beatings—once during an initiation and once because he reported his injuries to the school's administration.[4] Hazing practices were reported in secondary schools in the early 1900s. The first newspaper record of a high school student's death in a hazing incident occurred in 1905. A 13-year-old boy died as a result of contracting pneumonia after he was held down on the ground by upperclassmen who pushed snow down his clothes.[5] *The New York Times* published the article under the headline "Hazing Kills Schoolboy."

By 1933, educators at fourteen colleges had signed an agreement to eliminate detrimental hazing practices among fraternities and sororities.[6] Unfortunately, deaths from the practices—including excessive alcohol ingestion, falls, and drownings—continued throughout the century, including several well-publicized cases.[7] Toward the end of the twentieth century, the reported incidents had escalated; hazing and pledging activities were the cause of at least fifty-six fraternity and sorority deaths from 1970 to 1999.[8]

Prevalence of Hazing

Considering the presumed massive underreporting of incidents, defining the prevalence of hazing is extremely difficult, and few studies have attempted to quantify it. An investigator from Alfred University, however, conducted a national survey of a random sample of college athletes at National Collegiate Athletic Association (NCAA) institutions in early 1999. Out of the 325,000 athletes surveyed, 80 percent of respondents reported anonymously that they were subjected to "*questionable* or *unacceptable* activities as part of their initiation onto a collegiate athletics team." One in five was subjected to "unacceptable and potentially illegal hazing" including beatings, kidnapping, and abandonment.[9]

The number of patients who present to emergency departments with hazing-related injuries has never been reported. One study that attempted to catalogue fraternity hazing injuries and deaths up to 1982 indicated that students received medical care in 44.64 percent of the cases reported in the paper.[10] The authors stated that whether or not victims sought medical care was related to the severity of injury. Thus, victims of less severe injuries may not present to medical personnel. Conversely, some patients may be presenting but disguising the etiology of their injuries, resulting in an underreporting of patients who are victims of hazing-related practices presenting to health care providers. Beyond hypotheses, the true numbers have not been studied.

Methods of Hazing

The methods by which individuals are hazed vary. Knowledge of these practices is important for medical personnel who treat the victims. Sometimes hazed patients will conceal the cause or extent of their traumatic injuries. An emergency physician who is aware of the types of hazing practices will be better equipped to manage these patients.

Beating/Paddling/Whipping/Striking

Intraabdominal injuries, intracranial damage, and deaths are all documented consequences of blunt trauma caused by beatings as part of hazing practices. Excessive beating has also led to hemoglobinuria and renal failure.[11] A particularly disturbing hazing case occurred in 1994 at a state university in Missouri when a fraternity member died after being beaten and kicked by at least seven fraternity brothers during a pledge session. Fraternity members left the initiate dying in a vehicle while they ate at a fast-food restaurant. The college student's injuries included a massive subdural hemorrhage, fractured ribs, a fractured kidney, and a bruised thigh.[12] Another college student was slammed into a wall during a hazing incident in 1975, leading to a fractured skull, irreversible intracranial injury, and eventual death.[13] In 1991, a 22-year-old first-year law student was kicked, mauled, and beaten to death in a hazing incident.[14] Less injurious cases of hazers striking initiates with ropes, belts, or hands to cause welts or cuts on victims' chests and abdomens have also been reported.[15] A gang-initiation ritual called a "jump-in" or "beat-in" occurs when multiple gang members assault an initiate. The new member is required to endure the attacks for an allotted amount of time.[16]

Blood-Pinning

Blood-pinning, also called blood-winging, is most commonly seen in military hazing practices. In the ritual, a senior officer inserts the sharp points of ceremonial wings into the subcutaneous tissue of the new initiate.[17] Bleeding from wounds and severe pain have been reported.[18]

Branding/Tattooing/Cigarette Burning/Burning

Although branding has traditionally been associated with African-American fraternities, coerced tattoos, cigarette burns, and branding itself are all used to permanently mark members of a variety of organizations. In 1997 a predominantly white sorority conducted a ceremony that included using cigarettes to burn initiates. Some hazing incidents consist of other types of burning as well, including one in which grain alcohol was poured down initiates' lips, after which hazers lit matches, resulting in burn wounds.[19] Human branding is not uncommon in African-American, as well as white, fraternity and sorority organizations and has been reported in the medical literature to cause even third-degree burns. In a case reported in the burn literature, the branding injuries were so severe that the plastic surgeon consulted on the case recommended skin grafting.[20]

Calisthenics

Excessive calisthenics have claimed the lives and well-being of several initiates. A particularly famous episode occurred in 1901 when at West Point Academy, Douglas MacArthur was forced to do calisthenics over shards of glass until he had a syncopal episode. In 1980, a fraternity pledge died after being forced to perform calisthenics in a steam room. A college student was hazed to death by a local fraternity in 1981 when he was made to wear winter clothing on a hot day and do calisthenics.[21] These patients may present with symptoms of heat exhaustion or—in severe cases—exertional heat stroke, including confusion, bizarre behavior, seizure, and coma.

Confinement in a Restricted Area

Forcing initiates into confined spaces is another common hazing practice. A death occurred when a fraternity pledge suffocated after being forced to dig and climb into his own grave, which then collapsed on him.[22] Incidents among athletes have included putting an intoxicated player into a car trunk for a ride in the winter and stuffing rookies inside equipment bags.[23] Heat-related injuries and prolonged hypoxia are the principal emergency medical concerns in these cases.

Consumption of Nonfood Substances

Incidents that include consumption of distasteful substances are disconcerting but non-hazardous unless the substance consumed is toxic. One "benign" episode that occurred as part of a military initiation included coercing enlistees to consume shortening covered with hot sauce and tobacco juice.[24] Other initiates have reportedly been forced to eat pubic hair and others, corn flakes mixed with their own blood.[25] Potentially dangerous substances are also sometimes forced upon an initiate. In one case, a member consumed excessive quantities of laxatives during a hazing incident.[26]

Drowning, Near-Drowning

Forcing initiates to swim in untoward circumstances—sometimes after excessive alcohol ingestion—is a form of hazing that has led to death by drowning. In 1979, two African-American pledges disappeared and presumably drowned after being forced to swim to the center of a local river at dark. Fellow students did not report the disappearances until almost three hours later.[27]

Falls

Blunt trauma from falls is the harmful effect of hazing practices that include coercing initiates to climb roofs, ledges, and bridges—oftentimes after ingesting excessive amounts of alcohol. Conventional blunt-trauma issues including spinal cord, intracranial, intraabdominal, and orthopedic trauma all must be considered in this patient population. Since it is not uncommon that these patients are intoxicated, clinical evaluation is oftentimes unreliable, making an evaluation more difficult.

Immersion in Noxious Substances

As with cases in which initiates are coerced into consuming distasteful substances, episodes in which pledges are required to immerse themselves in foul materials are usually not harmful, but repugnant. Episodes including immersion in excrement, beer, raw eggs, mayonnaise, deer intestines, and vomit have all been reported. Clinically significant episodes can occur when initiates are submerged in excessively hot or cold substances. In one case, military enlistees were required to sit naked in tubs of ice water and refuse as part of a hazing incident.[28]

Psychological Abuse

Although usually not clinically pressing, no list of hazing activities would be complete without the mention of psychological abuse. According to the 1999 Alfred University study, two-thirds of those surveyed reported being subjected to this kind of humiliating hazing, including being yelled or sworn at, being forced to wear embarrassing clothing, or being forced to deprive themselves of sleep, food, or personal hygiene.[29] Other incidents have included upperclassmen's coercing victims into performing personal services for them.[30] Demeaning episodes have included making rookies carry veterans' equipment and food trays and coercing them to push pennies down the halls with their noses.[31]

Sexual Assaults

A particularly troubling and dangerous practice includes forced sexual activity as part of the hazing process. Pledges may be made to simulate sex, they may have to endure members' buttocks being shoved into their faces—a practice called "butting," they may be forced to attach objects to their genitalia, they may have undesirable materials rubbed on their bodies, they may be coerced into unwanted close proximity with a naked individual, and they may be forced to have unwanted sexual relations with members or be raped or sodomized with an object or digit.

In 1993, some high school novice cheerleaders were forced to pretend they were performing sexual acts on male students who were unrelated to the group while the older members watched.[32] This incident was subsequently exposed in the *Chicago Tribune*. In one reported episode, an initiate was coerced into attaching a chicken to his penis; in another incident, members of a high school football team forced initiates to disrobe and climb into a sleeping bag together.[33]

More dangerous, however, are episodes in which initiates are coerced into unwanted sexual activity. Being "sexed in" is a common practice among some gangs. This entails requiring initiates to have sexual relations with existing members in order to join.[34] Several episodes of anal rape with objects have been reported in hazing episodes. In 1997, older members of a high school wrestling team were accused of anally raping some younger wrestlers with a mop handle they jokingly nicknamed Pedro. No charges were ultimately lodged against the older wrestlers. One victim reported being teased afterward and being called a homophobic epithet.[35] Another episode occurred when a freshman football player was accosted by teammates in a locker room. There, the boy reported, his shorts and underwear were pulled down and he was sexually assaulted. When the case went to trial, the plaintiffs reported that they were indulging in mere horseplay.[36] In 1998, four high school football players pled guilty to misdemeanor hazing for forcing a soda bottle into a rookie's anus.[37] Sexually transmitted diseases; oral, vaginal, and anal injuries; and unwanted pregnancies are all potential physical consequences of these practices.

Influence of Alcohol

Alcohol abuse often is a major factor in hazing incidents. The peer pressure to drink alcohol has been divided into an *indirect* type, which includes the easy accessibility of alcohol and reinforcement to drink by observing others, and the *direct* type, the urging to drink or suffer social punishment, both of which are used in hazing behavior.[38]

Binge drinking in colleges has been an issue broached in the medical literature,[39] but scant clinical information exists regarding its blunt or penetrating traumatic secondary effects. According to the National Intrafraternity Conference, which in 1998 studied traumatic incidents among its members, alcohol was present in 95 percent of falls from high places, 94 percent of fights, 93 percent of sexual-abuse incidents, 87 percent of automobile accidents, 67 percent of all falls on fraternity property, and 49 percent of hazing incidents. Alcohol use was a factor in 80 percent of injuries resulting in paralysis and in just under 90 percent of deaths.[40] Excessive alcohol use in hazing incidents is not limited to college fraternities; it is infamous in high school and athletic initiations as well.

The impact of alcohol use on coercive sexual activities was recently studied in college undergraduates. Alcohol use was found to have a positive association with the victimization of women using certain types of coercive sexual strategies. Being a fraternity member was associated with the use of verbal coercion and physical force, and being a sorority member was associated with being a victim of alcohol/drug coercion and physical force.[41]

Acute alcohol intoxication itself is a consequence of hazing that has led to episodes of aspiration, alcoholic coma, and death.[42] According to the Alfred University NCAA study, half of all respondents were required to participate in drinking contests or alcohol-related hazing, and two in five consumed alcohol on recruitment visits even before enrolling.[43]

Recognizing Hazing Victims

Recognizing a patient as a hazing victim can be difficult. Like victims of domestic violence, these patients may disguise the cause of their injuries out of embarrassment or the desire to protect the perpetrator(s). Furthermore, patients may not want to be seen as the cause of their organization being disciplined if the injuries become public knowledge.

According to a forensic analysis of fraternity hazing episodes from the early twentieth century through 1982, several demographic factors can assist physicians in identifying hazed patients, including sex, race, calendar date, and geographical location. Hazing victims were predominantly males, and the number of hazing incidents involving white students was three times as many as those involving African-American students. Hazing episodes occurred most often in February, March, April, September, and October, likely because most hazing activities occur with the entrance of new students at a new semester. Episodes were less prevalent around final exams—May, June, and December; the fewest incidents occurred in July during summer break. Most hazing episodes reported were in the Mid-Atlantic and South Atlantic states.[44]

Treating Hazing Victims in the Emergency Department

It is important to treat hazing patients as victims of violent crime rather than as willing participants in their traumatic injuries. Individuals participate as initiates in hazing activities because of a wish to be accepted, well-liked, and successful. Furthermore, victims may fear even more deleterious injuries if they do not comply with the hazing activities, including severe harassment or worse physical violence. Victims of hazing may have been exposed to coercion and intimidation for months. This prolonged hazing can lead to a feeling of hopelessness or to the idea that after so much harassment, it would be foolish to "quit."[45] Initiates may pathologically take pride in being able to endure such abusive circumstances. They also may see their participation in hazing as an investment in a more powerful and satisfying social future.[46] The reasons initiates participate in hazing are complex, but emergency physicians' treatment of hazing patients as victims should include compassionate, nonjudgmental care.

Treatment of hazing victims who have been sexually assaulted is particularly complicated because it requires thorough emergency medical evaluations and treatment, meticulous documentation for potential legal purposes, and very sympathetic care. Rape exams need to be carefully completed and, depending on the situation, prophylaxis for pregnancy and sexually transmitted diseases, including HIV, need to be considered. In cases of excessive bleeding or severe mucosal tears, gynecology, gastroenterology, or surgical consults may be necessary. Social workers, particularly those trained in sexual-assault patient management, are helpful for these victims.

Guidelines for the treatment of hazing victims in the emergency department include the following:

1. Patients should be made to feel safe with no concern that retribution from the offending fraternity, sorority, military organization, athletic group, or gang will occur while the victim is in the emergency department. Security should be called if necessary to accomplish this goal. If the hazing incident was of a sexual nature, the patient should be

granted a health care provider of the gender that the patient requests, if available.

2. A complete history should be taken and physical examination done for clinical as well as legal purposes. Documentation should be thorough in case of legal action. Photographs of injuries should be taken if permitted.

3. Emergency physicians should explain clearly that hazing is a criminal act and that the patient has legal options. If a social worker or psychiatrist is available, the patient should be offered these services.

4. After the preliminary assessment is complete and while the patient is getting necessary diagnostic tests, law enforcement should be called if the patient wishes to report the crime. The victim can be reminded that he or she can withdraw a complaint in the future but that early reporting is important if legal action is eventually pursued. Law enforcement personnel and social workers should be asked to make suggestions regarding safe disposition if the patient is to be discharged home.

5. Patients who are victims of hazing can be referred to anti-hazing groups for support and information. Organizations include www.stophazing.org; the Committee to Halt Useless College Killings (CHUCK), P.O. Box 188, Sayville, New York, 11782; Cease Hazing Activities and Deaths (CHAD), P.O. Box 850955, Mobile, Alabama, 36685. Victims may require long-term support and psychological help to cope with the hazing episode(s).

Hazing Legislation

Hazing legislation is in effect in all U.S. states except seven: Alaska, Hawaii, Montana, Michigan, New Mexico, South Dakota, and Wyoming. All state hazing laws delineate penalties for the act of hazing, but some legislation goes beyond this fundamental step: Texas law states that medical personnel can report a hazing incident to the police with impunity. Florida's statue requires that each university adopt a written anti-hazing policy. And Massachusetts obligates secondary and postsecondary schools to provide all students with the state's hazing policy and includes a penalty for not reporting a witnessed hazing incident. Some states have statutes that have been interpreted to mean that individuals can still be guilty of hazing even if the victim consented. The legal concept is that individuals who are physically beaten or mentally abused cannot truly consent. Over the years, hazing laws in general have become stricter, but it is still unusual that individuals are charged with hazing as a crime and, if they are and are found guilty, most are given punishments of less than a few months of jail time.[47]

Another form of legal action in hazing incidents is civil. Parents of victims have brought civil suits against universities and local and national headquarters of fraternities. The results have been variable, but some families have won or settled for hundreds of thousands, even millions of dollars.[48]

Hazing Prevention

In light of the severity of injuries from hazing practices, some schools have developed strategies to halt these dangerous activities. Certain universities have taken a strong anti-hazing stance, including banning Greek chapters and athletic teams guilty of hazing practices.

In a well-publicized recent action, the University of Vermont cancelled its hockey season in January 2000 after administrators determined that athletes lied during the investigation of a hazing incident. A former hockey player reported that as a rookie in October 1999 he and his freshman colleagues were forced to drink excessively and participate in degrading acts such as walking in a line while holding each other's genitals. The freshman sued the university, administrators, and other members of the hockey team in federal court, saying that the defendants were negligent because the plaintiff had warned university officials of the hazing incident prior to its occurrence. The University of Vermont's president cancelled the remaining fifteen games of the hockey team's season and the university released guidelines intended to prevent hazing on campus. The incident also prompted Vermont's state legislature to pass new anti-hazing laws.[49] In the end, the case was settled when the university paid the player $80,000.

Hazing persists on many campuses, and one author suggests a variety of strategies for schools. These include keeping thorough and accurate records of hazing occurrences, appointing an ombudsperson who is well-versed in the dangers of hazing to hear hazing complaints, postponing rush to the second semester of a student's first year or eliminating it altogether, and establishing severe punishments for hazing transgressions. He also points out that illegal hazing, sexual assaults, and alcohol-related injury cases should be referred for criminal investigation, not just handled by the university administration.[50]

Several organizations promote anti-hazing prevention through public education. These groups also work to pass anti-hazing legislation. Relatives of hazing victims initiated many of these grassroots organizations.

Emergency physicians can help prevent hazing injuries by educating the medical staff of hazing's dangers. Treating these patients as victims of crime sets the tone, reminding fellow health care workers of the potential severity of injuries and the oftentimes-criminal nature of the activity.

Future/Conclusion

Hazing practices are so hazardous and increasingly prevalent that emergency physicians are now obliged to educate themselves about these activities so victims may be treated with adequate medical and psychiatric care. Emergency physicians need to be aware of the severity and range of traumatic inju-

Table 12.1. Summary List of Hazing Practices, Mechanisms, and Injuries

Hazing practices	Mechanism	Injuries
Alcohol, binge drinking	Acute alcohol intoxication	Aspiration, alcoholic coma, hematemesis, injuries associated with concomitant hazing practices
Beating/paddling/ whipping/striking	Blunt trauma	Intra-cranial, -thoracic, -abdominal; extremity
Blood-pinning	Penetrating trauma to chest	Superficial chest trauma
Branding/tattooing/ cigarette burning, burning	Burns	1st-, 2nd-, 3rd-degree burns; oropharyngeal and esophageal burns
Calisthenics	Heat-related	Syncope, vomiting, end-organ damage, including seizure and coma
	Cardiac	Ischemia in patients with underlying heart disease
Confinement in a restricted area	Heat-related	Syncope, vomiting, end-organ damage
	Hypoxia	Multi-organ system failure, hypoxic brain damage
Consumption of nonfood substances	Toxicity to GI tract	GI distress
Drowning, near-drowning	Hypoxia	Multi-organ system failure, hypoxic brain damage
Falls	Blunt trauma	Spinal cord/c-spine; intra-cranial, -thoracic, -abdominal; extremity
Immersion in noxious substances	Heat- or cold-related	Burns, cold-exposure, dermatitis
Psychological abuse	Verbal humiliation, coercion into performing demeaning acts, forced sleep deprivation	Depression, post-traumatic stress, poor self-esteem
Sexual assaults	Blunt trauma to mouth, vagina, anus	Anal, oral, vaginal trauma; HIV, hepatitis C and other STDs; unwanted pregnancy

ries in order to have a low threshold for suspected harm. Hazing prevention through legislation, university policies, grassroots organizations, and individual community activism may be effective in lessening the traumatic injuries presenting to emergency departments.

Notes

1. J. Leslie, M. Taff, and M. Mulvihill, "Forensic Aspects of Fraternity Hazing," *American Journal of Forensic Medicine and Pathology* 6 (1985): 53–67.
2. H. Nuwer, *High School Hazing* (New York: Franklin Watts, 2000), 17.
3. H. Nuwer, *Wrongs of Passage* (Bloomington: Indiana University Press, 1999), 238–250.
4. H. Nuwer, *Broken Pledges* (Atlanta: Longstreet), 291.
5. Ibid., 251.
6. Nuwer, *Wrongs of Passage,* 24–59.
7. Ibid., 238–250.
8. Nuwer, *High School Hazing,* 16.
9. N. Hoover and N. Pollard, *Initiation Rites and Athletics: A National Survey of NCAA Sports Teams* (Alfred, N.Y.: Alfred University and Reidman Insurance Co., Inc., 1999), 1, 4.
10. Leslie, Taff, and Mulvihill, "Forensic Aspects of Fraternity Hazing," 61.
11. B. A. Baker, K. A. Schwartz, D. J. Segan, et al., "Hemoglobinuria after Fraternity Hazing," *American Journal of Kidney Disorders* 1 (1982): 268–270; Leslie, Taff, and Mulvihill, "Forensic Aspects of Fraternity Hazing," 54.
12. Nuwer, *Wrongs of Passage,* 169–179.
13. Ibid., 238–250.
14. Ibid.
15. Nuwer, *High School Hazing,* 63–78.
16. Ibid., 101–111.
17. Ibid., 16–33.
18. J. McIntyre, Associated Press, "10 Marines to Be Disciplined for 'Blood Winging' Incident," *CNN Interactive,* July 11, 1997.
19. Nuwer, *High School Hazing,* 63–78.
20. W. Todd, "Human Branding in College Fraternities: Round-up Time at 'Animal House,'" *Journal of Burn Care and Rehabilitation* 14 (1993): 399–400.
21. Nuwer, *Wrongs of Passage,* 238–250.
22. Nuwer, *High School Hazing,* 101–111.
23. Ibid., 63–78.
24. Ibid., 16–33.
25. Ibid., 63–78; Nuwer, *Wrongs of Passage,* 169–79.
26. Leslie, Taff, and Mulvihill, "Forensic Aspects of Fraternity Hazing," 58.
27. Nuwer, *Wrongs of Passage,* 169–79.
28. Nuwer, *High School Hazing,* 16–33, 63–78; Nuwer, *Wrongs of Passage,* 24–59.
29. Todd, "Human Branding," 399.
30. Hoover and Pollard, *Initiation Rites and Athletics,* 1.
31. Nuwer, *High School Hazing,* 63–78.

32. Ibid., 16–33.
33. Ibid., 63–78.
34. Ibid., 101–111.
35. Ibid., 16–33.
36. Ibid., 63–78.
37. Ibid.
38. B. E. Borsari and K. B. Carey, "Understanding Fraternity Drinking: Five Recurring Themes in the Literature, 1980–1998," *Journal of American College Health* 48 (1999): 30–37.
39. Leslie, Taff, and Mulvihill, "Forensic Aspects of Fraternity Hazing," 54, 56–60.
40. Nuwer, *Wrongs of Passage*, 72.
41. K. A. Tyler, D. R. Hoyt, and L. B. Whitbeck, "Coercive Sexual Strategies," *Violence and Victims* 13 (1998): 47–61.
42. Leslie, Taff, and Mulvihill, "Forensic Aspects of Fraternity Hazing," 56–60.
43. Hoover and Pollard, *Initiation Rites and Athletics*, 1.
44. Leslie, Taff, and Mulvihill, "Forensic Aspects of Fraternity Hazing," 60.
45. Nuwer, *Wrongs of Passage*, 238–250.
46. I. Ramzy and K. Bryant, "Notes on Initiation and Hazing Practices," *Psychiatry* 25 (1962): 354–362.
47. Nuwer, *Wrongs of Passage*, 169–179.
48. Ibid.
49. W. Suggs, "Hazed Hockey Player Will Receive $80,000 from the U. of Vermont," *The Chronicle of Higher Education*, 31 August 2000.
50. Nuwer, *Wrongs of Passage*, 207–209.

13 A Carolina Soccer Initiation

Gregory Danielson and Hank Nuwer

Introduction

Hank Nuwer

Late in 2002, Gregory Danielson, a onetime University of North Carolina soccer player whose brush with death at a so-called team "party" was briefly mentioned in one of my books, wrote me an e-mail message. I asked Danielson to speak in my class. After hearing his story, I asked him to write an essay about his experience. I told him that I would need to get equal-time comments from his former coach, Elmar Bolowich, and UNC athletics director John Swofford, now commissioner of the Atlantic Coast Conference (ACC). Neither responded to requests for the lessons they had learned from the furor that might assist other coaches or athletic directors.

Gregory Danielson's essay must stand alone. Numerous photographs taken that night show players guzzling alcohol, wearing skimpy and silly outfits, and being cheered on by veterans, fellow rookies, and male and female partygoers. For rookies hungry to belong, attention from veterans and attractive women cheering them on can be as intoxicating as the alcohol they drink, and many have goofy celebratory smiles pasted on their faces. Nonetheless, these photographs tend to corroborate his story, as does the recollection of a teammate who describes his own nervousness and fear in the days before submitting to what had become an "annual initiation," in the claim of Danielson and his former teammate. Briefly, news accounts, hospital emergency-room reports, police records, and press accounts will verify that Danielson, then an 18-year-old rookie with a history of asthma, was admitted to an emergency room for acute alcohol poisoning on September 2, 1996. Afterward, instead of being treated as a victim, Danielson alleges that almost overnight he became a target of team and coaching-staff criticism, as very quickly the University of North Carolina (UNC) powers that be took pressure off the team and Chancellor Michael Hooker.

How? According to Danielson, instead of focusing on the real issue of hazing, UNC officials pushed the blame onto him by implying in every news release that some naive, dumb kid had swilled too much alcohol. And newspapers tended to print all quotations from the news releases without follow-up investigation.

"A kid comes to college and has some freedom for the first time," UNC women's soccer coach Anson Dorrance said after the event. "No longer do you have to go home and go through a gauntlet of parents. For the first time, literally, they are free to do what they want. They are adjusting to the responsibilities of this new freedom and that's when they tend to get irresponsible."

Dorrance made no mention of these people—the veteran players, who, according to Danielson, orchestrated the event and wrote the choreography that didn't change much from previous initiations—right down to the shaving of clumps of players' hair.

Also, Bolowich and Swofford looked to the public and press like disciplinarians, since the team would be made to back out of a trip to a Las Vegas tournament as a punishment and senior players would have to miss a game against Charleston Southern University. Moreover, the athletics office ordered the team to perform community service by participating as Habitat for Humanity volunteers, but Bolowich was present only in the afternoon to ride herd on the team, and the event became an excruciating exercise in torture for the landscape committee of Habitat for Humanity.

After the work-as-punishment day on September 21, 1996, the committee wrote the team this letter, which said, in part: "Most of you should re-evaluate your definition of community service. And for the few of you who complained, whined, and offered snide, rude, or insulting comments—You have a great deal to learn about group participation and common courtesy. . . . I was assured by Coach Bolowich that the proper attitude would prevail."

Athletic Director John Swofford, in strongly worded language, denounced the group's leadership and blasted "the underage drinking and the alcohol abuse that took place." There was no mention of hazing in his statement.

While Swofford's statement might be understandable in light of the fact that Alfred University's 1999 survey of initiation rites had not yet occurred, he nonetheless must have been or should have been aware that Kent State University had once cancelled an entire hockey season because of an initiation. Even minimal research would have shown him that a short list of athletes such as Western Illinois's Nick Haben, Nevada-Reno's John Davies, and American International's Jay Lenaghan had died during alcohol initiations. At any rate, contrast UNC's actions with those of Alfred University in 1998, when the president, athletic director, and coaching staff worked as one to suspend or expel hazers, send a clear public message, and even forfeit one game to emphasize the seriousness of an alcohol-related hazing close call. Or note the call of S. Daniel Carter of Security on Campus, Inc., that police investigate all hazings involving alcohol and/or criminal activities.

By constantly pointing the finger at him for his "alcohol abuse," alleges Danielson, the coaching staff unwittingly may have permitted the team to enjoy a measure of rationalization, the result being that many teammates began treating Danielson as less than an equal. If only he could have handled his liquor as they had, they could tell themselves, none of this trouble would have destroyed our soccer season.

Swofford in effect chided Danielson publicly in a press release. "Underage drinking is an issue that the chancellor and many on our campus are concerned about," he said, stressing that athletics had an "on-going alcohol educational program."

Swofford expressed concern for Danielson in a standard statement but then said "the team captains deny that this was an initiation for freshman team members." He said Bolowich shared his concern and that the Office of Student Affairs would hand over the "incident to the student attorney general's office for review." He failed to say why he did not call in Chapel Hill police officers to look into the matter to see if hazing, contributing-to-delinquency, or alcohol violations might be in order. Thus, no player was ever charged or given an opportunity to prove guilt or innocence. And, more important, no paper trail in police headquarters was created.

In fact, UNC had experienced serious hazing incidents all through the twentieth century, going back to the 1912 death of Isaac Rand, whose throat was slit on a broken bottle after older students apparently made him dance on a barrel. Back then, the governor of North Carolina himself took the UNC president to the woodshed in the press, but because Danielson had lived and his family expressed displeasure behind the scenes, no similar castigation befell Chancellor Hooker. Unfortunately for Danielson, although the University of North Carolina Hospitals that treated him in the emergency room gave him excellent care, no blood-alcohol measurement was taken that might have provided information to law enforcement personnel. Danielson read about his own "apparent binge" in the Chapel Hill newspaper.

Bolowich's team policy statement for the UNC men's soccer team makes interesting reading. Although the document says not one word about prohibitions on hazing, initiations, or underage drinking, it does prohibit drug abuse. Bolowich ordered his players to "wear Adidas jogging shoes for team travel," however.

After scrutinizing area newspapers for the month of September, the only paper I could find that pointed out any errors made by UNC's athletic department was the Durham *Herald-Sun*. Eight paragraphs deep into a story, a reporter wrote that Swofford's office had sent back-to-back conflicting news releases about whether the "party" had indeed been an initiation. Later, a sports information director said he had no idea where the paper had gotten a release that acknowledged an initiation had occurred.

Unlike the athletics department, UNC's public safety officials minced no words about what happened that night. An officer's report said this: "I learned that a UNC-Chapel Hill student was brought into the emergency room by South Orange Rescue for treatment of excessive alcohol consumption. They were at an [*sic*] UNC-Chapel Hill mens [*sic*] soccer initiation party. The party was at 505 North Greensboro Street. . . . Carrboro, NC 27510."

The Orange County Emergency Medical Services was equally explicit. Rescue workers interviewed witnesses who reported Danielson's repeated vomiting. They observed his "tremors & twitching—uncontrollably." They reported his regurgitating brown liquid as they transported him, and found him "confused" and only "able to answer some questions with constant prodding." In short, he might have slept it off as his fellow soccer players later said in mocking tones to his face later, but he also might have died, says Danielson.

While Bolowich declined to respond to my requests for input and lessons learned by his experience, Danielson's roommate and fellow soccer-team player Thomas Rijsman has no such qualms about keeping silence.

"I am nervous," Rijsman says he confided in Bolowich right before the party.

"For the Clemson game?" Bolowich replied, recalls Rijsman. "No, no for the initiation night."

Rijsman recalls this: "Elmar [Bolowich] took a little pause in his speaking. After a few seconds he told me not to worry. So he knew about the night. Yes, he knew about the night. He told me not to worry [and] that things will be OK that night. It's a thing that happens every year, I concluded. I honestly remember thinking, *Now I told him, I told him I'm scared, or at least nervous, now why can't he stop this thing?* But then again, I thought to myself, an initiation is just part of the deal. And Elmar probably thought the same. I compromised my thoughts to this rationale."

Rijsman also recalls a team captain picking him up and solicitously making sure that he and Greg had food in their stomachs by taking them to a fast-food eatery. At the party, he says, they were made to drink in a mock test of endurance, the biggest burden going to Greg and one other player, the heaviest of the rookies in weight. They were all given silly clothing with silly nicknames and their team numbers on the shirt. "I was 'The Painter' since I'm from Holland."

He also recalls the senior who brought razors to the party in spite of the fact that Coach Bolowich "explicitly told the team during a team meeting 'not to shave our heads this year,'" he recalls. He also recalls another individual on the team handing Danielson hard liquor in a bottle to drink in addition to the enormous supply of beer and booze they chugged from bottle and pretzel barrel and by bong.

That night, while Danielson staggered in the house and ended up alone in a closet with his hair in ragged clumps, Rijsman went out with players to town to drink some more, waking up in his own vomit in another fast-food eatery, he recalls.

Then, the UNC athletics department did take some action. Bolowich took away the captaincy from three players but failed to boot his stars off the team that prides itself on being an annual national contender for NCAA champion status. Because other disciplinary violations were committed by at least two UNC players unrelated to the party, one player was suspended for ill conduct at the party and after the party. Bolowich, unlike coaches at the University of Vermont or Kent State, who were lambasted in the press after an initiation, fared well at the hands of the media. "Thank you very much for all the support you have shown during the past few days," Bolowich wrote Swofford. He apparently tried to tighten team rules. "You can see on the attached sheet that we already had team rules in place prior to this season. I will fine-tune this page for the future and our players still have to sign that they are in agreement with my team policy. Thank you for your compassion in this matter."

The whole matter ended, until now, with this conclusion by Student Attorney General David Huneycutt, who released the results of his official "investigation" sixteen days after Danielson was taken to an emergency room. "The party which took place was not an 'initiation' party. The players who attended did not force the freshman [Danielson] to drink extra amounts of alcohol or to take part in activities which were 'highly offensive.'" If anything, the freshmen were excited about the chance to attend the party and accordingly consumed large quantities of alcohol of their own free will. . . . A senior captain on the team tried to prevent Greg Danielson from consuming any more alcohol by taking a bottle of vodka away from him. At least eight other people attending the party witnessed this act. . . . An additional factor which caused the officer to believe that hazing had occurred at the party was that all the freshman players had shaved heads. My investigation found that the freshman soccer players decided to shave each other's hair because they envied the already short hair possessed by one of their freshman teammates. Based on the above facts, I have concluded that there is insufficient evidence to support a charge."

In my book *Wrongs of Passage,* First Amendment expert Louis Ingelhart blasted colleges that have an embarrassing or criminal act occur on campus, then handle the investigation themselves instead of handing matters over to independent law enforcement authorities. But Huneycutt's findings—cc'd to just three people (Swofford, Bolowich, and UNC Chancellor Michael Hooker) —effectively capped a lid on the whole case. Before the findings, Chancellor Hooker had promised this to the *Chapel Hill Herald:* "The behavior, as reported, clearly is unacceptable and will not be tolerated at Carolina."

What follows is former UNC soccer player Gregory Danielson's statement of events. Draw your own conclusions about whether you side with UNC's investigation or Danielson's statement. I regret that neither Swofford nor Bolowich, the ACC's Coach of the Year in 2000, deigned to add their own insights and or criticisms of Danielson to complete this case study. Suffice it to say that Danielson claims that his UNC soccer career was ruined by this cloud. Finally, the University of Vermont hazing case ultimately resulted in a change of presidents and a heartfelt self-study of hazing by UVM. Nothing of the sort occurred at North Carolina. Chancellor Michael Hooker was never in danger of losing his job over what occurred on his watch. He died of cancer in 1999.

In February 2003, Associate Athletic Director for Communications Steve Kirschner issued this statement, reprinted verbatim:

> The University of North Carolina Department of Athletics and its men's soccer program regret any and all aspects of the unfortunate choices that were made by a number of student-athletes on the evening in question. We also regret Mr. Danielson did not have the type experience we hope all our student-athletes have while attending the University. However, our internal investigation found the acts committed that evening, while improper and dangerous, did not constitute hazing. The information we received in our investigation came directly from people who were in attendance that evening.

Mr. Danielson's assertion he was made to be a scapegoat after the fact is disputed by Coach Bolowich. Since Mr. Danielson and Mr. Bolowich have different opinions on the facts of this matter, the coach has declined to be interviewed for your book.

The Department of Athletics regarded the incident as serious and stands by its actions. The University cancelled the men's soccer team's two-game tournament in Las Vegas, rescinded the captaincy of several student-athletes, suspended the senior class for a game for a lack of leadership, among other disciplinary and educational measures it took.

Regardless of whether the activities on the evening in question met the level of hazing, the University has increased its anti-hazing educational message to its student-athletes and regards hazing and other alcohol-related actions as serious safety concerns. They are not to be taken lightly and the University feels it has taken proper steps to educate its teams about the dangers and consequences of hazing and other alcohol-related incidents. It is a continual educational process.

We wish Mr. Danielson and his family all the best.

Danielson's Account

The first time I was introduced to UNC-Chapel Hill as a potential school of interest was my junior year in high school when I attended Indiana University's Met Life Classic soccer tournament at Armstrong Stadium with a few soccer mates. Held in my hometown of Bloomington, Indiana, the Met Life Classic captivated me as a young soccer player with a dream of playing in college. The Met Life Classic hosted top collegiate soccer teams, including, that year, the University of North Carolina at Chapel Hill.

I remember sitting high in the stadium as I munched sunflower seeds with my fellow Bloomington High School South players as we awaited the final game between the Hoosiers and UNC. A teammate who was a good friend and a year older than I said he was thrilled that UNC was playing in the finals. So when UNC went on to win that year's Met Life Classic, I became hooked on the Carolina Blue.

That summer I visited the University as an exuberant summer camper ready to display my soccer talent to whatever authority could award me a spot on the soccer team. Because soccer is a small-revenue sport for most colleges, there typically is little recruiting outside of a school's own region. The camp, therefore, was a means of showcasing my skills.

The strategy paid off. By the end of the week, I had won camp Most Valuable Player honors, earning recognition from the team's head coach, Elmar Bolowich. I met Mrs. Bolowich and was on the top of the world when she told me Bolowich had expressed interest in my abilities. Coach Bolowich told me to keep in contact.

The middle of December, amid deadlines for collegiate signings, the pressure for me to make a decision began increasing. I wasn't getting much attention from Bolowich, so I took the initiative and called the coach. Just before the signing deadline, he offered me a position on the UNC men's varsity soccer team. I was nervous, thrilled, and happy.

I began training harder then I thought was humanly possible. I ran every day, twice a day, and still left room for soccer drills of all sorts. Nothing at that point was going to stop me, and if that meant I couldn't walk for a week from training so hard, then so be it.

I had prepared myself to face any obstacle with vigor, and I felt that no one could match my determination. I might add that I always tried to be humble with soccer. My philosophy was if you were good you didn't have to say anything, because it was evident by your presence. The great players did not have to say a word about their abilities. They were great because of their dedication and actions on the field.

When I arrived in Chapel Hill with my parents, the freshmen dorms were unavailable, so we freshmen soccer players stayed at a hotel for two weeks. After a few uncomfortable minutes we all began to connect. We all shared a common bond; we were all passionate about soccer.

Preseason started as the coaching staff conducted the Cooper Test, a measure of fitness designed by Dr. Kenneth Cooper. The Cooper Test consisted of a three-mile run; the first two miles in under twelve minutes, followed by a rest interval of six minutes, and a final mile completed in under six minutes. If the first two miles were completed under eleven and a half minutes, then you were excused from the third and final mile.

I ran two miles in a little over eleven minutes, which gave me the fastest time on the entire team. Afterward, I felt a little disappointed. I was certain I would run a good time, but I hadn't imagined my time would be the fastest on the team. I was joining one of the best teams in the nation—surely everyone took their conditioning as seriously as I did? But I saw that many players did not even pass the test and could not receive their UNC soccer gear until they passed, However, that lapse on their part wasn't going to sway me from pursuing anything ahead with determination and intensity, and that came to include the initiation the upperclassmen players would soon prepare us freshmen for.

The next two weeks became a grueling display of our desire and perseverance as we trained in hot and humid Carolina three times a day. Water weight was measured before and after each practice to ensure proper hydration during the hot temperatures. Everyone was mentally and physically exhausted after each practice, and little time was left for eating and sleeping. However, we freshmen were given constant reminders of a coming initiation, and it excited my nerves. The initiation was the final step in a freshman's realizing a true spot on the UNC men's varsity soccer team. Every break in practice action brought a reiteration of the coming event. Upperclassmen referred to it as a test of endurance, mentioning things like, "You guys better be ready for this," or "You are going to puke, but you have to keep drinking."

During a team meeting, Coach Bolowich said to everyone, "There will be no head shaving this year." His statement only made my suspicions about the mysterious initiation grow even more. At that point I began questioning to what extent he condoned such antics and where the line was going to be drawn in my case.

As freshmen we newcomers talked in secrecy in order to learn the same unknown answers. We had no idea what was about to take place, and that fear of the unknown was very real. One thing I did know was that I was not going to lessen my pace toward accomplishing my dream of playing for UNC.

Finally, a night for the initiation arrived but fell through for some reason, and in the additional days my anxiety heightened. Each day brought me new questions and assumptions about the initiation. It hindered my focus on important issues like my quality of play and the type of classes I was facing. Finally, the night of the initiation came up on me like a runaway freight engine. It had been rescheduled for Labor Day weekend because a Sunday presented the perfect night, with no Monday classes the next day.

On September 2, 1996, I remember waiting with my roommate outside our dormitory at the designated time to be picked up. Junior Co-Captain Carey Talley said he would transport us to his house, where other upperclassmen soccer players also resided. Carey informed us if we had not eaten we should grab something now. So Thomas and I both ordered meals at a Wendy's. My anticipation made it difficult to swallow each bite. When we arrived at the house, it and the surrounding area was illuminated with lights of all sorts. Most of the team had already gathered around the outside of the house socializing; the group included young men and women outside the team, acquaintances of players, and acquaintances of acquaintances.

The festivities, as I ironically refer to them, began when Thomas and I were given Dixie Cups® and then poured some so-called P.J., a concoction made from 100 percent grain liquor—customarily, I was told, 190-proof Everclear®, plus chopped fruit and punch. The fruit and grain liquor is marinated overnight so that the fruit absorbs most of the liquor, and the punch is then added. A whole Gatorade® vat—the multi-gallon Gatorade® vat seen on the sidelines of most football games—had been prepared with P.J., also known in some circles by other names like Sucker Punch. Everyone on the team, including the freshmen, began drinking and eating the fruit pieces.

I was not a big drinker, which my upbringing may have contributed to. My parents never stocked up on alcohol and I, at 18, was not legally able to drink. Midway through my second cup I began to feel intoxicated, and at that time we freshmen were summoned through a PA system attached to the house. We met at the side of the house and awaited further instruction.

A majority of the upperclassmen arrived and told us what we were about to face. The drinking event was called no other name than the "Cooper Test." This test began with a barrel of beer that had to be finished by the seven freshmen within the time slot of twelve minutes. If the barrel was not finished within twelve minutes we had to repeat the test until we were successful. Right before we started, we freshmen gathered around a circle to discuss our team strategy. We decided that the goalkeeper and I should be last in line because we were physically bigger than the other freshmen and should assume the anchor spot to pick up the slack if needed.

I remember lining up for the "Cooper Test" and hearing the entire team root us on. They scolded us if we dribbled any beer instead of consuming it. When the barrel reached me, it was a lot heavier than I expected. It took both hands to pick it up and, because it was filled with so much beer, it was hard not to slosh it around. I remember thinking that we were never going to finish it in time because, after the first round, it looked as if we hadn't even made a dent.

It was after the second round that most of us began to vomit. We would go through the line and chug as much beer as we could and return to the end of the line puking. This drinking and puking occurred for about four rounds. When we finally reached the last round we were given the passing time from a designated timekeeper. We then learned that this was but the first obstacle we had successfully completed.

As the night progressed, more and more people began to show up. How many people actually showed up amazed me. Young women and men clustered before the front porch of the house where, through the PA system, the freshmen had been ordered to reconvene. On the porch, which was serving as a stage, we were told to line up in twos. Due to the odd number of freshmen, I was the odd man out at the end of the line. I waited outside the door patiently as my fellow freshmen, in twos, entered the house within five minutes of each other. During that fifteen minutes, my mind was going crazy; I had no idea what was going on in the house. Finally, as I entered the house I was given a quick shot of liquor. I didn't see any of the other freshmen. I was told to open my hands and I looked down to see a miniature plastic cowboy hat, women's bikini underwear, and a halter top with my number and nickname printed on the back. I was told to go into the bathroom and put it on. I had "earned" this "team uniform," just as I had earned my real team uniform earlier by running the actual Cooper Test.

At this point, I was way past my alcohol limit, falling down and colliding with walls as I put this outfit on in the bathroom. I was thoroughly embarrassed when I saw my reflection in the mirror, but to my relief, when I exited the bathroom, I found the rest of the freshmen dressed in similar garb.

Samba music with loud thumps of bass played outside. An announcer on the intercom introduced us to the crowd of strangers and players. One by one we, in our demeaning outfits, attracted a rush of screams, yelps, and laughter from the audience. As the samba music blared, we lined up to funnel beer from a bong, which was administered in turn to another freshmen. As we were funneling beer, an upperclassman teammate approached with multiple fifths of vodka clenched in both hands. He entered the stage and proceeded to pour vodka down our bongs. I felt pain and gasped after taking two large chugs of vodka through the bong. At this point we freshmen were drenched in liquor, beer, and sweat.

The freshmen were then handed lit Tiki torches and sent on a scavenger hunt. The mission was to run down a main street and buy three Three Musketeers® bars from a Harris Teeter food market. After we exited the porch-stage, we ran into each other while attempting to reach the grocery store. Some fell down in the middle of the street and rolled around, while others dropped torches and stumbled to pick them up. When we finally reached our destination, incoherent, we attempted to bring our lit torches into the food market. Employees blocked us at the door. We finally left the torches outside and entered to retrieve the candy bars. People laughed in bewilderment when they saw our motley crew stagger toward the candy station in women's underwear and plastic cowboy hats. We began filing toward the register and spent the money the upperclassmen had given us. With our candy bars in hand, we headed, stumbling over one another, back to the house.

When we were back onstage the crowd cheered. We were lined up. While the crowd became increasingly loud, an upperclassman teammate handed us seven freshmen a full fifth of vodka and told us to finish it within twelve minutes. This was the final test of the mock Cooper conditioning test. I was the third one to receive the vodka and I tried to help my teammates finish the bottle. I can remember chugging the bottle of vodka and pretending that it was nothing but water. I quickly and easily downed a good portion of the bottle. The other freshmen finished the vodka expeditiously, and the crowd cheered once again.

Within minutes after the conclusion I began to feel extremely anxious. Something, a survival instinct I suppose, was telling me to flee the scene. In my confusion I began to feel that . . . I was going to die if I didn't find a place to hide. I staggered inside the house to find a place to hide. I recall going upstairs and seeing a nightlight, which I followed. When I reached the light, I realized I had entered a closet, and I collapsed on top of shoes with someone's clothes hanging above me. I started sweating, my palms began to burn, and I couldn't orient myself in terms of direction. I felt as if I was suspended in water not knowing which way was up. I began puking profusely, and had a hard time catching my breath in between. I couldn't stop puking until all that seemed left were the remnants of my stomach bile. I began slipping in and out of consciousness and my body began convulsing. I quickly became very cold, and it was all I could do to try and stay conscious. I remember thinking that if I passed out I would surely die. I continued to slip into unconsciousness and began pleading with myself to stay awake.

The rest is a blur. I was told afterward that while I was upstairs in what they called my "hiding place," the rest of the team was getting their heads shaved downstairs. I believe that is when the team set out to search for me. By no means were they out to rescue me, because when they found me nothing was done for me except to shave clumps of my head hair. I had no sense of time and I cannot tell you how long I was left upstairs. I did find out later that while I was left upstairs in that closet, the upperclassmen went uptown to the bars.

My next recollection is that I heard myself talking and I was aware an EMT (emergency medical technician) had arrived. I recall someone putting boxer shorts on me and I was carried away in a rescue vehicle. I remember the ride in the ambulance and some of the questions the rescuers were asking me. I recall a collage of images as I passed in and out of consciousness while I was in the hospital emergency room. I remember a police officer taking a police report, questioning bystanders. I heard him use the word "initiation," and this recollection was confirmed in his report, which I later read. I remember hearing Carey Talley's voice behind the curtain as he spoke to a doctor. At that point, I remember feeling safe, thinking it was okay to just let my body drift into sleep. I awoke early the next day and then learned that clumps of my head hair had been shaved.

I don't know how long I was at the hospital, but Mercer Reynolds graciously came and picked me up. Little did I know at the time that Mercer Reynolds and Curtis Jablanka had arrived at the aftermath of the party to find me in what they perceived was a desperate state that needed immediate attention. These two sophomore teammates did not participate in the hazing that I and my fellow freshman endured, and though they had experienced soccer initiation the year before, they acted sensibly when the situation called for it. (I couldn't be any more thankful or indebted to them.) Mercer drove me to my dormitory after I was dismissed from the hospital. There I saw someone I didn't recognize—my roommate. His head was completely shaved and he looked upset. When I spoke with him I found I didn't have much energy. I told him that I was going back to bed and that I didn't want to accept phone calls.

Nonetheless, I awoke and found Thomas pushing the telephone in my face. He gave me the phone against my wishes and I accepted it without a word. The lady on the end of the phone inquired how I was doing. Still dazed, I could only think she was from the hospital. She began asking me more details with regard to my condition, which I tried to pleasantly respond to. After a few moments I became a little suspicious as she began quizzing me on the details of initiation party. I finally realized I wasn't speaking with a nurse from the hospital. I asked her who she was and she told me she was a reporter. I asked her why she was calling me and she said that a police report was taken and that made it accessible to the public. I wasn't sure what I was supposed to do in that type of situation, and I told her to scratch everything I had said. I told her that I didn't realize she was a reporter. I began trying to cover up by ambiguously answering her questions. Concerned, I told her I wasn't sure if last night was an initiation or not and rambled some more.

The next day I was summoned by Coach Bolowich to meet him at the soccer hut. He was on the phone when I arrived and I didn't know what to expect. I just felt like I was in big trouble. I could hear him talking with people on the phone as I waited patiently. I remember that, as I was sitting alone, I heard him tell someone on the phone that when freshmen come to college they gain a whole new sense of freedom and that they are not responsible enough to handle it.

He called me in after a few minutes and told me to take off my hat. He saw that my head had been shaved in patches, and I could tell he was not pleased. He told me that I needed to answer some questions for John Swofford, the athletic director at the time. We got into his car and I was scared and didn't know what to say. When we arrived at John Swofford's office, Beth Miller, the senior associate athletic director for Olympic sports, was also there. Coach Bolowich and I entered the room and doors closed behind us. John Swofford sat us together and I felt really uncomfortable. I remember thinking that this was it; they are going to tell me I am off the team or expelled from school.

Swofford made a quick introduction and told me that Beth Miller was there to take notes. He began quizzing me on the initiation and I didn't know how to answer, because my coach was sitting right next to me. At that time I had no idea what hazing was, or that there was a university regulation against it. Swofford did not inform me of the definition of hazing or ask me if that was what had happened to me. My only thought was that I was going to be kicked out of school and how disappointed my parents would be. The whole time it felt as if I were being interrogated and I felt weak and vulnerable.

It was like a surprise attack and I didn't know what I, an 18-year-old boy who could have died the night before, was up against. At one point Coach Bolowich interjected a statement into the conversation, saying, "I heard you drank a full vodka bottle by yourself."

That is when I got defensive. I told Swofford and Bolowich that we were instructed by the seniors on the team to finish the vodka bottle within twelve minutes. I told them about the mock Cooper Test and everything else that happened that night. The meeting concluded, the last time any member of the athletic department or the administration of the University of North Carolina asked me any questions or inquired about my well-being. I received no apology, nothing at all, from anyone, including my coach. I was left to bear the full burden of what had happened alone.

When I got home, my parents called me and told me that they had talked with Bolowich, and he said that I had put the entire team and its season in jeopardy. He told my parents that I was the one to blame. I told my father everything that had happened. My dad also spoke with my roommate, who was also victimized in the incident, to confirm the details. My dad was angry. I later learned from my mother that my dad immediately called Bolowich back and rebuked him. My dad, according to my mother, said to Bolowich, words to this effect: "*How dare you for having the audacity to call me and tell me that my son put your team in jeopardy when your team almost killed my son? I put my son under your guidance and you victimized him.*"

These may not have been my father's exact words, but my father's meaning, his concern for me, and his scorn for the actions of the upperclassman and the coach's explanation is indisputable. He gave the coach a clear idea of his fury.

The next day at practice Coach Bolowich made us run as punishment. I continued to try hard. I was there to accomplish a dream, and I was still going to pursue my dreams; I was young and unaware of the full nuances of the situation. Many people commented how well I performed in the running drills and that, to them, it was evident that I hadn't been in need of medical attention two nights before. They could not know that my system had been flushed of all intoxication at the hospital and, under my mother's orders, I had been drinking bottle after bottle of Pedialyte®, an oral electrolyte-maintenance solution, to replenish my once-dehydrated body. In retrospect, I see that the only way I could have ever convinced some my teammates and the coaching staff that I had been wronged by them that night is if I had died. They didn't want to hear, see, or have anything to do with the truth, so I just tried to continue on.

I remember Assistant Coach Alan Dawson taking the team aside during practice shortly after the initiation. He sat us down and told us that we had killed his passion for soccer. At that second I felt my heart sink and my confidence shatter. I blamed myself for killing a man's passion for a game that I too loved. Dawson was a man that I held in such high regard, and he was someone whom I would have done anything for, connected with a team I would have done anything for. At that very second I couldn't breathe, my senses became numb to the world, and I just wanted to escape somewhere where nobody could find me. That, essentially, is what I attempted to do—escape. I no longer went to class. I couldn't stand people I didn't know quizzing me about the initiation. The media became ravenous for the story's details. Television cameras followed me about campus, begging for more information. I started hating people in general and grew cynical.

The things I saw as beautiful were beautiful to me no more. I began flunking classes, because I either didn't go or couldn't concentrate long enough to benefit. I had never received anything lower than a B throughout high school and now I was hanging on academically by a thread, but I didn't care. I lost hope, and then I became physically ill. I began checking into the health clinic again and again with the symptoms of walking pneumonia, sinus infections, and upper respiratory infections. Finally, I even had to take sleeping pills because I stayed up all night thinking about the initiation. I shut myself off to the world and only left my dormitory room when it was mandatory. Bolowich called me into his office. He told me that if I flunked English class from all the absences I had accrued he would kick me off the team. After our meeting I went straight to the hospital and collected all the days I had been seen by medical personnel and took them to my English teacher. I told my English teacher that I had been having rough time and asked if he would accept the documented visits at the sports medicine clinic as justification. He excused something like nine or ten absences that day.

I was crying out for help, but it didn't seem to me like anyone at North Carolina cared. No one asked me how I was doing, not my coaches, not the players, not anyone at the University. Moreover, coaches and players continually blamed me for bringing disgrace upon the team. Upperclassmen would literally come up to my face and blame me for all the bad press. I was repeatedly ridiculed and given nicknames like "Detox" and "Pump." The initiation did bring everyone closer together, but they were now close together—against me. I felt blacklisted and blackballed. It seemed I was the only one around with the plague, and everyone avoided me.

Most coaches and players could not even look me in the eyes. Even many of my fellow freshmen distanced themselves from me.

Yet, oddly perhaps, I didn't blame them. They wanted to play just as much as

I did, and siding with me would have jeopardized their chances, so I couldn't blame them. So instead, I continued blaming myself. What made it even worse, my mother and I learned from a story faxed by *The* [Durham] *Herald-Sun* that John Swofford sent out what the paper called successive "contradictory news releases" about whether or not my hospitalization was the result of a team initiation. As punishment, the team was suspended from a Las Vegas tournament, players were kicked off the team or suspended, and we all had to do community service. The cancelled tournament and punishments exacerbated a situation in which I already felt I wasn't welcome. Many teammates told me point-blank that I had ruined the season. The same people that had put me in the hospital began to believe what they wanted to believe. In spite of the dozens of witnesses that had attended the party, many of whom are pictured in photographs people took that evening on a disposable camera, several players were quoted as saying that no initiation had occurred. The implication was that I had drunk myself into a stupor and embarrassed my team.

I find it significant that John Swofford or someone in his office faxed my parents one press release on his letterhead which said, "This was evidently a type of initiation" and then a second in which he said the "Team captains deny that this was an initiation for freshman team members." When called about the discrepancy, Rick Brewer of the university's Sports Information Office told a reporter for *The Herald-Sun* that he had "no idea how you got that."

My name was in national news and I became perceived as the guy who got out of hand at a team party. As a consequence, my name and reputation had been slandered.

Neither my roommate nor myself as the one hospitalized were ever called in for questioning by David Huneycutt, the student attorney general. Nonetheless, Mr. Huneycutt was still able to enumerate six reasons why he found insufficient evidence to show a hazing violation according to the Code of Student Conduct. In a letter to the dean of students and John Swofford, Huneycutt states:

1. The party which took place was not an "initiation" party. The players who attended did not force the freshmen to drink extra amounts of alcohol or to take part in activities which were "highly offensive." If anything, the freshmen were excited about the chance to attend the party and accordingly consumed large quantities of alcohol of their own free will.
2. Several soccer players attending the party (including one freshman) decided to consume little or no alcohol. These players were not treated differently by their teammates because of their decision not to drink excessively.
3. A senior captain on the team tried to prevent Greg Danielson from consuming any more alcohol by taking a bottle of vodka away from him. At least eight other people attending the party witnessed this act.
4. The party was attended by non-soccer players including females. The freshman did not arrive any earlier than the other players on the team.
5. The nature of the party was not kept secret from the freshman players. All were well aware and excited about the prospect of getting drunk together.
6. An additional factor which caused the officer to believe that hazing occurred at

the party was that all the freshman players had shaved heads. My investigation found that the freshman soccer players decided to shave each other's hair because they envied the already short hair possessed by one of their freshman teammates. The seniors scolded [them about] this behavior because they were afraid that their coach would be upset.

Mr. Huneycutt was led to these false conclusions because of the fear of recrimination that we all felt would take place if the real facts came out. However, it is time to set the record straight, and while I have provided my own account of events surrounding the initiation party, I want to reiterate key elements from that evening in direct refutation of the points included in Mr. Huneycutt's report.

1. The event was an "initiation" party, as John Swofford declared in the initial press release faxed to my parents. The upperclassmen forced the freshman to drink excessive amounts of alcohol by conducting staged drinking tests. The activities were "highly offensive" when the freshmen were forced to wear women's underwear and miniature plastic cowboy hats and then coerced into going to a store. Other freshmen besides me were nervous about the idea of having to drink excessive amounts of alcohol.
2. Every single freshman participated in the hazing activities under the direction of upperclassmen. Not a single freshman decided to consume little or no alcohol; thus, the others could not have treated any of them any differently on this basis.
3. The senior captain on the team did not try to prevent me from consuming any more vodka because the senior captain was not in the vicinity to grab the vodka bottle away from me, as the photographs of the scene indicate. Furthermore, the vodka was then passed on to two more freshmen before being finished, again as indicated in the photographs.
4. The party was attended by individuals who were not soccer players, including females, which made it even more offensive to the freshmen who were showcased in women's underwear.
5. The nature of the party was not kept secret from the freshmen. For two weeks prior they were informed they would be forced to drink excessive amounts of alcohol and that they would not be able to stop. This information only heightened the already unsettled nerves of the freshmen, in particular Thomas Rijsman's. Thomas reported his feeling to Elmar Bolowich, who did not succeed in stopping the initiation. [*Ed. note:* He may have forbidden the head-shaving ritual, but his players disobeyed.]
6. The officer who filed a police report was correct in believing that an initiation had occurred based on the extent to which the freshmen's heads had been shaved. My head was shaved while in an unconscious state and thus unable to consent. I awoke in the hospital to find clumps of hair missing, which produced a very unappealing appearance, as proven by photos.

While Huneycutt's investigation exonerated the team of the more serious charges of hazing, my name gained national attention as the guy who got out of hand at a team party. I have had to live with the consequence of that notoriety, which falsely tarnished my reputation.

The incident always comes back to torment me. In the year 2000, while I was standing one evening on Franklin Street in Chapel Hill, I was blindsided with a football tackle. I fell off the curb and into the street. When I turned I saw two teammates who had graduated. They were drunk and growled at me for causing what they called "a shitty season."

I turned away from them and left. All I could think was, "Fucking grow up."

14 Hazing and Sport and the Law

R. Brian Crow and Scott R. Rosner

Editor's note: *Hazing activists such as Alice Haben, who lost her son in a lacrosse club initiation involving alcohol at Western Illinois University, have criticized professional athletes and their various umbrella leagues for cavalierly permitting hazing activities in public that set a bad example for amateur athletes. In this essay, the authors not only point to professional athletics as a source of toleration for silly and even dangerous hazing stunts but also point to serious liability issues the negligence of such initiations engenders. The authors also examine hazing in interscholastic and intercollegiate sports, finding that initiations at that level are increasing in number and severity.*

Although hazing was originally associated with stereotypical fraternal organizations, it is now common in both interscholastic and intercollegiate sports. Hazing, however, is not limited to amateur athletics. There is a long tradition of hazing rookies in professional team sports.[1] Hazing in sports has received a significant amount of media attention in the last several years, especially on high school and college campuses nationwide. More student-athletes are being prosecuted under state anti-hazing laws and more institutions are being held responsible for their care. This liability may soon be extended to professional athletes and sports organizations due to the frequent hazing of rookie players.

In attempting to determine the scope of the hazing problem and liability issues, a definitional question arises as to what actions or behaviors constitute hazing. Actions that are considered hazing by some are not considered hazing and are not objectionable to others. Hazing is defined as "any activity expected of someone joining a group that humiliates, degrades, abuses, or endangers, regardless of the person's willingness to participate."[2] Traditionally, athletic hazing was limited to relatively benign activities such as having rookies carry travel bags for veteran players or sing team songs in front of others. In recent times, however, these somewhat harmless behaviors have been replaced by potentially dangerous activities such as assault, binge drinking, sexual harassment, and exploitation.[3] Although it is difficult to know exactly how prevalent hazing is in intercollegiate and professional sports, the reporting of athletic hazing has increased dramatically since 1980, both in frequency and severity.[4] Additionally, it is obvious that most instances of hazing occur without being reported to coaches, school or team officials, or law enforcement,[5] despite the fact that hazing is illegal in forty-three states.[6]

Increasingly, however, students are being charged with criminal hazing.[7] Nonetheless, anti-hazing activists complain that there is no uniformity among the state statutes and that prosecutors are often not educated about the seriousness of hazing.[8] An analysis of current state hazing statutes demonstrates the following: 1) the majority of states consider hazing a misdemeanor that does not change the penalty or definition of any activity covered by other criminal statutes;[9] 2) statutes in seven of the forty-three states with anti-hazing laws include language that forbids observing or participating in hazing and failing to notify authorities;[10] 3) thirteen of the states with anti-hazing laws require anti-hazing policies to be developed and disseminated at public schools;[11] and 4) twenty states specifically state in their codes that implied or express consent, or a willingness on the part of the victim to participate in the initiation, is not an available defense.[12] Penalties for violation of these statutes are wide ranging and include: fines ($10 to $10,000), jail time (ten days to twelve months), a combination of fines and jail time, withholding of diploma, expulsion from school, or rescission of the right to assemble on campus.[13] A common penalty is three to twelve months in jail, a $1,000 fine, or both.[14]

Alfred University Study

In 1998, Edward Coll Jr., president of Alfred University, an NCAA Division III school, forfeited one of the school's football games after five players were arrested for hazing freshmen players, including minors, by restraining them with rope and requesting them to drink alcohol.[15] In the aftermath of the incident, administrators conducted a national survey of student-athletes, coaches, and administrators at NCAA-member institutions to identify: 1) the breadth and depth of initiation in college athletics; 2) perceptions of appropriate initiation behavior; and 3) strategies to prevent hazing.[16] Findings from the survey of student-athletes demonstrated the following:

- 45 percent of the respondents said they knew of, had heard of, or suspected hazing on their campuses.
- 80 percent reported being subjected to one or more of the listed hazing behaviors, yet only 12 percent characterized or labeled those activities as "hazing." [Ed. note: Hazing experts Nadine Hoover and Norm Pollard, who conducted the survey, and Hank Nuwer, who was a consultant on the NCAA project, agree that these results show that many people who participate in hazing rituals are reluctant to refer to what they have experienced as hazing.]
- 65 percent participated in some form of questionable initiation behavior.
- 51 percent claimed to be involved in alcohol-related initiation activities.
- 21 percent participated in unacceptable (dangerous) initiation activities, including 16 percent of female respondents.

• 60 percent of the respondent student-athletes said they would not report hazing to school officials.[17]

The athletes most at risk of being hazed were male swimmers and divers, lacrosse players, soccer players, and athletes whose institution was domiciled in a state with no anti-hazing law.[18]

University of Vermont Hockey Scandal

Some of the most heinous details of any athletic initiation surrounded the hazing incident at the University of Vermont. The initiation rites were so atrocious that the president of the university cancelled the remainder of the 1999–2000 hockey season after the players involved attempted to cover up the incident by lying during the subsequent investigation.[19] A former walk-on goalie (that is, a goalie who was not recruited by the university) and eight other freshmen players attended a team party in which they were coerced into lying on a basement floor while being spat upon and having beer poured over them. They were forced to engage in a "pie-eating contest." The pie consisted of seafood quiche doctored with ketchup and barbecue sauce and was accompanied by a community bucket into which several of them vomited nearby. They performed push-ups while naked as their genitals dipped into warm beer beneath them— the number of push-ups done determining whether they could drink their own glass of beer or someone else's. They also paraded around naked, performing an "elephant walk" in which the players held each other's genitals.[20]

The attorney general of Vermont rebuked the university for its inadequate investigation into the incident, and the state legislature subsequently enacted anti-hazing legislation.[21] [*Ed. note:* Testifying in favor of the Vermont law was Lizzie Murtie, a high school athlete who had to perform a simulated sex act on a male upon the orders of her teammates.] A university report produced fifty-three recommendations to remedy the problem, largely based on the Alfred University study. The university settled a lawsuit filed by former walk-on goalie Corey LaTulippe for $80,000.[22] The university estimated that the total cost to the institution in settlements, lost revenues, legal fees, and public-relations costs was $485,000.[23]

The University of Vermont is hardly alone among universities facing hazing scandals. Reports of hazing have recently occurred at many different types of institutions, from prestigious universities such as Yale University to state institutions including the University of Maryland and Georgia Southern University to small colleges such as Marian College, located in Wisconsin.[24] In addition, lawsuits have not been limited to hazing incidents involving male athletes.[25] A former University of Oklahoma female soccer player charged her former coach with "physical and mental abuse" in a federal lawsuit against the coach, her two assistants, and the university's board of regents stemming from an incident that occurred in 1997. The victim, then a freshman, was forced to perform simulated oral sex with a banana while blindfolded and wearing an adult diaper.[26] The humiliated victim, out of fear of losing her scholarship, did not report the incident for a year. She came forward after pictures of the hazing, taken by some teammates, were shown to the university athletic director. The coach resigned at the onset of the investigation, citing personal reasons, and the victim transferred to a smaller school closer to her family.[27] As of this writing, the original federal lawsuit had been dismissed, but the plaintiff plans to file an amended complaint.[28]

Given the increased frequency with which these incidents are being reported, it is important to understand the potential liability of colleges and universities for the hazing of its student-athletes. The primary theory that many plaintiffs rely upon is negligence.[29] In order to recover under this claim, a plaintiff must establish four elements: 1) the existence of a legal duty of care on the defendant's behalf to adhere to a standard of care to protect the plaintiff from unreasonable risks; 2) a breach of this duty; 3) actual and proximate causation; and 4) a resulting injury to the plaintiff.[30] The threshold requirement is a legally recognized duty of care.[31] Thus, an institution will not be held liable for the hazing injuries suffered by its student-athletes unless it can be proven that a duty of care was owed to them by the institution. There are three theories that these plaintiffs may rely upon to establish the presence of this duty of care: 1) the doctrine of in loco parentis; 2) the landowner-invitee theory; and 3) the existence of a special relationship between a university and its student-athletes. Each of these theories will be analyzed in the sections below.

In Loco Parentis

Traditionally, colleges and universities operated under the doctrine of in loco parentis, or "in place of the parents," as they dominated the lives of their students. Through this doctrine, schools were held responsible for the welfare of students in their care.[32] When society began to view college students as adults in the 1970s, however, courts began to hold that colleges had no duty to protect their students.[33] Consequently, the doctrine of in loco parentis seems to have met its demise on college campuses. It therefore seems unlikely that a student-athlete injured during a hazing incident could seek recourse under this doctrine. This wave of decisions that rule that the college or university has no duty to protect the safety and welfare of its students is changing course in the area of hazing activities.[34] The courts, however, have not reinstated the doctrine of in loco parentis to establish a duty of care. Instead, they are relying on traditional tort law to treat college and university defendants the same as landlords; that is, with a duty to act reasonably.[35]

Liability under a Landowner-Invitee Theory

A student-athlete injured during a hazing incident may be able to successfully recover against the institution under a landowner-invitee theory. Universities are considered landlords to their student-athletes based on the owner-ship of campus dormitories and buildings.[36] Generally, a landlord has a duty to aid or protect those invitees who enter his land.[37] This duty, which is one of reasonable care, extends only to reasonably foreseeable acts.[38] Hence, a landlord has no duty to ensure his visitor's safety.[39] In *Furek* v. *University of Delaware,* the Delaware Supreme Court held that a fraternity hazing incident, which oc-curred on university-owned property, was foreseeable.[40] The university was aware of both past and continuing hazing practices in fraternities and had pre-viously attempted to regulate it.[41] Because of this awareness, the university had a duty to regulate dangerous activities occurring on its property.[42]

While it was generally thought that the university's duty applied only to on-campus acts,[43] the Supreme Court of Nebraska has extended this duty to off-campus acts as well in *Knoll* v. *Board of Regents of the University of Nebraska.*[44] The court held that the university had an obligation to protect the plaintiff, who was severely injured while trying to escape a hazing incident.[45] Despite the fact that the fraternity house was privately owned and was located off campus, it was considered to be a student housing unit subject to the university's code of conduct.[46] The court concluded that the university owed their students a duty under a landowner-invitee theory to protect them from foreseeable acts of haz-ing.[47] The court reasoned that because the student's abduction occurred on the university's property, it was irrelevant that the harm occurred off campus.[48] The implication of this decision is that when hazing is foreseeable in a given situation, the school and administrators can be held responsible for not taking steps to prevent it regardless of whether the harmful incident occurs on or off campus.[49]

Pursuant to the court's holding in *Furek,* a victimized student-athlete may recover damages if the hazing occurred on university-owned property[50] and was reasonably foreseeable. The court's holding in *Knoll* may allow an injured student-athlete to recover against the institution even if the foreseeable hazing occurred off the university's property.[51] In either case, hazing will be foreseeable only if the university knew or should have known about it. This standard can be easily satisfied if there has been a tradition of hazing at the university. On the other hand, it may be argued that all hazing incidents are foreseeable given the prevalence of hazing among student-athletes.[52] Institutions may have a duty to protect the student-athletes from hazing if the landlord-invitee theory is es-tablished, but recovery may be constrained by the location in which the hazing occurs.

Liability Arising out of the Special Relationship between Student-Athletes and Colleges

Student-athletes injured in hazing accidents might also argue that the special relationship between the university and its student-athletes creates a duty of care.[53] A basic tenet of tort law is that no duty of care exists between two parties unless they have a special relationship.[54] Common examples of special relationships are parent and child, common carrier and passenger, innkeeper and guest, and landowner and invitee.[55] Although this list is not exhaustive,[56] courts are reluctant to find that a special relationship exists between a university and its students[57] and therefore generally find that universities do not owe a duty of care to their students.[58] Courts view college students as adults who can take care of themselves and protect their own interests.[59] Furthermore, colleges have been viewed not as custodial institutions[60] but rather as educational institutions that do not ensure the safety of their students.[61] Courts have maintained that to decrease college students' autonomy by making the students' own safety the responsibility of the institution would "produce a repressive and inhospitable environment, largely inconsistent with the objectives of a modern college education."[62]

Despite the general failure of courts to recognize a special relationship between a university and its students that gives rise to a duty of care, several courts have found the existence of a special relationship between a university and its student-athletes.[63] In Kleinknecht v. Gettysburg College, the Third Circuit held that an intercollegiate athlete participating in a college-sponsored athletic activity for which he was recruited was owed a duty of reasonable care while acting in this capacity.[64] The court focused on three factors in finding that a special relationship existed between the university and the student-athlete.[65] First, the student-athlete was actively recruited by the institution to play intercollegiate lacrosse.[66] The court stated that "we cannot help but think that the College recruited [the student-athlete] for its own benefit, probably thinking that his skill at lacrosse would bring favorable attention and so aid the College in attracting other students."[67] Second, the student-athlete was participating in his college team's practice session when he was stricken.[68] The court distinguished this class of individuals from those students injured while pursuing their own private interests;[69] the former group is owed a duty of care, while the latter group is not.[70] Third, the court recognized that the duty of care is owed only when the foreseeable risk of harm is unreasonable.[71] Noting that it was reasonably foreseeable that a life-threatening injury could occur during athletic participation, the court held that the college owed a duty of care to take precautions against such an injury.[72]

If a special relationship between a university and its student-athletes exists, it is still unclear whether a student-athlete injured during a hazing incident may succeed in recovering under this theory. The court's finding of a special relationship between the university and the student-athlete in Kleinknecht was based on three enunciated factors: 1) the injured athlete must be "actively recruited"; 2) the athlete must be acting in an athletic capacity while injured; and 3) both the hazing and the resulting injury must be reasonably foreseeable. The absence of any of these factors could preclude a similar finding in future hazing litigation. First, the injured student-athlete must have been "actively recruited" to play the sport.[73] If walk-ons are excluded from this definition, then any such individuals who are injured during a hazing incident would likely be unable to recover against the institution. They would lack the requisite "special relation-ship" with the institution and thus no duty of care would be owed to them. This distinction seems arbitrary and would result in the university owing a duty of care to team members recruited out of high schools but not to others. Though a court may be unwilling to engage in such line-drawing, the Third Circuit's decision allows this to remain a possibility.

Most problematic for student-athletes injured during hazing incidents is the court's requirement that the intercollegiate student-athlete should be acting in an athletic capacity in order to be owed a duty of care.[74] The Third Circuit's inconsistent descriptions of this factor make it very difficult to determine when the duty of care is owed.[75] Although the differences in these phrases appear slight, the linguistic subtleties may have a substantial impact on whether a uni-versity owes a duty of care to a student-athlete injured during a hazing incident. However, the court did note that a special relationship existed when the student-athlete was "participating in a scheduled athletic practice for an intercollegiate team sponsored by the College under the supervision of College employees";[76] "participating as one of its intercollegiate athletes in a school-sponsored ath-letic activity";[77] "in his capacity as an intercollegiate athlete engaged in school-sponsored intercollegiate athletic activity";[78] and "[participating in] an athletic event involving an intercollegiate team of which he was a member."[79]

These standards imply that the existence of a special relationship between a university and its student-athletes depends on the circumstances involved and arises only when the individual is actually playing the sport. A student-athlete faced with these standards is unlikely to recover damages. Hazing injuries do not occur during either "intercollegiate athletic activity" or "athletic events" and are not "school-sponsored."

In describing when a duty of care is owed to the student-athlete, the court also used phrases such as "participating in an intercollegiate athletic pro-gram,"[80] "participating as an intercollegiate athlete in a sport for which he was recruited,"[81] and "in his capacity as a school athlete."[82] These phrases may establish a basis upon which a student-athlete may recover for hazing injuries, as they imply a looser standard of liability based mainly on the individual's status as an intercollegiate athlete.[83] Hazing is traditionally a de facto require-ment of participation on intercollegiate athletic teams. A student-athlete has no choice but to be hazed, and failure to do so may negatively affect his athletic experience because of the numerous social costs that will be imposed. If a court recognizes this and interprets hazing as an aspect of "participating in an inter-collegiate athletic program," then universities will owe its student-athletes a duty of care to protect them from hazing injuries.[84] Under this interpretation, student-athletes injured during a hazing incident will likely recover damages in a negligence suit.

Finally, both the hazing itself and the resulting injury must be reasonably foreseeable before a university will owe its student-athletes a duty of care to take precautions against both the incident and the injuries.[85] This is the easiest hurdle for plaintiffs to overcome. Based on the prevalence of hazing among intercollegiate athletes, it is likely that a hazing incident may be considered foreseeable. It is also foreseeable that serious injuries will be suffered by hazing victims.[86] Therefore, institutions must take reasonable precautions to prevent hazing from occurring.

Hazing in Professional Sports

There is also a long tradition of hazing in professional team sports. Similar to the hazing that occurs at the high school and collegiate levels, hazing in professional team sports is meant to indoctrinate nascent professional athletes into their new surroundings and promote team bonding.[87] In addition, hazing supposedly serves the purpose of keeping players who are freshly minted with lucrative contracts from getting the enhanced ego that often comes with sudden affluence.[88] Beyond keeping the rookie's "feet on the ground" and amusing the veteran players, the hazing is meant to teach respect for the culture of the sport at the professional level.[89]

Although all rookies in every league are forced to perform chores such as carrying the veterans' bags on road trips,[90] the form of the hazing varies slightly from sport to sport. In Major League Baseball, players are often forced to wear dresses and other embarrassing outfits in public[91] after returning to their lockers after a game or practice and finding their clothes either missing or destroyed.[92] Rookies have not always accepted these pranks without anger or resentment, the way Baltimore Orioles player Jerry Hairston did when veteran teammates made him put on a full Baltimore Ravens football uniform in full public view out of Yankee Stadium in New York after a game.[93] When a similar prank was played on former Oriole and current New York Met pitcher Armando Benitez during his rookie season, Benitez was so angry that he nearly asked to be traded.[94]

In the National Hockey League, rookies traditionally have been subjected to a full-body shave. This physical mistreatment has been replaced on some teams by a financial one, with rookies paying for prohibitively expensive team dinners at upscale restaurants.[95] For example, during the 1999–2000 Vancouver Canucks season, three rookies were forced to split the cost of a $10,000 team dinner.[96]

Due to the physical nature of the sport, perhaps it should not be surprising that the hazing in the National Football League (NFL) is traditionally a bit more extreme than in other sports.[97] Beyond carrying veterans' helmets and shoulder pads off of practice fields and singing their colleges' fight songs at training-camp meals,[98] rookies are exposed to a variety of physical hazings, many of which are potentially dangerous. Activities such as head-shaving,[99] wrestling teammates,[100] taping teammates to goalposts,[101] and setting off fireworks inside players' rooms and automobiles[102] have been de rigueur in the NFL for a long time but, despite their hazards, were largely ignored by the NFL teams.[103] This attitude was changed by an outrageous hazing incident involving the New Orleans Saints on their last night of training camp in 1998. This event led to an increased awareness of hazing and the adoption of a no-hazing policy by several NFL teams.[104]

New Orleans Saints Hazing Incident

The last night of training camp is usually cause for great celebration among professional football players, as it marks the end of the most intense period of preseason practices. For the New Orleans Saints, however, the celebration on August 20, 1998, devolved into something much more serious when the team was involved in a hazing incident in the players' dormitory at University of Wisconsin-LaCrosse.[105] As a veteran player read the names of the rookies off a list, each one was forced to wear a pillowcase over his head and run down a dormitory hallway as a gauntlet of twenty to thirty veterans punched, kicked, elbowed, and swung bags of coins at them.[106] Three of the five players who ran the gauntlet before campus security guards arrived required medical treatment.[107] Defensive tackle Jeff Danish required thirteen stitches in his left arm after crashing through a window at the end of the hallway; tight end Cam Cleeland suffered a detached fluid sac in his retina after getting hit in the eye with a bag of coins; and wide receiver Andy McCullough underwent an MRI after becoming dizzy and suffering a bloody nose due to blows to the head.[108] While Cleeland missed one week of practice and an exhibition game because of his injury, Danish was not as fortunate.[109] His wound opened in an exhibition game several days later, causing him to leave the game; he was released by the team shortly thereafter.[110] The players responsible for the hazing went largely unpunished, though the Saints traded the only player who admitted his involvement.[111] Two other players were alleged to be involved in the hazing.[112] The NFL did not impose punishment on any player after conducting its own investigation.[113]

As a result of this incident, Danish filed a lawsuit against the Saints, six players, and an assistant coach, seeking $650,000 in damages for lost wages, medical expenses, pain and suffering, residual scarring, public ridicule, humiliation, and loss of enjoyment of life.[114] The lawsuit alleged that the Saints "knew or should have been aware of the training-camp incident before it happened and did nothing to prevent it."[115] The lawsuit alleged a lack of any team staff located in close proximity to the team's living quarters. It also averred that an announcement of the planned hazing was written by a veteran or veterans on a blackboard hours after Coach Mike Ditka specifically instructed the players a second time not to haze rookies during training camp.[116] Danish and the Saints reached an out-of-court settlement for an undisclosed sum in early 1999.[117] The Saints adopted a zero-tolerance policy toward hazing the next season and vowed to release any player involved in a hazing incident, including the victim.[118] The players were notified of this policy by team president and general manager Bill Kuharich and Coach Ditka at a meeting on the first day of training camp.[119] The team also moved the team's training staff closer to the players in the dormitories and urged the veteran players to display stronger leadership to prevent any hazing incidents.[120]

While the Saints incident received considerable media attention, hazing in professional sports is not limited to any one organization. Hazing is prevalent in professional sports and it is likely that similar cases will arise in the future. Although the lawsuit that resulted from the New Orleans Saints incident settled before there were any trial court proceedings, it is appropriate to review the legal principles that would apply in a lawsuit against a professional sports team by an athlete injured during a similar incident.

Application of Legal Principles to Hazing in Professional Sports

Due to the dangerous nature of hazing and the surging number of well-publicized incidents among college and high school students, forty-three states have enacted or have encouraged the enactment of anti-hazing laws.[121] The vast majority of these statutes, however, only address hazing within the educational context. Only Indiana, Mississippi, New York, and Utah do not limit the application of hazing laws to student groups.[122] Thus, only professional athletes and teams located in these four states are subject to anti-hazing laws. In the absence of an applicable statute, common law remedies are available for professional athlete hazing victims against both the employer team and employee teammates. The following sections outline these theories of liability.

Workers' Compensation

Employees injured during the course of their employment typically must file a claim under the applicable state's workers' compensation statute in order to be compensated for their injuries.[123] Because of the exclusive nature of these statutes, employees are precluded from recovering in tort against their employers for their injuries.[124] [*Ed. note:* That is, successfully bringing a civil suit for negligent or intentional wrong or harm.] These employees forfeit their tort claims in exchange for "timely, scheduled payments" for their injuries. But an intentional tort exception exists that allows an employee to avoid the reach of the workers' compensation statute and pursue tort remedies against the employer.[125] In order for this exception to apply, the employer must either act intentionally or deliberately with a specific intent to harm the employee.[126] This exception extends to an employer with suspicion or knowledge of a potentially harmful condition who allows the condition to persist.[127] While workplace violence lawsuits arising under the intentional tort exception may vary in their results,[128] claims of contributory negligence, assumption of risk, and employee negligence are unavailable to employers as defenses.[129] These lawsuits may include the negligence-derived claims of negligent hiring and retention, negligent supervision, and breach of a voluntary assumption of a duty to protect. Under any of these theories, a plaintiff needs to prove "the elements of common law negligence—duty, breach, cause, and harm."[130] A determination of employer liability often turns on the issue of whether a duty of care was owed to the employee. The existence of any legal duty is an issue for the court, while foreseeability is determined by the trier of fact—that is, whether the case is heard before the jury or, in a bench trial, the judge.[131] Foreseeability depends on whether the defendant's conduct is likely to cause the type of injury suffered by the plaintiff.[132] An injury may be foreseeable based on either "prior similar incidents" or the "totality of the circumstances," alternative tests that are used by most courts in determining this issue.[133]

In each cause of action, the injured employee alleges that the employer did not exercise due care to prevent the intentional acts of the co-employees.[134] As one commentator noted, "Two common fact scenarios surround allegations of managerial negligence: (1) the plaintiffs allege that the employer should have screened applicants more scrupulously and (2) plaintiffs attempt to advance some proof that the employer failed to respond to actual or constructive knowledge of the facts."[135]

Negligent Hiring and Retention

Claims of negligent hiring and negligent retention arise when an employer hires or retains an individual whose dangerous propensities, unfitness, or incompetence were known or should have been known to the employer and this employee harms another person.[136] In a negligent-hiring scenario, the employer is obligated to conduct a reasonable background check of the employee to satisfy its duty of care.[137] Further, after the hiring, an employer who learns of an employee's harmful proclivities has a duty to take precautions to protect others from the employee in order to avoid liability for negligent retention.[138] In both negligent-hiring and negligent-supervision cases, the plaintiff must also establish that there existed a foreseeable risk of injury because of these harmful proclivities.[139] Courts have proven to be flexible in determining whether an injury is foreseeable, though they have provided differing guidelines as to what constitutes a reasonable background search.[140]

Because of the enormous investment made in athletes and fear of negative media attention, professional sports teams conduct background checks of many of their prospective employees prior to the league's entry draft.[141] While some teams search more extensively than others, at a minimum, most teams research arrest and conviction records and check the references of and administer screening tests to their potential top draft picks.[142] Despite the results, however, many teams ignore known dubious backgrounds and instead hire athletes because of their substantial playing abilities.[143] If these athletes are subsequently involved in a hazing incident where another player is injured, the team will likely be liable for negligent hiring. Similarly, once employed, a team gaining actual or constructive knowledge [reliable facts derived from reliable sources] of a player's harmful tendencies has a duty to protect their other employees from this individual. Thus, if an employee is subsequently hazed and injured at the hands of this individual, the team will likely be liable for negligent retention.[144] An example is the case involving Andre Royal, the only New Orleans Saints player to admit his involvement in the team's hazing. Royal was signed to a free-agent contract by the team despite a checkered background that included four suspensions during his college career at Alabama and an incident involving a Bourbon Street dancer.[145] [*Ed. note:* Royal was sued by a New Orleans dancer who said he groped her, although witnesses and employees disagreed with her version and charges of public drunkenness against the player were dismissed.] While it is unclear whether the Saints had conducted a background search or had actual knowledge of Royal's history when he was acquired,[146] it is reasonable to conclude that the team should have been aware of his background. If this constructive knowledge was present before employment, then the Saints could be liable for negligent hiring because a reasonable background check would have uncovered the information. If constructive knowledge was present after employment, then the team could be liable for negligent retention if it were demonstrated that the Saints needed to protect their other employees from Royal.

Negligent Supervision

Closely related to a negligent-retention claim is one for negligent supervision. Negligent supervision occurs when an employer's failure to properly train or supervise an employee leads to a foreseeable injury to another employee.[147] An employer with actual or constructive knowledge of an employee's harmful proclivities must properly supervise the situation so as to prevent any injuries from occurring.[148] Doing so is quite burdensome, however, because an employer that monitors its employees too closely raises privacy concerns that may negatively impact their employees' morale and consequently hamper productivity.[149] Supervising is even more difficult when a collective bargaining agreement exists restricting the ability of the employer to monitor and discipline employees.[150]

As previously mentioned, hazing of rookies has long been a fixture of professional team sports.[151] This tradition has also long been known by the management of professional sports teams, yet it is ignored out of a fear of hurting the esprit de corps.[152] This general knowledge heightens the duty owed by any one team to supervise its employees because a court may hold the organization lacking actual knowledge liable based on its constructive knowledge of the hazing tradition. In the New Orleans Saints incident, the presence of an announcement of a planned hazing on a meeting-room blackboard—whether or not it was seen and ignored by the assistant coaches, as alleged—is indicative of the extent to which hazing is accepted in professional sports. The players made little attempt to keep their hazing plan a secret; if hazing had been verboten, surely the players would have attempted to conceal it. The team has a duty to take affirmative steps to prevent hazing, particularly during training camps when hazing incidents are prevalent. The placement of coaches in training-camp residences and enforcement of a strict zero-tolerance policy with clearly enunciated consequences are two measures that all teams could take to reduce the risk of hazing.[153] Simply warning players about hazing without additional penalties or enforcement policies is not likely to absolve teams of liability. In the New Orleans Saints incident, the players ignored the head coach's two warnings about hazing, including one given just hours before the hazing occurred.[154] The impetus for this warning was a hazing incident on the final night of training camp of the prior year in which harm was done to the dormitory rather than to the rookies themselves.[155] Thus, it is likely that a court would have found the Saints to have actual or constructive knowledge of the planned hazing. Its failure to prevent the hazing therefore constituted a breach of its duty to its employees, and the team would have been liable for its negligent supervision.

Voluntary Assumption of Duty to Protect

An organization that volunteers or contracts to protect others from a third party's harmful acts owes a duty of care under the theory of voluntary assumption.[156] The employer's implied or express promise to provide security measures at its facilities establishes a duty to protect its employees from third-party criminal acts.[157] An employer that provides security must do so in a manner that is sufficient to prevent any foreseeable crimes against its employees from occurring.[158] The foreseeability of this criminal activity is typically based on the existence of any prior similar incidents.[159]

In professional sports, the voluntary-assumption theory is applicable in instances of hazing that occur either in the team's practice or locker-room facilities or during residential training camps in which the team provides dormitory-style housing for all of the players. Security is either provided by the team itself or by a third party pursuant to a contract. This security must be adequate to protect the team employees from any foreseeable criminal acts, including those associated with hazing incidents. If the team was on notice of any prior hazing incidents, a court may consider hazing a foreseeable act. Once deemed foreseeable, the occurrence of any hazing by employees, despite the provision of security by the team, would render the organization liable for breach of the voluntary assumption of duty.

Recommendations and Conclusion

Intercollegiate-athletics and professional-sports administrators and coaches must be diligent in monitoring the initiation activities of their athletes and must be cognizant of applicable institutional and organizational regulations as well as local, state, and national laws that govern hazing and group initiations. These sport administrators must be aggressive in investigating complaints by athletes and should stop initiation rites before they reach the level of criminal hazing. This can be achieved through development and enforcement of a clear, comprehensive anti-hazing policy.

Unfortunately, initiation rites are a traditional part of athletic team membership that will not likely disappear soon. There are, however, several ways that coaches and administrators can prevent initiations from becoming criminal hazing that endanger the innocence, and even the lives, of student-athletes. Respondents in the Alfred University study made three recommendations for the prevention of athletic hazing:

1. Send a clear anti-hazing message by developing a written anti-hazing policy; educating administrators, coaches, and athletes; developing a contract for athletes to sign; establishing a record of strong corrective action; and immediately notifying law enforcement of any suspected hazing incident.
2. Promote responsibility, integrity, and civility by involving high-level administrators, screening recruits for behavioral problems, establishing a recruitment visit policy, and making an athlete's behavior on and off the field part of the coach's evaluation.
3. Offer team-building initiation rites by training coaches on the importance of initiation rites and the proper ways to conduct them, require organized initiation rites prior to each season, and incorporating initiations into team goal-setting.[160]

These recommendations are applicable to both intercollegiate and professional sports. In addition to these recommendations, it is particularly important for coaches to be educated about hazing and to be made aware of its warning signs. As individuals with the most contact with athletes, coaches must be especially vigilant of obvious, relatively benign behaviors that may indicate that more serious hazing is occurring.[161] Institutions and organizations may also adopt proactive practices to prevent hazing such as having supervision in locker rooms and player living facilities during residential training sessions where many hazing incidents occur.[162] Athletes should be encouraged to notify the appropriate internal officials of any hazing by designing an anonymous reporting system. Athletes might prove more willing to disclose the hazing if they can avoid the negative consequences associated with doing so.[163]

When a hazing incident is reported, officials should immediately conduct a fair investigation[164] and take prompt, strong remedial action to punish those involved and ensure that the behavior is stopped.[165] In the context of professional sports, the league office and players' association should be notified so that they, too, may take appropriate action in the form of investigations, fines, or suspensions. If appropriate, the activity should be referred to law enforcement officials.[166] A subsequent discovery of any criminal activity by law enforcement officials should be followed by vigorous prosecution of the perpetrators.[167]

It is clear that hazing is widespread, harmful, and misunderstood.[168] The pervasiveness of hazing in intercollegiate sports should be cause for concern to athletic administrators throughout the NCAA. This deeply ingrained behavior continues when athletes reach the professional leagues, though it is somewhat surprising because of the tremendous amount of money that professional teams have invested in their athletes. Clearly, however, until these policy recommendations are adopted, these senseless initiation rites will continue unabated and more educational institutions and professional sports organizations will be subjected to liability.

Notes

1. See "Men Behaving Badly," (New Orleans) *Times-Picayune,* 26 August 1998, B6 (noting that "hazing . . . is an old NFL tradition," and reporting that five rookies on the National Football League's New Orleans Saints were forced to wear pillowcases over their heads and walk by team veterans, "who punched and pushed them").

2. Nadine Hoover and Norm Pollard, *Initiation Rites and Athletics: A National Survey of NCAA Sports Teams* (Alfred, N.Y.: Alfred University and Reidman Insurance Co., Inc., 1999).

3. See "Sports Hazing Incidents," available online at http://espn.go.com/otl/hazing/list.html (a listing of confirmed instances of hazing incidents occurring in competitive sports context, compiled by Hank Nuwer and Tom Farrey; accessed May 7, 2003); see also Tom Farrey, "Like Fighting, Part of Game," available online at http://espn.go.com/otl/hazing/thursday.html (accessed May 7, 2003).

4. "Sports Hazing Incidents"; Hoover and Pollard, *Initiation Rites and Athletics.*

5. See Farrey, "Like Fighting, Part of Game."

6. Only Alaska, Hawaii, Michigan, Montana, New Mexico, South Dakota, and Wyoming do not have anti-hazing statutes. See "State Anti-Hazing Law," available online at http://www.stophazing.org/laws.html (accessed May 7, 2003).

7. See "Eight Potsdam Players Hit With Hazing Charges," *Times Union,* 4 April 1998, C2; "Twelve Seniors Face Hazing Charges against Freshmen," Associated Press Newswires, 8 July 2000.

8. See Hank Nuwer, *Wrongs of Passage: Fraternities, Sororities, Hazing, and Binge Drinking* (Bloomington: Indiana University Press, 1999). The Delaware anti-hazing law provides a very comprehensive definition of hazing: "Any action or situation which recklessly or intentionally endangers the mental or physical health or safety of a student or which willfully destroys or removes public or private property for the purpose of initiation or admission into or affiliation with, or as a condition for continued membership in, any organization operating under the sanction of or recognized as an organization by an institution of higher learning. The term shall include, but not be limited to, any brutality of a physical nature, such as whipping, beating, branding, forced calisthenics, exposure to the elements, forced consumption of any food, liquor, drug or other substance, or any other forced physical activity which could adversely affect the physical health and safety of the individual, and shall include any activity which would subject the individual to extreme mental stress, such as sleep deprivation, forced exclusion from social contact, forced conduct which could result in embarrassment, or any other forced activity which could adversely affect the mental health or dignity of the individual, or any willful destruction or removal of public

or private property. For purposes of this definition, any activity as described in this definition upon which the admission or initiation into or affiliation with or continued membership in an organization is directly or indirectly conditioned shall be presumed to be 'forced' activity, *the willingness of an individual to participate in such activity notwithstanding.*" Del. Code Ann. tit. 14, 9302 (1999) (emphasis added). Other state statutes offer vague definitions of hazing, making prosecution under these statutes harder. See Andrew Jacobs, "Violent Rites; High School Hazing," *New York Times Upfront,* 24 April 2000, 8.

9. See "State Anti-Hazing Laws"; see also Michael John James Kuzmich, "Comment, In Vino Mortuus: Fraternal Hazing and Alcohol-Related Deaths," *McGeorge Law Review* 31 (2000): 1087, 1097.

10. Kuzmich, "Comment, In Vino Mortuus," 1097. Alabama, Arkansas, New Hampshire, North Carolina, South Carolina, Texas, and Washington all require notification. See "State Anti-Hazing Laws."

11. See "State Anti-Hazing Laws." Arizona, Delaware, Florida, Kentucky, Maine, Minnesota, Missouri, Oklahoma, Pennsylvania, Tennessee, Vermont, West Virginia, and Wisconsin all require schools to adopt anti-hazing policies.

12. Ibid. Arizona, Connecticut, Delaware, Florida, Indiana, Iowa, Missouri, Nebraska, Nevada, New Hampshire, New Jersey, North Dakota, Ohio, Oklahoma, Pennsylvania, South Carolina, Texas, Utah, Vermont, and Washington do not allow the defense.

13. Kuzmich, "Comment, In Vino Mortuus," 1097.

14. Ibid.

15. "Alfred Cancels Game over Hazing," Associated Press Online, 1 September 1998.

16. Hoover and Pollard, *Initiation Rites and Athletics.*

17. Ibid.

18. Ibid.

19. "Vermont Ends Season over Hazing Scandal," available online at http://espn.go.com/nch/news/2000/0114/290846.html (accessed May 7, 2003).

20. "Report Faults U. of Vermont's Investigation of Hockey Team Hazing," *Chronicle of Higher Education,* 18 February 2000, A63; see also Bob Duffy, "A Matter of Rite and Wrong in the Wake of the UVM Case: Debate Is Renewed on Whether Initiations Are Harmless Bonding Rituals or Outright Abuse," *Boston Globe,* 13 February 2000.

21. "State Report on Hazing Case," *USA Today,* 4 February 2000, 2C.

22. Andy Gardiner, "Hazing Scandal Rips Apart Town, School, University of Vermont Still Has Scars," *USA Today,* 5 February 2001, 1C.

23. Ibid.

24. "Sports Hazing Incidents."

25. Greg Garber, "It's Not All Fun and Games," available online at http://espn.go.com/otl/hazing/Wednesday.html (accessed May 7, 2003).

26. Ibid.

27. Ibid.

28. "Judge Dismisses University from Lawsuit," Associated Press Newswires, 13 April 2000.

29. Jenna MacLachlan, "Dangerous Traditions: Hazing Rituals on Campus and

University Liability," *Journal of College and University Law* 26 (2000): 511, 512.

30. W. Page Keeton et al., *Prosser and Keeton on the Law of Torts,* Citation 30, 5th ed. (St. Paul: West, 1984), 164–165.

31. Ibid.

32. MacLachlan, "Dangerous Traditions," 512, 514.

33. Ibid., 515; see also *Knoll v. Bd. of Regents of the Univ. of Neb.,* 601 N.W.2d 757 (Neb. 1999); *Furek v. Univ. of Del.,* 594 A.2d 506 (Del. 1991).

34. See MacLachlan, "Dangerous Traditions," 539 (noting that the "decisions indicate that the trend toward university responsibility for hazing incidents will continue").

35. Ibid., 513.

36. See Gil B. Fried, "Illegal Moves Off-the-Field: University Liability for Illegal Acts of Student-Athletes," *Seton Hall Journal of Sport Law* 7 (1997): 69, 77.

37. See Restatement (Second) of Torts, 314A(3) (1965). This section, entitled "Special Relations Giving Rise to Duty to Aid or Protect," provides that "[a] possessor of land who holds it open to the public is under a [duty to aid or protect] to members of the public who enter in response to his invitation."

38. See Restatement (Second) of Torts 344 (1965). A possessor of land who holds it open to the public for entry for his business purposes is subject to liability to members of the public while they are upon the land for such a purpose; for physical harm caused by the accidental, negligent, or intentionally harmful acts of third persons or animals; and by the failure of the possessor to exercise reasonable care to (a) discover that such acts are being done or are likely to be done, or (b) give a warning adequate to enable the visitors to avoid the harm, or otherwise to protect them against it.

39. Ibid. This Restatement comment states that a landowner with knowledge of the likelihood that the safety of his invitees will be endangered by third parties may have a duty to protect the invitees.

40. See *Furek v. Univ. of Del.,* 594 A.2d 506, 522 (Del. 1991).

41. Ibid., 510–511.

42. Ibid., 522.

43. See Jennifer L. Spaziano, "It's All Fun and Games until Someone Loses an Eye: An Analysis of University Liability for Actions of Student Organizations," *Pepperdine Law Review* 22 (1994): 213, 221–222 (analyzing the university's liability for actions resulting in harm on the university campus after the university has taken protective measures for student safety); see also Michelle D. McGirt, "Do Universities Have a Special Duty of Care to Protect Student-Athletes from Injury?" *Villanova Sports and Entertainment Law Journal* 6 (1999): 219, 221; Edward H. Whang, "Necessary Roughness: Imposing a Heightened Duty of Care on Colleges for Injuries of Student-Athletes," *Sports Law Journal* 2 (1995): 25, 32.

44. See *Knoll v. Bd. of Regents of the Univ. of Neb.,* 601 N.W.2d 757 (Neb. 1999).

45. Ibid., 765.

46. Ibid., 761–762, 764.

47. Ibid., 762, 765.

48. Ibid., 764.

49. Ibid., 764–765.

50. This includes locker rooms, athletic facilities, dormitory rooms, and many off-campus housing units.

51. This is particularly problematic for universities, as most intercollegiate hazing incidents occur in the off-campus homes of team upperclassmen.

52. See *Tanja H. v. Regents of the Univ. of Cal.*, 278 Cal. Rptr. 918, 922 (Cal. Ct. App. 1991) (holding that statistical evidence of a general level of criminal activity does not, in and of itself, create the requisite level of foreseeability). See generally *Kleinknecht v. Gettysburg College*, 989 F.2d 1360 (3d Cir. 1993); *Kennedy v. Syracuse Univ.*, No. 94-CV-269, 1995 WL 548710 (N.D.N.Y. Sept. 12, 1995).

53. See Spaziano, "It's All Fun and Games until Someone Loses an Eye," 228–230 (noting that courts have been reluctant to apply this special relationship to university-student relationships).

54. See Restatement (Second) of Torts 315 (1965). This section provides: "There is no duty to control the conduct of a third person as to prevent him from causing physical harm to another unless (a) a special relation exists between the actor and the third person which imposes a duty upon the actor to control the third person's conduct, or (b) a special relation exists between the actor and the other which gives rise to the other a right to protection." See also Whang, "Necessary Roughness," 33.

55. See Restatement (Second) of Torts 314A (1965). The Restatement (Second) of Torts provides:

> (1) A common carrier is under a duty to its passengers to take reasonable action
> (a) to protect them against unreasonable risk of physical harm, and
> (b) to give them first aid after it knows or has reason to know that they are ill or injured, and to care for them until they can be cared for by others.
> (2) An innkeeper is under a similar duty to his guests.
> (3) A possessor of land who holds it open to the public is under a similar duty to members of the public who enter in response to his invitation.
> (4) One who is required by law to take or who voluntarily takes the custody of another under circumstances such as to deprive the other of his normal opportunities for protection is under a similar duty to the other.

56. See ibid. ("The duties stated in this Section arise out of special relations between the parties. . . . The relations listed are not intended to be exclusive, and are not necessarily the only ones in which a duty of affirmative action for the aid or protection of another may be found.")

57. Spaziano, "It's All Fun and Games until Someone Loses an Eye," 228.

58. See *Bradshaw v. Rawlings*, 612 F.2d 135, 141–142 (3d Cir. 1979); *Univ. of Denver v. Whitlock*, 744 P.2d 54, 55 (Colo. 1987) (holding no duty where a student was injured while using a trampoline in an unsafe condition located on the front lawn of a house leased from the university); *Rabel v. Ill. Wesleyan Univ.*, 514 N.E.2d 552, 560–561 (Ill. App. Ct. 1987); McGirt, "Do Universities Have a Special Duty?" 225. See generally *Beach v. Univ. of Utah*, 726 P.2d 413 (Utah 1986).

59. Whang, "Necessary Roughness," 35.

60. *Beach,* 726 P.2d at 419.

61. *Bradshaw,* 612 F.2d at 138.

62. *Whitlock,* 744 P.2d at 60 (quoting *Beach,* 726 P.2d at 419).

63. See *Kleinknecht* v. *Gettysburg College,* 989 F.2d 1360, 1369 (3d Cir. 1993) (predicting that the Supreme Court of Pennsylvania would hold that the university owed a duty of care to a student engaged in school-sponsored collegiate athletic activity for which he had been recruited); *Kennedy* v. *Syracuse Univ.,* No. 94-CV-269, 1995 WL 548710, at 2 (N.D.N.Y. Sept. 12, 1995). Interestingly, neither the university nor the defendant denied that the university owed a reasonable duty of care to the student-athletes. Nonetheless, the court granted the university's motion for summary judgment due to the plaintiff's inability to establish proximate cause. Idem at 4. But see *Orr* v. *Brigham Young Univ.,* 108 F.3d 1388 (10th Cir. 1997) (refusing to recognize a special relationship between a university and its student-athletes); *Fox* v. *Bd. of Supervisors of La. State Univ. and Agric. and Mech. Coll.,* 576 So. 2d 978, 983 (La. 1991) (holding that Louisiana State University had no affirmative duty to act in protection of the visiting student-athlete since there was no special relationship).

64. F.2d at 1369. In *Kleinknecht,* the parents of a student-athlete who suffered a fatal heart attack during a supervised practice session brought a wrongful death action against the institution for its failure to provide prompt medical treatment. Ibid., 1362.

65. See McGirt, "Do Universities Have a Special Duty?" 232–233.

66. *Kleinknecht,* 989 F.2d at 1367.

67. Ibid., 1368.

68. Ibid.

69. Ibid.

70. Ibid. The court noted that had the plaintiff been injured while acting as a private student in a fraternity football game, the college may not have owed him a duty of care.

71. Ibid., 1369.

72. Ibid., 1370.

73. Ibid., 1367. The Third Circuit did not delineate whether this term applies only to athletes recruited from high schools or whether it includes those recruited from the institution's student body.

74. Ibid., 1367–1368.

75. See notes 63–72 above and accompanying text.

76. *Kleinknecht,* 989 F.2d at 1367.

77. Ibid., 1373.

78. Ibid., 1369.

79. Ibid., 1368.

80. Ibid., 1367 n.5.

81. Ibid., 1368.

82. Ibid., 1372.

83. See notes 8–19 above and accompanying text.

84. See *Kleinknecht,* 989 F.2d at 1367 n.5.

85. Ibid., 1370.

86. See notes 10–12 above and accompanying text.

87. See Josh Peter, "Ditka's Order Fails to Stop Brutal Hazing, Foul Play Casts Cloud over Saints," *Times-Picayune,* 30 August 1998, A1.

88. Richard Hoffer and Kostya Kennedy, "Praising Hazing," *Sports Illustrated,* 13 September 1999, 31.

89. Jim Parque, "Rookie Hazing Fun If You're Not the Victim," *Chicago Sun-Times,* 30 July 2000, 139. Parque, a veteran pitcher for the Chicago White Sox, stated, "Veterans utilize this degrading form of teasing as a tool to teach the youngsters how to act and hold themselves as professionals. The hazing, if done properly, teaches the rookies respect for the game, respect for their elders and respect for themselves. It is a way of introducing these young men into the world of major-league baseball and also a way of getting to know what a rookie is like on the inside."

90. John Eisenberg, "Humiliation, Pain Are Its Only Products," *Baltimore Sun,* 17 September 1999, 1D.

91. Parque, "Rookie Hazing Fun If You're Not the Victim."

92. Eisenberg, "Humiliation, Pain Are Its Only Products."

93. Ibid.

94. Ibid.

95. Michael Farber, "Bumper Crop," *Sports Illustrated,* 22 November 1999, 54.

96. Ibid.

97. See notes 86–87 above; see also notes 99–104 below.

98. Brian Allee-Walsh, "Rookies Keep Cool-Headed during Hazing," *Times-Picayune,* 3 August 1997, C4.

99. Gary Myers, "Rookie Hazing Has No Place in NFL Camps," *New York Daily News,* 30 August 1998, 10.

100. Allee-Walsh, "Rookies Keep Cool-Headed during Hazing." NFL Hall-of-Famer Mike Ditka was forced to do this as a rookie with the Chicago Bears in 1961.

101. Hoffer and Kennedy, "Praising Hazing." The Cleveland Browns have engaged in this activity.

102. Mark Heisler, "The Inside Track," *Los Angeles Times,* 3 September, 1998, C2. NFL player Albert Lewis suffered the indignity of having his bed set on fire with him in it as a rookie with the Kansas City Chiefs. Stoney Case was subjected to both mistreatments as a rookie quarterback with the Arizona Cardinals.

103. Mike Freeman, "Hazing, a Longtime NFL Tradition, May Have Seen Its Last Days," *New York Times,* 25 October 1998, 2.

104. Myers, "Rookie Hazing Has No Place in NFL Camps." Former Cleveland Browns coach Chris Palmer had a policy forbidding any form of hazing. See Aaron Portzline, "No Hazing for Browns, Palmer Won't Allow Vets to Abuse Rookies," *Columbus Dispatch,* 24 July 1999, 7E; see also Mark Potash, "A Nice Reception for Rookie McNown," *Chicago Sun-Times,* 4 August 1999, 116.

105. "Former Saints Rookie Describes Hazing," *New York Times,* 28 August 1998, C4.

106. Ibid.; see also Jonathan Rand, "Hazing Incident Simply a Disgrace," *Kansas City Star,* 30 August 1998, C4.

107. Peter, "Ditka's Order Fails to Stop Brutal Hazing"; Tom Archdeacon, "Saints Struck Dumb by Brutal Hazing," *Dayton Daily News,* 5 September 1998.

108. Peter, "Ditka's Order Fails to Stop Brutal Hazing"; Archdeacon, "Saints Struck Dumb by Brutal Hazing." Two other players, offensive guard Kyle Turley and linebacker Chris Bordano, did not require medical treatment, and other Saints rookies were spared the gauntlet after the security guards arrived.

109. Dave Lagarde, "NFL's Probe of Hazing Is Sham," *Times-Picayune,* 22 September 1998, E1.

110. Peter, "Ditka's Order Fails to Stop Brutal Hazing." According to the campus report filed in connection with the incident, perhaps Danish should be considered fortunate. The report stated that had a board not been in place across the window, Danish likely would have gone completely through it and plunged three floors to the ground. Josh Peter, "Report on Hazing Mentions Blood," *Times-Picayune,* 16 September 1998, D8.

111. Linebacker Andre Royal was dealt to the Indianapolis Colts shortly after his admission. Mike Strom and Brian Allee-Walsh, "Hazing Decision Not Surprising," *Times-Picayune,* 22 September 1998, E4.

112. See speculation by John DeShazier in "Saints' Silence Proving Less Than Golden," *Times-Picayune,* 22 October 1998, D1. It should be noted that neither player's involvement was proven, nor did the club confirm that the players, linebacker Brian Jones and guard Isaac Davis, were released because of the incident. The speculation was based on the fact that the two players were vying for starting positions and were named as defendants in a lawsuit later brought by Danish.

113. Strom and Allee-Walsh, "Hazing Decision Not Surprising."

114. Mike Strom and Brian Allee-Walsh, "Saints, Players Sued by Danish," *Times-Picayune,* 22 October 1998, D1. The six players were Brady Smith, Keith Mitchell, Troy Davis, Andre Royal, Brian Jones, and Isaac Davis. The assistant coach was defensive line coach Walt Corey.

115. Ibid.

116. Ibid.; see also Mike Strom, "Ditka Warns against Hazing," *Times-Picayune,* 30 July 1999, D1 (emphasizing that there was an individual stationed at the dormitory's front desk and a security guard patrolling inside and outside the building at the time of the incident). At least one NFL team, the New York Giants, has two weight coaches reside in the dormitories with the players during training camp to prevent any incidents. See Myers, "Rookie Hazing Has No Place in NFL Camps."

117. Josh Peter, "[Jeff] Danish, Saints Settle Lawsuit," *Times-Picayune,* 2 February 1999, E1. The settlement covered the team, the assistant coaches, and every player except Andre Royal. The suit against Royal was later dismissed after Danish's attorneys did not pursue it any further. "Court Dismisses Danish's Lawsuit," *Times-Picayune,* 16 April 1999, 7D.

118. Strom, "Ditka Warns against Hazing."

119. Ibid. This "zero-tolerance" policy is a misnomer, as it applied only to physical contact; rookies could still be forced to sing their fight songs and carry veterans' shoulder pads and helmets. Head Coach Mike Ditka addressed the provision of the policy that would release the hazed player as well by stating, "If he won't fight back and resist, then I want him out of here, too. . . . If we'd had guys that would have stood up last year and said, 'Hey I don't want no part of this,' then it would have ended right there."

120.   Strom, "Ditka Warns against Hazing."

121.   "State Anti-Hazing Law."

122.   Ind. Code 34-30-2-150 (1998); Miss. Code Ann. 97-3-105 (2001); N.Y. Penal Law 120.16 (McKinney 1998); Utah Code Ann. 76-5-107.5 (1999). All other state hazing laws are available online at http://www.stophazing. org/laws.html.

123.   Ann E. Phillips, "Comment, Violence in the Workplace: Reevaluating the Employer's Role," *Buffalo Law Review* 44 (1996): 139, 150.

124.   Ibid.; see also Janet E. Goldberg, "Employees with Mental and Emotional Problems: Workplace Security and Implications of State Discrimination Laws, The Americans With Disabilities Act, The Rehabilitation Act, Workers' Compensation, and Related Issues," *Stetson Law Review* 24 (1994): 201, 233.

125.   See David Minneman, "Annotation, Workers' Compensation Law as Precluding Employee's Suit against Employer for Third Person's Criminal Attack," 49 *American Law Review* 4th 926, 932 (1986).

126.   Ibid.

127.   Ibid.

128.   See Robert L. Levin, "Workplace Violence: Navigating through the Minefield of Legal Liability," *Labor Lawyer* 11 (1995): 171, 175 (discussing results of cases resulting in millions of dollars in settlements and bad publicity).

129.   Terry S. Boone, "Violence in the Workplace and the New Right to Carry Gun Law: What Employers Need to Know," *South Texas Law Review* 37 (1996): 873, 877.

130.   Stephen J. Beaver, "Comment, Beyond the Exclusivity Rule: Employer's Liability for Workplace Violence," *Marquette Law Review* 81 (1997): 103, 108.

131.   Ibid., 108–109.

132.   Ibid., 109.

133.   Phillips, "Comment, Violence in the Workplace," 169–170. The prior-similar-incidents test looks at factors such as "the proximity, time, number, and types of prior violent incidents in determining whether the particular harm was foreseeable," while the totality-of-the-circumstances test examines past criminal acts, the "nature of the business, the condition of the premises, and the surrounding neighborhood." Beaver, "Comment, Beyond the Exclusivity Rule," 109.

134.   J. Hoult Verkerke, "Notice Liability in Employment Discrimination Law," *Virginia Law Review* 81 (1995): 273, 305–306. This doctrine applies even though the employees' actions were beyond the scope of their employment.

135.   Beaver, "Comment, Beyond the Exclusivity Rule," 109.

136.   See Verkerke, "Notice Liability in Employment Discrimination Law," 305–306.

137.   Katrin U. Byford, "Comment, The Quest for the Honest Worker: A Proposal for Regulation of Integrity Testing," *Southern Methodist University Law Review* 49 (1996): 329, 359.

138.   Goldberg, "Employees with Mental and Emotional Problems," 215.

139.   Ibid., 216.

140.   Byford, "Comment, The Quest for the Honest Worker," 359–360.

141.   L. C. Johnson, "The NFL Takes a Hit: With Pending Legal Troubles of All-

Pro Ray Lewis and Former Receiver Rae Carruth, As Well As the Arrests and Disturbing Cases of Other Players, Does the League Have a Problem with Off-the-Field Violence That It Cannot Control?" *Orlando Sentinel Tribune,* 27 February 2000, C8. ("Before an athlete is allowed to strap on a pair of shoulder pads, buckle a chinstrap or make a fresh set of teeth marks on a mouthpiece in the National Football League, he must endure a battery of physical and psychological tests used to assess his overall health and state of mind.")

142. NFL teams are most vigilant in doing so, subjecting most prospective draftees to a battery of psychological tests, interviews, and reference checks (Ibid.).

143. For example, Lawrence Phillips, a star football player at the University of Nebraska, was selected in the NFL draft by the St. Louis Rams despite well-publicized run-ins with the law involving violent behavior. See Kevin Mannix, "The NFL: Time Has Come—Glenn's Arrest Should Be Final Straw for Pats," *Boston Herald,* 17 May 2001, 96.

144. See Verkerke, "Notice Liability in Employment Discrimination Law," 306 (explaining that "notice liability" demands that "employers that learn of a tendency toward violence . . . must respond with appropriate precautions against further harm").

145. Lonnie White, "Sinners and Saints; It's Not Team's Play That Bothers Ditka, It's Off-the-Field Activity that Wears on Him," *Los Angeles Times,* 15 November 1998, D1. Royal signed a four-year, $3.8 million contract earlier that year. He was traded to the Indianapolis Colts shortly after his admission and never played a regular-season game for the Saints.

146. Mike Ditka, then head coach of the New Orleans Saints, claimed to be unaware of Royal's past (Ibid.).

147. Boone, "Violence in the Workplace," 880.

148. Verkerke, "Notice Liability in Employment Discrimination Law," 306.

149. Beaver, "Comment, Beyond the Exclusivity Rule," 120.

150. Ibid., 122. Collective bargaining agreements are present in all four major North American professional sports leagues.

151. "Men Behaving Badly."

152. See Freeman, "Hazing, a Longtime NFL Tradition."

153. The consequences must not run afoul of the maximum penalties prescribed by each league's collective bargaining agreement, lest they be subjected to a grievance arbitration process.

154. Strom and Allee-Walsh, "Saints, Players Sued by Danish."

155. Peter, "Ditka's Order Fails to Stop Brutal Hazing."

156. See Linda A. Sharp, "Annotation, Employer's Liability to Employee or Agent for Injury or Death Resulting from Assault or Criminal Attack by Third Person," 40 *American Law Reports* 5th 1, 32–35 (1996). This duty is as follows: "One who undertakes, gratuitously or for consideration, to render services to another which he should recognize as necessary for the protection of a third person or his things, is subject to liability to the third person for physical harm resulting from his failure to exercise reasonable care to protect his undertaking, if (a) his failure to exercise reasonable care increases the risk of such harm, or (b) he has undertaken to perform a duty owed by the other to the third person, or (c) the harm is suffered because of reliance of

the other or the third person upon the undertaking." Restatement (Second) of Torts 324 A (1965).

157.   Phillips, "Comment, Violence in the Workplace," 160.

158.   Beaver, "Comment, Beyond the Exclusivity Rule," 125.

159.   Ibid.

160.   See Hoover and Pollard, *Initiation Rites and Athletics.* 161. See Kevin Bushweller, "Brutal Rituals, Dangerous Rites," *American School Board Journal,* available online at http://www.asbj.com/2000/08/0800coverstory.html (accessed May 7, 2003).

162.   Ibid.

163.   See Michael I. Levin, "Hazing: Debunking the Myths about This 'Right' of Passage," *Pennsylvania School Boards Association Bulletin,* available online at http://www.nsba.org/nepn/newsletter/500.htm (Accessed October 1999); Kelley R. Taylor, "Hazing: Harmless Horseplay?" *Principal Leadership,* March 2001, 78.

164.   See Levin, "Hazing: Debunking the Myths."

165.   Bushweller, "Brutal Rituals, Dangerous Rites"; Levin, "Hazing: Debunking the Myths."

166.   Bushweller, "Brutal Rituals, Dangerous Rites"; Levin, "Hazing: Debunking the Myths."

167.   See David S. Doty, "No More Hazing: Eradication through Law and Education," *Utah Bar Journal,* (November 1997): 18, 19, microformed on *Hein's Bar Journal* (William S. Hein & Co., Inc.).

168.   Levin, "Hazing: Debunking the Myths."

15 Institutional Liability and Hazing—Mainly Athletics-Related

R. Brian Crow and Scott R. Rosner

Hazing has been a part of life on college campuses throughout the United States since the founding of the first college in the colonies.[1] Athletic hazing is becoming a serious problem on both high school and college campuses nationwide.[2] This type of hazing is widespread, harmful, and misunderstood.[3] More student-athletes are being prosecuted under state anti-hazing laws, and more institutions are being held responsible for the care of their students.[4] The question of what actions or behaviors constitute hazing often arises. A clear concept is important because actions that are considered hazing by some are not considered hazing and are not objectionable to others. Hazing is defined as "any activity expected of someone joining a group that humiliates, degrades, abuses, or endangers, regardless of the person's willingness to participate."[5] Athletic hazing can range in scope from relatively harmless initiation rites, such as having rookie team members carry the travel bags of veteran players or sing team songs, to potentially dangerous activities such as kidnapping, binge drinking, sexual harassment, and exploitation.[6] While it is impossible to know exactly how prevalent hazing is in recreation and sport, the incidence of reported athletic hazing has increased dramatically since 1980, both in frequency and severity.[7] In addition, hazing often goes unreported, despite the fact that hazing constitutes an illegal activity under anti-hazing statutes enacted in forty-three states.[8]

Though an increasing number of students are being charged with criminal hazing, the application of these statutes is still quite rare. This is not surprising, given the issues of prosecutorial discretion that exist because the penalties for conviction are not generally significant enough to warrant the pursuit of criminal charges. The majority of states consider hazing a misdemeanor that does not change the penalty or definition of any activity covered by other criminal statutes.[9] Penalties for violating these state statutes include fines ranging from $10 to $10,000, jail time from ten days to twelve months, a combination of fines and jail time, withholding of diplomas, expulsion from school, and rescission of the right to assemble on campus.[10] A common penalty is three to twelve months in jail, a $1,000 fine, or both.[11]

In addition, the anti-hazing legislation of any one state tends to be flawed in at least one of several manners. First, hazing may be defined too narrowly. Though the definition varies from state to state,[12] it often includes only pre-initiation or initiation activities;[13] thus, it does not apply to any hazing that occurs after initiation. The definition often excludes athletic teams[14] and frequently applies only to institutions of higher education and not to secondary schools.[15] In these states, the limited definition allows much of the sports-related hazing activity to fall outside the scope of the law. Some states require bodily harm to result before hazing laws will apply.[16] Numerous other states allow the consent of the victim to be a defense to hazing,[17] though twenty-five of the forty-three states with hazing laws specifically state in their codes that implied or express consent, or a willingness on the part of the victim to participate in the initiation, is not an available defense.[18] Beyond these definitional issues, seven states penalize those who observe but fail to report hazing incidents.[19] Thirteen states require educational institutions to adopt anti-hazing policies;[20] however, not all specifically require secondary schools to do so,[21] and there are no significant penalties connected with these provisions.[22] This should not be surprising given the rather soft penalties prescribed by hazing laws in many states.

Hazing in Interscholastic Sports

High School Hazing Studies

In addition to numerous newspaper reports chronicling hazing incidents at high schools throughout the United States,[23] the findings of two recent studies suggest that hazing is pervasive in interscholastic athletics. The findings of a national survey of 1,541 high school juniors and seniors indicate that, of the athletes responding, 35 percent reported being subjected to some form of hazing.[24] Forty-five percent of these individuals were subjected to humiliating hazing,[25] 22 percent participated in hazing involving substance abuse, and 22 percent were subjected to dangerous hazing.[26] Extrapolating this data to the nationwide population, the survey estimated that approximately 800,672 high school athletes are hazed every year.[27] While boys were more involved than girls in all forms of hazing behaviors, girls were involved in all forms of hazing at very high levels.[28] Finally, 40 percent of students said that they would not report hazing.[29] These results have been supported by the findings of a survey of student-athletes at five suburban New York high schools.[30] According to this survey, 17.4 percent of high school athletes were subjected to hazing activities;[31] boys and girls were hazed in similar numbers.[32] While it is clear from these surveys that hazing is common in high school athletics,[33] anecdotal evidence arising from two recent high school incidents indicates the seriousness of athletic hazing in the new millennium. [Ed. note: Members of the Investigative Reporters of America criticized the study because it was based on a less than 25 percent response rate. However, the researchers in a single survey were able to collect personal accounts by respondents that arguably will be extremely valuable for the information contained therein when future researchers consult these materials.]

Recent High School Hazing Incidents

A recent high school wrestling incident has the potential to symbolize the dangerous nature of athletic hazing in the new millennium. Eight members of the Trumbull (Connecticut) High School wrestling team were arrested in connection with a hazing scandal.[34] Over a three-month period, the victim was "hog-tied" with athletic tape, stuffed inside a locker, thrown against a wall, and repeatedly sodomized with a plastic knife.[35] This hazing is even more heinous because the 15-year-old victim is a special-education student diagnosed with attention deficit disorder and a hyperactivity condition.[36] The victim had been counseled by school officials to join the wrestling team.[37] Seven of the eight assailants were expelled from school;[38] the five individuals charged as juveniles spent a week in juvenile detention.[39] The three wrestlers who were charged as adults pleaded guilty to assault and conspiracy charges and were sentenced to two years of probation, ordered to perform 300 hours of community service each, and ordered to reimburse the victim's family for $7,500 in medical expenses.[40] It was alleged by team members accused in the incident that school officials knew about the hazing for years[41] and that the school's basketball and wrestling coaches saw the victim hog-tied, yet did nothing.[42] The coaches of the wrestling team were subsequently dismissed.[43] [*Ed. note:* Records of the students will eventually be cleared if they follow all conditions set by the court.]

Another hazing incident involving male athletes which led to both criminal and civil charges occurred at Winslow (Arizona) High School during the 1999–2000 academic year.[44] Five basketball players and three track and field athletes were indicted in May 2000 on twenty-two sexual assault and kidnapping charges stemming from the hazing of at least ten other team members;[45] the basketball coach was indicted on three counts of felony child abuse for failing to prevent the attacks despite his prior knowledge of them.[46] During the hazings that occurred over a two-month period, younger athletes were held down by their older teammates, who pulled down their pants and inserted markers, pencils, fingers, and other objects into their rectums.[47] The incidents took place behind the school's pole-vault pit, on school buses traveling from competitions, and in locker rooms and parking lots at the school.[48] Seven of the athletes pleaded guilty to lesser charges of aggravated assault; of these individuals, the three "ringleaders" received sentences of nine months in jail, two to three years of probation, and community service; two perpetrators were sentenced to six months in jail and two others received sentences of two months in jail.[49] In reaction to this scandal, Arizona became the forty-third state to pass an antihazing law.[50] Eight of the hazing victims have filed civil lawsuits against the school district, the former basketball coach, and the individuals convicted of assault.[51]

While most hazing incidents are unreported,[52] those that do get reported often involve civil rather than criminal charges.[53] In addition to suing the perpetrators of these acts for intentional torts such as assault and battery as well as negligence-based actions, the plaintiffs file lawsuits against the school district and its employees under a variety of theories in both federal and state courts.[54]

Federal Law Claims Arising from Hazing

Fourth and Fourteenth Amendment Claims

Public schools may be held liable for both monetary damages and injunctive relief under 42 United States Code 1983.[55] Plaintiffs who are deprived of an independently existing federal right may seek remedy via 1983.[56] The U.S. Supreme Court has held that a student's right to bodily integrity is a constitutionally protected liberty interest.[57] Therefore, students who are victims of athletic hazing may argue that they have been deprived of an existing federal right.[58] In order to successfully raise this claim, the plaintiff must prove that the school acted with "deliberate indifference" to the student's constitutional rights by failing to prevent future harm against the student despite its knowledge of prior violent behavior.[59] A federal district court has ruled that hazing impacts one's right to bodily integrity.[60] Despite this ruling, courts have been reluctant to hold schools liable for hazing under 1983, relying heavily on the Supreme Court's decision in *DeShaney v. Winnebago County Department of Social Services*.[61] In *DeShaney*, the Court held that states do not have a general affirmative duty under the Constitution to protect their citizens,[62] though a duty to protect can arise if a state restrains personal liberty by taking a person into custody.[63] Most courts have refused to recognize that school attendance laws restrain students' liberty interests, which would have created a custodial relationship between the schools and students, giving rise to an affirmative duty to protect students.[64]

The federal courts that have heard and rejected victims' claims in athletic hazing cases have relied heavily on *DeShaney*. In *Reeves v. Besonen and Owendale Gagetown Area Schools*,[65] a freshman football player suffered a broken nose and bruised ribs during a "hit line" hazing ritual inflicted by older teammates while returning from a game on the team bus.[66] Despite the presence of coaches on the bus and the fact that both the head coach and at least one school-board member had long known about the ritual,[67] the court refused to find a violation of 1983 and granted the defendants' motion for summary judgment.[68] The plaintiff's claim that the hazing violated his Fourth Amendment right to be free from an unreasonable seizure and unreasonable and excessive force was summarily dismissed because the court found that no search or seizure by any state actor had occurred.[69] In addition, the plaintiff claimed that his Fourteenth Amendment substantive due process rights were violated by the defendants' failure to prevent the hazing ritual despite their knowledge of it.[70] The court relied on *DeShaney* in rejecting this argument and finding no constitutional violation.[71] Because the plaintiff voluntarily participated on the football team, his riding the school bus did not amount to "'incarceration' or 'involuntary commitment,' or 'police custody,' or anything of that sort."[72] The court held that "in the absence of such State coercion, DeShaney makes clear that the Constitution imposes no duty on the state to care for the Plaintiff's safety."[73] Finally, the court stated that "the remedies for such negligence . . . are adequately addressed in state tort law."[74]

In *Seamons* v. *Snow*,[75] the Tenth Circuit Court of Appeals considered the 1983 claims of another high school football player. As the plaintiff left a locker-room shower, he was attacked by his teammates, who forcibly restrained him and bound him naked with athletic tape to a towel bar while also taping his genital area; subsequently, a girl that the plaintiff had dated was brought into the locker room to view him.[76] The plaintiff claimed that he suffered violations of, among other things, his Fourteenth Amendment right to procedural and substantive due process.[77] The court first considered the plaintiff's procedural due process claims, including being forced to attend a school far removed from his parents, his dismissal from the Sky View High School (Utah) football team, and damage to his reputation.[78] Recognizing the plaintiff's constitutional right to receive a public education,[79] the court nonetheless found that the defendants failed to take any deliberate action to remove him from school; rather, the plaintiff made the decision to transfer on his own.[80] In addition, the court refused to recognize a constitutionally protected right to any specific aspect of education; therefore, the plaintiff had no right to participate in sports, take advanced placement courses, or attend a particular school.[81] Finally, as to the plaintiff's injured reputation, the court stated that "damage to an individual's reputation alone, apart from some more tangible interest, is not enough to establish a due process violation."[82]

After disposing of the procedural due process claims, the court turned to the plaintiff's substantive due process arguments. Interestingly, these claims were not based on the locker-room incident itself; rather, they were premised on the argument that the defendants' removal of the plaintiff from the football team and failure to investigate the incident, discipline the students involved, or adopt or follow procedures to protect the plaintiff's property interests constituted a violation of his rights.[83] Though acknowledging the plaintiff's removal from the football team, the court found that the plaintiff's liberty interests were not affected because he lacked a constitutional right to play high school sports.[84] The court also denied the plaintiff's "failure to protect" claims.[85] Because there was neither state action nor the existence of the *DeShaney* requirement of a custodial or other "special relationship" between the plaintiff and the school district, the defendant did not have a duty to protect the plaintiff.[86] The court then attempted to find liability under an alternative "danger creation" theory.[87] This theory is premised on the notion that state officials can be held liable for the acts of third parties if the officials engaged in extremely reckless or intentional acts sufficient to create a danger that caused harm to the plaintiff.[88] The court found that the defendants did not engage in such behavior because they did not intend to harm the plaintiff or place him at an unreasonable risk of harm;[89] although the defendants may have acted in a negligent, incorrect, and ill-advised fashion, their behavior did not rise to the level required to find liability under the danger-creation theory.[90] The federal court of appeals thus affirmed the district court's dismissal of the plaintiff's substantive due process claims.[91]

The case ended on an interesting note. In 2001, according to *The Salt Lake Tribune* (March 24, 2001), Seamons won partial vindication when a jury awarded him $250,000 against his former coach for alleged violation of his First Amendment rights, in effect accepting the player's testimony that his coach asked him to apologize to his teammates, including hazers. The coach lost in spite of his denial that he asked for an apology.

Despite some adverse rulings, at least two courts have allowed hazing victims' constitutional-law claims to proceed against school officials. In *Hilton* v. *Lincoln-Way High School*,[92] the court addressed the 1983 claims of a freshman student hazed during a marching-band retreat. The new members of the marching band were forced to wear paper bags over their heads on bus rides to and from the band's initiation ritual, where they were led into the woods and forced to participate in a medieval knighting ceremony that included "sword-wielding" men dressed in costumes resembling those of the Ku Klux Klan.[93] The plaintiff alleged that she was so frightened that she hyperventilated and subsequently blacked out;[94] she claimed that the hazing constituted an illegal seizure violative of her Fourth Amendment rights.[95] In denying the defendant's motion for summary judgment, the court found that the plaintiff sufficiently alleged a pattern of unconstitutional conduct that was participated in by school officials on the retreat who had policymaking authority.[96] Because many hazing incidents involve similar acts of kidnapping, blindfolding, or transporting of victims;[97] plaintiffs alleging such behavior may rely on *Hilton* in alleging Fourth Amendment violations.

In *Nabozny* v. *Podlesny*,[98] the Seventh Circuit Court of Appeals refused to dismiss a homosexual student's claims that the failure of school officials to intervene in a pattern and practice of male-on-male harassment constituted a violation of his Fourteenth Amendment equal protection rights.[99] The plaintiff alleged that school officials refused to stop the longtime physical and mental harassment of him by fellow male students despite receiving numerous reports of this behavior.[100] The court found that while students involved in male-on-female harassment were aggressively punished under the school's discipline code, school officials did not react similarly to the plaintiff's complaints; instead, the officials allegedly laughed at the plaintiff's complaints and told him that he deserved the abuse because he was a homosexual.[101] Upon remand for trial, a jury also found in the plaintiff's favor, and a $900,000 settlement offer from the school district was accepted shortly before jury deliberations on damages began.[102] As most hazing cases involve same-sex harassment that school officials are frequently aware of yet fail to prevent,[103] *Nabozny* provides an important precedent upon which plaintiffs may rely in asserting their constitutional rights. However, courts may choose to limit the case to its facts and apply it only in instances of harassment of homosexual students.

To avoid a court decision about its 1983 liability for an alleged Fourteenth Amendment violation, a suburban Philadelphia school district recently settled a lawsuit brought by a hazed student-athlete. In *Nice v. Centennial Area School District*, a tenth-grade wrestler at William Tennent High School was subjected to various forms of hazing, including a ritual where the victim was forcibly held down while a teammate sat on his face with his buttocks exposed.[104] The student sued the school district, school administrators, the team coaches, and his teammates who were involved in the hazing and their parents, claiming that his Fourteenth Amendment right to protection of his bodily integrity was violated when the school district failed to prevent the incidents despite its knowledge of the hazing.[105] The plaintiff received a settlement in the amount of $151,000.[106]

Title IX Claims Arising from Hazing

Title IX of the Education Amendments of 1972 is a federal law prohibiting sex discrimination in education programs and activities receiving or benefiting from federal funding.[107] In *Davis v. Monroe County Board of Education*,[108] the Supreme Court determined that Title IX applies to peer sexual harassment that occurs in schools.[109] Specifically, students are protected from being "excluded from participation in" or "denied the benefits of" an "education program or activity receiving federal financial assistance" on the basis of sex.[110] The Supreme Court defines "hostile environment sexual harassment" under Title IX as unwelcome behavior "so severe, pervasive, and objectively offensive" that it amounts to a denial of or exclusion from the school's educational opportunities or benefits.[111] A school district may be liable for "subjecting their students to discrimination where [it] is deliberately indifferent to known acts of student-on-student sexual harassment and the harasser is under the school's disciplinary authority."[112] In order to rise to this level, the harassment must have a "specific, identifiable, negative effect on [the victim's] ability to receive an appropriate education."[113] A single incident of peer sexual harassment is generally insufficient to cause such effects under Title IX;[114] rather, the complained-of behavior must be so "serious" and "persistent" that it systematically denies the victim access to educational benefits or opportunities.[115] School districts can be held liable only for their actions and not for those of the harassing student.[116] In *Gebser v. Lago Vista Independent School District*,[117] the Supreme Court determined that even if sexual harassment is occurring at the school, liability does not arise unless the school had actual notice of the behavior and acted in a deliberately indifferent manner by failing to remedy it.[118] Actual notice of the harassment by a school official "with authority to take corrective action to end the discrimination" must occur before a school district may be held liable.[119] A plaintiff may prove that the school district acted with deliberate indifference by establishing that its response to allegations of harassment was "clearly un-reasonable"[120] and thus was tantamount to an "official decision . . . not to remedy" the harassment.[121]

The high standards established by the Supreme Court in both *Davis* and *Gebser* make it very difficult for student-athletes injured during hazing incidents to recover for peer sexual harassment under Title IX. At the outset, the student must establish that the discrimination occurred on the basis of sex;[122] this may be done only if the student shows that "the harasser treated him or her differ-ently from other students based on gender."[123] In order to do so, a hazed athlete would likely have to prove that peer same-sex hazing attacks were treated dif-ferently by the school than peer opposite-sex hazing attacks. Second, it would be necessary to prove that the hazed athlete was "denied the benefits of" or "ex-cluded from participation" in "any education program or activity";[124] this may be shown if it can be established that the student-athlete's participation on a school-sponsored athletic team was negatively affected by the hazing. Third, the student-athlete must prove that the hazing was so "severe" and "pervasive" that it constituted a denial of education opportunities;[125] this is more easily accom-plished if the hazing consisted of a series of incidents rather than only one egre-gious act. Fourth, the student-athlete must prove that a school official "with authority to take corrective action to end the discrimination" had actual notice of the hazing;[126] this may be shown if the team's coach or an administrator had knowledge of the hazing.[127] Finally, the student-athlete must prove that the school's response to actual knowledge of the hazing was so "clearly unreason-able" that it reached the required deliberate indifference standard;[128] the student would need to show that the school officials' acts or omissions in response to the hazing were the functional equivalent of no response at all.[129]

Seamons v. *Snow*[130] describes one court's analysis of a hazed athlete's claims under Title IX and highlights the difficulty a plaintiff may have establishing this particular cause of action. In *Seamons,* the Tenth Circuit evaluated the plain-tiff's Title IX claim in addition to his aforementioned constitutional due process claims.[131] Seamons argued that he was excluded from participation in an edu-cational program on the basis of sex because of the school district's creation and tolerance of a hostile educational environment.[132] Specifically, the plaintiff alleged that the school district: 1) "failed to adopt and publish Title IX grievance procedures"; 2) "knew or should have known of the prior occurrences of sexual harassment" at the school; and 3) failed to properly investigate the incident or discipline the students involved.[133] The plaintiff argued that this constituted sex discrimination because it imposed masculine stereotypes on him, as per the coach's statements that he "should have taken it like a man" and that the con-duct complained of was simply a matter of "boys will be boys."[134] The court held that neither the coach's comments nor any other aspect of the defendants' behavior constituted sex discrimination.[135] The school's cancellation of the final football playoff game had the unfortunate effect of increasing the hostile envi-ronment in the school toward the plaintiff.[136] The court, noting that the school's action was intended to punish those involved in the hazing, held that the cancellation did not constitute an attempt to "exacerbate or create a hostile sexual environment for" the plaintiff.[137] In other words, the plaintiff was treated hostilely not because of his sex but because the student body felt that he had betrayed the team by reporting the incident and failing to apologize for doing so.[138]

State Law Claims Arising from Hazing

In addition to the aforementioned federal claims, student-athletes injured in hazing incidents may file lawsuits under state laws. Indeed, several plaintiffs have pursued civil litigation under state laws with varying degrees of success.[139] Though no consistent results have been reached, there appear to be several principles gaining increased acceptance in the courts. Many plaintiffs seeking remedies against a secondary educational institution believe that the common law doctrine of in loco parentis[140] establishes a responsibility on the behalf of the school to ensure the welfare of students.[141] Specifically, a parent "may . . . delegate part of his parental authority, during his life, to the tutor or schoolmaster of his child; who is then in loco parentis, and has such a portion of the power of the parent committed to his charge, viz.: that of restraint and correction, as may be necessary to answer the purposes for which he is employed."[142]

Along with this power comes an obligation for schools to maintain order and use reasonable care to prevent negligent conduct and physical attacks by other students.[143] One court has interpreted the doctrine of in loco parentis by stating that a teacher's "relationship to the pupils under his care and custody differs from that generally existing between a public employee and a member of the general public. . . . In such a relationship, he owes his pupils the duty of supervision."[144] A failure to so supervise may result in a lawsuit brought by a student-athlete injured during a hazing incident under a theory of negligent supervision. This occurs when a school's failure to properly train or supervise a student leads to a foreseeable injury to another student.[145] Under this theory, the plaintiff must prove the existence of the elements of common law negligence—duty, breach, cause, and harm. Typically, the key issues are whether a duty of care exists on behalf of the school and, if so, what the applicable standard of care is.

In *Benitez* v. *New York City Board of Education*,[146] the New York Court of Appeals held that a school owes a duty of reasonable care to protect interscholastic student-athletes from injuries resulting from "unassumed, concealed, or unreasonably increased risks."[147] In doing so, the court rejected the trial court's heightened standard that a school owes a student-athlete the duty of a reasonably prudent parent.[148] Similarly, the Indiana Supreme Court held that school officials owe a duty of reasonable care and supervision to high school athletes.[149] While noting that schools are not intended to be ensurers of their student-athletes' safety nor are they strictly liable for the injuries suffered by those student-athletes, the court rejected the lower standard of care proffered by the school district that it should only be liable if it acted with "deliberate, willful, or with a reckless disregard" for the safety of its student-athletes.[150]

In addition to the existence of a legal duty of care, a hazing injury also must be foreseeable for liability to arise. For example, in *Rupp* v. *Bryant*,[151] a case involving a student injured while participating in an unsupervised extracurricular club hazing, the Florida Supreme Court held that certain student misbehavior is itself foreseeable and therefore is not an intervening cause which will relieve principals or teachers from liability for failure to supervise: "We should not close our eyes to the fact that . . . boys of seventeen and eighteen years of age, particularly in groups where the herd instinct and competitive spirit tend naturally to relax vigilance, are not accustomed to exercise the same amount of care for their own safety as persons of more mature years."

Recognizing that a principal task of supervisors is to anticipate and curb rash student behavior, our courts have often held that a failure to prevent injuries caused by the intentional or reckless conduct of the victim or a fellow student may constitute negligence. Courts following this standard find that a lack of deportment in unsupervised students is to be expected. Thus roughhousing or hazing at a high school club initiation is behavior which is not so extraordinary as to break the chain of causation between the school's failure to supervise and the injury to the student.[152]

Nonetheless, it is unclear whether state courts require actual or constructive notice of hazing incidents at schools in determining whether or not a particular incident was foreseeable. However, based on the court's holding in *Rupp*, it is possible that the prevalence of hazing in high school athletics indicated by the two studies conducted on the issue provides the requisite level of foreseeability necessary to impose liability for injuries arising out of hazing incidents. It appears that schools will be held liable for any foreseeable hazing injury that is proximately caused by the absence of supervision.[153]

The three defenses most frequently asserted by schools in response to hazing-related claims arising under state laws are assumption of the risk, comparative negligence, and immunity. In *Siesto* v. *Bethpage Union Free School District*, the Nassau County (New York) Supreme Court granted summary judgment for the plaintiff, a junior varsity football player who required fifty-eight stitches after being hit in the forehead by a weighted football practice pad during a traditional locker-room hazing ritual that occurred a short distance from the coaching staff's office.[154] The plaintiff alleged that the school district was negligent in allowing the hazing to occur, arguing that school officials knew or should have known about the ritual based on its long history and the players' discussions of it in the presence of the coaches.[155] The trial court dismissed the affirmative defenses of comparative negligence and assumption of risk proffered by the defendant, summarizing that:

> While a student athlete assumes the risk of injury from the risks inherent in the sport in which he or she participates, such students do not assume the risk of

injury from a hazing ritual or tradition, which has no place in organized student athletics, even if they have knowledge that such rituals or traditions exist.[156]

School districts and their employees often claim to be free from liability for negligence in hazing litigation, citing an immunity doctrine as a defense. This issue is addressed in *Caldwell* v. *Griffin Spalding County Board of Education.*[157] In 1994, a high school freshman football player accompanying his team to their annual summer training camp was attacked in a dormitory, severely beaten, and knocked unconscious.[158] He sued the football coach, the principal, and the school board, alleging that school officials had knowledge of these hazings and, therefore, had a duty to protect him from the attack.[159] In upholding the trial court's summary dismissal of the case, the Georgia Court of Appeals ruled that the coach and principal, as school board employees, were immune from civil liability because their actions arose out of the discretionary act of supervising student safety.[160] In his concurring opinion, Judge John H. Ruffin Jr. called for stricter Georgia laws regarding immunity, stating that "school officials should not be immune from suit when they are . . . acting in the place of the students' parents, but then fail to take precautionary measures . . . when the potential for harm is known."[161] Thus, the distinction between whether supervision of students constitutes a discretionary or ministerial act will be determinative as to whether a school district and its employees are entitled to immunity from hazing litigation arising under state laws.

Recommendations and Conclusion

It is imperative that athletes, coaches, athletic administrators, and school officials be aware of the anti-hazing statutes in their jurisdictions and appreciate the fact that they can be held liable for injuries resulting from hazing activities. In light of this fact, these sport administrators must be aggressive in investigating athlete complaints and should stop initiation rites before they reach the level of criminal hazing. Numerous other proposals regarding the curtailment of hazing in interscholastic and intercollegiate athletics have been made.[162] Schools must adopt a clearly written zero-tolerance hazing policy with a plain-language explanation of both the definition of hazing and the consequences of engaging in this behavior.[163] All parents and students should sign a form stating that they have read and agree to abide by the policy.[164] Pursuant to the adoption of this policy, educational institutions should educate students, parents, coaches, and both athletic and school administrators about hazing by conducting informational presentations and team meetings and by posting educational materials about hazing and its dangers.[165] It is particularly important for coaches to be educated about hazing and made aware of its warning signs.[166] As the individuals with the most contact with the athletes, coaches must be especially vigilant of obvious, relatively benign behaviors that may indicate that more serious hazing is occurring.[167] Schools may also adopt proactive practices to prevent hazing such as adult supervision in locker rooms, where many hazing incidents occur.[168] Knowledge of specific hazing activity may be gleaned by conducting a survey of alumni, who may be more willing to disclose the hazing after graduation than they were during their active playing careers at the school.[169] In addition, schools should encourage athletes to notify school officials of any hazing by designing an anonymous reporting system; perhaps students would be more willing to disclose the hazing if they could avoid the negative consequences associated with doing so.[170]

If a hazing incident is reported, school officials should immediately conduct a fair investigation,[171] take prompt, strong remedial action to punish those involved, and ensure that the behavior is stopped.[172] The school board should keep a thorough record of the incident and its aftermath.[173] If appropriate, the school should refer the activity to law enforcement officials.[174] The subsequent discovery by law enforcement officials of any criminal activity should be followed by vigorous prosecution of the perpetrators.[175]

It is clear that hazing is widespread, harmful, and misunderstood.[176] School officials, administrators, and coaches must be proactive in their approach to hazing. Hazing is dangerous, contemptuous behavior that does nothing to enhance "team chemistry" and certainly does not help a team win its contests. All it does is harm innocent young individuals and prevent them from maximizing their athletic experiences because they may walk away with memories of torture and humiliation rather than athletic glory. Important lessons and lifetime friendships are gained from meaningful competition in interscholastic sports, not from senseless initiation rites. There is no reason for these two activities to be connected, nor should they be. The time for the eradication of hazing in interscholastic sports is past due. However, until these policy recommendations are adopted, these senseless initiation rites will continue unabated and more educational institutions will be subjected to liability.

Notes

1. See Hank Nuwer, *High School Hazing: When Rites Become Wrongs* (New York: F. Watts, 2000), 17.

2. For a thorough discussion of the legal issues surrounding hazing in this context, see Chapter 14 of this volume.

3. Michael I. Levin, "Hazing: Debunking the Myths about This 'Right' of Passage," *Pennsylvania School Boards Association Bulletin,* October 1999, available online at http://www.yk.psu.edu/~jlg18/484/pdf__files/rdg_hazing.PDF (accessed May 7, 2003).

4. See Kevin Bushweller, "Brutal Rituals, Dangerous Rites: High School Hazing Grows Violent and Humiliating," *American School Board Journal,* August 2000 (noting that some hazing incidents have been followed by "lawsuits filed against school districts for failing to prevent hazing"), available online at http://www.asbj.com/2000/08/0800coverstory.html (accessed May 7, 2003).

5. Nadine C. Hoover and Norm Pollard, "Initiation Rites and Athletics for NCAA Sports Teams," 30 August 1999, 8, available online at http://www.alfred.edu/news/html/hazing_study_99.html (accessed May 7, 2003).

6. Ibid., 8–11 (sorting hazing activities into categories ranging from "acceptable behaviors" such as attending preseason training to "unacceptable behaviors" such as being paddled, kidnapped, and/or abandoned).

7. See ESPN, "Sports Hazing Incidents," 17 April 2000 (providing a detailed list of reported hazing incidents in sports since 1980), by Tom Farrey and Hank Nuwer, available at http://espn.go.com/otl/hazing/list.html (accessed May 7, 2003); Kim Wilson, "It *Is* News . . . and It Has a Sensational Twist!" (discussing the increased media coverage of high school hazing incidents since 1981), available online at http://stophazing.org/high_school_hazing/kwilsonpaper.htm (accessed May 7, 2003).

8. Refer to Appendix 15.1 above. Only Alaska, Hawaii, Michigan, Montana, New Mexico, South Dakota, and Wyoming do not have anti-hazing statutes.

9. Refer to Appendix 15.1 above (showing that thirty-one states make hazing a misdemeanor).

10. See StopHazing.org (listing the various penalties for violating state hazing statutes), available online at http://www.stophazing.org/laws.html (accessed May 7, 2003); see also Melissa Dixon, "Hazing in High Schools: Ending the Hidden Tradition," *Journal of Law & Education* 30 (2001): 357, 359–60.

11. See, for example, Cal. Educ. Code 32051 (West 1994) (assessing a fine, imprisonment, or both for violation of the statute).

12. See Dixon, "Hazing in High Schools," 359 (recognizing the variation in anti-hazing laws and calling for stricter laws).

13. For example, California defines hazing in this fashion. See Cal. Educ. Code 32050 (West 1994).

14. See, for example, La. Rev. Stat. Ann. Tit. 17:1801 (West 2001) (limiting the definition of hazing to include only initiations into fraternal organizations at publicly funded educational institutions).

15. Pennsylvania limits the definition of hazing in this manner. Pa. Stat. Ann. Tit. 24, 5352 (West 1992); see also Dixon, "Hazing in High Schools," 359 (noting that only three states specifically apply their anti-hazing policies to primary or secondary schools).

16. See, for example, 720 Ill. Comp. Stat. Ann. 120/5 (West 1993 & Supp. 2001). In 1995, the Missouri Supreme Court ruled the state's anti-hazing law constitutional after a fraternity member claimed the statute's reference to "beating" was vague and ambiguous. Elisa Crouch, "Hazing Law Upheld," *Missouri Digital News,* 19 September 2000, available online at http://www.mdn.org/1995/stories/haze.htm (accessed May 7, 2003).

17. There are currently eighteen states with this provision. Refer to Appendix 15.1 above.

18. See, for example, Ariz. Rev. Stat. Ann. 15-2301 (West Supp. 2001).

19. Refer to Appendix 15.1 above. A constitutional challenge to this type of provision on Fifth Amendment grounds was recently rejected by the Texas Court of Criminal Appeals. See Armando Villafranca, "Ex-Cadets Can Be Tried in Texas A&M Hazing," *Houston Chronicle,* 8 February 2001, 27A (referring to *State* v. *Boyd,* 38 S.W.3d 155 [Tex. Crim. App. 2001]).

20. Included in this list are Arizona, Florida, Kentucky, Maine, Minnesota, Tennessee, Vermont, and West Virginia. Refer to Appendix 15.1 above.

21. For example, Florida and Kentucky do not require secondary schools to adopt anti-hazing policies. See Fla. Stat. Ann. 240.262 (West 1998 & Supp. 2002) (prohibiting hazing for purposes of admission or initiation into university organizations); Ky. Rev. Stat. Ann. 164-375 (Michie 1999) (requiring state universities and colleges to adopt statements of campus policy prohibiting hazing). Tennessee recently expanded its anti-hazing laws to require public school systems to adopt a written policy prohibiting hazing. See Tenn. Code Ann. 49-2-120 (Supp. 2001).

22. See Dixon, "Hazing in High Schools," 359–360 (comparing the various penalties among the states making hazing a criminal offense).

23. Wilson, "It *Is* News."

24. Nadine C. Hoover and Norman J. Pollard, "Initiation Rites in American High Schools: A National Survey," August 2000, 6 (hereinafter "High School Hazing Study"), available online at www.alfred.edu/news/html/hazing_study.html (accessed May 7, 2003). The reliability of this study has been questioned due to a low response rate, as only 1,541 of the 18,500 students selected (8.28 percent) returned their surveys. STATS Statistical Assessment Service, "Facts Hazy on High School Hazing," September 2000, available online at http://www.stats.org/newsletters/0009/hazing.htm.

25. "High School Hazing Study, 8."

26. Ibid.

27. Ibid., 6.

28. Ibid., 9.

29. Ibid., 11.

30. See Jeffrey C. Gershel et al., "Hazing of Suburban Middle and High School Athletes," Paper presented at the Pediatric Academic Societies' Annual Meeting, Baltimore, Maryland, April 30, 2001, (describing hazing as a "largely unrecognized issue for younger age groups").

31. Ibid.

32. Ibid.

33. Due to privacy concerns, neither of the aforementioned studies directly surveyed sexually exploitative hazing activity. See "High School Hazing Study," 4; Telephone interview with Jeffrey Gershel, M.D., June 7, 2001 (on file with author).

34. Denise Lavoie, "Eight High School Wrestlers Charged in Brutal Attack on Teammate," Associated Press Newswires, 2 March 2000; see also Associated Press, "High School Wrestlers Arrested," 2 March 2000, available online at http://abcnews.go.com/onair/closerlook/wnt_000302_cl_hazing_feature.html (accessed May 7, 2003).

35. Lavoie, "Eight High School Wrestlers Charged."

36. Associated Press, "Trumbull Teens Charged with Hazing Apply for Special Probation," *The News Times,* 9 July 2000, available online at http://www.newstimes.com/archive2000/jul09/rgc.htm (accessed May 7, 2003).

37. Rick Green, "Disability Made Hazing Victim a Target: School Move Backfired on Special-Ed Student," *The Hartford Courant,* 8 March 2000, A1.

Appendix 15.1. State Anti-Hazing Laws[1]

State	State Hazing Statute	Classification of Crime	Is Failure to Notify a Crime?	Is Anti-Hazing Policy Required in Schools?	Victim's Willingness to Be Initiated Is a Defense
Alabama	16-1-23	Class C misdemeanor	Yes	No	Yes
Alaska	–	–	–	–	–
Arizona	–	–	No	Yes	No
Arkansas	6-5-201	Class B misdemeanor	Yes	No	Yes
California	32050-1; 1411	Misdemeanor	No	No	Yes
Colorado	18-9-124	Class 3 misdemeanor	No	No	Yes
Connecticut	53-23(a)	–	No	No	No
Delaware	68, c.400, 9302-04	Class B misdemeanor	No	Yes	No
Florida	240.262		No	Yes	No
Georgia	16-5-61	High and aggravated misdemeanor	No	No	No
Hawaii	–	–	–	–	–
Idaho	18-917	Misdemeanor	No	No	Yes
Illinois	720 ILCS 120	Class A misdemeanor Class 4 felony	No	No	Yes

State		Misdemeanor–felony[2]			
Indiana	IC 35-4-2-2		No	No	No
Iowa	708.10	Serious or simple misdemeanor	No	No	No
Kansas	21-3434	Class B misdemeanor	No	No	Yes
Kentucky	164.375	–	No	Yes	Yes
Louisiana	17:1801	–	No	No	Yes
Maine	20-A;5;401	–	No	Yes	Yes
Maryland	27-268H	Misdemeanor	No	No	Yes
Massachusetts	269-17	–	No	No	Yes
Michigan	–	–	–	–	–
Minnesota	127.465	–	–	Yes	Yes
Mississippi	97-3-105	Misdemeanor	No	No	Yes
Missouri	578.360	Class A or C misdemeanor	No	Yes	No
Montana	–	–	–	–	–
Nebraska	28-311.06	Class II misdemeanor	No	No	No
Nevada	200.605	Misdemeanor	No	No	No
New Hampshire	631.7	Class B misdemeanor	Yes	No	No
New Jersey	2c:40-3	4th degree crime	No	No	No

Appendix 15.1. *Continued*

State	State Hazing Statute	Classification of Crime	Is Failure to Notify a Crime?	Is Anti-Hazing Policy Required in Schools?	Victim's Willingness to Be Initiated Is a Defense
New Mexico	—	—	—	—	—
New York	120.16	Class A misdemeanor	No	No	Yes
North Carolina	9:14:35-38	Class 2 misdemeanor	Yes	No	Yes
North Dakota	12.1-17-08	Misdemeanor	No	—	No
Ohio	2307.44; 2903.31	4th degree misdemeanor	No	No	No
Oklahoma	21-1190	Misdemeanor	No	Yes	No
Oregon	163.197	Misdemeanor	No	No	Yes
Pennsylvania	5352	3rd degree misdemeanor	No	Yes	No
Rhode Island	11-21-1	Misdemeanor	No	No	Yes
South Carolina	16	Misdemeanor	Yes	No	No
South Dakota	—	—	—	—	—
Tennessee	49-7-123	—	No	Yes	Yes
Texas[3]	37.152	Misdemeanor	Yes	No	No

Utah	76-5-107.5	Misdemeanor or felony	No	No	No
Vermont	16-§11 (a)(30)	—	No	Yes	No
Virginia	18.2-56	Class I misdemeanor	No	No	Yes
Washington	28B.10.901	Misdemeanor	Yes	No	No
West Virginia	18-2-33	—	No	Yes	Yes
Wisconsin	948.51	Misdemeanor felony	No	Yes	Yes
Wyoming	—	—	—	—	—

1. The authors developed this table for "Institutional Liability for Hazing in Interscholastic Sports," *Houston Law Review* 39, no. 2 (Summer 2002).

2. Misdemeanor likely, felony theoretically possible.

3. Tex. Educ. Code 37.51–37.157.

38. Ibid.

39. Ibid.

40. Diane Scarponi, "Judge Grants Probation to Three Trumbull Wrestlers in Hazing Abuse Case," *The News Times,* July 25, 2000, available online at http://www.newstimes.com/archive2000/jul25/rga.htm (accessed May 7, 2003); see also Lavoie, "Eight High School Wrestlers Charged."

41. See Lavoie, "Eight High School Wrestlers Charged."

42. See ESPN, "Sports Hazing Incidents."

43. See David M. Herszenhorn, "Trumbull: Coaches Dismissed," *New York Times,* 13 October 2000, B4.

44. See Mark Shaffer, "Winslow 7 Get Jail Time: Hazing Caused 'So Much Trouble,'" *Arizona Republic,* 19 October 2000, A1. It must be noted that hazing among high school–aged athletes is not the sole province of school-sponsored teams. In youth hockey, reliance upon veteran players for guidance is prevalent because the players spend an inordinate amount of time together on-ice, traveling, in social settings, and in the locker room. See Tom Farrey, "Like Fighting, Part of Game," 14 April 2000, available online at http://espn.go.com/otl/hazing/thursday.html (accessed May 7, 2003). This reliance on veterans led to a serious hazing incident in 1994, when thirteen veteran members of the Tilbury Hawks of the Ontario Hockey Association were charged with 135 criminal violations stemming from an initiation party at the home of one of the team owners. Many of the charges involved sexual assault and exploitation, resulting in the team trainer and team captain pleading guilty to committing indecent sexual acts.

45. Mark Shaffer, "Athletes Indicted in Sex Assaults," *Arizona Republic,* 10 May 2000, B1.

46. Mark Shaffer, "Winslow Coach Indicted in Hazing," *Arizona Republic,* 23 May 2000, A1. At this publication there have been no updates as to whether the charges will still stand or be dropped.

47. Shaffer, "Winslow 7 Get Jail Time."

48. Mark Shaffer, "Winslow Star May Face Jail in Hazing," *Arizona Republic,* 26 August 2000, A1. See also Shaffer, "Winslow Coach Indicted in Hazing."

49. See Shaffer, "Winslow 7 Get Jail Time."

50. The law requires all public educational institutions in the state to adopt and enforce a zero-tolerance hazing policy. See Ariz. Rev. Stat. Ann. 15-2301 (West Supp. 2001); see also Robbie Sherwood, "Battle against Hazing," *Arizona Republic,* 12 February 2001, A1 (discussing the upcoming hearing of Senate Bill 1096, which creates a new crime of hazing and recognizes that the incident at Winslow High School focused attention on the practice of hazing).

51. See Mark Shaffer, "Hazing Victims File New Suit," *Arizona Republic,* 25 January 2001, B4 (noting that a $4 million lawsuit against the school district alone alleges negligence, while a separate personal-injury lawsuit has been filed against all of the aforementioned parties seeking an unspecified amount of damages).

52. ESPN, "Sports Hazing Incidents."

53. See David S. Doty, "No More Hazing: Eradication through Law and Education," *Utah Bar Journal* 18 (November 1997): 19 (discussing Utah's newly enacted statute). This is frequently due to the narrow scope of some state

laws. Refer to notes 12–22 above and the accompanying text (discussing how some states' hazing statutes define hazing narrowly). In April 2001, no criminal hazing charges were filed in the touching and prodding of new members of the Bel Air (Maryland) High School wrestling team, because the Maryland anti-hazing law prohibits hazing only for the purpose of initiation; the hazed individuals were already on the team, and thus no initiation was involved. See Tim Craig, "Police, School Look into Bel Air High Hazing Allegation," *Baltimore Sun,* 5 April 2001, 2B. The deputy chief of the local police department stated, "it is hazing in a broad sense, but not hazing in a legal sense."

54. See Tom Farrey, "Laws Get a Workout," 17 April 2000 (discussing options for recourse available to hazing victims), available online at http://espn.go.com/otl/hazing/Friday.html (accessed May 7, 2003).

55. Section 1983 states: "Every person who, under color of any statute, ordinance, regulation, custom, or usage, of any State or Territory or the District of Columbia, subjects, or causes to be subjected, any citizen of the United States or other person within the jurisdiction thereof to the deprivation of any rights, privileges, or immunities secured by the Constitution and laws, shall be liable to the party injured in an action at law, suit in equity, or other proper proceeding for redress." 42 U.S.C. 1983 (1994).

56. See *Wood* v. *Strickland,* 420 U.S. 308, 326 (1975) (holding that a 1983 action is not available to review evidentiary questions in school disciplinary proceedings, to interpret school regulations, or to review the exercise of discretion by school officials unless that exercise involved violations under the Constitution).

57. See *Ingraham* v. *Wright,* 430 U.S. 651, 673–674 (1977) (holding that freedom from bodily restraint and punishment is within the liberty interest protected by the Fourteenth Amendment).

58. Despite the fact that Ingraham addressed the corporal punishment of students, federal courts have "readily accepted it as the foundation for other types of school violence actions in federal court." Deborah Austern Colson, "Safe Enough to Learn: Placing an Affirmative Duty of Protection on Public Schools under 42 U.S.C. Section 1983," *Harvard Civil Rights-Civil Liberties Law Review* 30, 169, 172 (1995).

59. Landra Ewing, "When Going to School Becomes an Act of Courage: Students Need Protection from Violence," *Brandeis Journal of Family Law* 36 (Fall 1997–1998): 627, 642 (discussing the dangers students face at school).

60. *Alton* v. *Hopgood,* 994 F. Supp. 827, 836–837 (S.D. Tex. 1998) (holding that university officials are shielded by qualified immunity because they acted with reasonable efforts to protect plaintiff's constitutional rights). See also David S. Doty, "Enough Is Enough: The Legal Responsibility of Public Schools and Universities to Prohibit Hazing," *Educational Law Reporter* 134 (1999): 423, 426–427 (discussing a federal civil rights claim filed against eight members of the Texas A&M Corps of Cadets in which the court addressed the issue of bodily integrity in a hazing situation).

61. U.S. 189 (1989).

62. Ibid., 195. The Court stated: "Nothing in the language of the Due Process Clause itself requires the State to protect the life, liberty, and property of its citizens against invasion by private actors. The Clause is phrased as a

limitation on the State's power to act, not as a guarantee of certain minimal levels of safety and security. . . . Nor does history support such an expansive reading of the constitutional text. . . . Its purpose was to protect the people from the State, not to ensure that the State protected them from each other" (195–196).

63. Ibid., 198–200. The Court further stated: "It is true that in certain limited circumstances the Constitution imposes upon the State affirmative duties of care and protection with respect to particular individuals. . . . But these cases . . . stand only for the proposition that when the State takes a person into its custody and holds him there against his will, the Constitution imposes upon it a corresponding duty to assume some responsibility for his safety and general well-being. . . . The affirmative duty to protect arises . . . from the limitation which it has imposed on his freedom to act on his own behalf."

64. See Laura Beresh-Taylor, "Preventing Violence in Ohio's Schools," *Akron Law Review* 33 (2000): 311, 319–320 (evaluating the impact of alternative schools on school violence); see also Colson, "Safe Enough to Learn," 171–180 (discussing 42 U.S.C. 1983 as a possible theory under which a school may have a duty to protect its students).

65. F. Supp. 1135 (E.D. Mich. 1991).

66. Ibid., 1137 (explaining that the "hit line" was a hazing ritual that usually consisted of some team members "roughing up" the other members of the team).

67. Ibid., 1136–1138 (noting that both the football coach and the one member of the school board had been aware of the "hit line" hazing ritual for over ten years).

68. Ibid., 1139 (concluding that the plaintiff failed to prove that he was deprived of a constitutionally protected right, privilege, or immunity by a person acting under the color of state law).

69. Ibid.

70. Ibid. (noting that the plaintiff contended that, in the event the due process clause did not impose an affirmative duty to protect, such a duty may arise under a "special relationship" created or assumed by the state).

71. Ibid., 1140.

72. Ibid.

73. Ibid.

74. Ibid., 1141. In support of this argument and its concern about creating a slippery slope for such federal claims, the court wrote: "If the Court were to accept the Plaintiff's argument here that the Constitution somehow imposes a duty on school officials to provide for the safety of students with respect to extracurricular activities, even though their participation in those activities is wholly voluntary, then there would no longer be any practical distinction between ordinary state-law negligence claims and federal constitutional violations, so long as the negligent party was acting under the color of state law. It is foreseeable, for example, that the Plaintiff's reasoning could be extended to school sports in general. The Plaintiff's theory here, if accepted, might be thought to impose a constitutional duty on school officials to protect student athletes—and, perhaps, others—from unreasonable risk of injury during athletic events both on and off the field. Similarly, the consti-

tution might be construed to require school officials to make school property safe, not only with respect to students and others on the premises for legitimate purposes, but to outsiders (such as vandals or thieves) whose presence on public property is unauthorized, but nevertheless foreseeable" (1140).

75. F.3d 1226 (10th Cir. 1996).

76. Ibid., 1230. The plaintiff reported the incident to the coach shortly thereafter. After talking to the individuals involved, the coach required the plaintiff to apologize to the team for reporting the incident in order to avoid any internal disharmony on the squad. When the plaintiff refused to do so, the coach removed him from the team. Upon further complaints to the school principal, the principal immediately cancelled the remainder of the team's season. The plaintiff was continually threatened and harassed at school thereafter, and eventually transferred to another high school at the principal's suggestion.

77. Ibid. The plaintiff also claimed a violation of Title IX as well as his First Amendment rights pursuant to section 1983. The Tenth Circuit allowed the First Amendment claims to survive summary judgment. *Seamons* v. *Snow,* 206 F.3d 1021, 1028 (10th Cir. 2000). Seamons eventually was awarded $250,000 against the coach on the First Amendment decision by a jury.

78. *Seamons,* 84 F.3d at 1234–1235. The plaintiff claimed "that he had constitutionally protected property interests (1) in his education at Sky View [Utah] High School, (2) the advanced placement courses and credits, and (3) participation in interscholastic athletics. He also claimed he had constitutionally protected liberty interests in: (1) attending public school in the district where he resides; (2) bodily integrity, which includes the right to be free from sexual assault and harassment at school; (3) living with his family and not being forced to attend school in a district far removed from his family; (4) not being dismissed from the Sky View football team; and (5) his reputation and standing in the community" (1234).

79. Ibid. (citing *Goss* v. *Lopez,* 419 U.S. 565, 573 [1975]).

80. Ibid.

81. Ibid., 1234–1235 (recognizing that there are "innumerable separate components" within the educational context not protected by the Constitution).

82. Ibid., 1235 (citing *Paul* v. *Davis,* 424 U.S. 693, 701 [1976]).

83. Ibid. The plaintiff relied on the Fifth Circuit Court of Appeals decision in *Doe* v. *Taylor Independent School District,* 15 F.3d 443 (5th Cir. 1994), in support of his claim that he had a liberty interest in his bodily integrity for which the defendants could be held liable for their omissions, if such omissions constituted a "deliberate indifference" to his rights. However, the court distinguished Doe on its facts because that case involved teacher-student sexual abuse in which the plaintiff clearly possessed liberty rights and state action was not present.

84. Ibid.

85. Ibid. (stating that the due process clause was not intended to protect individuals against private violence).

86. Ibid., 1235–1236 (noting that taking an individual into custody against his or her will is an example of a situation in which the state owes some measure of constitutional protection).

87. Ibid., 1236.
88. Ibid. (citing *Uhlrig* v. *Harder*, 64 F.3d 567, 572 [10th Cir. 1995]).
89. Ibid. (citing as evidence the fact that the school cancelled the remainder of the team's season in addition to requiring the team to send the plaintiff a written apology letter).
90. Ibid. (concluding that the defendants' conduct did not satisfy the "shock the conscience" standard required by the danger-creation theory).
91. Ibid., 1229–1230, 1239. The plaintiff's only surviving claim of a violation of his right to freedom of speech was remanded on the finding that there was no overriding school interest in denying the plaintiff's right to report the incident.
92. No. 97–C-3872, 1998 WL 26174 (N.D. Ill. January 14, 1998).
93. Ibid., 1–2 (recounting that the plaintiff was forced to kneel before one of the "Grand Dragons" who then tapped her on the shoulder with his "sword").
94. Ibid., 2.
95. Ibid. The plaintiff also asserted several state claims including battery, false imprisonment, hazing, negligence, and intentional infliction of emotional distress.
96. Ibid., 5. The band director and his assistant were among those on the retreat (1). The court dismissed the plaintiff's federal claim of racial discrimination as well as one made under the Illinois hazing statute; the plaintiff failed to allege that the school's actions were motivated by race, as is required in order to find a violation (3–4).
97. See, for example, *Psi Upsilon of Philadelphia* v. *Univ. of Pa.*, 591 A.2d 755, 757 (Pa. Super. Ct. 1991) (upholding sanctions levied against fraternity for kidnapping a student during a hazing ritual); *Ohio* v. *Brown*, 630 N.E.2d 397, 404–406 (Ohio App. 3d 1993) (stating that although paddling and other acts of hazing occurred in one county, venue was proper as to a general hazing charge in the county from where the victim was transported).
98. F.3d 446 (7th Cir. 1996).
99. Ibid., 460.
100. Ibid., 449 (noting that the plaintiff reported these incidents in both middle school and high school).
101. Ibid., 451, 454–455. This particular incident reported by the plaintiff involved two other male students who pushed the plaintiff to the floor and then proceeded to mock-rape the plaintiff as twenty students looked on and laughed.
102. Linda Jacobson, "Gay Student to Get Nearly $1 Million in Settlement," *Education Week*, 27 November 1996, 7 (disclosing that the plaintiff also received up to $62,000 for potential medical expenses related to the injuries he suffered).
103. See Thomas A. Mayes, "Confronting Same-Sex, Student-to-Student Sexual Harassment: Recommendations for Educators and Policy Makers," *Fordham Urban Law Journal* 29 (2001): 641, 660–663 (providing several possible reasons why school officials might be reluctant to interfere with same-sex harassment among students).
104. F. Supp. 2d 665 (E.D. Pa. 2000).

105. Levin, "Hazing: Debunking the Myths."
106. 98 F. Supp. 2d at 666 (approving the settlement agreement).
107. U.S.C. 1681(a) (1994) provides in relevant part that "no person in the United States shall, on the basis of sex, be excluded from participation in, be denied the benefits of, or be subjected to discrimination under any education program or activity receiving Federal financial assistance."
108. U.S. 629 (1999).
109. See ibid., 632–633 (emphasizing that Title IX is applicable to situations in which a school responds with deliberate indifference to known acts of harassment).
110. Ibid., 638 (citing 20 U.S.C. 1681[a]).
111. Ibid., 651 (clarifying that it is not necessary to show physical exclusion to prove a denial of educational opportunity based on gender).
112. Ibid., 646–647.
113. Anne-Marie Harris and Kenneth B. Grooms, "A New Lesson Plan for Educational Institutions: Expanded Rules Governing Liability under Title IX of the Education Amendments of 1972 for Student and Faculty Sexual Harassment," *American University Journal of Gender, Social Policy & the Law* 8 (2000): 575, 604 (discussing *Davis*, 526 U.S. at 629).
114. *Davis*, 526 U.S. at 652–653.
115. Ibid., 650; see generally Harris and Grooms, "A New Lesson Plan for Educational Institutions," 604–606.
116. *Davis*, 526 U.S. at 642. In addition, the Department of Education's sexual harassment guidance provides that: [A] school's failure to respond to the existence of a hostile environment within its own programs or activities permits an atmosphere of sexual discrimination to permeate the educational program and results in discrimination prohibited by Title IX. Conversely, if, upon notice of hostile environment harassment, a school takes immediate and appropriate steps to remedy the hostile environment, the school has avoided violating Title IX. Thus, Title IX does not make a school responsible for the actions of harassing students, but rather for its own discrimination in failing to remedy it once the school has notice. "Sexual Harassment Guidance: Harassment of Students by School Employees, Other Students, or Third Parties," *Federal Register* 62 (March 13, 1997): 12034, 12039–12040.
117. U.S. 274 (1998).
118. Ibid., 290.
119. Ibid.
120. See *Davis*, 526 U.S. at 648.
121. See *Gebser*, 524 U.S. at 290 (noting that a school district's response must amount to deliberate indifference to establish liability).
122. See 20 U.S.C. 1681 (1994) (prohibiting discrimination by educational institutions on the basis on sex).
123. See Harris and Grooms, "A New Lesson Plan for Educational Institutions," 597 (discussing the elements needed to prove Title IX liability under the deliberate indifference standard).
124. U.S.C. 1681.
125. See *Davis*, 526 U.S. at 650 (explaining when an educational institution may be liable for damages under Title IX).

126. *Gebser,* 524 U.S. at 290.
127. This may be a difficult hurdle for a plaintiff to overcome, given the general reluctance of student-athletes to report hazing to coaches and administrators and the inability of many student-athletes to discern hazing activities from non-hazing activities. See Hoover and Pollard, "Initiation Rites in American High Schools," 6, 11 (reporting that "most high school students did not perceive even the most dangerous initiation activities as hazing" and that 40 percent would not report hazing).
128. See *Davis,* 526 U.S. at 648.
129. See *Gebser,* 524 U.S. at 290.
130. F.3d 1226 (10th Cir. 1996). Notably, this case was decided prior to the Supreme Court's decision in Davis.
131. Ibid., 1232.
132. Ibid.
133. Ibid. (citing factors Seamons alleged created a hostile educational environment).
134. Ibid.
135. Ibid., 1233 (determining that the defendants' actions or inaction reflected their sense that Seamons betrayed the team and did not rise to the level of sex discrimination).
136. Ibid.
137. Ibid.
138. Ibid. While the court dismissed the plaintiff's Title IX claims, Judge McKay's concurrence was noteworthy: "The authors cannot agree that the alleged harassment in this case was not based on sex within the meaning of Title IX. The majority writes that statements such as 'boys will be boys' and 'take it like a man' are not sufficiently sex related to state a claim. I believe, however, that these statements can only be understood as a response to the original hazing incident. In my view, this incident was clearly sexual in nature. Members of the football team taped Plaintiff to a towel rack while he was naked, taped his genitals, and then displayed their captive to a girl Plaintiff had dated. These actions clearly derive their power to embarrass and to intimidate from their sexual and sex-based nature. It is hard for me to believe that the display of the male genitalia to a female for other than medical or educational reasons has a non-sexual connotation. The coach's statement that 'boys will be boys' clearly relates to and flows out of the original sexual harassment. As such, it may be considered to be a continuation by the school official of the student-initiated sexual harassment, even if the statement by itself is not sexual in nature." Ibid., 1239–1240 (McKay, J., concurring).
139. Compare *Rupp* v. *Bryant,* 417 So. 2d 658, 660 (Fla. 1982) (finding a valid cause of action against the school board, principal, and teacher for injuries a student received during a hazing incident) with *Caldwell* v. *Griffin Spalding County Bd. of Educ.,* 503 S.E.2d 43, 43–44 (Ga. Ct. App. 1998) (dismissing a suit brought against the school board, the principal, and a coach for injuries suffered during a hazing incident).
140. Literally, "in the place of a parent." *Black's Law Dictionary,* 7th ed. (St. Paul: West Group, 1999), 791.

141. See, for example, *Eastman* v. *Williams,* 207 A.2d 146, 148 (Vt. 1965) (noting that some courts utilize the doctrine of in loco parentis in order to impose a duty of supervision on an educational institution).

142. William Blackstone, Commentaries 453, "In Loco Parentis: A Balance of Interests," 61 *Illinois Bar Journal* 638 (1973).

143. See W. Page Keeton et al., *Prosser and Keeton on the Law of Torts,* 5th ed. (St. Paul: West, 1984), 358 (discussing a person's duty to exercise reasonable care).

144. *Eastman,* 207 A.2d at 148.

145. It has generally been held that, with respect to school athletics, "the duty owed an athlete takes the form of giving adequate instruction in the activity, supplying proper equipment, making a reasonable selection or matching of participants, providing nonnegligent supervision of the particular contest, and taking proper post-injury procedures to protect against aggravation of the injury." Allan E. Korpela, Annotation, Tort Liability of Public Schools and Institutes of Higher Learning for Accident Occurring during School Athletic Events, 35 A.L.R. 3d 725, 734 (1971) (citations omitted).

146. N.E.2d 29 (N.Y. 1989).

147. Ibid., 33 (dismissing a student's claim because there was insufficient evidence to show the school breached its duty of care).

148. Ibid., 32 (rejecting the reasonably prudent parent standard and applying the ordinary reasonable care standard).

149. See *Beckett* v. *Clinton Prairie Sch. Corp.,* 504 N.E.2d 552, 553 (Ind. 1987) (rejecting the theory that a lower standard of care is warranted when supervising high school as opposed to elementary school students).

150. Ibid., 553–554.

151. *Rupp* v. *Bryant,* 417 So. 2d 658 (Fla. 1982).

152. Ibid., 668–669 (citations omitted) (quoting *Dailey* v. *Los Angeles Unified Sch. Dist.,* 470 P.2d 360, 364 [Cal. 1970]).

153. See *Siesto* v. *Bethpage Union Free Sch. Dist.,* as reported in "Student Athletes Do Not Assume the Risk of Injury From Hazing Rituals," *New York Law Journal,* 30 December 1999, 21, 29 (finding the doctrine of assumption of risk does not bar the claims of a student-athlete injured in a hazing incident).

154. Ibid.

155. Ibid.

156. Ibid. Courts have differentiated student-athlete hazing from fraternity hazing with regard to the assumption of risk defense to negligence. In *Barran* v. *Kappa Alpha Order, Inc.,* the Alabama Supreme Court upheld a summary judgment in favor of the defendant fraternity stating that, by voluntarily subjecting himself to hazing for more than one year, the victim assumed the risk of being hazed. 730 So. 2d 203, 206–207 (Ala. 1998). The plaintiff argued that "peer pressure created a coercive environment that prevented him from exercising free choice," but his testimony that 20 to 40 percent of the members of his pledge class dropped out convinced the court that he could have quit at any time. Ibid., 207.

157. S.E.2d 43, 44 (Ga. Ct. App. 1998) (analyzing the state's immunity statutes as applied to hazing incidents).

158. Ibid., 43–44.

159. Ibid., 44.

160. Ibid.

161. Ibid., 46–47 (Ruffin, J., concurring) (arguing that student supervision involves a ministerial rather than a discretionary act).

162. See, for example, Doty, "No More Hazing," 18, 19–20 (proposing a plan of action "to ensure that a concerted effort is made to eradicate hazing"); Kelley R. Taylor, "Hazing: Harmless Horseplay?" *Principal Leadership* (March 2001): 75, 77–78 (recommending the needed elements for a model anti-hazing policy).

163. See Doty, "No More Hazing," 19 ("School [as well as university and Greek] officials must, by means of carefully drafted and well-communicated policy, unequivocally prohibit hazing and firmly discipline students who participate in hazing."). One commentator explains the need for a zero-tolerance policy as follows: "Splitting hairs over the seriousness of the incident is a bad idea when you're dealing with high school students; when it comes to teenagers, they often don't know when to quit. Allowing room for conjecture as to what is and what isn't acceptable in hazing is an invitation to more disaster. . . . Better they understand that they should never get started in the first place." Brad Rock, "Memo to Hazers: Read the Handbook," *Deseret News,* 12 September 1996, D1; see also Levin, "Hazing: Debunking the Myths"; Bushweller, "Brutal Rituals, Dangerous Rites," 18 (noting that "anti-hazing policies should define hazing and identify behaviors that are unacceptable"); Taylor, "Hazing: Harmless Horseplay?" 77–78 (noting the necessary components for an effective anti-hazing policy).

164. See Taylor, "Hazing: Harmless Horseplay?" 78 (recommending that school districts make their policy available to students and parents).

165. See ibid.; see also Bushweller, "Brutal Rituals, Dangerous Rites," 21 (analyzing effective methods for implementing an anti-hazing policy).

166. See Bushweller, "Brutal Rituals, Dangerous Rites," 21 ("Many coaches participated in hazing rituals when they were younger, and some might believe the experience made them tougher.").

167. Ibid.

168. Ibid.

169. Ibid. (recognizing that some hazing forms may be passed from one class to the next).

170. See Taylor, "Hazing: Harmless Horseplay?" 78 (outlining a model anti-hazing policy that includes an anonymous reporting system).

171. Ibid. (emphasizing that an effective anti-hazing policy requires unbiased investigations).

172. See Bushweller, "Brutal Rituals, Dangerous Rites," 21 (calling for "immediate" and "aggressive" responses to allegations of hazing); see also Levin, "Hazing: Debunking the Myths" (suggesting possible actions such as discipline, expulsion, or counseling).

173. See Levin, "Hazing: Debunking the Myths" (emphasizing the need to prove and to publicize its responses to hazing); see also Taylor, "Hazing: Harmless Horseplay?" 78 ("As with any complaint or serious issue in your school, it is extremely important to document every step of an investigation.").

174. See Taylor, "Hazing: Harmless Horseplay?" 78; see also Levin, "Hazing: De-

bunking the Myths" (analogizing hazing to other forms of criminal activity such as weapon or drug offenses).

175. See Doty, "No More Hazing," 19 (propounding a plan of action to eliminate hazing).

176. See Levin, "Hazing: Debunking the Myths" (correcting the myths that hazing is rare, not harmful, and includes innocuous activities such as carrying books).

16 Initiating Change: Transforming a Hazing Culture

Susan VanDeventer Iverson and Elizabeth J. Allan

Editor's note: *Numerous experts have identified characteristics of hazing cultures. In this essay, two veteran educators offer hope that such a culture can be changed. Susan VanDeventer Iverson and Elizabeth J. Allan have experienced some success at their institutions in halting hazing and in introducing hazing reforms.*

We approach this chapter with more than twenty-five years of combined experience working in postsecondary education in various capacities, including positions in offices of student activities and Greek life, student judicial affairs, residence life and housing and as faculty in a college of education. While we have been involved with the issue of hazing in numerous capacities, the majority of the insights we share have been garnered from in-depth work at two different institutions; one a small private women's college in the mid-Atlantic region, the other a state flagship research university in the northeast (we have selected the pseudonyms IC for Independent College and SU for State University, respectively). In each of these cases, we were privileged to work with students and colleagues who inspired us with their passion and courage to take a stand against the ugly and often-deadly hazing rituals that plague student organizations and athletic teams on college campuses throughout the country.

Each week, www.StopHazing.org (an educational website co-run by author Allan) receives numerous inquiries asking what can be done to end the abuses of hazing. Many concerned students, family members, and educational professionals want to end dangerous and degrading hazing traditions. Unfortunately, relatively few success stories serve as guideposts for organizational and institutional change. Our hope is to contribute to such change by sharing some of the positive images that have inspired us. We also describe some theories of culture and student development that help to explain how such change occurs. We believe that anyone can make a difference and perhaps save a life by speaking out.

At first glance, the dynamics of hazing seem to defy common sense. Why would anyone hesitate to intervene in the sorts of senseless group practices that have resulted in scores of student deaths? Yet the reality is that many people are reluctant to intervene. Hazing traditions are often cloaked in secrecy and silence and are sustained by powerful cultural norms that make it exceptionally difficult for victims and others to speak out against it. Those who do break the silence are often vulnerable and frequently endure emotional and physical abuse in retaliation for their stance. Even those who are not directly involved as victims or participants may hesitate to report hazing because they fear reprisal by the group—or, perhaps more commonly, dismiss hazing rituals as harmless pranks. Many simply consider hazing activities to be the result of individual choices and thus a private rather than public matter. Nevertheless, there are some who do take a stand, and they are the focus of this chapter.

What spurs an individual to take action against hazing? What are some key characteristics of collective action to eliminate hazing? In this chapter, we describe real-life accounts of undergraduate students as well as the stories of college and university staff, faculty, and administrative leaders who have taken courageous actions to eliminate hazing on their campuses.[1] While our work with students has occurred at diverse institutions (small private schools, a women's college, research universities, and state flagship campuses) in different regions of the country over the past decade, we have discovered that our experiences dealing with the issue of hazing share marked similarities. Based on these experiences, we suggest that some key elements seem to characterize success stories. We begin by providing a snapshot of our individual experiences in order to provide readers with a fuller context for considering the themes and recommendations we set forth in this chapter.

Elizabeth Allan's Story

My personal efforts to address the problem of hazing in student organizations began at a state university (henceforth SU) in 1991 where, as a new professional in the Office of Student Affairs, I became increasingly concerned with issues of peer harassment, violence, and victimization on campus. As I became more familiar with the student culture, I was alarmed by the prevalence of humiliating, degrading, and often physically dangerous hazing traditions that pervaded Greek life, athletics, and other student organizations. Concurrently, I read Hank Nuwer's *Broken Pledges* (1990) and his account of Eileen Stevens's experience of losing her son Chuck Stenzel, who died as a result of fraternity hazing. This tragic story motivated me to take a tough stand against hazing practices despite resistance that came in many forms, including threats of physical harm against students made by students who were deeply invested in sustaining hazing traditions. I was committed to learning more about this complex issue in order to intervene before a tragedy like Alfred's befell SU. The hazing stories shared with me by students were chilling. I was truly frightened for their safety. I knew that some of the hazing practices could be life-threatening and I felt compelled to take action.

Addressing the issue of hazing was a contentious process. It involved the exposure of ugly secrets and threatened to shift power away from those who had built individual and group identities around these dangerous traditions. Ongoing efforts to educate and hold student groups accountable for hazing practices as violations of the student code of conduct seemed at times futile, largely due to the lack of visible community support. Inspired by the story of Eileen Stevens's pioneering work to enact a law prohibiting hazing in the state of New York, I decided to draft a proposal for a state law that would make hazing in my state an illegal practice. This endeavor also represented an opportunity to challenge institutional complicity in the problem of hazing, represented largely by the failure of key leaders to take a strong stand against it. Although I knew that legislation alone would not eradicate hazing, I believed it could serve as a strong deterrent and, at the very least, cause more people to become aware of the problem.

Within three months, the proposal for a state law moved from an idea to a centerpiece for a student activist group. Although I was the person who had taken the initiative to draft the proposal for legislation, the primary support and far-reaching community education came from the students who chose to become involved in the effort. These students came together from different backgrounds and personal experiences. Many had been hazed and had participated in hazing others, while others had no direct experience with hazing. Some took personal risks to speak publicly about their experiences of victimization as a result of hazing. Some testified before the state legislature; others wrote letters to the editors of major newspapers, and some voiced support through television and radio interviews. While all these actions were courageous, some of the most difficult challenges that faced these young people was in day-to-day interactions with their peers.

In addition to student activists, some faculty, staff, and community members were instrumental in anti-hazing efforts as well. The director of student activities, the director of the student conduct system, the coordinator of the Sexual Harassment and Rape Prevention Program, residence life staff, and the chief of campus police were particularly instrumental in taking strong stands against hazing violations. The collaborative efforts of these key staff members as well as a number of courageous and committed fraternity and sorority alumni/ae advisors was crucial to sending a clear message to the campus that hazing would no longer be tolerated.

During this time, students were slowly learning that hazing was no longer going to be ignored by university officials. Nearly half of the fraternity chapters and one sorority were held accountable for hazing and for other violations of the student conduct code. In a few cases, the violations were so severe that the chapters were suspended from operation by both the university and the national organization affiliated with the local chapter. Alongside the prohibitive effect of formal sanctions against hazing, a number of productive efforts were underway, including peer-education workshops, a hazing hotline, and letters sent home to parents. Following about six months of coordinated lobbying, the state's governor signed the proposed anti-hazing bill into law in the late spring of 1993. The president of the university held a celebratory reception at his house for the students involved in the lobbying efforts, symbolically marking a change in the tide. The anti-hazing team had achieved a significant victory by winning the passage of a law—and the campus hazing culture was slowly eroding after months of focused dialogue and debate.

Susan VanDeventer Iverson's Story

My exposure to hazing had been nearly nonexistent prior to arriving at a private women's college, but all that soon changed. Hazing practices disguised as rivalries and games were part of the fabric of the institution. I was shocked by stories I heard, incidents that were reported, and activities I saw. Humiliating and degrading traditions were prevalent in club activities and class rivalries. I asked questions and raised concerns, I challenged students to ask themselves and others similar questions about what was happening to women in our community, and I kept senior administrators informed in an effort to engage them in problem-solving.

Many behaviors were rarely hidden. The games and rivalries were pervasive; they rang through the residence halls at all hours of the night and they were present in the classrooms, in the dining commons, and on the quad. Photos and articles were in the student newspaper. In one article in the student newspaper, a sophomore admitted to "witnessing" (participating in) hazing; she identified first-year students as inferior and deserving of "hate." A faculty member in anthropology tried to convince her students of the insidious effects of symbols in ritual performance by having students in her senior seminar classes write reflective essays and analyze the images. At times I felt powerless, as I am sure many individuals did, about how to respond. Students would report disruptions, harassment, and abuse to me, but I had no procedural recourse. A state law against hazing existed, but the college did not have a policy; in fact, the state law was not even published in the student handbook.

Change did not begin formally for a few months. Students, faculty, and staff wanted to join the effort to make change but were unaware that others shared their motivations. I initiated informal conversations with students. By gathering and sharing stories, I built networks and allies. The deleterious effects of the ridicule and humiliation were striking, and the need for a policy to support a response was clear. The president, advised by others, and I decided to call attention to these behaviors and develop a plan to address hazing. In a memo to the campus community, the president charged an advisory task force to draft a policy on hazing, to include sanctions for hazing, and to develop a plan for educating the community about these issues. The task force was co-chaired by a student and a faculty member and was made up of faculty, staff, alumnae, and students. The students represented all four class years; some had hazed, others had participated in hazing. None could say they had no direct experience since its effects were so pervasive on this campus.

I directed the hazing task force, providing administrative and emotional support to the members. Meetings were frequent; a draft policy was produced and brought before the community in an open meeting that was divisive and polarized. Continued conversations, meetings, focus groups, and discussions in the dining commons all contributed to further revisions and the final policy, which included processes for adjudication and sanctioning. In addition to students, individual faculty, staff, and alumnae were instrumental in escorting change. This collaborative effort sent a clear message to the community that the culture, rituals, and traditions were changing. Once the policy was final, I spent as much, if not more, time working with the leadership of clubs and organizations on how to survive and thrive as a club under the terms of the new hazing policy. As challenging and demanding as it was to develop a hazing policy, the implementation of the policy was just as important and time-consuming. I believe that students felt like partners in developing solutions. They were educating themselves and others, and the campus community was learning that hazing was not acceptable and no longer tolerated.

So You Want to Eliminate Hazing?

Any organizational or cultural change process is dynamic and therefore impossible to predict or analyze in any sort of linear way. In our experience, successful anti-hazing initiatives have been multilayered and often unpredictable. Yet, based on our experiences, several themes have emerged that help us characterize key components of changing an organizational and/or institutional hazing culture. The specific hazing incidents and environmental nuances vary depending on the individuals, organization, and institutions involved, but the themes are relatively constant and typically include the development of new heroes, symbols, and rituals; the power of individual voices as catalysts for change; the involvement of leaders who are willing to disrupt the status quo; and the reshaping of cultural norms that support a hazing culture through accountability measures and education/awareness programming.

Hazing Cultures

In the field of anthropology, traditions, heroes, symbols, ceremonies, rituals, and sagas are considered central elements of culture (Manning 2000; Masland 2000). Culture can be loosely defined as the shared assumptions, beliefs, and "normal behaviors" (norms) of a group. These assumptions and beliefs are powerful influences on the way people live and act, and they define what is "normal" and how to sanction those who do not conform (Schein 1992). More specifically, culture includes the "symbolic processes, ideologies and sociohistorical contexts" that influence the ways in which participants make sense of their reality (Tierney 1993, 7). Many social scientists argue that individual behavior is largely shaped by cultural norms (Masland 2000; Schein 1992; Tierney 1989).

Volumes have been published on culture and change in many diverse arenas, including education (Manning 2000; Rhoads 1995; Tierney 1991) and the private sector (Frost, Moore, Louis, Lundberg, and Martin 1985; Martin 1992; Schein 1992). Researchers in higher education often rely on anthropological literature as a theoretical lens for making sense of seemingly ordinary experiences on college campuses (Manning 2000; Tierney 1991). Anthropological perspectives provide a focus on "how people build, learn, and transform culture in ways that create meaning and give definition to their existence" (Manning 2000, 2). For instance, the campus tour "is one of many formal rituals that transmit the institution's political, social, environmental, and cultural expectations and norms for prospective members" (Baxter-Magolda 2001, 2).

Our focus in this chapter, however, is specific to describing themes of cultural change related to groups or organizations in colleges and universities in which hazing has become a norm. We refer to these groups or organizations as having "hazing cultures." We suggest that hazing cultures exist when members of a group (such as a team, a Greek-letter society, or a student club) or larger organization (such as a school or college) accept hazing practices as part of the ordinary functioning of their group. A "hazing culture" includes those groups who are actively participating in hazing practices as well as those groups and individuals who tacitly sustain hazing practices by virtue of their silence on the issue.

In all cultures, pressure to behave in acceptable ways, to conform to established norms, is significant, and being on a college campus is no different (Kuh and Whitt 1988). "A dominant culture presents difficulties to newcomers or members of underrepresented groups when trying to understand and appreciate the nuances of behavior" (163). The concept of culture can be used as a lens through which to understand many of the dynamics of hazing organizations. At its worst, "culture can be an alienating, ethnocentric force that goads members of a group, sometimes out of fear and sometimes out of ignorance, to reinforce their own beliefs while rejecting those of other groups" (Gregory, quoted in Kuh and Whitt 1988, 163).

We contend that the description provided in this quote often characterizes the culture of secret societies[2]—particularly when much of their group identity has been shaped around hazing traditions. Nonetheless, the message and lure of secret societies (and groups with high social status such as athletic teams) are powerful and pervasive with minimal, if any, marketing or promotion.

While we use the term "hazing culture" to characterize specific groups, this is not meant to imply that those groups somehow exist apart from the larger social context. Rather, we subscribe to the view that hazing behaviors are powerful and pervasive largely because they are supported by societal attitudes that make it more likely for hazing to be practiced and accepted or ignored. Sanday (1990) describes this dynamic in her analysis of fraternity gang rape where she specifically examines "the values, social expectations, and institutional practices encouraging male sexual aggression . . . in the university setting" (9). While her focus in this research was the practice of "pulling train" (multiple men with one woman, who was often too inebriated to consent) in college fraternities, she clearly links this behavior with "a broader social ideology of male dominance" (11). In much the same way, hazing behaviors in particular groups are typically supported by broadly accepted social norms and ideologies that make many abuses of hazing seem quite normative. For instance, cultural expectations about manhood and the social acceptability of binge drinking among college students is reflected in college fraternity hazing as described by Sweet (see Chapter 1 in this book): "At Alfred University's Klan Alpine house . . . considerable social pressure was put on pledges to consume alcohol in excessive quantities. So important was heavy alcohol consumption to this fraternity's subculture that members would actually photograph each other vomiting."

Like this account, numerous descriptions of student hazing rituals portray the abuses that are shaped by powerful cultural forces (Nicoletti, Spencer-Thomas, and Bollinger 2001; Nuwer 1999; Rhoads 1995; Sanday 1990; Sweet 2001). In our experience, individuals or groups who have worked to eradicate hazing in a group or organization were involved with reshaping some important elements of culture. In particular, they have worked to replicate some of the elements of culture that are attractive to those who participate in secret societies. For example, heroes are often established and become part of the cultural context of secret societies. They may be current members in the group or past members whose contributions have become a sort of legend. Or a hero may be represented in a particular role or leadership position independent of the particular personality of the person holding the post. These heroes are pivotal to maintaining the group's culture over time. In working to shift a culture away from hazing, new heroes are likely to emerge. These heroes serve as role models and provide a powerful moral example, which is conveyed through their personal commitment and action (Dalton 1985).

Emergence of Heroes and Role Models

Marjorie (a pseudonym, as are other first names in this essay) is an example of a student who provided a moral example. She was an active student leader and the current leader of one of the most prominent secret societies at IC. She was asked by the president of IC, and agreed, to serve on the task force charged with eliminating hazing. Marjorie was deeply conflicted about how to combine her role on the task force with her role as a member of a secret society. She was withdrawn and reflective as she wrestled with how to provide leadership to change groups while she was an active member of the one of the groups she sought to change. Marjorie realized that she might be witnessing, if not engaging, in the behaviors she was working to stop.

After months of deliberation and many conversations with Susan VanDeventer Iverson and others, Marjorie announced her resignation as the leader of the secret society and disassociated with the group altogether. I (Iverson) admired her strength of conviction but was also concerned. I didn't want her to endure the alienation and hostility I anticipated she would encounter from her peers. And she did. Many challenged her with anger and disappointment. Others felt that if Marjorie wanted to work for change, she could have best done so from within. The previous year's members were particularly hostile. The former president wouldn't acknowledge Marjorie at all, even if they were using the same toaster in the dining hall. Spring tapping[3] was only weeks away, and the group didn't have active leadership. But Marjorie was not swayed. She realized that she could gain strength and influence change by working with others rather than trying to influence change in organizations that were, at this point, fighting against her.

Her actions spoke volumes to the community. At the time, the decision was painful and Marjorie feared that no good would come of it. Yet later that year Marjorie was elected as president of the Student Government Association. She had run against four other students, all but one of whom were active in secret societies. Marjorie clearly stood out as the type of student leader which the IC student body was seeking. She could make tough decisions and she stood up for what she believed. Under Marjorie's leadership, the Student Government Association was restructured to create a strong club council, which would serve as the oversight body for the administration of the hazing policy and education for clubs.

On a different campus, other students were emerging as heroes for change. One of these students was Brendan—a member of an SU fraternity who decided to speak out against hazing rituals that included forcing pledges to sit unclothed on an ice-cold keg of beer while the active members took turns shouting at them and demanding humiliating acts of subservience. For some it involved crawling on a basement floor stained with urine and beer; others were egged, paddled, and sometimes punched. During one initiation, Brendan witnessed two pledges being burned as brothers sprayed oven cleaner on their bare chests.

According to Brendan (a third-year member of the fraternity) and Derek (a recent alumnus of the same fraternity chapter), a typical semester in this fraternity chapter house would be filled with hazing activities that spanned the continuum and grew more reprehensible as hell week approached. The implicit threat of retribution for violating the code of silence among the brotherhood prevented both young men from reporting the fraternity.

Nevertheless, Brendan became increasingly troubled by his knowledge of the abuse. He decided to talk with chapter officers. He urged them to call off hell week activities. He even offered to serve as a new pledge educator and develop a non-hazing program. They laughed at him; they told him, "No one will go for it." Faced with such entrenched hazing attitudes, Brendan decided to take the next step. He called the national fraternity, identified himself, and asked for their support.

The national fraternity intervened and after a swift and intense interview process with the membership, elected to revoke the charter of this chapter. Enraged by this, fraternity members lashed out at Brendan—verbally harassing him, vandalizing his car, threatening him, and spreading rumors intended to humiliate him. As a result of these incidents, Brendan decided to send a letter to the campus newspaper in an effort to address the rumors and misinformation circulating about why the fraternity's charter was revoked.

Not surprisingly, publication of this letter in the campus paper caused an uproar within the Greek system and captivated the attention of many who were not involved with fraternity and sorority life. By breaking the code of silence, Brendan had ignited change. To the surprise of many, a number of fraternity and sorority leaders publicly supported him. People phoned to tell him they were inspired by his strength and courage. Others gained the courage to join Brendan in making a difference and taking a stand against hazing in their own chapters. As one SU student reflected, "Brendan's courage was inspiring. If he could do it, we could do it." A ripple effect had begun throughout the Greek system and the larger student body.

Developing New Rituals

Rituals are another means of identifying cultural values, beliefs, and ideologies. "Rituals are useful tools for uncovering culture because they translate culture into actions" (Masland 2000, 148). The anthropological literature delineates a number of forms and types of rituals across cultures. For instance, rites of passage, cultural ceremonies, and performances are forms of ritual that have been the focus of scholarly inquiry (Manning 2000). Additionally, Manning has identified seven types of rituals (reification, revitalization, resistance, incorporation, investiture, entering/exiting, and healing) that are particularly relevant to college campuses as cultural sites.

Many rituals exist within secret societies. It is perhaps, along with tradition, one of the terms most often associated with such groups. It is therefore essential when changing a hazing culture not to eliminate all rituals but rather to identify the importance and value of rituals and create new ones to replace those that involve hazing. As Manning (2000) notes, "If one remembers as well as takes advantage of the created reality of rituals and culture, successful 'new' traditions are possible. Humans can do anything within the bounds of culture because it is their creation" (126). New elements of culture such as rituals are not "created anew" but rather emerge from aspects of culture "inherited from the past" (2). Thus, for a new ritual to be relevant and meaningful for a group, it must have ties to the cultural context from which it emerges.

For example, at IC, Iverson's college, the memorizing of the honor pledge (vow) gave relevance and meaning to the new hazing policy. During the same year that the hazing policy was being drafted, the honor pledge was under review. Under the new honor pledge, instead of pledging only regarding one's academic conduct, students now had to pledge to uphold standards of nonacademic conduct as well. Students were pledging not only to report themselves but also the actions of others, including the actions of others in secret societies. By hanging signs around campus with words of the new honor pledge and requiring students to memorize the new pledge, students had identified a ritual that would publicly expose the secretive anti-hazing culture and transform the pledge into actions.

At SU, a number of new rituals were developed in the process of changing a hazing culture. According to McLaren (1986), rituals of revitalization are an "event that functions to inject a renewal of commitment into the motivations and values of the ritual participants" (as quoted in Manning 2000, 5). An example of a revitalizing ritual can be seen in the implementation of a Greek awards banquet at SU. In an effort to spotlight fraternity and sorority chapters who were making positive efforts to eliminate hazing in their groups and promote positive environments for academic achievement and service, annual Greek awards were established and celebrated at a formal banquet each spring. Chapter leaders and members who were accustomed to rituals for marking achievements generally greeted this initiative with enthusiasm. This Greek awards provided an extra incentive to avoid violating campus policies (including the non-hazing policy; points were deducted from chapters on judicial sanction). More important, this new ritual served as a public acknowledgment of chapters that had taken affirmative steps to educate and eliminate hazing by holding training sessions and workshops and by developing creative new member education programs.

Rituals of reification are those that acknowledge the choices that are made by participants in a culture. On college campuses, convocation ceremonies where students are ushered into a new academic year and assured that their choice to attend the college or university are of value to the institution serve as rituals of reification (Manning 2000). Similarly, these types of rituals can play an important role in efforts to transform a hazing culture. For instance, at SU, students who were involved in the efforts to lobby for the passage of the statewide anti-hazing bill were invited to the university president's home for a reception in their honor. This ritual provided an opportunity for the students to hear from the institution's chief executive that their choices (and sometimes sacrifices) were valued by the community. Similarly, a special ceremony offered by the state governor marked the occasion of signing the anti-hazing bill into law. Both of these events provided important opportunities for reflection, recognition, and closure.

Establishing New Symbols

The use of symbols is another element of changing a hazing culture. Symbols reside in many places—an act, an event, a story, an insignia, a language, dress, structural roles, ceremonies, or even a position within an organization (Tierney 1989). The key to understanding organizational symbols lies in delineating the symbolic forms whereby the participants communicate, perpetuate, and develop their knowledge about and attitudes toward life (Geertz, referenced in Tierney 1989, 224).

In addition to representing culture, symbols represent identity. The importance of a group's identity formation should not be underestimated. Though many elements contribute to a group's identity, the power of a name should not be minimized. A group's name, like an individual's name, is perhaps one of the most important aspects of identity. We each saw evidence of the power of name with the groups with whom we worked.

At IC, the president named the group charged with developing a policy on hazing. We were the Presidential Advisory Task Force on Hazing. Many abbreviated this name to Antihazing Task Force. Someone within the group pointed out, early on, that the acronym was the ATF, otherwise known as Alcohol, Tobacco and Firearms. That was the level and nature of what we felt we were dealing with, so the acronym seemed appropriate. It caught on and was how we self-identified in meetings. Baseball caps with club letters were popular on campus, and for a while we (almost seriously) considered getting ourselves hats with ATF sewn on them. We were serious because we knew that we would seem like the new club on campus and it would catch on; people would want to join the ATF. Hats would be the symbol for our identity. The whole idea may seem amusing, but in terms of cultural change, it holds an important meaning. An identity which represents a group's message and a way to communicate the identity/message through symbols are essential.

Individual Voices Inspired to Make a Difference

In an analysis of how student development occurs, Chickering and Reisser (1993) subscribe to the perspective that student development occurs through sequences of differentiation and integration. Differentiation requires a dissonance or challenge to one's way of thinking. Hazing forces individuals to reexamine values and beliefs in the face of challenging moral situations. Important contributions have been made in research on students' ethical and moral development (Kohlberg 1971; Perry 1968; Gilligan 1982). According to these theories, the encounter and struggle with experiences that challenge one's own beliefs and values is important for promoting moral development in college students. The dissonance produced through decisions involving moral conflicts helps motivate students to speak out, get involved, and make a difference.

In our experiences, students who became involved with anti-hazing efforts had often experienced dissonance as a result of a moral dilemma related to hazing—and this dissonance contributed to their motivation to take action. For instance, many of the students at SU became involved in anti-hazing efforts only after they had been hazed and had participated in hazing others. They faced a moral dilemma when they realized that their silence was making them complicit with the problem of hazing and, in turn, contributing to an environment that placed others in danger. In terms of developmental theory, these students faced a moral crisis of sorts when they recognized an opportunity to speak out against hazing but also wanted to preserve their membership in the hazing organization.

Stephen Sweet (1999) draws on symbolic interactionist theory from the field of sociology to examine the particular challenges fraternity and sorority members face when they recognize that hazing is a problem and that they do not want to perpetuate the problem. He writes, "Hazing is not simply the result of psychologically flawed individuals, but is the result of a confluence of symbols, manipulated identities, and definitions of situations that are organized in the context of fraternity initiation rites" (362). Students who have pledged a fraternity or sorority (the same can be said of athletes as well) have invested tremendous energy and time in the process of becoming a member. Often their friendships have become restricted to the group; in fact, according to Sweet's analysis, fraternities "deliberately and systematically limit the social relations of their pledges, forcing them to form tight groups with intimate contact" (359). Student affiliation with such organizations becomes a part of one's identity, and speaking out against the organization is an implicit challenge to one's sense of self. Thus, it can be exceedingly difficult to find students who are willing to speak out against hazing.

Mary, a junior at SU, reported that previously positive relationships with her sorority sisters turned sour when she took a stand against hazing. At the same time, however, new pledges were coming to her secretly to get support because they were afraid of rejection and possible reprisal for not conforming. It was at this point that Mary decided to come forward and publicly speak out in support of a state law against hazing. Her commitment solidified as she became a part of the collective effort and saw other students who had made similar decisions. Eventually, Mary became one of the students who not only spoke out against hazing but also became involved with multiple visits to the statehouse, where she testified before legislators and gave interviews to reporters from newspapers around the state.

It seemed that time and time again, we were both witness to seemingly ordinary people doing extraordinary things. For example, Rachel, a first-year student at IC, wrote a letter to the dean of students regarding her participation in an "unfortunate incident." First-year students had been invited to a senior class meeting under the guise of being asked to help plan Senior Week. During the meeting it was announced that the first-years would participate in a "scrubbing." Rachel said that she tried to exercise her right not to participate but was told that she had to and that if she opted to leave she would be "hunted down and chastised." Rachel wrote that the seniors yelled at them while they scrubbed, calling them profanities such as "bitch." First-year students who admitted feeling threatened were called "stupid" and were told that they were "acting like babies." Rachel closed her letter by writing, "I thought this college would be a place for me to unite with other women." The dean of students recognized the courage it took for Rachel, a first-year student, to write this letter and to speak out against hazing.

Pam, a sophomore, is another individual voice that made a difference. She didn't feel like she fit into the school community. Pam was active in theatre and wanted to connect with other students. She was aware of the secret societies on campus, including one group in particular whose members were active in theatre, but Pam didn't think they represented the type of group of which she wanted to be a member. She decided to start her own group. She posted a sign, recruiting students to join her in developing a comedy improv troupe. She made clear in the sign that this group would be different from that other group and would not involve hazing of members. A few nights later, Pam had a knock on her room door. Outside her door were members of a secret society. They claimed to admire her ideas about a comedy improv troupe and said she was the type of student they wanted in their group. Pam paused to wonder if she had this group all wrong; maybe they were the group for her. She'd paused too long. The individuals laughed and mocked her and made threatening and hurtful comments. That night Pam got on her computer and began searching other schools' Web pages with the intention to transfer. But Pam did something else. She sent an e-mail to the president regarding the actions of secret societies. "I hope this letter in some way informs you of what is happening on campus from the point of view of a student who has experienced hazing and will encourage you and the rest of the faculty to do something about it," she wrote.

Many times the person who speaks out against hazing is a student who has participated in hazing. Like Maryann, she was a part of the campus community and even a member of a secret society. Other students were vocal about "tradition" and promoted rituals that she had once participated in but now questioned and wanted to challenge. She was against what groups were doing; her beliefs and values were different, and she was against hazing. This struggle, feeling within and yet against, leaves many students silent. But it only takes one voice, one person to speak up. A number of students have had a profound impact on the movement to eradicate hazing on campus. Each one took the courageous first step to speak out.

Insights from student development theory make clear that opportunities to speak out against hazing can provide an important developmental challenge for students. It is crucial for parents, teachers, staff, and administrators to understand the dynamics of hazing and work to provide students with real opportunities to face a moral crisis related to hazing and then provide them with a balance of support to help them work through the crisis productively. Faculty, staff, students, and family members can offer support for students dealing with the moral dilemma of whether or not to speak out against hazing by helping them understand how their voice can make a difference.

Believing they could make a difference was a theme voiced by a number of undergraduate students at SU when asked to reflect on their role in working for the passage of anti-hazing legislation:

> It gave me a sense of responsibility and made me feel involved in a worthwhile endeavor.

> It amazed me that the thoughts and views of an individual, a student, myself, could influence government.

> I felt I was involved in an uphill battle. I enjoyed the challenge and the feeling of accomplishment.

[We were] working toward something and achieving it. Learning about courage, risk, and putting one's self on the line for something we felt strongly about.

Students who are facing the developmental challenges of moral dilemmas need to have support from those they trust and respect. In fact, theories of student development contend that in order for students to develop a solid sense of self, there must be a balance between challenge and support. Students who are overwhelmed by a developmental challenge will likely regress developmentally, while students who are coddled with too much support will remain stagnant in the developmental process (Evans, Forney, and Guido-DiBrito 1998). It is important that students who get involved in anti-hazing efforts receive the appropriate support and validation so they know that their involvement can make a difference.

Margaret Mead said, "Never doubt that a small group of thoughtful, committed citizens can change the world." The importance of a single voice in promoting community awareness and igniting collective action should not be underestimated. "The impact of the general culture may vary substantially after it has been interpreted by two different reference groups, and the impact of a reference group may be modified as a close friend describes his [sic] view of what the group 'really stand[s] for'" (Chickering 1969, 268). Dissonance and disruption challenge the values of individual students. As these individuals speak out, other students shift their moral positions and change allegiances. This can have a ripple effect that engages other students, who form coalitions and serve as a potent force for change.

Tonya, a student at IC, used her voice to motivate others. She was senior class president: outgoing, popular, and highly respected. Susan VanDeventer Iverson worked with her and other class officers on changing a tradition on campus, one that had escalated over the years to involve excessive drinking, abuse, and vandalism. An advocate of the tradition wrote in the campus newspaper that this "hedonistic delight" stood "perilously on the brink of extinction." Students were going to defend their rights to drink to excess and "trash" student rooms.

The class officers working with administrators to change this abusive tradition were named "sellouts." Tonya was so angry with her peers. "Why can't they get it? This is not an unrestricted party!" And she wrote just that and more to the student newspaper. "We're not eliminating tradition; we're fostering it. We're not stifling a good time; we're preserving it." Tonya and other class officers repeated this message at the senior and junior class meetings. They received much heat from her peers, but they stood tall and defended decisions to make changes in policies and programs in order to stop the abuse.

Leadership

Change as we are describing it requires a different type of leadership. Instead of leadership being one individual as an architect of a bold initiative, power is found in networks and through coalitions. Decentralized leadership enables different voices to arise and enables oppositional voices to speak (Tierney 1993, 99). This is very different from the leadership of secret societies, which is hierarchical, where leaders are exercising power, modeling behaviors that position some students higher on the hierarchy than others. Some students are dominant, exercising their power and potential abusiveness, and others are subordinate, marginalized, and possibly victimized.

In contrast, leadership within grassroots change efforts is more egalitarian. Leaders are coordinators or facilitators of ongoing activities. Team leadership allows for the communication of multiple voices, stories, and perspectives. Leadership is symbolic; leadership isn't held (like a position) but rather is shared. By recognizing this, individuals can feel empowered to make change. Leadership provides a vision, a symbolic sense of direction. If the leadership of secret societies is providing one direction, change agents can provide an alternate vision. "I saw myself as a team player. I tried to be a 'supporter,' especially for those who were more emotionally/personally connected with the issue. I also saw myself as an advocator, educator and lobbyist" (SU undergraduate student).

These individuals were active participants in the change process, a role for which Belenky and colleagues use the metaphor of "midwife." Individuals leading change can serve as midwives, "focusing on the others' knowledge and contributions" (Belenky, Clinchy, Goldberger, and Tarule 1986, 218). These midwives provide support and facilitate conversation, listening, and mutual sharing. "They question and listen to others, urging them to speak, so that they might better know the world from the other person's vantage point" (145).

Jill, a senior, was a strong leader at IC who was able to hold her own in challenging situations. She had agreed to serve as the task force co-chair from the perspective of her position as chair of the campus judicial committee. In this new role, Jill was faced with reconstructing her understanding and approach to leadership. Jill was also the former leader of a highly respected secret society on campus and was now being challenged by her peers to recall her role as the so-called supreme ruler of all that is evil within the secret societies. Jill wished that in some way her identity, and her leadership role, could have been masked. "Why couldn't the memo that announced the task force, not have named the task force members? The task force could meet in secret and produce a document that would be distributed by the President" (Jill, personal correspondence).

The task force membership was not anonymous, and that reality came crashing down on Jill sooner than she expected. Jill had chaired the judicial committee; she'd made controversial decisions. She was now receiving harassing phone calls and threatening e-mails. In an e-mail to Susan VanDeventer Iverson, Jill wrote, "I was very concerned about the letter that went out to the student body because I thought that I was labeled the fall guy. Well, I have gotten some very interesting email, much of which is not very nice. . . . The student body is very upset with me. . . . I just wish the letter was different." Jill had always been within a group, and now she was working against a group. She was struggling with where to stand, what position to take. She knew and agreed that hazing was wrong, but she suddenly was viewed as the leader of this change; it was more controversy than she had bargained for.

Jill talked with Iverson, her faculty advisor, the president, the task force co-chair, and students on and off the task force. She began to realize that she wasn't alone in providing leadership for change. A web of people were involved in initiating change. "I have talked with some students and feel better about the whole thing. I am excited about the task force and I think it is a good thing" (Jill, personal correspondence).

Leadership can be seen at all levels of the institution. Concerned individuals initiated change at IC. Their voices informed the president, who made the formal decision to organize the task force to develop a policy on hazing. In a memo to the community outlining her observations, the president wrote:

> Tradition binds us together as a community by serving as a meaningful link between past and future. But not all tradition is worth preserving, and I have come to realize that some of what we do in the name of "tradition" is, to put it bluntly, hurtful to individuals and harmful to the College. Specifically, much of what occurs under the aegis of ritual "games" and "initiation rites" for various class and club rivalries is hazing. Hazing is illegal. . . . Even if this behavior were not illegal, however, it would have to end. To the degree that any students are deliberately intimidated or degraded, or made to feel discriminated against, this behavior makes a mockery of what is best about any college, and in fact perpetuates patterns of behavior that are antithetical to the community values . . . students, faculty, and alumnae care most deeply about.

The president could have easily endorsed the policy initiative privately, and the task force co-chairs could have sent a memo that announced the task force to the campus community, if one was sent at all. However by taking a stand in what she believed and knew was right, the president sent a message (literally and figuratively) to the community that this was serious business. Such action creates dissention that not every administrator is prepared to invite. To develop an ally or advocate in a senior position, it is essential to keep senior-level administrators informed, educated, and aware of issues and incidents and to create opportunities when it is possible or necessary to speak on behalf of change.

Accountability

Developing policy is one approach to changing a hazing culture. While publishing the state's law on hazing is important, it is not enough for the institution to stop there. Not all states have laws, and many of the laws that do exist are not comprehensive enough to cover the nature and scope of offenses. Institutions are encouraged to develop their own standards for group behavior. This eliminates the use of statutory language. But more important, it allows an institution to define norms for its culture. It is desirable to educate a community around norms for good citizenship and community standards. Students need to be discouraged from making their own definitions about what is and what isn't hazing.

The introduction of policy alone, however, does not change a culture. Some institutions may already have a policy but need to change a hazing culture. Determining a strategy for the implementation of the policy and the adoption of the policy, or standards, by groups is essential. At IC, when the policy was developed, students were eager (and not all for good reasons) to know how the policy would be implemented. Prior to the development of the hazing policy, clubs were encouraged to review their group's constitution every four years, but no further expectations existed regarding the clubs' missions, training methods, purposes, or activities. In fact, in an annual student government report there is a reference to a meeting of club leadership at which they were reminded of the hazing law. In discussion of how to preserve tradition in light of the law on hazing, the clubs were told to use "good taste and good judgment."

Secret societies need much more direction than advice to use good judgment. With the development of the IC policy, club heads and their advisors were expected to affirm their understanding and commitment to the following expectations by signing and submitting an agreement to the club council, a governing body. By signing this agreement, the group was agreeing to:

- Annually review the policy on hazing with their membership.
- Participate in regular club officer meetings and training, including a session on hazing.
- Review their mission, purpose, and activities to ensure none are in violation of the policy.

A review of a group's purpose and activities was time-consuming and challenging. Some clubs were very creative in their approaches with their club's activities; this was the opportunity they had needed. Others felt they would become extinct when the policy was implemented; they were angry and stubborn. However, the essential element was make sure that all groups realized that they would be accountable if they did not determine how to be in compliance with the hazing policy. This agreement was a symbol of the policy; a signed form signified the group's commitment to an anti-hazing culture.

Still, even with the agreement, groups were most curious about how (or if) they would be held accountable. The policy outlined the following procedures: A violation would be reported, as all offenses were, to the judicial chair of a student disciplinary group. During the investigation, the club president would be notified of the offense. If the club was responsible, the club president would represent the group by standing before a hearing with the judicial board. If the violation was committed by an individual within the club, the individual could be held responsible separately from the club.

Students were eager to test the legitimacy of the policy, and Susan VanDeventer Iverson had an opportunity, unfortunately, to do just that within the first semester. A sophomore reported to Iverson that during a class activity, a junior spit on her and called her profane names. She didn't know the name of the junior, but she knew the club because the junior was wearing the club's colors. Iverson met with Lucy, the club's president, and informed her of the incident. Iverson informed her that either Lucy would be called before the judicial board or she could identify the individual student who would be brought forward as an individual rather than as a club member. Lucy said, "Give me twenty-four hours. We have informed our members of the policy. This is not okay and they know that. I think this person was acting on her own, but give me twenty-four hours." The next day she arrived at Iverson's office with the junior. Lucy said that the individual student had not acted on behalf of the club and that this was an individual violation of policy. The junior was referred to the judicial board, and Lucy served as her advocate through the process.

Jake, a student at SU, is an example of individual action resulting in group accountability. Jake, along with other members of his pledge class, was hazed repeatedly. He endured the abuse, thinking all the while that he would "change the system" once he became a brother. During his sophomore year, Jake became more involved in a serious relationship. Preoccupied with his girlfriend, he easily distanced himself from the fraternity during pledging and became less active as a brother. As he entered his junior year, however, Jake and his girlfriend parted ways and he found himself drawn back to the fraternity.

Soon the pledging process began again at his fraternity, and Jake became increasingly uncomfortable with the hazing (forced drinking, long periods of sleep and hygiene deprivation, servitude, verbal abuse, physical paddling, and calisthenics were among the hazing practices in this particular chapter). He decided he would not participate, but even having the knowledge of the abuse and degradation began to trouble him more and more. Jake obliquely voiced some of his concerns with me (Allan). Since he was not willing to officially report the fraternity for hazing, I encouraged him to talk with the leadership of the chapter to recommend that hazing be eliminated from the pledge process. At the next chapter meeting he spoke out. While there were one or two brothers who seemed sympathetic to his concern, the majority overruled and insisted that hazing was essential to the brotherhood.

Finally, after a few more weeks passed and the levels of hazing seemed to intensify, Jake agreed to talk with Bill, an alumnus of the fraternity and a prominent community member. When Jake shared the hazing accounts, Bill was immediately concerned for the health and safety of the pledges as well as the legal liability of the chapter and any alumni formally associated with the group. Together, they both decided to intervene.

Jake informed Bill of the time and place of hell week activities. Bill, flanked by other concerned alums, arrived at the chapter house to witness and interrupt the abuses of hell week. Pledges were removed from the chapter house and brought immediately for individual questioning by university officials. While some pledges were not willing to disclose their experiences, many did, and these individual accounts provided ample evidence to charge the fraternity with violating the SU's hazing policy without implicating Jake as the lone whistleblower.

Education and Awareness: Shifting Perspectives

Due to differences in experience and/or education, individuals may hold markedly different views. Hence, education [about hazing] is less an act of describing the "facts" and more about shifting another's perspective.

—SU undergraduate student

Making a difference and feeling as though one matters in the larger scheme of things are crucial—but a necessary prelude to individual action against hazing is one's belief that the issue is an important one (Berkowitz 1994; 2003). Whether or not one can engender the support of individual voices to change a hazing culture is largely dependent upon the attitudes and beliefs of those individuals about the issue of hazing. When an individual dismisses hazing as "harmless pranks" or as an isolated issue particular to specific student groups, it is unlikely that that person will be motivated to join in efforts to eliminate it. Initiating grassroots support against hazing requires that hazing myths be dispelled and replaced by accurate understandings of what constitutes hazing and why it is dangerous for individuals and harmful for the community as a whole. Thus, promoting community awareness about hazing is a key starting point.

As with many public health issues, it is generally understood that increasing the level of awareness is an exceedingly important step toward the prevention of harmful behaviors. Sadly, however, such awareness is often achieved as a result of a hazing tragedy. In the wake of such tragic events, we often wonder whether or not such events might have been prevented had there been more awareness about the potential risks or warning signs of dangerous and potentially lethal hazing practices. While we can never know the answer to that question for sure, prevention specialists have underscored the importance of education for reducing the prevalence of high-risk behaviors (Benard 1986; Roberts 1995). One participant spoke about this realization: "I learned that education and awareness are key to understanding; to change something it is necessary to change the way people think—not just how they act."

Educating the community is a necessary first step toward eliminating the dangers and abuses of hazing. But even this first step seems a rather daunting undertaking. Aren't these public awareness campaigns better left to social service organizations and schools? Sure—schools and social service organizations play a valuable role in community education, but should this absolve individuals from taking responsibility too? As the familiar saying goes, if you're not part of the solution, you're part of the problem. In our experience, anyone can play an instrumental role in building community awareness about the problem of hazing. One does not need to be an expert—a professionally trained teacher, educator, social worker, or public speaker. One simply needs to care! "I realized how much people did not understand about the issue of hazing and I felt I had to do my part to inform them" (SU undergraduate student).

When the IC hazing policy was being drafted, and after it was finalized, the club presidents began meeting to discuss the implications of the hazing policy on their groups' identities. Their identities were wrapped up in hazing rituals and traditions. Simply distributing a policy, without education about how to implement it, would not have been a productive way to lead change. It was important that these secret societies determine how to survive, even thrive, under the umbrella of a hazing policy.

Iverson, along with the chair of the club council, decided to convene meetings with the club leadership. These meetings were held at a staff person's home, which represented neutral territory and a place of comfort and emotional safety. Groups were not told they had to change. Instead, it was acknowledged that the hazing policy represented a challenge to their groups. They were invited to analyze their group's identity, norms, practices, rituals, and games. They were told that they had the option at the end of the self-analysis exercise to affirm their current group's identity. But they did need to ensure that their groups' activities were not in violation of the hazing policy. For some clubs, this was an exciting opportunity, and they exhibited creativity beyond Iverson's imagination; for others they simply rounded the edges of existing rituals. All of them, however, took risks, asked questions, were self-reflective, and became educated about hazing and its effects.

Crafting the Message

Promoting awareness about the dangers of hazing is an important step for garnering individual and community support to transform a hazing culture. In our experience, we have found that some educational strategies work better than others. Even the most well-intended awareness campaigns will likely be ineffective if they do not first establish that hazing is problem. This approach is borrowed from the literature on social norms and from Berkowitz's (2003) adaptation of "interventions for reducing the causes of bystander behavior" (11). This model suggests that the following steps are essential for changing behavior and shifting cultural norms around related to health and social justice issues: 1) it is necessary for people to notice the event (i.e., hazing); 2) the event must then interpreted as a problem; 3) people need to recognize they have both the responsibility and capacity to change the problem; 4) individuals must have the necessary skills to act on the problem; and 5) people need to take action to intervene with the problem (Berkowitz 2003).

Since Chuck Stenzel's death at Alfred University in 1978, many dedicated individuals have worked to help the nation notice the problem of hazing in colleges and universities and, more recently, in high schools as well (Nuwer 2000). As a result of these efforts, several helpful books provide recommendations for approaches to educating about hazing (Nicoletti, Spencer-Thomas, and Bollinger 2001; Nuwer 1999, 2000; Sweet 1999, 2001). Additionally, the professional leaders of fraternity and sorority national organizations have been developing anti-hazing policies and educational campaigns for nearly two decades and can serve as tremendous resources for campus leaders working to change hazing cultures.

Unfortunately, as we have seen from the rash of hazing incidents reported in the national news over the past several years, including eight deaths linked to pledging from January 2002 to January 2003, much more work needs to be done to eliminate hazing. In order to sustain and enhance effective education efforts, it is crucial that common misperceptions about hazing be corrected with accurate information. Asking the public to relinquish antiquated ideas about hazing as simply a matter of harmless pranks and juvenile antics can be accomplished by offering new definitions to replace the old. The importance of a definition for hazing is discussed by Sweet, who points out the resistance to labeling the abuse, humiliation, and degradation of initiations as hazing.

Building on the model shared by Berkowitz (2003) and borrowing directly from the work done in the field of sexual assault prevention education (Rape Education and Prevention Programs), we offer the following points as a framework for redefining hazing for students and community members:

1. Hazing is a serious social problem. It is not simply harmless pranks. Hazing can result in physical, psychological, and emotional harm—even death.
2. Hazing is about a process of wielding power and control over others.
3. Hazing is humiliating and degrading. It ultimately weakens rather than strengthens a group. Hazing does not build respect or trust. Groups can be stronger without hazing.
4. Hazing is a community issue. Hazing and the attitudes that support hazing cultures are pervasive and affect us all.
5. Your help is needed to eliminate hazing. You can make a difference by speaking out and educating others about the dangers of hazing; reporting hazing incidents to school, college, and university officials; insisting that educational institutions take hazing seriously and hold students accountable in meaningful ways; and finding creative alternatives to hazing.

Lessons Learned

In reflecting back on our experiences, it is clear that working to transform a hazing culture within a school, college, or university requires a team effort. Mutual respect and trust among group members are integral components of this process, as evidenced by the following comments made by SU students involved in anti-hazing efforts:

There are so many valuable aspects to the experience, but probably the most valuable aspect is that I came to respect other group members and I finally realized that there are people out [there] who care about others and stand up for what they believe in—very empowering!

We remained individuals with our own vignettes, each struggling to teach a resistive group . . . about an issue that is of paramount concern. . . . Through it all, we never lost sight of the "I"—the individual . . . and that became the key to our success.

Additionally, having clear goals, developing a group identity, and incorporating a sense of humor can play a crucial role in sustaining momentum for changing a hazing culture. Initially, when students at SU began to gather together to learn more about lobbying for the passage of a statewide anti-hazing law, they were simply an ad hoc group of about ten to fifteen individuals who were drawn together because of a mutual interest in working to end the abuses of hazing. When it became clear that the passage of the law would require more strategy than was initially anticipated, the group gathered more frequently. It began to develop its own identity, calling themselves the MJTF, or the Multi-Jurisdictional Task Force against hazing. The name began simply as a joke among a few group members, who borrowed the term from a popular 1980s comedy (*Beverly Hills Cop*). As part of the joke, one of the students created letterhead with the group's name and an accompanying logo. Somehow, the letterhead found its way into the hands of a newspaper reporter and suddenly the MJTF was making headlines! What began as simply a joke and a parody of the political system evolved into a group identity that also served as an inside joke and a continual reminder to keep things in perspective, especially when the going got tough. It is crucial to incorporate humor in the work against hazing, as making change can be discouraging, especially when students are living among peers who are deeply entrenched in a hazing culture and may actively resist any change-making efforts.

In each of the campus-wide anti-hazing initiatives in which we have been involved, the voices and actions of an early few appeared to be instrumental in prompting others to become involved. The following quotes from SU students evidence this theme:

I saw how much faith people had in Betsy [Allan] and how much we felt empowered by her. It was great that we all owned it by the end.

We definitely had group cohesion and . . . there was definitely commitment to the group—as a result, I think some sort of bond formed within our group. We were more of a team rather than a hierarchical group.

Finding one's voice and being a leader are therefore essential to changing the hazing culture. For Brendan at SU, the process changed his life and the lives of many others. One can never predict with certainty what changes might occur as a result of speaking out against hazing. While he was initially shunned and harassed by members of his chapter and others in the Greek system on campus, Brendan became an influential participant in the effort to enact hazing legislation and coordinated a student peer-education program on hazing. Through his efforts, the Inter-Fraternity Council passed a bill making hazing-education programs mandatory for all chapters. In the spring of the following year, he received the Annual Leadership and Service Award at the annual Greek Awards Banquet—an honor reserved for that man and woman who have most contributed to the enhancement of Greek life at the university.

Individuals are not powerless against a hazing culture. Such a culture has been constructed and can therefore be dismantled and reconstructed. Change occurs by introducing doubt. Core beliefs are questioned. "People develop their power to perceive critically the way they exist in the world . . . ; they come to see the world not as a static reality, but as a reality in process, in transformation" (Freire 1970, 83). Individuals will feel empowered to initiate action and make change that has meaning. The individuals with whom we have worked have initiated change, spoken up, raised questions. They in turn re/wrote the language (policies) and ideas (education) that impel action.

Change too often occurs as a result of a tragedy. But that doesn't have to be the case. Individual voices, like those of the students we worked with, can be role models for change. Some students with whom we worked made significant changes; others took small steps. Above all, however, these individuals made the problem of hazing everyone's business. The honorable and courageous acts of a few motivated many others and resulted in new sagas, rituals, and symbols for transforming culture.

Notes

1. Author's note of disclosure: The quotes and stories we share from students were drawn from either public documents or were given to us with permission from each individual. When names are provided however, they are pseudonyms. Two years following Elizabeth Allan's departure from SU, she and Brendan (pseudonym) were married.
2. We use the term "secret societies" to refer to fraternities, sororities, tap clubs, and other similar groups because we believe secrecy is one of the elements that is alluring.
3. Spring tapping is the time when new members are "tapped," or invited to pledge.

17 Hazing and Gender: Analyzing the Obvious

Elizabeth J. Allan

> Editor's note: *While hazing occurs in male and female fraternal organizations, the way men and women haze reflects differences in gender. In this essay, Elizabeth J. Allan discusses such behaviors and cautions readers against forming preconceptions based on gender stereotypes.*

Over the decade of my involvement in anti-hazing education, I have been interviewed numerous times by reporters preparing news stories on the topic of hazing. Inevitably, I am asked about my view of the differences in hazing traditions between the genders—or sexes—that is, girls/women and boys/men. My understanding and analysis of sex/gender differences deepened markedly when I became familiar with gender theory after having spent several years educating about hazing. In this chapter, I draw upon gender theory to describe both similarities and differences in hazing practices/group initiations for girls/women and boys/men. I also consider how predominant understandings of hazing are shaped by social norms related to gender.

It seems that the general public is often captivated by talk about the differences between women and men, as evidenced by best-selling books with titles such as *Men are from Mars, Women are from Venus.* News programs, talk shows and magazines often feature programs and articles related to the (assumed) difference between the sexes. Of course, the question is an age-old one. Nevertheless, people nearly always seem to be interested in new (and often old, disguised as new) perspectives about how and why men and women are so different. The talk of differences is so common that the assumption that women and men are different is rarely questioned. One problem with much of the talk about sex/gender differences is the facility with which gender stereotypes can be unintentionally reinforced.

Gender Stereotypes and Research on Gender Differences

A stereotype is a belief about a group that is applied to all individuals perceived to be a part of that group. Stereotypes are rigid and not open to revision—which is a major problem, since they are often based on misinformation. This isn't to say that we can't draw any generalizations about women as a group or men as a group, but generalizations based on research (called empirical generalizations) are different from stereotypes. Empirical generalizations are based on research that takes differences within a group into account (typically through statistical tests of significance) and can be revised when new data emerges that differs from previously drawn conclusions.

When considering research on sex/gender differences the often-referenced question of nature versus nurture does indeed muddy the waters. It is frequently difficult to sort out how much of a measured difference between the sexes may can be attributed to one's biological composition (anatomy, chromosomes, and hormones) and how much of the difference may be attributed to learned behavior—behaviors reinforced through powerful social norms. For instance, consider the idea that men are hard-wired to be better map readers than women or that women are hard-wired to be better housekeepers than men. Are these ideas more likely stereotypes or empirical generalizations? If a research study tested a group of randomly selected men and women on map reading and housekeeping and came to these conclusions, we might accept it as valid, but how do we know if the behavior is truly sex-based? In other words, is there something on the X or Y chromosome that predisposes men and women to be better map readers and housekeepers, respectively? Or could it be that people tend to be better at things they have practiced more and for which they've received positive reinforcement over the years?

It is exceedingly difficult to know scientifically to what extent biological differences (anatomical, hormonal, chromosomal) between women and men shape behavioral differences. In fact, there are few scientific studies that currently support a biological basis for substantial differences between the way women and men think. Rather, research indicates that there is more variation among women (or men) on cognitive, emotional, and psychological variables than between the two groups (Fausto-Sterling 1992; Kimmel 2000; Kivel 1999). Despite this, however, the idea persists that women and men are vastly different in their thinking and that they are hard-wired to assume different social roles. In my view, this speaks to the power of gender-role expectations that have become so familiar and taken for granted that they are often invisible—and it this very invisibility that often prevents us from considering their influence on behavior.

Sex/Gender and Hazing

National news accounts of hazing and anecdotal evidence point toward gender differences in hazing activities. In general, a common conclusion drawn is that hazing among men is more likely to be violent in nature and hazing among women is more likely to be psychological/emotional in nature. For example, *The Courier-Journal* of Louisville, Kentucky, (Woolhouse 2000) quoted

Gary Powell, a Maryland attorney who has represented fraternities and sororities charged with hazing, as saying that hazings involving "females tend to be less physically violent than those involving males." Such perspectives align with and also reinforce predominant understandings of differences between women and men.

Empirical research on gender differences and hazing is limited, however. In a study sponsored by Alfred University and the NCAA, differences in hazing practices among male and female athletes were documented but were not the focus of the study. The vast majority of research on hazing, and media attention to particular incidents, has focused on male groups. In the few studies with a focus on women, hazing has been found to be prevalent. For example, in a survey distributed nationally to professionals who advise fraternities and sororities on college campuses, 44 percent said that hazing incidents among sororities had been reported to them. "Of the incidents reported, 20 percent considered them psychological, 2 percent considered them physical and 28 percent considered them both" (Shaw and Morgan in Holmes 1999, 4).

Nuwer details accounts of hazing in college sororities (1999) and on athletic teams and pom-pom and cheerleading squads in high schools (2000). According to his research, far more hazing incidents among sorority women have been reported in the decade from 1988 to 1998 than in the previous ten-year period. It is possible, however, that these numbers may reflect an increase in reporting rather than an increase in incidents (Nuwer 1999). "Although some violent hazing, alcohol misuse and even branding have occurred in college sororities, hazing has been far less a problem in female clubs than in male fraternities" (Nuwer 2000, 36). At any rate, experts agree that sororities on the whole experience far less hazing than do fraternities.

A number of authors have examined male group behavior and hazing from various disciplinary and interdisciplinary perspectives (Nuwer 1990, 1999, 2000; Rhoads 1995; Robinson 1998; Sanday 1990; Sweet 1999, 2001; Tiger 1984). Of these, the ethnographic studies of fraternity culture rely substantially on theories of gender, sexism, and homophobia to explain aspects of fraternity life that increase the probability of violence against women who come into contact with these groups (Sanday 1990; Rhoads 1995). Sanday describes how "pulling train," or gang rape, becomes a normative part of a fraternity's behavior and group identity. She also identifies the pledging process as an important means of socializing men to endorse such attitudes and behaviors.

Gender Theory

Analyzing the phenomenon of hazing through the lens of gender theory provides some helpful insights on both similarities and differences in hazing behaviors between female and male groups. Gender theory is especially helpful for providing tools to shed new light on facts whose interpretation seems clearcut. Since gender norms are so often taken for granted, they can be easily overlooked. Gender theory works against this omission because it makes gender the focus of analysis and thus illuminates some of the ways in which gender influences hazing behaviors and works to reinforce hazing cultures.

I use the term *gender theory* to denote a body of theories that examines how cultural expectations about femininity and masculinity shape understandings of women and men as gendered selves. Gender theory contends that versions of masculinity and femininity are largely learned through a process of socialization rather than being essential to one's biological sex. As Jennifer Coates explains, "Doing femininity can be paraphrased as 'doing being a woman'" (1996, 232). In other words, femininity refers to abstract qualities associated with being feminine, and masculinity refers to abstract qualities associated with being masculine. Gender theory challenges dominant understandings about gender that are typically rooted in the assumption that masculinity and femininity are "natural" outcomes of being male and female, respectively.

The use of the term *gender,* then, refers to the discussion of both masculinity and femininity. However, I want to be careful to point out here that a discussion of gender should not imply that there are only singular conceptualizations of these terms. As Michael Kimmel says: "Within any one society at any moment, several meanings of masculinity and femininity coexist. Simply put, not all American men and women are the same. Our experiences are also structured by class, race, ethnicity, age, sexuality, region. Each of these axes modifies the others" (2000, 10). Nevertheless, particular versions of femininity and masculinity rise to ascendancy during particular social periods. Bem (1993) points out that even while the predominant versions of masculinity and femininity may shift periodically, they generally operate as two poles of a gender binary where the masculine (man) is positioned as active and the feminine (woman) is positioned as passive. In other words, whatever traits are understood to characterize the feminine also serve to connote the antithesis of what is taken to be masculine—or, that which is culturally defined as masculine oppositionally defines feminine. Active/passive, strong/fragile, aggressive/submissive, independent/dependent, and invincible/vulnerable are further examples of gender binaries that depict masculinity and femininity as polar opposites of a vast gender divide. While this particular construction is rooted in perceptions of ideal womanhood for white women specifically, it is relevant to all women because it remains a powerful and pervasive image or standard against which all women are often compared.

Another perspective gained from gender theory, one that is important to an understanding of gender dynamics and hazing, is the analysis that gender norms are typically cast in ways that privilege masculinity over femininity. An exception to this occurs when women behave in ways that are perceived to be *too* masculine. As a result, women find themselves in a lose/lose situation where the performance of femininity is often devalued (and is disempowering to them), yet the alternative performance of masculinity often results in negative consequences as well. The dominant discourse of heterosexuality also supports the shaping of this dynamic. For example, a woman whose behavior is interpreted as "overly aggressive" (i.e., masculine), will likely be labeled in ways that are perceived negatively (i.e., "bitch," "dyke") in the context of heterosexist/homophobic culture. Thus, women are in a double bind—they are disadvantaged when they act in gender-appropriate ways *and* when they don't (Frye 1983; Kimmel 2000).

Scholars who use gender theory to analyze society generally agree that women and men actively participate in the construction of subjectivity by choosing to subvert and/or reinforce the dominant expectations for ideal masculinity and femininity. While individuals are active in defining themselves as masculine and/or feminine, alternatives to the dominant cultural expectations are often overshadowed by the power of the ascendant images—thus making it more difficult to assume alternatives that are marginalized or rendered invisible. Those who wish to adopt alternatives or stretch beyond the narrow confines of normative gender roles are further deterred by the likelihood that these alternatives will be labeled as somehow deviant.

Femininity and Masculinity as Social Constructions

A number of scholars have described how social norms around gender and heterosexuality may powerfully influence one's sense of self (Butler 1990; Coates 1996; Kimmel 2000; Messner 1989, 2001; Mills 1997; Smith 1990). Some studies look specifically at the dominant expectations of femininity in Western society and the ways in which it contributes to women's subjective sense of self—the ways in which women experience and act upon their bodies (Bartky 1988; Brumberg 1997; Smith 1990). Researchers have examined how a dominant discourse of femininity shapes use of cosmetics, eating disorders, perceptions of menstruation, programs of exercise, styles of dress, and types of adornment. These are examples of what Bartky describes as "part of the process by which the ideal body of femininity—and hence the feminine body subject—is constructed; in doing this, they produce . . . a body on which an inferior status has been inscribed" (1988, 71).

A social-constructionist view of gender posits that masculine and feminine behaviors are largely a result of learning what is expected in a particular culture (rather than what is imprinted on one's genetic material, for instance). Thus, gendered behavior is historically and contextually situated and can change over time or can differ among cultures. For instance, Deborah Rhode notes that a trade journal on children's clothing published in 1918 pointed out that a clear popular consensus indicated that "the accepted rule is pink for the boy and blue for the girl" (Mahoney quoted in Rhode 1997, 43). While there may indeed be some biological predispositions to gendered behavior, it seems that the overriding tendency when it comes to gender is to assume that biology is destiny.

I do not subscribe to the view that individuals are simply a blank slate waiting for a cultural imprint. Rather than negating the role of biology, considering gender as a socially constructed performance highlights the strong and pervasive messages children receive from the time of birth about sex-appropriate behavior. "These messages often involve unconscious, subtle, or indirect signals, rather than intentional instruction" (Rhode 1997, 44). Many adults are largely or even completely unaware of their role in the gender-socialization process. For instance, when my son was three years old in 1999, his grandfather made him a toolbox and included some real tools (a screwdriver, a hammer, a tape measure, etc.) as a gift. Now that my daughter is three years old and capable of safely handling such implements with adult supervision, I asked her grandfather if he would be willing to make a toolbox for her as well, and he was taken by surprise by this request. Indeed, the thought had never crossed his mind.

Over the past few decades, many writers have documented the differential treatment of boys and girls and the probable implications of those differences. Feminist scholars have examined how girls have been placed at a disadvantage as a consequence of gender stereotyping (AAUW 1998; Pipher 1995; Rhode 1997; Sadker and Sadker 1994; Sandler, Silverberg, and Hall 1996). Studies in educational settings have documented gender bias—most often unintentional—by well-meaning teachers who simply give boys more attention and attention of a quality that is more likely to promote cognitive development and substantive learning. According to the Sadkers' (1994) research, even though girls and boys are sitting in the same classrooms day after day, on average, boys are receiving a better-quality education than the girls.

Studies also document how children themselves police each other's behavior according to stereotypes (Thorne 1997). For instance, if a young boy plays with a doll in the presence of older boys, it is likely that he will be teased and will quickly learn that having a doll is outside the bounds of acceptable masculine behavior. This is particularly troubling when one considers that having a doll is an important way for young children to develop important human qualities of nurturing and caregiving. Beginning in early childhood, boys learn to devalue activities that are associated with female-identified qualities while they simultaneously learn that rough and aggressive play is acceptable for boys, as evidenced by the maxim "boys will be boys."

Over the past decade there has been increased attention to the examination of how dominant understandings of masculinity shape a sense of self for boys and men. For instance, in his book *Boys Will Be Men* (1999), Paul Kivel describes the predominant social construction of masculinity as harmful for boys because it confines them to the "act like a man" box (Fig. 17.1) and prevents them from experiencing a range of emotions and thus being fully human.

The center column within the box lists the range of emotions that boys/men feel but which they often hide because of the cultural pressures to "act like a man." The columns on the left and right within the box are the predominant cultural norms of Western masculinity that have come to define manhood in many respects. When boys attempt to step out of the box, or reveal some of their true feelings (from the center column), they are often pushed back into the box with verbal and/or physical abuse—or the threat of these.

"Act Like a Man" Box

VERBAL ABUSE:

PHYSICAL ABUSE:

tough		have money
aggressive		never ask for help
competitive	anger	angry
	sadness	
in control	love	yell
	connection	
no feelings	confusion	intimidate
don't cry	low self-worth	responsible
	resentment	
take charge	curiosity	take it
	excitement	
don't make	isolation	don't back down
mistakes		
		have sex with women
succeed		

Verbal Abuse labels (left): wimp ▲, girl ▲, sissy ▲, mama's boy ▲, nerd ▲, fag ▲, punk ▲, mark ▲, bitch ▲

Physical Abuse labels (right): ▲ hit/beat up, ▲ teased, ▲ isolated, ▲ rejected, ▲ forced to play sports, ▲ sexual assault

Source: Oakland Men's Project in Kivel 1992, 12.

As Kivel explains,

> If we pay attention we can easily see the Box's effects on boys. Just watch a group of them together. They are constantly challenging each other, putting each other down—testing to see who is in the Box. They are never at ease, always on guard. At an early age, most start to hide their feelings, toughen up and make a huge emotional effort not to cry. Many boys stop wearing colorful clothing or participating in activities that they think might make them vulnerable to being labeled gay. (1999, 13)

Both Kivel and Katz and Earp (1999) contend that the ways in which masculinity is currently conceptualized creates environments where boys/men are more likely to learn be aggressive and sometimes violent. William Pollack also describes the confines of masculinity in his highly acclaimed book *Real Boys.* According to Pollack, "Studies show that boys at a very early age are pushed to suppress their vulnerable and sad feelings[;] they also demonstrate that boys are pressured to express the one strong feeling allowed them—anger" (1998, 44). He draws on the term "emotional funnel" to describe what unfortunately happens for most boys when anger becomes "the final common pathway to express their vulnerability and powerlessness" (44). These experts point out that aggressive and even violent behavior is more likely to be tolerated and/or excused precisely because gender norms are so powerful and pervasive that they are rarely questioned (Katz and Earp 1999; Kimmel 2000; Kivel 1999; Pollack 1998).

The Problem of Homophobia

It is impossible to provide an analysis of gender without attending to the role homophobia plays in reinforcing rigid and confining expectations of masculine and feminine behavior. This is clearly indicated when you ask a group of high school students to think about what happens if a man is a little bit *too* nurturing or a bit *too* emotional. They are quick to respond, "He's a sissy," or "He's a fag." Women who cross the line of normative expectations for femininity face similar social consequences by being called "butch" or "dyke." Of course, these terms are unlikely to serve as deterrents unless they are perceived negatively. Homophobia—the fear of homosexuality in oneself and/or others— serves as just such a deterrent for many. These attitudes are so powerful and pervasive that they reinforce what has been termed a "gender straitjacket," ensuring that boys and girls do not deviate substantially from culturally proscribed beliefs about appropriate behavior for men and women (Kimmel 2000; Kivel 1999). While a full discussion of the multiple and complex connections between gender and homophobia is outside the scope of this chapter, it is essential for any gender analysis to delineate how homophobia reinforces rigid (and sometimes harmful) expectations of acceptable behavior for girls/women and boys/men.

Those working to eliminate hazing need to be mindful of the ways in which masculinity—that is, the predominant social construction of masculinity—and homophobia work in tandem to create a climate in which violent and demeaning hazing practices are more likely to be tolerated and even considered beneficial for young men. Gender theory provides an important lens for deepening our understanding about the prevalence and persistence of hazing.

Masculinity and Hazing

The results of a national study on hazing among NCAA athletes (Hoover and Pollard 1999) revealed differences between the types of hazing experienced by male and female athletes. "Women were much less likely than men to be subjected to unacceptable acts: destroying or stealing property, beating up others, being tied up or taped, being confined to small places, being paddled, beaten, kidnapped or transported and abandoned" (3). This finding supports the assertion that sex/gender differences in hazing experiences do exist. For some, this distinction is simply attributed to innate biological differences between the sexes. An analysis from a social-constructionist perspective, however, would argue that these differences are largely the result of learning to perform gender roles differently. In other words, how men and women are taught to live in the world affects patterns of violence, abuse, and other factors involved in hazing.

The connection between masculinity and hazing is not a difficult one to make. Nonetheless, it is a connection that is not often thoroughly addressed or even articulated. One need not look very far to find examples of how hazing behaviors in male groups often serve as a test of masculinity or as an opportunity to prove one's masculinity. Listed below are attributes commonly associated with the ascendant version of masculinity in the U.S.:

Aggressive
Analytical
Strong
Dominant
In Control
Tough
Independent
Competitive
Rational
Self-reliant
Brave

When hazing occurs among men, regardless of the type of group, it is often framed as a test of "strength," "courage," and "determination." For instance, accounts of hazing incidents among high school boys and college men frequently include tests of physical endurance, forced/coerced alcohol consumption, paddling, and other forms of physical assaults/beatings (Nuwer 1990; 1999; 2000). In their research on fraternity cultures, Martin and Hummer found that fraternities emphasize "toughness, withstanding pain and humiliation, obedience to superiors, and using physical force to obtain compliance" (1989, 462). In support of hazing, men will often say that such "traditions" are necessary to "weed out" those unworthy of membership. Some men who have been hazed are firm believers in the process of hazing and insist that they "enjoyed the challenge." Such arguments are firmly embedded in cultural expectations around masculinity and what we are taught to expect of "real men."

Drawing on gender theory helps to illuminate why it can be so difficult to eradicate hazing practices. For instance, in a fraternity, "'becoming a brother' is a rite of passage that follows the consistent and often lengthy display by pledges of appropriately masculine qualities and behaviors" (Martin and Hummer 1989, 463). Since hazing can serve as an opportunity for men to prove their masculinity (and heterosexuality), the elimination of hazing traditions can be quite threatening on multiple fronts. Steven Sweet (1999) points out that the pledging process forces many students to terminate or sharply curtail social interactions outside the fraternity, ensuring that the sense of self for pledges, and eventual brothers, becomes closely tied with the organization itself. This increases the "exit costs" of leaving a hazing organization; fraternity members can "literally lose a major part of themselves by withdrawing," notes Sweet. Adding gender theory to this analysis provides an additional perspective on the challenges of speaking out against hazing or leaving a hazing organization. When hazing is so closely tied to the performance of masculinity, it is difficult to untangle the two.

Hence, boys and young men who identify with predominant cultural constructions of masculinity are likely to fear that their manhood will be called into question if they resist an opportunity to prove their masculinity via hazing practices. This also explains, at least in part, why some pledges and rookies will ask to be hazed even if the fraternity chapter, club, or team is working to eliminate such traditions. They know they will likely be subject to scrutiny by other members of the group who were hazed and hence proved their masculinity. Such scrutiny is not entirely external; it is also self-imposed because many boys/men have been taught to think of manhood in terms of physical prowess, toughness, and conquest.

Social anxieties around masculinity are central to the continuation of hazing practices. The more that boys/men are fearful of being labeled as weak, the more likely they are to participate in hazing practices that are often dangerous and even life-threatening. For example, in her examination of violence in Canadian hockey, Robinson interviewed a 16-year-old boy subjected to hazing as a junior hockey player. His comment is illustrative of the way in which hazing preys upon anxieties around proving one's masculinity: "They were persistent in giving us alcohol. Lots of beer. We might look like a wimp if we turned it down" (Robinson 1998, 66).

Some researchers have considered how the learning of gender may affect patterns of health and well-being. For instance, an argument has been made that we can understand the phenomenon of longer life expectancy among women through a social learning lens (rather than simply as a consequence of biology). Research indicates that higher mortality rates for men are attributable to higher accident rates for younger men and to heart disease for men at older ages (Krieger and Fee 1994). However, as Krieger and Fee point out, "the higher accident rates of younger men are not accidental" (62) but are due to hazards related to gender-role expectations, including more hazardous occupations, higher rates of illegal drug use and alcohol abuse, and injuries related to firearms and motor vehicle accidents. While heart disease is the leading cause of death for both men and women, many of the risk factors may be associated more with gender than with biology; higher rates of cigarette smoking and fewer sources of social/emotional support among men, for example. A similar connection can be made between gender and deaths due to hazing. Nuwer's (1999) chronology of hazing fatalities reveals that men are far more likely to die from hazing activities than are women. Of the more than seventy documented hazing deaths, only five have been women, according to Nuwer's documentation.

Table 17.1. Attributes Associated with Traditional Views of Masculinity
and Femininity.

FEMININE	MASCULINE
Passive	Aggressive
Nurturing	Analytical
Gentle	Strong
Submissive	Dominant
Yielding	In Control
Tender	Tough
Dependent	Independent
Collaborative	Competitive
Emotional	Logical
Supportive	Self-reliant
Fragile	Brave

Femininity and Hazing

Like masculinity, femininity serves as a powerful cultural force for defining womanhood. In the interdisciplinary field of women's studies, numerous scholars have examined how women's subjective sense of self is influenced by predominant cultural expectations of femininity. Feminist thinkers have been instrumental in identifying the ways in which the predominant social construction of femininity has often undermined women's chances for sociopolitical equality (Rhode 1997). In sum, feminist and gender theories generally support the contention that dominant understandings of femininity shape women's desire to appeal to men in ways that limit their power and reinforce male power. Table 17.1 presents a list of attributes associated with a traditional and predominant version of femininity. When placed beside the list of masculine attributes, gender polarization is evident. Further, as I have described, homophobia serves to reinforce compliance with these narrowly defined versions of gender.

The disempowering effects of the dominant discourse of femininity can be seen by the ways in which femininity becomes "imprinted" on female bodies. Brumberg uses the term "project" to describe the relationship girls/women learn to have with their bodies. In her book *The Body Project* (1997), she shares her research on girls' diaries produced throughout the twentieth century with a focus on how a girl's sense of self has become increasingly tied to her appearance, evidenced, for example, by one of the most popular New Year's resolutions for white girls: to lose weight. In his text *Ways of Seeing* (1972), John Berger draws on images from high art and pop culture to describe "the gaze" in Western society, where images of women are often presented from a male vantage point. This, however, is not only an issue of men looking at women—the gaze is so pervasive that girls/women internalize it as well and unconsciously come to see themselves and their bodies through this male gaze. This is not surprising when women's bodies can serve as a source of cultural capital in a sense. In other words, a certain degree of power is gained from being able to display a body that somehow "fits" the largely unattainable ideals of beauty presented in the popular media. Women's drive to achieve this "ideal body" is evidenced by excessive dieting among white women (and the disproportionate numbers of girls and women with eating disorders), "body sculpting" classes in fitness centers, hair removal procedures, breast implants, and other types of cosmetic surgery that are largely oriented toward girls/women becoming more attractive (to men). I don't mean to imply that women do not find these ideals attractive as well. Women themselves actively participate in, and often achieve a great deal of satisfaction from, achieving a particular kind of "look."

When considering the social construction of gender, race and ethnicity cannot be overlooked, as these are cultural factors that also influence the shaping of what is deemed acceptable behavior for women and men. The lists of masculine and feminine attributes I have provided are based primarily on a white middle-class dominant ideal that is often, but not always, replicated by members of other racial and socioeconomic groups. So while these are not neat and tidy category schemes that can be generalized to all members of U.S. society, I offer them because these are the characteristics that tend to pervade the culture through dominant discourses of gender reflected and reinforced by media representations, public school curricula, and public policy (Kimmel 2000). This does not imply that alternatives do not exist; rather, I want to emphasize that alternatives to the dominant white middle-class conceptualizations of masculinity and femininity do exist. However, they are most often overshadowed, marginalized, or labeled deviant. One example of this is how African-American girls often find themselves labeled as "loud black girls" when they don't conform to the predominant image of white femininity (Fordham 1993).

Gender and Sexism

Sexism. Explanation is warranted here. I have learned through my six years of experience teaching women's studies at the college level that this concept is often misunderstood and is confusing to many. The term "sexism" itself often evokes strong reactions ranging from denial to defensiveness, resentment, and defiance. These reactions are understandable from a number of vantage points. One of the most crucial reasons for discomfort with the term is that the concept of sexism requires an acceptance that sex/gender inequality exists. This is difficult for many to see, especially when there have been numerous gains for women in education, employment, and public policy (i.e., Title IX) over the past several decades. It is not as easy to see that there have also been setbacks and stagnation in a number of arenas (Rhode 1997; Valian 1998).

Another major barrier to understanding the concept of sexism is that the term is often equated with the "blame game" or "male-bashing," as some like to call it. No one wants to be blamed for gender inequality, and the use of the term "sexism" is often perceived as an indictment of all men. As Allan Johnson points out,

> It's become almost impossible, for example, to say *sexism* or *male privilege* without most men becoming so uncomfortable that the conversation is impossible. They act as [if] sexism names a personality flaw found among men, and just saying the word . . . is heard as an accusation of a personal moral failure. (2001, 12)

These defensive reactions are unfortunate because they can preclude an important opportunity for analysis.

Sexism refers to systematic and structural conditions (patterns of privilege and power) that contribute to and/or sustain discrimination against women. These patterns include individual attitudes and prejudicial behavior (intended or not) as well as systematic and institutionalized practices that cannot be attributed to any single person. Men do stand to benefit from sexism in many ways because they inherit social power in a society where women are disadvantaged—just as whites stand to benefit from race privilege in a society where people of color are systematically disadvantaged. However, this does not imply that all men want women to be second-class citizens or that all whites are bad people. The dynamics of sexism are complex and need to be considered in relation to race, social class standing, sexual identity, and other forms of identity differences. However, a basic understanding of the concept of sexism is crucial to examining the dynamics of gender and how the social construction of femininity is implicated in hazing practices for women's groups.

In *The Gendered Society*, Michael Kimmel (2000) succinctly summarizes important connections between gender and sexism. Drawing on Connell's concept of "emphasized femininity," Kimmel explains that "emphasized femininity is organized around compliance with gender inequality" and is "oriented to accommodating the interests and desires of men" (Connell as quoted in Kimmel 2000, 11). According to this view, emphasized femininity serves as an amplification of perceived differences between women and men and is used as a strategy of adapting to male power. In other words, women learn to perform femininity both consciously and unconsciously as a strategy to cope with sexism. Emphasized femininity can be seen in "the display of sociability rather than technical competence, fragility in mating scenes, compliance with men's desire for titillation and ego-stroking in office relationships, [and] acceptance of marriage and childcare as a response to labor-market discrimination against women" (ibid.).

Emphasized femininity is closely connected to the concept of androcentrism, or the tendency to see men and masculinity as the center of the social world. Bem (1993) contends that androcentrism is an important factor in sustaining sex/gender inequality in society. Androcentrism is manifested in many ways, including language, school curricula, and textbooks in which women's contributions have been marginalized or omitted; in medical studies and psychological theories, to name a few. Another example of androcentrism is the tendency to valorize the attributes that have historically been associated with men and masculinity. Since gendered attributes are so sharply polarized, the valorization of one (masculinity) tends to result in the devaluation of the other (femininity). For example, we are all familiar with the differences in pay and prestige afforded to occupations (engineer, computer technician, attorney) that are considered to require more masculine qualities (analytic, rational, logical thinking) and those considered more feminine (teacher, social worker, secretary) because they involve more emotional labor and are oriented around nurturing and fulfilling the needs of others.

Sexual Objectification

The sexual objectification of women is another outcome of sexism that is often implicated in hazing behaviors. I am using the term sexual objectification here to refer to the ways in which women's bodies are commodified—made into objects of heterosexual male desire. This can be seen on a daily basis in the popular media, where women's bodies or particular parts of women's bodies are used to sell products. In a society where heterosexual men hold more fiscal, political, and institutional power than women (on the whole), the objectification of women's bodies occurs with a far greater frequency and intensity than objectification of male bodies.

In her analysis of fraternity little-sister groups, Stombler uses theories of gender, sexism, and sexual objectification, describing sexual objectification as a "fundamental process in maintaining male dominance" (1994, 299). A number of scholars have argued that the ways in which women's bodies are objectified in the media tends to have a dehumanizing effect; women may come to be seen as objects rather than human beings. Some contend that the sheer volume, the cumulative and often unconscious effects of seeing women's bodies as "things," may contribute to a greater cultural tolerance for violence against women (Kilbourne 2000). Rhoads's analysis of a fraternity culture supports this contention: "Women were frequently characterized in ways that depicted them as something less than human beings. . . . They were discussed as 'tools' or 'whores' and were frequently seen as targets for sexual manipulation" (1995, 314).

The sexual objectification and victimization of girls/women is often a component of hazing among both single-sex and mixed groups (i.e., ski clubs, pep clubs, marching bands). At both high school and college levels, sexual simulation is a common hazing/initiation practice among women's groups (athletic teams, sororities, clubs); men are almost always present as voyeurs during the simulations. This was the scenario that fueled an anti-hazing bill for the state of Vermont in the wake of the highly publicized case of a high school gymnast in the state, who, along with other new recruits to the team, was asked to simulate oral sex with a banana while circled by members of the football team (Nuwer 2000). Interestingly, it is most often the female members and leaders of the group who are responsible for planning and executing such activities and inviting boys/men to witness and/or assist. Here lies one of the paradoxes of sexism:

women themselves actively participate in sustaining the "object" status of other women. This dynamic works especially well in the context of hazing—a practice that is designed to humiliate, degrade, and disempower people. Hazing practices generally prey on particular vulnerabilities. While the stated intent may be "to have a good laugh," "build character," and "create unity"; girls/women who haze other girls/women are purposefully designing scenarios that are intended to humiliate, degrade, cause discomfort for, and/or frighten new members to achieve these goals. Creating conditions for sexual objectification and preying on women's fear of sexual victimization (participants in these simulations are often blindfolded), sexual simulation is used by groups of women for hazing initiations.

In my own experience working with college students in both student activities and student conduct offices at several universities, I have been involved in a number of investigations where the sexual objectification (and possible victimization) of women was central to hazing activities. In one instance, sorority pledges were required to visit each of ten fraternity houses (where alcohol was served). To prove they had accomplished this, the pledges were required to have signatures written on their skin by a member of each fraternity. One of these young women was found intoxicated and passed out in the bushes adjacent to her residence hall. This activity was one that clearly placed this sorority pledge in harm's way—not only from the toxic affects of the alcohol but because the risks for sexual assault were heightened as well. Another example of sexual objectification in hazing was evidenced in a recently publicized case in Maine, where a sorority chapter lost its university recognition after a series of hazing activities, one of which involved having pledges dress in seductive clothing and visit an adult video store (Fish 2001). [*Ed. note:* At one university that shall not be named, male football players stood while female athletes, intoxicated, knelt before them in a demeaning posture that made at least one weep afterward with the recollection, according to one female athlete.]

Sexual objectification of women is also used in hazing activities among men but reflects a markedly different dynamic. Among women, sexual objectification of the initiates often serves as the hazing activity. This is less the case among men. More typical is the scenario where the sexual objectification of women is used as a "prop" for what often results in homoerotic-type hazing. For example, Robinson (1998) describes how new teenage players on a hockey team were ushered into a room where pornographic videos were playing and then encouraged to masturbate in the group while older team members observed. When nudity or sexually explicit activities are involved in hazing among men's groups, the spectators are most often male teammates, fraternity brothers, and (sometimes) male coaches. In cases where sexual simulation involves both male and female participants, the boys/men usually assume the dominant role characteristic of traditional heterosexuality (Millett 1990). While this scenario is meant to be humiliating and degrading for all involved, the power dynamics are such that women are typically cast in the most vulnerable positions.

Sexual Victimization

Simply put, sexual assault refers to sexual contact that is not consensual. Consent is a choice that is made without coercion and without impaired judgment (induced by alcohol, other drugs, or other conditions). Since hazing activities are generally predicated upon an abuse of power involving intense peer pressure, coercion, and alcohol and/or other drugs, any hazing activities that are sexual in nature are likely to fall into the category of sexual assault and victimization.

Sexual victimization in hazing is a deeply disturbing trend. Among boys/ men, the frequency of same-sex assaults, particularly sodomies performed with broomstick handles or other objects, appears to have increased dramatically over the past twenty years, particularly among male high school athletic teams (Nuwer 2000). Other documented examples of demeaning and potentially sexually violating hazing behaviors include forced nudity and smearing of initiates' bodies with food products; using duct tape or athletic tape to immobilize nude recruits; "butting"—where the rookie player is held down while a veteran puts his naked buttocks in the player's face; connecting a string weighted with a heavy object to a new recruit's penis; and immobilizing initiates in a chair while strippers perform in their laps (Nicoletti, Spencer-Thomas, and Bollinger 2001; Nuwer 2000; Robinson 1998).

In many cases, sexual objectification can also be a form of sexual victimization. Statistically speaking, one out of four women will be sexually assaulted in her lifetime and one in eight children is sexually abused, so it is quite probable that someone in a group (female or male) has experienced a sexual assault and may be highly traumatized by any hazing activity that involves sexual simulation or situations where control over one's sexual decision-making is perceived to be jeopardized (Greenfeld 1997).

Identity Differences and Hazing: Gender, Race, Sexuality, and Poverty

Hazing activities among women's groups sometimes mimic the kinds of hazing behaviors typically associated with men and masculinity. Girls and women gain credibility and status by proving they are tough, rugged, and strong. This plays out in hazing; for instance, in the excessive consumption of alcohol (especially in predominantly white organizations and teams), forced sleep deprivation, ingestion of vile substances, brandings, paddlings, and beatings that have all been documented among groups of women. Recently, a study from Finland found that violence is carrying an increasingly positive connotation among girls and is something "that makes the girl feel powerful, strong, and makes her popular" (Kimmel 2000, 250).

While there is a tendency for girls/women's groups to mirror some hazing practices that are typically associated with masculinity, it is far less likely for male groups to mimic the kinds of hazing activities typically associated with female groups. Since masculine attributes are generally valued more highly than feminine attributes, it is not surprising then that many hazing activities among women's groups are shaped around the valorization of masculinity and gendered vulnerabilities associated with womanhood. Nevertheless, the social stigma that was once attached to those who challenged the expected passive and fragile role of "true femininity" (as black women and working-class women have done for many years) has been substantially eroded. This is not always the case; the classic double bind is a common experience for women. Even though violent hazing practices have been documented among women's groups, reports of this are relatively rare in comparison to male groups (Hoover 1999; Nuwer 1999, 2000).

In addition to sexual objectification among female groups and physically violent hazing among male groups, other hazing activities are shaped around gendered vulnerabilities as well. I want to be clear here that I do not consider these vulnerabilities to be innate to girls/women or boys/men, but rather a consequence of complex and powerful social forces that contribute to sustaining unequal power relations as a consequence of sexism, racism, homophobia, poverty, and other systems of disadvantage that render certain groups of individuals vulnerable in particular ways.

For instance, over the past decade, the very slim "waif look" (with large breasts) has become a standard of beauty among white women. Many women spend inordinate amounts of time and money trying to achieve this "look," which is largely unnatural and cannot be attained without significant risks to one's health (not to mention the investment of time, money, and energy that could be used in other ways). It is not surprising then that some hazing activities among women's groups capitalize on this gendered vulnerability. In my own work at a university, I encountered a sorority that required pledges to stand on a table in their underwear while the sisters circled areas of the pledges' bodies that they deemed "too fat." In this case, the differences in beauty ideals for men and women shape types of hazing activities. It would be highly unlikely that this same activity would occur as a form of hazing among a group of men.

Another gender-based difference is that groups of men are more likely than groups of women to engage in homoerotic activities as a form of hazing. When boys/men are *subjected* to homoerotic activity (rather than freely entering into horseplay such as giving wedgies and wrestling), they often consider such activity a threat to heterosexual masculine identity. Defending one's heterosexuality is paramount to securing one's status as a "real man," and homoerotic activities run the risk of threatening this status. In the much-publicized case of hazing on the University of Vermont ice hockey team, an initiate sued the university, alleging sexual assault after being directed to drink, eat vile substances, and "parade naked holding one another's genitals" during a team initiation (Rosellini 2001, 1). Reports of activities such as this are becoming increasingly common, it seems, and when consent is not clear, charges of sexual assault may be likely.

Researchers have noted the seemingly paradoxical frequency of homoerotic activities in male groups that are deeply invested in sustaining highly masculinized environments (Martin and Hummer 1989; Rhoads 1995; Robinson 1998). They theorize that this may be due largely to the need for men to have socially sanctioned outlets for expressing same-sex intimacy, especially in groups where the "culture stresses a very macho conception of manhood" and other types of physical contact and sensitivity are viewed as objectionable (Rhoads 1995, 318). The sanctioning of homoerotic activities in highly masculinized environments such as fraternities and male athletic teams occurs within an intensely homophobic culture. According to Rhoads, the emphasis on machismo is also reflected in the strong disdain for gay students, whom the brothers tend to see as lacking masculinity (319). Researchers have also noted that male groups who ascribe to very rigid and narrow definitions of masculinity (which are common to fraternities and male athletes) exhibit not only an intense hatred for but also a fascination with homosexuality (Martin and Hummer 1989; Sanday 1990).

Consent is a key factor in determining the ways in which homoerotic activity is experienced and interpreted by others. When initiates are subjected to hazing practices involving homoerotic activity, they are placed in a subordinate position, peer pressure is strong, and alcohol may be involved—all factors that make the line between sexual consent and nonconsent blurry at best. This is why such activity may be considered sexual assault when practiced during an initiation activity but may be interpreted differently when practiced under other circumstances where the power dynamics are operating more evenly among participants.

Just as hazing differs for male and female groups and reflects gendered (and heterosexist) power dynamics in the larger culture, hazing practices are also shaped in relation to other vulnerabilities that are produced as a consequence of inequitable power relations operating in society. According to Walter Kimbrough, a scholar of higher education who has written about historically black fraternities, "Organizations are always greatly affected by the culture of the larger society" (in Nuwer 1999, 184). As a cultural construction, gender is historically situated and influenced by other culturally mediated factors (such as race and poverty) that affect the ways in which individuals experience the social world.

Michael Messner (1989) points out how the development of a masculine identity is structured in relation to race and socioeconomic status. If hazing among men is shaped by cultural expectations around masculinity, then it is also shaped by race, socioeconomic status, and other identity-related factors. For example, scholars John Williams (2001) and Paula Giddings describe their own experiences and reflections on how pledging and hazing in National Panhellenic Council (historically black) fraternities and sororities was specific to conditions resulting from centuries of racial oppression in the U.S. For instance, in her book on the history of Delta Sigma Theta, Giddings writes, "Hazing had always been a part of the initiation period . . . but may have a particular meaning and character among Blacks" (in Nuwer 1999, 180). She cites the "stripping away of individuality" and the emphasis on unity and unconditional respect for sisters as having "a particular resonance in terms of the black experience" (ibid.). Patricia Hill Collins (1991) provides a detailed account of how black women's experiences of sexism are in some ways parallel and also markedly different from the experiences of white middle-class women. Clearly, cultural differences among women—of different racial and ethnic backgrounds, economic statuses, and sexual identities—must be taken into account when considering how gender influences hazing. Much more research needs to be done in this area in order to broaden and enhance understanding of these dynamics.

In his essay "Hazing in Black Fraternities," Williams describes how hazing in historically black fraternities is often justified by appealing to the desires of young males to prove their manhood/masculinity (as in "only the strong survive") and by appealing to the need to promote racial pride by reminding a pledge "that the pressure he is expected to endure from 'the brothers' is nothing compared to what the 'real world' will put on him" (2001, 1). Types of hazing practices also reflect cultural differences among groups of men in fraternities. According to Nuwer (1999), beatings, paddling, and other forms of violent pledging practices are the primary cause of injury and death within historically black fraternities, while pledging deaths among predominantly white fraternal groups are more likely to involve alcohol poisoning and other substance abuse as well as violence. [*Ed. note:* That is not to say that white pledges have not been savagely beaten by members and that black pledges have not been coerced into drinking.]

Messner points out that "within a social context that is stratified by social class and by race, the choice to pursue—or not to pursue—an athletic career is explicable as an individual's rational assessment of the available means to achieve a respected masculine identity" (1989, 83). He draws on the work of sociologist Maxine Baca Zinn to explain the particular salience of athleticism for men who have been oppressed by racism or poverty. "When institutional resources that signify masculine status and control are absent, physical presence, personal style and expressiveness take on increased importance" (Messner 1989, 82). Understanding the complexity of cultural forces that operate in the shaping of gender is exceedingly important. While many white, economically privileged boys and young men wrestle with fulfilling dominant expectations around masculinity, the available options for achieving "real man" status are increased by access to education and well-paying occupations. In contrast, boys/men from disadvantaged backgrounds may have much more at stake when it comes to developing their gendered identity. As Messner asserts, "For lower-status young men . . . success in sports was not an added proof of masculinity; it was often their only hope of achieving public masculine status" (80).

Implications and Recommendations

Attending to the cultural construction of gender and homophobia and the influences of race and social class is key to promoting more complex understandings and developing effective solutions to the problem of hazing. Interventions in all arenas need to take gender theory into account in order to design educational and policy initiatives that will work. Speaking specifically about masculinity, anti-violence educator Jackson Katz (1999) points out,

> Making masculinity visible is the first step to understanding how it operates in the culture and how definitions of manhood have been linked, often unconsciously, with dominance and control. Making masculinity a key part of the equation is therefore step one to dealing effectively with the problem of violence in our society.

The social construction of femininity, sexism, and homophobia also need to be made visible to help draw attention to the ways in which girls/women as well as boys/men are made more vulnerable to particular types of hazing practices.

More research is needed to help sort out the ways in which hazing may be shaped by gender and other identity differences. The vast majority of research studies on hazing have examined its occurrence among groups of white men. One unfortunate outcome of this is that definitions of hazing and policies in response to hazing often reflect how it occurs among white male groups. While there are similarities in hazing practices across all groups, there are many differences. In her research on sorority hazing, Holmes found that many women defined hazing as "a fraternity issue involving physical activities including drinking, running and calisthenics" (1999, 81). So even though these women described their own participation in activities that constitute hazing (i.e., pledge drops, servitude, not allowing friendships outside the chapter, and verbal abuse), they did not define it as such.

In my view, as a mother of three young children and a professor of education, it is exceedingly important that parents, teachers, coaches, and school administrators become more aware of how rigid gender-role expectations can have harmful consequences for children. Fathers in particular can do more to model an expanded version of masculinity that does not valorize aggressive sexuality and violence (Kivel 1999). Primary and secondary schools as well as colleges and universities would be wise to expand opportunities for meaningful dialogue with students, teachers, parents, and community members about the potentially harmful consequences of narrow and confining conceptualizations of gender.

In this chapter, I have described how rigid and narrow versions of gender work in tandem with homophobia to create environments that are more likely to tolerate and perpetuate hazing practices, particularly forms of hazing among different types of groups. If we are truly committed to circumventing the harm that is often produced through hazing, we need to become more cognizant of how gender, race, social class, and other social hierarchies shape our understandings and tolerance of the role of hazing—even in light of the emotional and physical damage and sometimes lethal consequences that can result. Working to expand narrow and confining gender norms and eliminating homophobia is not only important for understanding and preventing hazing, it is an important step toward providing children (and adults) with opportunities for lives that are more fully human.

Appendix
Hazing Information Resources

Activist and Educational Individuals/Organizations

Center for the Study of the College Fraternity
CSCF Membership Records
Franklin Hall 206
Bloomington, IN 47405
http://www.indiana.edu/~cscf/
President: Charles Eberly

Rita Saucier
P.O. Box 850955
Mobile, AL 36685

Security On Campus, Inc.
601 South Henderson Road Suite 205
King of Prussia, PA 19406
http://www.campussafety.org/
Contact Person: S. Daniel Carter

Eileen Stevens (retired)
P.O. Box 188
Sayville, NY 11782

StopHazing
Web site: StopHazing.Org
Membership site: http://www.stophazing.org/join.htm
Officers: Brian Rahill, Elizabeth Allan

U.S. Department of Education
Higher Education Center for Alcohol and Other Drug Prevention
55 Chapel Street
Newton, MA 02458
voice (800) 676-1730 x2719 or (617) 618-2719
http://www.edc.org/hec
Contact: Linda Langford, Sc.D., Associate Director

Hazing News List

E-mail list for journalists and educators that provides a forum for news and occasional discussion of hazing issues. No charges or fees.

To join, write SUBSCRIBE HAZING in the body of an e-mail message and send to
LISTSERV@LISTSERV.IUPUI.EDU
To quit, write UNSUBSCRIBE HAZING in the body of an e-mail message and send to
LISTSERV@LISTSERV.IUPUI.EDU
Contacts: The list co-owners are Hank Nuwer and Jim Brown.

Hazing Policywriting Assistance Guide (free)

http://www.stophazing.org/nuwer/hazingpolicy.htm

Hazing Speakers or Speaker Representatives (fee-paid)

Miscellaneous, Listed at StopHazing
http://www.stophazing.org/speakers.htm

Hank Nuwer
http://www.ciaspeakers.com/speakerroster2.htm
Exception: Does not charge Greek headquarters or schools he has written
about in accordance with Society of Professional Journalists guidelines

Lawrence C. Ross, Jr.
http://www.peopletalk2000.com/speakers.html

CampusSpeak
http://www.campuspeak.com/speakers/barnes/

Hazing Law Page

Douglas Fierberg
http://www.hazinglaw.com/

Hazing Information Web Sites

StopHazing
http://stophazing.org

Unofficial Clearinghouse of Hazing Deaths and Injuries
http://hazing.hanknuwer.com

References

AAUW (American Association of University Women). *Gender Gaps: Where Schools Still Fail Our Children*. Washington, D.C.: AAUW, 1998.

Alexander, C. N., and E. Q. Campbell. "Peer Influences on Adolescent Drinking Behaviors." *Quarterly Journal of Studies on Alcohol* 28 (1967): 444–453.

Applebome, P. "Lawsuit Shatters Code of Silence over Hazing at Black Fraternities." *New York Times*, 21 December 1994, B8, B15.

Arnold, J. C., and G. D. Kuh. *Brotherhood and the Bottle: A Cultural Analysis of the Role of Alcohol in Fraternities*. Bloomington, Ind.: Center for the Study of the College Fraternity, 1992.

Aronson, E., and J. Mills. "The Effect of Severity of Initiation on Liking for a Group." *Journal of Abnormal and Social Psychology* 59 (September 1959): 177–181.

Arthur, L. B. "Role Salience, Role Embracement, and the Symbolic Self Completion of Sorority Pledges." *Sociological Inquiry* 67 (1997): 364–379.

Asante, M. *Afrocentricity*. Trenton, N.J.: Africa World Press, 1988.

Augustine. *Confessions*. Books I–XIII. Trans. F. J. Sheed. Indianapolis: Hackett, 1993.

Baier, J. L., and E. G. Whipple. "Greek Values and Attitudes: A Comparison with Independents." *NASPA Journal* 28 (1990): 43–53.

Baker-White, R. "The Politics of Ritual in Wole Soyinka's *The Bacchae of Euripides*." *Comparative Drama* 27, no. 3 (Fall 1993): 377.

Barnes, B. "Our Common Bonds." Paper presented at the Southeastern Intrafraternity Conference, Atlanta, Georgia, 1994.

Bartky, S. L. "Foucault, Femininity, and the Modernization of Patriarchal Power." In I. Diamond and L. Quinby, eds., *Feminism and Foucault: Reflections on Resistance*, 61–86. Boston: Northeastern University Press, 1988.

Baxter-Magolda, M. *Making Their Own Way*. Sterling, Va.: Stylus, 2001.

Beattie, M. *Beyond Codependency*. San Francisco: Harper & Row, 1989.

Beck, K. "Psychosocial Patterns of Alcohol Abuse in a College Population." *Journal of Alcohol and Drug Education* 28, no. 2 (1983): 64–72.

Beck, R. *Planetary Gods and Planetary Orders in the Mysteries of Mithras*. Leiden: E. J. Brill, 1987.

Becker, H., B. Geer, E. C. Hughes, and A. Straus. *The Boys in White: Student Culture in the Medical World*. Chicago: University of Chicago Press, 1961.

Bem, S. L. *The Lenses of Gender*. New Haven, Conn.: Yale University Press, 1993.

Belenky, M. F., B. M. Clinchy, N. Goldberger, and J. Tarule. *Women's Ways of Knowing*. New York: Basic Books, 1986.

Benard, B. "Characteristics of Effective Prevention Programs." *Prevention Forum* 6, no. 4 (1986): 57–64.

Berg, P. "Organizational Change as a Symbolic Transformation Process." In P. J. Frost, L. F. Moore, M. R. Louis, C. C. Lundberg, and J. Martin, eds., *Organizational Culture*, 281–299. Beverly Hills, Calif.: Sage, 1985.

Berger, J. *Ways of Seeing*. London: Penguin Books, 1972.

Berkowitz, A.D., ed. *Men and Rape: Theory, Research, and Prevention Programs in Higher Education.* San Francisco: Jossey-Bass, 1994.

——. "Applications of Social Norms Theory to Other Health and Social Justice Issues." In H. W. Perkins, ed., *The Social Norms Approach to Preventing School and College Age Substance Abuse.* San Francisco: Jossey-Bass, 2003.

Berkowitz, A., and W. Perkins. "College Students' Attitudinal and Behavioral Responses to a Drinking-Age Law Change: Stability and Contradiction in the Campus Setting." Paper presented at the annual meeting of the New York State Sociological Association, Rochester Institute of Technology, Rochester, New York, 1985.

Blumer, H. *Symbolic Interactionism: Perspective and Method.* Englewood Cliffs, N.J.: Prentice Hall, 1969.

Boudervijnse, B., ed. *Current Studies in Rituals: Perspectives for the Psychology of Religion.* Atlanta: Rodopi, 1990.

Brooks, M., S. Walfish, D. E. Stenmark, and J. M. Cagner. "Personality Variables in Alcohol Abuse in College Students." *Journal of Drug Education* 11 (1981): 185–189.

Brown, S. A. "Expectancies versus Background in the Prediction of College Drinking Patterns." *Journal of Consulting and Clinical Psychology* 53 (1985): 123–130.

Brown, S. A., M. S. Goldman, A. Inn, and L. R. Anderson. "Expectations of Reinforcement from Alcohol: Their Domain and Relation to Drinking Patterns." *Journal of Consulting and Clinical Psychology* 48 (1980): 419–426.

Brumberg, J. J. *The Body Project: An Intimate History of American Girls.* New York: Random House, 1997.

Brunson, J. E. *Frat and Soror: The African Origin of Greek-Lettered Organizations.* Southfield, Mich.: Cleage Group, 1991.

Burawoy, M., et al. *Ethnography Unbound: Power and Resistance in the Modern Metropolis.* Berkeley: University of California Press, 1991.

Bushweller, K. "Brutal Rituals, Dangerous Rites." *American School Board Journal* (August 2000). Available online at http://www.asbj.com/2000/08/0800coverstory.html (accessed May 7, 2003).

Butler, E. M. *Ritual Magic.* New York: Cambridge University Press, 1979.

Butler, E. R. "Alcohol Use by College Students: A Rites of Passage Ritual." *NASPA Journal* 31 (1993): 48–55.

Butler, J. *Gender Trouble: Feminism and the Subversion of Identity.* New York: Routledge, 1990.

Calasso, R. *The Ruin of Kasch.* Cambridge, Mass.: Belknap Press of Harvard University, 1994.

Carnes, M. *Ritual and Manhood in Victorian America.* New Haven, Conn.: Yale University Press, 1989.

Cartwright, D. "The Nature of Group Cohesiveness." In D. Cartwright and A. Zander, eds., *Group Dynamics.* 3rd ed. New York: Harper & Row, 1968.

Chagoya, S. "Online Exclusive: Adrian Heideman 9-1-1-Tape." *The Orion,* February 14, 2001. Available online at http://orion.csuchico.edu/Pages/Vol46issue4/online/911call.html (accessed May 8, 2003).

Chickering, A. W. *Education and Identity.* San Francisco: Jossey-Bass, 1969.

Chickering, A. W., and L. Reisser. *Education and Identity.* 2nd ed. San Francisco: Jossey-Bass, 1993.

Coates, J. *Women Talk.* Oxford: Blackwell Publishers, 1996.

Collins, P. H. *Black Feminist Thought: Knowledge, Consciousness, and the Politics of Empowerment.* New York: Routledge, 1991.

Cooley, C. H. *Human Nature and the Social Order*. New York: Schocken Books, 1970.

Cox, W. "Joining a Fraternity Should Not Result in Death." *Black Issues in Higher Education* 1 (March 1994): 88.

Crump, W. *The Story of Kappa Alpha Psi*. Philadelphia: Kappa Alpha Psi Fraternity, Inc., 1991.

Curry, S. "Hazing and the 'Rush' Toward Reform: Responses from Universities, Fraternities, State Legislatures, and the Courts." *Journal of College and University Law* 16 (1989): 93–117.

Dalton, J. D., ed. *Promoting Values Development in College Students*. Monograph Series, vol. 4. Washington, D.C.: National Association of Student Personnel Administrators, 1985.

Daly, M. J. "Hazing: What's the Harm?" *AmericanCatholic.org* (July 2001). Available online at http://www.americancatholic.org/Newsletters/YU/ay0701.asp (accessed May 8, 2003).

DiConsiglio, J. "Hazed and Confused." *Scholastic Choices* (September 2000). Available online at http://teacher.scholastic.com/products/classmags/choices.htm (accessed May 8, 2003).

Engs, R. C. "Drinking Patterns and Drinking Problems of College Students." *Journal of Studies on Alcohol* 38 (1977): 2144–2156.

———. "Drinking Patterns and Drinking Problems of College Students." *Journal of Alcohol and Drug Education* 31 (1985): 65–83.

———. "University Students' Drinking Patterns and Problems: Examining the Effects of Raising the Purchase Age." *Public Health Reports* 103 (1988): 667–673.

Engs, R. C., and D. J. Hanson. "Boozing and Brawling on Campus: A National Study of Violent Problems Associated with Drinking over the Past Decade." *Journal of Criminal Justice* 22 (1994): 171–180.

Evans, N.J., D. S. Forney, and F. Guido DiBrito. *Student Development in College: Theory, Research, and Practice*. San Francisco: Jossey-Bass, 1998.

Faulkner, K. K., J. Alcorn, and R. B. Gavin. "Prediction of Alcohol Consumption among Fraternity Pledges." *Journal of Alcohol and Drug Education* 34 (1989): 12–20.

Fausto-Sterling, A. *Myths of Gender: Biological Theories about Women and Men*. Revised ed. New York: Basic Books, 1992.

Feldman, A. *Formations of Violence*. Chicago: University of Chicago Press, 1991.

Fischer, J. M. "A Historical Perspective: Alcohol Abuse and Alcoholism in America and on Our Campuses." In J. S. Sherwood, ed., *Alcohol Policies and Practices on College and University Campuses*, 1–17. Washington, D.C.: National Association of Student Personnel Administrators, 1987.

Fish, J. "USM Suspends Gorham Sorority for Hazing." *Portland Press Herald*, December 12, 2001.

Fordham, S. "Those Loud Black Girls: (Black) Women, Silence, and 'Passing' in the Academy." *Anthropology and Education Quarterly* 24, no. 1 (1993).

Friere, P. *The Pedagogy of the Oppressed*. New York: Herder and Herder, 1970.

Frost, P. J., L. F. Moore, M. R. Louis, C. C. Lundberg, and J. Martin. *Organizational Culture*. Beverly Hills, Calif.: Sage Publications, 1985.

Frye, M. *The Politics of Reality: Essays in Feminist Theory*. Trumansville, N.J.: Crossing Press, 1983.

Geertz, C. *The Interpretation of Cultures*. New York: Basic Books, 1973.

Gilligan, C. *In a Different Voice: Psychological Theory and Women's Development*. Cambridge, Mass: Harvard University Press, 1982.

Gilmore, D. D. *Manhood in the Making: Cultural Concepts of Masculinity.* New Haven, Conn.: Yale University Press, 1990.

Girard, R. *Violence and the Sacred.* Baltimore: Johns Hopkins University Press, 1989.

Globetti, G., J. T. Stem, F. Marasco, and S. Haworth-Hoeppner. "Student Residence Arrangements and Alcohol Use and Abuse: A Research Note." *The Journal of College and University Student Housing* 18, no. 1 (1988): 18–33.

Goffman, E. *The Presentation of Self in Everyday Life.* New York: Anchor, 1959.

———. *Asylums.* Chicago: Aldine, 1961.

Gonzalez, G. M., and Broughton, E. A. "Status of Alcohol Policies on Campus: A National Survey." *NASPA Journal* 24, no. 2 (1986): 49–59.

———. "Changes in College Student Drinking, 1981–1991." *Journal of College Student Development* 34 (1993): 222–223.

Goodwin, L. "Explaining Alcohol Consumption and Related Experiences among Fraternity and Sorority Members." *Journal of College Student Development* 30 (1989): 448–458.

———. "Social Psychological Bases for College Alcohol Consumption." *Journal of Alcohol and Drug Education* 36 (1990): 83–95.

Gose, B. "Efforts to End Fraternity Hazing Have Largely Failed, Critics Charge." *Chronicle of Higher Education* (18 April 1997): A37, A38.

Greenfield, L. A. *Sex Offenses and Offenders: An Analysis of Data on Rape and Sexual Assault.* (NCJ-163392). Washington, D.C.: U.S. Department of Justice, Office of Justice Programs, Bureau of Justice Statistics.

Gusfield, J. R. "The Structural Context of College Drinking." *Quarterly Journal of Studies on Alcohol* 22 (1961): 428–443.

Haines, M., and A. F. Spear. "Changing the Perception of the Norm: A Strategy to Decrease Binge Drinking among College Students." *Journal of American College Health* 45 (1996): 134–140.

Handler, L. "In the Fraternal Sisterhood: Sororities as Gender Strategy." *Gender and Society* 9, no. 2 (1995): 236–255.

Hendren, C. E. "A Comparative Study of Alcohol Problems among Greek and Independent Collegians." Ph.D. diss., United States International University, 1988.

Hill, F. E., and L. A. Bugen. "A Survey of Drinking Behavior among College Students." *Journal of College Student Personnel* 20 (1979): 236–243.

Hilliard, A. "Pedagogy in Ancient Kemet." In M. Karenga and J. Carruthers, eds., *Kemet and the African Worldview.* Los Angeles: University of Sankore Press, 1985.

Hirschorn, M. W. "Alcohol Seen No. 1 Campus Abuse Problem Despite Concerns about Students' Drug Use." *Chronicle of Higher Education* (March 25, 1987): 1, 34.

Holmes, H. "The Role of Hazing in the Sorority Pledge Process." Ph.D. diss., State University of New York at Buffalo, 1999.

Hong, L. "Redefining Babes, Booze and Brawls: Men Against Violence—Towards a New Masculinity." Ph.D. diss., Louisiana State University, 1998.

Hoover, N., and N. Pollard. *Initiation Rites and Athletics: A National Survey of NCAA Sports Teams.* Alfred, N.Y.: Alfred University and Reidman Insurance Co. Inc., 1999.

Horowitz, H. L. *Campus Life: Undergraduate Cultures from the End of the Eighteenth Century to the Present.* Chicago: University of Chicago Press, 1987.

Igra, A., and R. Moos. "Alcohol Use among College Students: Some Competing Hypotheses." *Journal of Youth and Adolescence* 8 (1979): 393–405.

James, W. *The Principles of Psychology*. Cambridge, Mass.: Harvard University Press, 1983.

Johnson, A. *Privilege, Power and Difference*. New York: McGraw Hill, 2001.

Kaplan, M. S. "Patterns of Alcoholic Beverage Use among College Students." *Journal of Alcohol and Drug Education* 24 (1979): 26–40.

Karenga, M. *Selections from the Husia: Sacred Wisdom of Ancient Egypt*. Los Angeles: University of Sankore Press, 1984.

———. *The Book of Coming Forth by Day: The Ethics of the Declarations of Innocence*. Los Angeles: University of Sankore Press, 1990.

———. *Introduction to Black Studies*. 2nd ed. Los Angeles: University of Sankore Press, 1993.

Katz, F. *Ordinary People and Extraordinary Evil: A Report on the Beguilings of Evil*. Albany, N.Y.: SUNY Press, 1993.

Katz, J. and J. Earp. *Tough Guise*. Video. 1999. Available online at http://www.mediaed.org/videos/MediaGenderAndDiversity/ToughGuise#vidinfo (accessed May 8, 2003).

Kershner, F. D., Jr. "Hazing: A Throwback to the Middle Ages." *Delta Tau Delta Rainbow Magazine* 140 (Summer 1977): 3–42.

———. "Report on Hazing, Pledging and Fraternity Education in the American Social Fraternity System." Indianapolis: National Interfraternity Conference, 1989.

Kilbourne, J. *Killing Us Softly 3*. Video. Available online at http://www.mediaed.org/videos/MediaGenderAndDiversity/KillingUsSoftly3#vidinfo (accessed May 8, 2003).

Kimbrough, W. M. "A Comparison of Involvement, Leadership Skills and Experiences for Black Students Based on Membership in a Black Greek-Lettered Organization and Institutional Type." Ph.D. diss., Georgia State University, 1996.

Kimmel, M. S. *The Gendered Society*. New York: Oxford University Press, 2000.

King, W. D. "Dionysus in Santa Barbara: Wallace Shawn's Euripidean *Fever*." *Theater* 23, no. 1 (1992): 83.

Kivel, P. *Boys Will Be Men: Raising Our Sons for Courage, Caring and Community*. Gabriola Islands, B.C.: New Society Publishers, 1999.

Klein, H. "Helping the College Student Problem Drinker." *Journal of College Student Development* 30 (1989): 323–331.

Kohlberg, L. "Stages of Moral Development." In C. M. Beck, B. S. Crittenden, and E. D. Sullivan, eds., *Moral Education*. Toronto: University of Toronto Press, 1971.

Kohn, A. *Punished by Rewards*. New York: Houghton Mifflin, 1993.

Kozicki, Z. A. "The Measurement of Drinking Problems among College Students at a Midwestern University." *Journal of Alcohol and Drug Education* 27 no. 3 (1982): 61–72.

Kraft, D. P. "The Prevention and Treatment of Alcohol and Drug Problems on a College Campus." Paper presented at the Tenth Anniversary Symposium, Alcohol/Drug Studies Center, Jackson State University, 1985.

Krieger, N. and E. Fee. "Man-Made Medicine and Women's Health: The Biopolitics of Sex/Gender and Race/Ethnicity." *International Journal of Health Services* 24, no. 2 (1994).

Kuh, G. D. *Environmental Influences on Alcohol Use by College Students*. Washington, D.C.: Office of Educational Research and Improvement, U.S. Department of Education, 1991 (ED 331 336).

Kuh, G. D., and J. C. Arnold. "Liquid Bonding: A Cultural Analysis of the Role of Alcohol in Fraternity Pledgeship." *Journal of College Student Development* 34 (1993): 327–334.

Kuh, G. D., and F. K. Stage. "Student Development." In B. R. Clark and G. R. Neave, eds., *The Encyclopedia of Higher Education,* 1719–1730. Oxford: Pergamon Press, 1992.

Kuh, G. D., and E. J. Whitt. "The Invisible Tapestry: Culture in American Colleges and Universities." ASHE-ERIC Higher Education Report no. 1. Washington, D.C.: Association for the Study of Higher Education, 1988. Reprinted in M. C. Brown, ed., *Organization and Governance in Higher Education,* 5th ed., 160–169. Boston: Pearson Custom Publishing, 2000.

James, G. G. M. *Stolen Legacy.* Newport News, Va.: United Brothers Communications Systems, 1989.

Jones, R. "The Hegemonic Struggle and Domination in Black Greek-letter Fraternities." *Challenge* 10, no. 1 (1999): 1–26.

Lakoff, G., and M. Johnson. *Metaphors We Live By.* Chicago: University of Chicago Press, 1980.

Leemon, T. A. *The Rites of Passage in a Student Culture.* New York: Teachers College Press, 1972.

Lefkowitz, M. *Not Out of Africa: How Afrocentrism Became an Excuse to Teach Myth as History.* New York: Basic Books, 1996.

Longino, C. F., Jr., and C. S. Kart. "The College Fraternity: An Assessment of Theory and Research." *Journal of College Student Personnel* 14 (1973): 118–125.

Luckok, H. M. *The Ritual Crisis: How It May Be Turned to the Best Account.* New York: Longmans & Green, 1899.

Luyster, R. "Dionysus: The Masks of Madness." *Parabola* 20, no. 4 (Winter 1995): 43.

Magolda, P. M. "A Quest for Community: An Ethnographic Study of a Residential College." Ph.D. diss., Indiana University, 1994.

Magolda, P. M., and B. M. Robinson. "Doing Harm: Unintended Consequences of Fieldwork." Paper presented at the American Educational Research Association Annual Meeting, Atlanta, Georgia, April 1993.

Malaney, G. D. "Student Attitudes toward Fraternities and Sororities." *NASPA Journal* 28 (1990): 37–42.

Mandelbaum, D. G. "Alcohol and Culture." *Current Anthropology* 6 (1965): 281–288.

Maney, D. W. "Predicting University Students' Use of Alcoholic Beverages." *Journal of College Student Development* 31 (1990): 23–32.

Manning, K. *Rituals, Ceremonies and Cultural Meaning in Higher Education.* Westport, Conn.: Bergin and Garvey, 2000.

Martin, C. M., and M. A. Hoffman. "Alcohol Expectancies, Living Environment, Peer Influence, and Gender: A Model of College Student Drinking." *Journal of College Student Development* 34 (1993): 206–211.

Martin, J. *Cultures in Organizations: Three Perspectives.* New York: Oxford University, 1992.

Martin, P. Y. "Fraternities and Rape on Campus." *Gender and Society* 3, no. 4 (1989): 457–473.

Martin, P., and R. Hummer. "Fraternities and Rape on Campus." *Gender & Society* 3, no. 4 (1989): 457–473.

Masland, A. T. "Organizational Culture in the Study of Higher Education." In M. C.

Brown, ed., *Organization and Governance in Higher Education*, 5th ed., 145–152. Boston: Pearson Custom Publishing, 2000.

McMinn, B. "A Content Analysis of the Esoteric Ritual Manuals of National College Social Fraternities." Ph.D. diss., University of Mississippi, 1979.

Mead, G. H. *Mind, Self, and Society*. Chicago: University of Chicago Press, 1934.

Mellody, P. *Facing Codependence: What It Is, Where It Comes From, How It Sabotages Our Lives*. San Francisco: Harper & Row, 1989.

Messner, M. "Masculinities and Athletic Careers." *Gender and Society* 3, no. 1 (1989): 71–88.

———, and M. Kimmel. *Men's Lives*. 5th ed. Boston: Allyn and Bacon, 2001.

Millett, K. *Sexual Politics*. New York: Simon & Schuster, Inc., 1990.

Mills, K. C., B. Pfaffenberger, and D. McCarty. "Guidelines for Alcohol Abuse Prevention on the College Campus: Overcoming the Barriers to Program Success." *Journal of Higher Education* 52 (1981): 399–414.

Mills, S. *Discourse*. London: Routledge, 1997.

Miser, K. "The Fraternity and Alcohol Abuse: A Challenge for the '80s." *Phi Gamma Delta* 1, no. 6 (Spring 1981).

Moffatt, M. *Coming of Age in New Jersey*. New Brunswick, N.J.: Rutgers University Press, 1989.

Moos, R. H., B. S. Moos, and J. A. Kulik. "College Student Abstainers, Moderate Drinkers, and Heavy Drinkers: A Comparative Analysis." *Journal of Youth and Adolescence* 5 (1976): 349–360.

Morgan, G. *Images of Organization*. Beverly Hills, Calif.: Sage, 1986.

Newcomb, T. M. "Student Peer-Group Influence." In N. Sanford, ed., *The American College*, 469–488. New York: John Wiley & Sons, 1962.

Nicoletti, J., S. Spencer-Thomas, and C. Bollinger. *Violence Goes to College: The Authoritative Guide to Prevention and Intervention*. Springfield, Ill.: Charles C. Thomas, 2001.

Nurius, P., J. Norris, L. Dimeff, and T. Graham. "Expectations Regarding Acquaintance Sexual Aggression among Sorority and Fraternity Members." *Sex Roles* 35 (1996): 427–444.

Nuwer, H. "Dead Souls of Hell Week." *Human Behavior* 7, no. 10 (October 1978): 50–56.

———. *Broken Pledges: The Deadly Rite of Hazing*. Atlanta: Longstreet Press, 1990.

———. *Wrongs of Passage: Fraternities, Sororities, Hazing and Binge Drinking*. Bloomington: Indiana University Press, 1999.

———. *High School Hazing: When Rites Become Wrongs*. New York: F. Watts, 2000.

———. "In My View." *The Beta Theta Pi* 80, no. 3 (Winter 2003): 8.

Nicholson, O. "The End of Mithraism." *Antiquity* 69, no. 263 (June 1995): 358.

Olmert, M. "Points of Origin." *Smithsonian*, September 1983, 150–154.

Perkins, W., and A.D. Berkowitz. "Collegiate COAs and Alcohol Abuse: Problem Drinking in Relation to Assessments of Parent and Grandparent Alcoholism." *Journal of Counseling and Development* 69 (1991): 237–240.

Perry, W. *Forms of Intellectual and Ethical Development in the College Years*. New York: Holt, Rinehart, and Winston, 1968.

Peterson, J. "Internal-External Control and Motivations for Alcohol Use among College Students." *Psychological Reports* 52 (1983): 692–694.

Pipher, M. *Reviving Ophelia: Saving the Selves of Adolescent Girls*. New York: Ballantine, 1995.

Pollack, W. *Real Boys: Rescuing Our Sons from the Myths of Boyhood.* New York: Owl Books, 1998.

Presley, C. A., and P. W. Meilman. *Alcohol and Drugs on American College Campuses: A Report to College Presidents.* Carbondale: Southern Illinois University Press, 1992.

Presley, C. A., P. W. Meilman, and R. Lyerla. *Alcohol and Drugs on American College Campuses: Use, Consequences, and Perceptions of the Campus Environment.* Vol. 1: *1989–1991.* Carbondale: Southern Illinois University, 1993.

Raphael, R. *The Men from the Boys: Rites of Passage in Male America.* Lincoln: University of Nebraska Press, 1988.

Reiskin, H., and H. Wechsler. "Drinking among College Students Using a Campus Mental Health Center." *Journal of Studies on Alcohol* 42 (1981): 716–724.

Rhoads, R. "The Brothers of Alpha Beta: An Ethnographic Study of Fraternity Oppression of Women." Paper presented at the annual meeting of the Association for the Study of Higher Education, Minneapolis, Minnesota, October 1992.

Rhoads, R. A. "Whales Tales, Dog Piles, and Beer Goggles: An Ethnographic Study of Fraternity Life." *Anthropology and Education Quarterly* 26 no. 3 (1995): 306–323.

Rhode, D. L. *Speaking of Sex: The Denial of Gender Inequality.* Cambridge, Mass.: Harvard University Press, 1997.

Roberts, Scott W. "Effectiveness of Drug Education Components: Knowledge, Attitudes, Decision Making, Motivations, and Self-Esteem." *Journal of Health Education* 26, no. 3 (1995): 146–150.

Robinson, L. *Crossing the Line: Violence and Sexual Assault in Canada's National Sport.* Toronto, Canada: McClelland & Stewart, 1998.

Rogers, E. M. "Reference Group Influences on Student Drinking Behavior." *Journal of Alcohol Studies* 19 (1958): 244–254.

Rosellini, L. "Unsporting Athletics: Four in Five NCAA Athletes Are Subjected to Hazing." *U.S. News and World Report,* September 11, 2000, 102. Available online at http://www.usnews.com/usnews/edu/college/articles/brief/sthazing.htm (accessed May 8, 2003).

Rosenbluth, J., P. E. Nathan, and D. M. Lawson. "Environmental Influences on Drinking by College Students in a College Pub: Behavioral Observation in the Natural Environment." *Addictive Behaviors* 3 (1978): 117–121.

Sadker, M., and D. Sadker. *Failing at Fairness: How Our Schools Cheat Girls.* New York: Simon and Schuster, 1994.

Saltz, R., and D. Elandt. "College Student Drinking Studies, 1976–1985." *Contemporary Drug Problems* (Spring 1986): 117–159.

Sanday, P. R. *Fraternity Gang Rape: Sex, Brotherhood and Privilege on Campus.* New York: New York University Press, 1990.

Sandler, B. R., L. Silverberg, and R. M. Hall. *The Chilly Classroom Climate: A Guide to Improve the Education of Women.* Washington, D.C.: National Association of Women in Education, 1996.

Schaef, A. W. *Women's Reality: An Emerging Female System in a White Male Society.* Minneapolis: Winston, 1985.

———. *Co-dependence: Misunderstood—Mistreated.* New York: Harper & Row, 1986.

———. *When Society Becomes an Addict.* San Francisco: Harper & Row, 1987.

———. *Escape from Intimacy.* New York: Harper & Row, 1989.

———. *Beyond Therapy, Beyond Science: A New Model for Healing the Whole Person.* San Francisco: HarperSanFrancisco, 1992.

Schaef, A. W., and D. Fassel. *The Addictive Organization*. San Francisco: Harper & Row, 1988.

Schein, E. H. "Organizational Culture." *American Psychologist* 45, no. 2 (1990): 109–119.

———. *Organizational Culture and Leadership: A Dynamic View*. 2nd ed. San Francisco: Jossey-Bass Publishers, 1992.

Schofield, A. "The Search for Iconographic Variation in Roman Mithraism." *Religion* 25, no. 1 (January 1995): 51.

Scott, W. A. *Values and Organizations: A Study of Fraternities and Sororities*. Chicago: Rand-McNally, 1965.

Schwartz, M., R. Burkhart, and S. B. Green. "Turning On or Turning Off: Sensation Seeking or Tension Reduction as Motivational Determinants of Alcohol Use." *Journal of Consulting and Clinical Psychology* 46 (1978): 1144–1145.

Shaw, D. "A National Study of Sorority Hazing Incidents in Selected Land-Grant Institutions of Higher Learning." Ph.D. diss., Auburn University, 1992.

Shaw, D. L., and T. E. Morgan. "Greek Advisors' Perceptions of Sorority Hazing." *NASPA Journal* 28 (1990): 60–64.

Sherry, P., and V. Stolberg. "Factors Affecting Alcohol Use by College Students." *Journal of College Student Personnel* 28 (1987): 350–355.

Sherwood, J. S., ed. *Alcohol Policies and Practices on College and University Campuses*. Washington, D.C.: National Association of Student Personnel Administrators, 1987.

Shibutani, T. *Society and Personality: An Interactionist Approach to Social Psychology*. Englewood Cliffs, N.J.: Prentice Hall, 1961.

Shore, E., C. Rivers, and J. J. Berman. "Resistance by College Students to Peer Pressure to Drink." *Journal of Studies on Alcohol* 44, no. 2 (1983): 352–361.

Singer, M. T., with J. Lalich. *Cults in Our Midst*. San Francisco: Jossey-Bass, 1995.

Smith, D. E. *Texts, Facts, and Femininity: Exploring the Relations of Ruling*. London: Routledge, 1990.

Southwick, L., C. Steel, A. Marlatt, and M. Lindell. "Alcohol-Related Expectancies Defined by Phase of Intoxication and Drinking Experience." *Journal of Consulting and Clinical Psychology* 49 (1981): 713–721.

Stombler, M. "'Buddies' or 'Slutties': The Collective Sexual Reputation of Fraternity Little Sisters." *Gender and Society* 8, no. 3 (1994): 297–323.

Sweet, S. "Understanding Fraternity Hazing: Insights from Symbolic Interactionist Theory." *Journal of College Student Development* 40, no. 4 (1999): 355–363.

———. *College and Society: An Introduction to the Sociological Imagination*. Boston: Allyn & Bacon, 2001.

Talbot, M. *The Holographic Universe*. New York: HarperCollins, 1991.

Tampke, D. R. "Alcohol Behavior, Risk Perception, and Fraternity and Sorority Membership." *NASPA Journal* 28 (1990): 71–77.

Thomas, W. I. *The Child in America*. Chicago: University of Chicago Press, 1928.

Thorne, B. *Gender Play: Girls and Boys in School*. New Brunswick, N.J.: Rutgers University Press, 1997.

Tierney, W. G., "Critical Leadership and Decision Making in a Postmodern World." In *Building Communities of Difference: Higher Education in the Twenty-First Century*. Westport, Conn.: Bergin & Garvey, 1993. Reprinted in M. C. Brown, ed., *Organization and Governance in Higher Education*, 5th ed., 537–549. Boston: Pearson Custom Publishing, 2000.

———. "Symbolism and Presidential Perceptions of Leadership." *Review of Higher Edu-*

cation 12, no. 2 (1989). Reprinted in M. C. Brown, ed., *Organization and Governance in Higher Education,* 5th ed., 223–231. Boston: Pearson Custom Publishing, 2000.

Tierney, W. G., ed. *Culture and Ideology in Higher Education: Advancing a Critical Agenda.* New York: Praeger Publishers, 1991.

Tiger, L. *Men in Groups.* 2nd ed. New York: Marion Boyars Publishers, 1984.

Tulin, A. "A Note on Euripides' *Bacchae.*" *Mnemosyne* 47, no. 2 (April 1994): 221.

van Gennep, A. *Rites of Passage.* Paris: Nourry, 1909; reprinted Chicago: University of Chicago Press, 1960.

van Maanen, J. "People Processing: Strategies of Organizational Socialization." *Organizational Dynamics* 7 (1978): 18–36.

———. "The Moral Fix: On the Ethics of Fieldwork." In R. M. Emerson, ed., *Contemporary Field Research: A Collection of Readings,* 269–287. Prospect Heights, Ill: Waveland Press, 1983.

———. "Doing New Things in Old Ways: The Chains of Socialization." In J. L. Bess, ed., *College and University Organization: Insights from the Behavioral Sciences,* 211–247. New York: New York University Press, 1984.

van Maanen, J., and E. H. Schein. "Toward a Theory of Organizational Socialization." In B. M. Staw and L. L. Cummings, eds., *Research in Organizational Behavior,* 209–264. Greenwich, Conn.: JAI Press, 1979.

Walsh, W. *Secret Societies of the Ritualists.* Leamington: J. Beck, 1884.

———. *The Ritualistic Reaction in the Present Century: Important Lecture.* Liverpool: Protestant Standard, 1899.

Warner, H. "Alcohol Trends in College Life: Historical Perspectives." In G. Maddox, ed., *The Domesticated Drug: Drinking among Collegians,* 45–80. New Haven, Conn.: College and University Press, 1970.

Wechsler, H. "Alcohol and the American College Campus: A Report from the Harvard School of Public Health." *Change* 28 (1996): 20–25.

Wechsler, H., and N. Isaac. "'Binge' Drinkers at Massachusetts Colleges: Prevalence, Drinking Style, Time Trends, and Associated Problems." *Journal of the American Medical Association* 267 (1992): 2929–2931.

Wechlser, H., and M. McFadden. "Drinking among College Students in New England: Extent, Social Correlates and Consequences of Alcohol Use." *Journal of Studies on Alcohol* 40 (1979): 969–996.

Wegscheider-Cruse, S. *Another Chance: Hope and Health for the Alcoholic Family.* Palo Alto, Calif.: Science and Behavior Books, 1981.

Weinhold, B. K., and J. B. Weinhold. *Breaking Free of the Codependency Trap.* Walpole, N.H.: Stillpoint Publishing, 1989.

Weir, W. "The Fraternity System and a Changing University." *Banta's Greek Exchange* 49 (1961): 186–189.

Williams, J. "Hazing in Black Fraternities." Available online at http://www.stophazing.org/fraternity_hazing/blackfrat.htm (accessed May 8, 2003).

Woolhouse, Megan. "Cheerleaders." *Louisville Courier-Journal,* November 6, 2000, A1.

Wright, L. S. "Correlates of Reported Drinking Problems among Male and Female College Students." *Journal of Alcohol and Drug Education* 28, no. 3 (1983): 47–58.

Contributors

Elizabeth J. Allan is an assistant professor of Higher Educational Leadership at the University of Maine. She also teaches in Women's Studies and is co-founder and executive director of the educational Web site www.StopHazing.org.

James C. Arnold is an Oregon educator and consultant. His scholarship on college students, Greek life, alcohol, and hazing is frequently cited in the academic literature. This excerpt comes from his dissertation, entitled "Alcohol and the Chosen Few: Organizational Reproduction in an Addictive System." He earned his Ph.D. in Higher Education Administration from Indiana University.

R. Brian Crow is Assistant Professor of Sport Management at Slippery Rock University. He is also the editor-in-chief of *Sport Marketing Quarterly* and founding board member of the Sport Marketing Association. He has presented extensively and written on hazing in interscholastic, intercollegiate, and professional sport.

Gregory Danielson is a former professional soccer player. He resides in California. His once-promising soccer career at the University of North Carolina was cut short by hamstring strain and the fallout from an initiation party that landed him in an emergency room.

D. Jason DeSousa is vice president for student affairs at Savannah State University in Savannah, Georgia. He is past Assistant Executive Director of Kappa Alpha Psi Fraternity and a life member of that organization.

Jonathan R. Farr is a graduate student in the northeast studying Higher Education Administration. He has been an advisor in Greek Affairs and currently works in Residence Life.

Michelle A. Finkel, M.D., is a faculty member in the Department of Emergency Medicine at Massachusetts General Hospital. Her academic interests include violence prevention.

Michael V. W. Gordon is former Executive Director of the National Panhellenic Council, Inc. He resides in Ghana and is Professor Emeritus from Indiana University—Bloomington. He is also Past Vice Chancellor of Student Affairs at Indiana University and a life member of Kappa Alpha Psi.

Susan VanDeventer Iverson is a doctoral student in Higher Education Leadership at the University of Maine. She also works as Assistant Director of Offender Accountability Initiatives for the Safe Campus Project, a federal grant–funded initiative to reduce sexual assault, relationship violence, and stalking on campus.

Irving L. Janis (1918–1990) became a member of the Yale University Psychology Department in 1947. His book *Victims of Groupthink* (1972) gained a wide audience, and the term "groupthink" became an international catchword.

Ricky L. Jones is an associate professor in the Department of Pan-African Studies at the University of Louisville. He is author of *Black Haze: Violence, Sacrifice, and Manhood in Black Greek-Letter Fraternities.* He is a member of Kappa Alpha Psi Fraternity. His Web site is http://www.blackvanguard.com.

Walter M. Kimbrough serves as the Vice President for Student Affairs at Albany State University in Albany, Georgia. He is the author of *Black Greek 101: The Culture, Customs, and Challenges of Black Fraternities and Sororities.* The past regional vice president for the Association of Fraternity Advisors, he is a nationally known researcher and author on African-American fraternities and sororities. Kimbrough is a life member of Alpha Phi Alpha fraternity.

Holiday Hart McKiernan is the former executive director of Alpha Chi Omega, a women's social fraternity. With her legal background and work with Greek organizations, she is a frequent speaker on finding solutions to campus high-risk alcohol use and hazing issues.

Hank Nuwer is the author of three books on hazing (*Broken Pledges, Wrongs of Passage,* and *High School Hazing*). He teaches journalism for the Indiana University School of Journalism, Indianapolis, and for Franklin College in Indiana. His Web site is http://hazing.hanknuwer.com.

Scott R. Rosner writes frequently on the legal aspects of hazing. He is a former assistant professor of Finance and Legal Studies at Seton University's Center for Sports Management. He now teaches at the Wharton School, University of Pennsylvania.

Stephen Sweet has written numerous articles on education, work, family, and the life course. He currently teaches at Ithaca College. He formerly worked at SUNY Potsdam and Cornell University.

Lionel Tiger is Darwin Professor of Anthropology at Rutgers University. His books include *The Decline of Males* and *Men in Groups.* He also has written

on hazing for the *Wall Street Journal* and the *New Yorker.* His Web site is http://
anthro.rutgers.edu/faculty/tiger.shtml.

Donna Winslow is the former coordinator of the Programme for Research on
Peace Security and Society at the University of Ottawa, Canada. She currently
holds the Chair of Social Anthropology at the Vrije Universiteit in Amsterdam
and is conducting a major research project for the Canadian Department of National Defence on the regimental system and its relationship to army ethos.

Index